Changing Party

Changing Party Systems in Western Europe

Edited by

David Broughton and Mark Donovan

PINTER

London and New York

Pinter

A Cassell imprint

Wellington House, 125 Strand, London WC2R 0BB
370 Lexington Avenue, New York, NY 10017-6550

First published 1999

British Library Cataloguing-in-Publication Data
A catalogue record for this book is available from the British Library.

ISBN 1 85567 327 4 (hardback)
1 85567 328 2 (paperback)

Library of Congress Cataloging-in-Publication Data

Changing party systems in Western Europe / edited by David Broughton and Mark Donovan.
p. cm.
Includes bibliographical references and index.
ISBN 1-85567-327-4. — ISBN 1-85567-328-2 (pbk.)
1. Political parties—Europe, Western. 2. Europe, Western—
Politics and government. I. Broughton, David. II. Donovan, Mark,
1955–
JN94.A979C43 1998
324.2'094'09049—dc21   98–15093
                                             CIP

Typeset by York House Typographic Ltd, London
Printed in Great Britain by Biddles Limited, Guildford and King's Lynn

Contents

List of figures and tables   vii
About the Contributors   ix
Preface   xiii
Abstracts of the Chapters   xiv

1   Introduction and Guide to Key Sources and Texts
     David Broughton and Mark Donovan   1

2   The Changing British Party System: Two-Party Equilibrium or the
     Emergence of Moderate Pluralism?
     Paul Webb and Justin Fisher   8

3   Ireland: A Party System Transformed?
     David M. Farrell   30

4   France: Living with Instability
     David Hanley   48

5   Italy: Rupture and Regeneration?
     Philip Daniels   71

6   Germany: From Hyperstability to Change?
     Charlie Jeffery   96

7   Austria: From Moderate to Polarized Pluralism?
     Kurt Richard Luther   118

8   Sweden: A Mild Case of 'Electoral Instability Syndrome'?
     David Arter   143

9   The Netherlands: Resilience Amidst Change
     Hans-Martien ten Napel   163

10   Belgium: Party System(s) on the Eve of Disintegration?
     Lieven de Winter and Patrick Dumont   183

11 Spain: Political Parties in a Young Democracy
    Jonathan Hopkin   207

12 Portugal: Party System Installation and Consolidation
    José M. Magone   232

13 Party System Change in Western Europe: Positively Political
    Mark Donovan and David Broughton   255

Glossary of Key Terms   275
References   279
Index   308

List of Figures and Tables

Figures

10.1 Rae fractionalization index, Belgium, 1946–95 186
10.2 Number of effective parties, Belgium, 1946–95 186

Tables

2.1 United Kingdom general election results, 1945–97 9
2.2 Government composition in the UK, 1945–97 9
3.1 Government composition in the Republic of Ireland, 1948–97 33
3.2 Irish national election results, 1948–97 39
3.3 Party system volatility and fragmentation, Republic of
    Ireland, 1950s–97 41
4.1 French National Assembly elections, 1958–97 59
4.2 French presidential elections, 1965–95 60
4.3 Government composition in the French Fifth Republic,
    1959–97 66
5.1 Italian election results, Chamber of Deputies, 1946–92 73
5.2 Italian election results, Chamber of Deputies, 1994 82
5.3 Italian election results, Chamber of Deputies, 1996 83
6.1 Weimar Republic, election results, 1919–32 98
6.2 Federal Republic of Germany, election results, 1949–94 103
6.3 Government composition in the Federal Republic of
    Germany, 1949–94 104
7.1 Austrian national election results, 1945–95: votes and seats 127
7.2 Government composition in Austria, 1945–97 135
8.1 Swedish general election results, 1970–94 145
8.2 Government composition in Sweden, 1970–98 147
8.3 Average electoral volatility in the Nordic countries, 1948–77 148
8.4 The level of cross-bloc volatility in Sweden, 1970–94 150
9.1 Dutch election results, 1946–98 173
9.2 Government composition in the Netherlands, 1945–94 175

List of figures and tables

10.1 Belgian general election results, 1946–95   185
10.2 Belgian traditional parties' vote shares, 1946–95   194
10.3 Total core party vote, Belgium, 1946–95   194
10.4 Government composition in Belgium, 1946–95   204
11.1 Spanish general election results, major parties, 1977–96   215
12.1 Portuguese general election results, major parties, 1975–95   236
12.2 Government composition in Portugal, 1974–98   237
12.3 Trends in electoral volatility, Portugal, 1976–91   249
13.1 Systemic properties of party systems   258
13.2 Stages and phases of party system development in
      Western Europe   262
13.3 Possible impacts of (new) parties on party systems   267

About the Contributors

David Arter is Professor of Nordic Politics and Director of the Nordic Policy Studies Centre at the University of Aberdeen. He has published extensively on European and Nordic politics and is an active participant in a number of European projects including the EU's PHARE project on Democracy and Security-Building in the Baltic States. His most recent publications include *Parties and Democracy in the Post-Soviet Republics* (Dartmouth 1996) and *The Politics of European Integration in the Twentieth Century* (Dartmouth 1993). His *Scandinavian Politics Today* (Manchester University Press) is due to be published in 1998.

David Broughton is a Lecturer in Politics in the School of European Studies at Cardiff University. He is the author of *Public Opinion Polling and British Politics* (Prentice Hall 1995) and he was the co-editor of the first six volumes of the *British Elections and Parties Yearbook 1991–1996* (Harvester Wheatsheaf and Frank Cass). He is currently working on a book entitled *German Government and Society*.

Philip Daniels is a Lecturer in European Politics at the University of Newcastle upon Tyne. He has published widely on Italian politics and he is currently completing a study of the post-war Italian party system (with Mark Donovan).

Mark Donovan is a Lecturer in European Politics in the School of European Studies at Cardiff University. He is editor of *Italy* (1997) in the Dartmouth series of readers on Comparative Government and Politics and has written several articles on Italian politics including contributing to the special issue of *International Political Science Review* on electoral reform (1995).

Patrick Dumont is a researcher at the Université Catholique de Louvain-la-Neuve in Belgium. His current interests include parties and party systems in

Europe, especially in the Benelux and Nordic countries. His doctoral thesis focuses upon the process of government formation in Belgium.

David M. Farrell is the Jean Monnet Senior Lecturer in European Politics at the University of Manchester. He has held previous appointments in Dublin and Cardiff. In 1997, he was a fellow at the Joan Shorenstein Center, Kennedy School of Government, Harvard University. He is co-editor of the journal *Party Politics*. His latest book is *Comparing Electoral Systems* (Prentice Hall 1996). He is currently working on a book on comparative election campaigning.

Justin Fisher is a Lecturer in Political Science at London Guildhall University. He is the author of *British Political Parties* (Prentice Hall 1996) and he has published widely in the field of party finance. He is the co-editor of the recent *British Elections and Parties* volumes published by Frank Cass.

David Hanley is Professor and Head of the School of European Studies at the University of Wales, Cardiff. He has previously taught at the Universities of Ulster and Reading. His research interests lie in the field of French government and politics, Christian Democracy and social democracy. He is the editor of *Christian Democracy in Europe: A Comparative Perspective* (Pinter 1994). His other interests include French parties in an historical context and the European People's Party (EPP).

Jonathan Hopkin is a Lecturer in European Politics at the University of Birmingham. He was previously a Lecturer in the Department of Politics at the University of Durham and before that, a researcher at the European University Institute, Florence. In 1995, he was awarded his PhD from the European University Institute for his thesis entitled *Party Development and Party Collapse: The Case of the Union de Centro Democratico (UCD) in Post-Franco Spain*. He has also published articles on the UCD and the Spanish party system and on the theory of party organization.

Charlie Jeffery is Deputy Director of the Institute of German Studies at the University of Birmingham. He was previously a Lecturer in the Department of Politics at the University of Leicester. He has worked on Austrian political history, although his more recent work has focused on party politics, federalism and European policy in Germany as well as regional politics in the European Union. He is co-editor of *Regional and Federal Studies* (Frank Cass) and he has also published articles in *Political Studies*, *West European Politics* and *German Politics*.

Kurt Richard Luther is a Lecturer in Politics at the University of Keele, and researches into Austrian politics, focusing in particular on political parties, consociational democracy and federalism. He has co-edited *Politics in Austria. Still a Case of Consociationalism?* (Frank Cass 1992), *Austria 1945–95: Fifty Years of the Second Republic* (Ashgate 1998), *Austria and the European Union Presidency: Background and Perspectives* (Keele European Research Centre 1998) and *Party Elites in Divided Societies: Political Parties in Consociational Democracy* (Routledge 1998). He is currently preparing a monograph on the Austrian Freedom Party.

José M. Magone is a Lecturer in European Politics in the Department of Politics at the University of Hull. He has published extensively on Portuguese and southern European politics. Among his most recent publications are *The Changing Architecture of Iberian Politics* (Mellen University Press 1996) and *European Portugal: The Difficult Road to Sustainable Democracy* (Macmillan 1996). He is currently working on a project on trade unions and European integration in Spain and Portugal.

Hans-Martien ten Napel is a Lecturer in the Department of Political Science at the University of Leiden in the Netherlands. He is the author of *Een Eigen Weg. De Totstandkoming van het CDA (1952-1980)* (1992), an analysis of the origins of the Dutch CDA, as well as being co-editor and co-author of *Geloven in Macht* (1993), *Christelijke Politiek en Democratie* (1995) and *De Strijd om de Ether* (1997), three studies of Dutch Christian democracy. His other research interests include the judiciary and politics and in that field, he has recently published *Inleiding Staatkunde* (1995), a handbook on Dutch government and constitutional law.

Paul Webb is a Senior Lecturer in Government at Brunel University in West London, and was formerly a visiting fellow in Social Sciences at Curtin University in Western Australia. He has numerous publications in the fields of party politics and voting behaviour including *Trade Unions and the British Electorate* (Dartmouth 1992). He is reviews editor of the journal *Party Politics*, and he is currently writing a book on British political parties for Sage.

Lieven de Winter is Professor of Politics at the Université Catholique de Louvain-la-Neuve and at the Katholieke Universiteit, Brussels. His current research interests include the relationships between parliaments, parties and cabinets in comparative perspective, regionalist parties in Europe, political clientelism and electoral behaviour in Belgium. In 1996, he co-edited (with Kris Deschouwer and Donatella della Porta) a special issue of *Res Publica* entitled *Partitocracies Between Crises and Reforms: The Cases of Italy and Belgium*.

Preface

———

Most of the chapters contained in this book were first given as draft papers to a seminar series held at the School of European Studies, University of Wales, Cardiff (UWC) between November 1993 and March 1995. Only after extensive revision and updating did they reach the form in which they are presented here. We felt strongly that such a close degree of co-operation between all the contributors was essential if our principal aims of coherence and a high degree of comparability between the different chapters were to be achieved.

On that basis, we must express our sincere thanks to all our contributors for their patience and willingness to co-operate in our requests for yet further revisions and extra information. The whole project was encouraged and supported from the start by Professor David Hanley as Head of the School of European Studies at UWC. He not only agreed to fund the original seminar series but also to write the chapter on France. Our gratitude to him for both these major contributions must be fully acknowledged here.

In the course of planning, developing, writing, re-writing and editing this book, a number of other individuals played vital roles. We would like to thank Karen Owen (as usual) for her all-round help in preparing the book and Peter Dorey for reading earlier draft chapters. In addition, we would like to thank some of our students (Heidi Hampton, Claire Lewis, Kim Morgan, Jim Pirie and Zoë Taylor) who read some of the draft chapters and who suggested constructive changes, particularly the inclusion of a glossary of key terms.

The inevitably enthusiastic encouragement of Nicola Viinikka at Pinter for the whole project at its conception must be recalled and the supportive efforts of Petra Recter at its completion must also be gratefully acknowledged.

David Broughton
Mark Donovan
Cardiff
November 1997

Abstracts of the Chapters

The Changing British Party System: Two-Party Equilibrium or the Emergence of Moderate Pluralism?

Paul Webb and Justin Fisher

This chapter reviews the various challenges to which the orthodox 'two-party, two-class' post-war British party system has been subjected since 1970. These challenges comprise, *inter alia*, the emergence of new cleavages, new issue agendas and new forms of political communication, and they have produced changes in electoral behaviour, party ideology and party organization. As a result of these changes, the orthodox account of the Westminster model of two-party politics no longer seems convincing, and we discuss the implications of change for the classification of the party system in the conclusion; in particular, attention is drawn to the issue of whether the British model is restabilizing at a two-party equilibrium or moving towards a new two-and-a-half party system of moderate pluralism.

Ireland: A Party System Transformed?

David M. Farrell

Contemporary party politics in Ireland is very different from twenty or thirty years ago. The system has shifted from being a two-and-a-half party system to a more conventional multi-party system. The predominance of Fianna Fáil has been weakened and the system now bears the hallmarks of being moderately pluralist in Sartori's terms. Having been one of the most stable party systems of Western Europe, with governments changing very irregularly, the system is now very much less stable. Governments change from one election to the next; coalitions have become the norm; Irish voter volatility is among the highest in Europe and new parties have entered the system. So far, the established parties have successfully adapted their policies and organizations to meet these challenges. Like elsewhere, there are signs of the parties starting to pay more attention to demands for greater internal democratization. This is a party system still undergoing transformation.

France: Living with Instability

David Hanley

The French party system is one of the oldest and most sophisticated in the world. It has very deep roots, the study of which suggests much continuity beneath the high degree of apparent fluctuation. Institutional change and the response of party actors to it have, to some extent, reshaped the French party system. It retains, however, most of its abiding historical characteristics. Sociological and cultural variables continue to guarantee the existence of a Left/Right polarity. In the 1990s, the French party system has settled into a kind of stability or at least it seems able to manage the demands of a varied society (albeit less polarized than before) without enormous difficulty. It provides governments which function. The system allows the voters to enforce change easily enough, and of late they have made full use of that facility. If the French party system has worked well up to now, it speaks volumes for the quality of party elites.

Italy: Rupture and Regeneration?

Philip Daniels

Italian party politics has undergone a rapid and unprecedented change in the 1990s. Traditional parties have disappeared, others have taken on new names and identities and entirely new political movements have achieved significant electoral success. The roots of this transformation can be traced back over many years but the principal catalysts for change in the 1990s were the extensive judicial enquiries into political corruption and the reform of the electoral system. The national elections of 1994 and 1996 confirmed the transformation of the party landscape. In terms of the structural features of the party system such as the number of parties, ideological polarization and competitive dynamics, the changes are less clear-cut. In the electoral arena, there has been a simplification of party competition and the alternation of competing alliances in government was finally achieved in 1996 when the Centre–Left Olive Tree coalition took office. At the parliamentary level, however, the system remains multi-party and, as a result, it reproduces many of the problems of governmental instability which have afflicted postwar Italy.

Germany: From Hyperstability to Change?

Charlie Jeffery

This chapter considers the evolution of the German party system against the background of the turbulent historical experience that Germany has undergone in the twentieth century. In tracing party system development across the historically and territorially discontinuous Weimar and Federal Republics, it is argued that only limited evidence exists for the long-term party system 'freezing' claimed by Lipset and Rokkan. It also shows that, following an interlude of unusual party system stability from the mid-1960s to the mid-1980s, forces supporting the dealignment of voter–party relations, and more recently the impact of German unification in 1990, have combined to embed the contemporary party system in a new context of instability and change.

Austria: From Moderate to Polarized Pluralism?

Kurt Richard Luther

Long regarded as an example of consensus and hyperstability, the Austrian party system has of late been characterized by polarization and in part, profound change. This chapter first outlines the genesis of the party system and its rebirth in 1945. The chapter then identifies the key institutional and cultural factors that contributed to the 'freezing' of the post-war party system. Five key aspects of the structure of party competition in Austria are then examined: the number and relative size of the parties, polarization, volatility, government–opposition relations and the 'sites of decisive encounters'. Having identified the nature and extent of change to the 'core features' of the post-war party system, the chapter concludes with a consideration of the causes and possible consequences of that change.

Sweden: A Mild Case of 'Electoral Instability Syndrome'?

David Arter

The Swedish five-party system showed no sign of change until the late 1980s, and even then a resistance to change had apparently built up. Only very mild symptoms of the conditions associated with electoral instability were experienced. There has been a slight increase in the number of parties and the new Green and Christian Democratic parties modestly challenge the long-established domination of the Left–Right spectrum. However, the resilience of the party system in the face of new conflicts and high levels of electoral instability has to be noted, with the major impact being the fluctuating fortunes of the three 'bourgeois' parties. By far the greatest change has been in the sphere of government–opposition relations. Elite co-operation between the bourgeois parties has brought about the end of one-party, social democratic dominance and the establishment of a system of bipolar alternation.

The Netherlands: Resilience Amidst Change

Hans-Martien ten Napel

The Netherlands has not only had a multi-party system but also a *multi-dimensional* party system since the 1870s. Both before and after the Second World War, at least five political parties have been 'relevant'. This chapter deals with the historical development of the Dutch party system before 1945, the contextual variables of most relevance, the post-1945 party system and then the processes of change and adaptation up until the present. The concept of the 'core' of a party system is particularly useful to describe the developments which have taken place in the Dutch party system since 1945. The 'core' of the Dutch party system has been preserved, although it remains to be seen whether the outcome of the parliamentary election of 1994 and the formation of the first cabinet without the participation of the Christian Democrats since 1917, will mark the beginning of an era of more radical change.

Belgium: Party System(s) on the Eve of Disintegration?

Lieven de Winter and Patrick Dumont

The Belgian party system has undergone dramatic change since the 1960s, from a simple three-party system to an extreme case of centrifugal multi-partism. While not polarized along its founding religious and socio-economic cleavages, it is polarized along the linguistic dimension. Indeed, since 1978, there have been two distinct party systems in Belgium – one Flemish and one Walloon. All the traditional parties have split along language lines, success-fully trumping the challenger language parties which emerged in the 1960s, but also strengthening the centrifugal tendencies in the party system. Entrenched clientelism and party domination akin to that in Italy and the rise of a wave of protest parties in the 1980s and 1990s put further strain on the system. The interaction of protest, scandal and regional quasi-autonomy makes an 'ethnic big bang' a real possibility.

Spain: Political Parties in a Young Democracy

Jonathan Hopkin

This chapter examines the evolution of the Spanish party system from the democratic elections after Franco's death to the defeat of the Socialist government in March 1996. It is argued that the historical cleavages which structured the Spanish party system before the Civil War remained relevant in the 1970s, in particular the centre–periphery cleavage, which was directly responsible for the fragmentation of the system into regional party sub-systems. However, there is evidence that institutional variables such as the electoral system, and the strategic decisions of party elites, have had a significant role in shaping the system. Organizational factors and the autonomous choices of party elites, rather than changes in the cleavage structure, explain the radical realignment of the party system in 1982, and the re-emergence of a balanced Left–Right competition for power in the 1990s. Although the party system shows signs of consolidation, the organizational fragility of Spanish parties provides the potential for new re-alignments.

Portugal: Party System Installation and Consolidation

José M. Magone

The Portuguese party system is a product of the country's still recent democratization. The 1975–76 transition to democracy (the 'Revolution of the Carnations') in Portugal was the first instance of the so-called 'third wave of democratization'. The construction and development of the party system have been marked by past practices, notably clientelism, patronage and personalism. These are briefly examined in the light of the exclusion of the masses from the political sphere in the period 1822–1974. The construction of the party system in the 1970s and the changes that occurred in the 1980s and 1990s are then analysed. In the 1980s, the party system developed towards a two-party system, with the decline of the parties to the left and right of the centre. This trend was halted in the election of October 1995 when the four-party system regained vitality. The Portuguese party system in the late 1990s, however, remains ultra-stable.

Party System Change in Western Europe: Positively Political

Mark Donovan and David Broughton

This conclusion summarizes the main findings of the case study chapters, identifying three major developments in contemporary Western European party systems: the weakening of the old 'people's parties'; the virtual disappearance of predominant party systems; and territorial differentiation. Rather than seeing these changes as symptoms of instability or crisis, it argues that they are signs of flexibility, innovation and experimentation within substantially stable systems, structured by competition for government. Consequently, the relative autonomy of the political sphere and the role of party elites in maintaining and in changing patterns of coalition formation is emphasized.

1

Introduction and Guide to Key Sources and Texts

DAVID BROUGHTON AND MARK DONOVAN

Studying political parties and their interaction within competitive party system structures and the process of party system change remain a staple of academic research in political science as well as teaching at both undergraduate and postgraduate levels. Whole academic careers have been selflessly devoted to the study of parties and their struggle with one another for governmental office and political power. It is very rare indeed for the annual European Consortium for Political Research (ECPR) Joint Sessions of Workshops not to have at least one workshop on various aspects of parties in Europe. The most recent of these workshops, specifically concerned with party system change, was convened in Oslo in Spring 1996 and was co-directed by Paul Pennings and Jan-Erik Lane. In addition, the Stein Rokkan lecture, also given at the ECPR sessions in memory of the vastly influential social scientist who died in 1979, is often devoted to a party-related theme.

The reasons for this major and continuing interest in parties and party systems are straightforward. Parties remain central to analysing and understanding key questions of mass representation, democratic participation and policy action and reaction. Despite the seemingly irrefutable evidence from all around the world that parties are less respected, less valued and less trusted than immediately after 1945, the major, 'core' parties in most countries have survived by adapting to new challenges and innovating in response to rapid socio-economic change. These changes have rendered the political arena more uncertain and much less predictable than in the world of stable cleavages and loyal electors which characterized party systems in the past.

The precise significance of these changes requires some differentiation since their impact varies both by nature and degree in different countries. There is, however, enough commonality in terms of such factors as ever increasing economic interdependence, vast structural economic change from industrial to tertiary employment and a seemingly unstoppable decline in the hold of organized religion on ordinary people to draw broad conclusions about the main trends and developments. The chapters in this book consider these changes as the backdrop to the development of the various national party systems and their 'fallout' in terms of party system conflict.

Our particular focus in this book concerns the changing pressures and demands placed on parties and party systems in eleven countries of Western Europe since 1945. The questions raised in the process of considering such a broad canvas inevitably do not provide easy answers. However, even if the answers have to be narrower and more specifically subtle than the questions, they still provide vital components in our understanding of the nature of the challenges that party systems in Western Europe will have to face as we rapidly approach and enter the twenty-first century.

The immediate problems facing any editor of a volume such as this centre upon which countries to choose and which authors to ask to contribute, as well as how best to achieve a high degree of coherence and compatibility between the different national chapters. In this book, we have concentrated upon eleven countries of Western Europe. The book includes studies of the party system in the 'big four' Western European countries, namely, Britain, France, Italy and Germany, as well as studies of seven other nations of considerable significance: Spain, Portugal, Ireland, Sweden, Austria, Belgium and the Netherlands.

The most obvious 'absentees' from the above list are Denmark and Norway. The decision to omit both Denmark and Norway was taken with regret, given the inherent interest in the party systems of both countries derived from the establishment of the Progress parties and Christian People's parties in recent years as well as the regularly cited 'earthquake election' of 1973 in Denmark. Our inability to find contributors in time and the length of the book already with eleven countries left us with no choice. However, David Arter's chapter on Sweden makes a number of comparative points which include both Denmark and Norway.

We should stress that the decision to concentrate solely on the countries of Western Europe is not an attempt to prolong the former Cold War division of the continent. It is more a recognition of the fact that after 1945, under the conditions of the Cold War, the continent of Europe increasingly grew apart. The history of Western Europe in the twentieth century is characterized by long-term, socio-economic and structural trends which have brought Western European societies closer to each other. This process of convergence makes comparison much easier to perform, not only for the number of similarities which emerge, but also for the remaining differences which reveal important individual facets of Western European nation–states. The specific concentration on Western Europe continues elsewhere, most recently in Rhodes *et al.* (1997).

The study of party systems in Central and Eastern Europe has, of course, gathered pace and vigour since 1989 and a number of publications in Europe as well as the United States suggest that this broad theme will remain a growth area for academic study as newly democratic political systems emerge into the sometimes harsh and uncertain arena of mass scrutiny in the 1990s. For now at least, questions of comparability with the 'mature' party systems of Western Europe render the inclusion of the nascent, if already interesting, party systems of Eastern Europe hard to justify. One article of particular interest in the context of recent party and party system developments in Eastern Europe is by Perkins (1996).

As editors, we developed and refined the analytical framework which each of the contributors of the country chapters was asked to follow. This framework was designed to produce a coherent feel to the book as a whole. Consequently, all contributors followed guidelines as to the structure of their chapters. In particular, all the contributors were expected to address five major themes.

First, the broad development of the party system in each country had to be summarized, along with a brief introductory discussion of the different party system typologies and the ways in which they had been applied to each country. Second, a detailed discussion of the historical background to party system developments was needed, dealing with the structure of the party system and the main underpinning cleavages derived from the typology of Lipset and Rokkan. Third, the most important contextual variables were to be considered, specifically, the 'electoral environment' within which the party system operates, most obviously in terms of the prevailing electoral system but also the 'rules of the game' which might help some parties and hinder others. Fourth, consideration had to be given to the major question of the degree of 'unfreezing' of the party system since 1945 (later in Spain and Portugal) and a discussion was needed of the changing balance between stability, continuity and change. The potential of 'anti-system' parties could be dealt with here along with the role and significance of 'extreme' parties and 'flash' parties in the context of electoral volatility.

Fifth, and finally, the contributors were asked to tackle major questions of change and adaptation to bring their accounts of the party system in each country into the 1990s. The rise of new issues and new parties, the importance of European integration, major themes such as electoral de-alignment and realignment as well as questions of policy development, changes in party strategies, intra-party conflict comprised the main themes under this heading.

This may appear to be an overly rigid and prescriptive approach to the study of Western European party systems. We felt, however, that such an approach was necessary if a coherent and complementary volume was to result from the project. Not all of the authors have followed the framework to the letter on the grounds that some of the specified questions and themes were not relevant or important in 'their' country. However, the chapters do broadly follow the framework and they do all attempt to answer the principal questions arising from it in the context of a particular national party system.

In addition, we decided to start the book by giving some general guidance via brief reviews of the 'classic' books and sources on party systems that together provide the main concepts that the contributors employ in the country chapters that follow. These sources should be consulted in tandem with our book. We have omitted works specifically on parties by authors such as Ostrogorksi, Michels, Duverger, Downs, Epstein, von Beyme and Panebianco, while recognizing that the division between parties and party systems is often problematic to draw with any precision.

Guide to Key Sources and Texts on Party Systems and Party System Change (in Chronological Order)

Kirchheimer, O. (1966) The transformation of the West European party systems, J. LaPalombara and M. Weiner (eds), *Political Parties and Political Development*, Princeton, NJ: Princeton University Press, pp. 177–200.

A chapter that is impossible to ignore. Kirchheimer was the key author in the labelling and analysis of the 'catch-all' party in Europe. Parties were now looking to attract voters by whatever means they could and from whichever social groups they could. Change in party systems therefore became possible as appeals based on social attachment and loyalty to particular parties broke down. The idea of 'catch-all' parties tied in with ideas of the 'end of ideology' in the 1960s and the weakening of social cleavages that had previously underpinned stable party systems.

Lipset, S. M. and Rokkan, S. (eds) (1967) *Party Systems and Voter Alignments: Cross-National Perspectives*, New York: Free Press.

A magisterial work whose reputation remains largely undiminished even thirty years after publication. Its main value is rooted in the seminal introductory chapter by the editors in which they set out a developmental approach to party systems, based on an explicitly comparative and historical model. Lipset and Rokkan discuss two 'revolutions' (National and Industrial) from which four major cleavages (subject/dominant culture, church/ government, primary/secondary economy and workers/employers) are derived. They believed that party systems in the 1960s were still based on the cleavage structures of the 1920s (although there were significant exceptions), arguing a strong case for continuity at the party system level.

Sartori, G. (1976) *Parties and Party Systems: A Framework for Analysis*, Cambridge: Cambridge University Press.

An important work for its classification and typologization of different party systems and its use of measures of party system fragmentation and the ideological distance between parties. The type and direction of party competition (centripetal or centrifugal) are stressed and the degree of polarization is seen as an important influence. This book gets far beyond mere description and the simple counting of parties to wrestle with important ideas of party system structure, giving rise to ideas such as 'blackmail potential' and 'segmented multipartism'. Although the book is stated to be volume one, volume two has never been published.

Merkl, P. H. (ed.) (1980) *Western European Party Systems*, New York: Free Press.

A substantial work containing four parts, 25 chapters and more than 600 pages. Studies of the major countries, the smaller democracies, comparative research topics such as cabinet stability, ideological trends and party competition are all included, along with a variety of other themes such as the 'decline of parties' thesis, the aggregation of party systems and citizen lobbies. This is a very useful collection of chapters which acts as a solid introduction to the state of party system research in 1980.

Daalder, H. and Mair, P. (eds) (1983) *Western European Party Systems: Continuity and Change*, London: Sage Publications.

Another very useful collection of chapters covering the main themes and topics. Electoral volatility, voting turnout, incumbency, the European Left, party membership, regionalism, the 'catch-all' thesis tested and the structure of power in parties are all dealt with in a comparative context. The introductory chapter by Hans Daalder and the concluding chapter by Peter Mair provide the best starting points for the general reader.

Mair, P. and Smith, G. (eds) (1989) *Understanding Party System Change in Western Europe*, London: Frank Cass.

This book is also available as a special issue of *West European Politics*, October 1989. The introductory chapter by Smith and Mair provides an excellent introduction to a series of country studies on Austria, Belgium, Denmark,

France, the Netherlands, West Germany, Italy, Ireland and Norway. There then follow two important articles (one by Smith, the other by Mair) on the ideas of 'core persistence' and the people's party, and the 'vulnerability' of party.

Mair, P. (ed.) (1990) *The West European Party System*, Oxford: Oxford University Press.

An excellent starting point for students of party systems since this reader contains many of the 'classic' articles which deal with party systems and party system change over time. The authors chosen include Duverger, Neumann, Kirchheimer, Sartori, Lipset and Rokkan, Rose and Urwin, Pedersen, Inglehart, Lijphart, Dahl and Blondel. In other words, this is the place to start for easy access to the key primary material.

Katz, R. S. and Mair, P. (eds) (1994) *How Parties Organize. Change and Adaptation in Party Organizations in Western Democracies*, London: Sage Publications.

Katz and Mair's work in the 1990s is important for the development of the idea of the 'cartel party' specifically (see also their article in the first issue of *Party Politics* in 1995) and the shifting of emphasis onto the internal workings and structures of parties generally. The first publication from this project was a huge sourcebook of data on parties in many countries of Europe published in 1992. The above book, edited by Katz and Mair and a team of country specialists, is an analysis of these internal structures in detail.

Ware, A. (1996) *Political Parties and Party Systems*, Oxford: Oxford University Press.

A substantial book of more than 400 pages, divided into three parts (parties, party systems and moving towards government). The party systems section focuses upon comparing party systems, the causes of the differences between party systems and the question of party system change. The book is consistently structured, with a discussion of the main themes followed by examples, followed by a consideration of the themes in five countries: France, Germany, Britain, Japan and the United States. Data in five appendices provide the empirical context for the analyses.

Mair, P. (1997) *Party System Change: Approaches and Interpretations*, Oxford: Clarendon Press.

This book focuses upon the interpretation of change and stability in contemporary party systems. How do party systems survive and how best may party system change be analysed and understood? The questions of persistence and change along with ideas of vulnerability and endurance are discussed. Party organizations and their 'invasion' of the state are considered as are the themes of structure and competition in Western European party systems. Post-Communist party systems are also considered, in particular the problems of consolidation that such systems face.

Wolinetz, S. B. (ed) (1997) *Party Systems*, Aldershot: Ashgate.

This is another reader of important journal articles on party systems intended to provide the starting point for students and researchers alike. There is an introduction to the volume written by Wolinetz, and the various articles are reproduced as they were first published. Wolinetz has also edited a companion volume in this series on political parties.

Having now set out the ideas behind the project, the framework of the volume as a whole and the 'classic' and other texts to consult for initial information and ideas, we can now move on to the first substantive chapter of the book: a consideration of the development of the party system in Britain.

2

The Changing British Party System: Two-Party Equilibrium or the Emergence of Moderate Pluralism?

PAUL WEBB AND JUSTIN FISHER

Introduction

For some time after 1945, it was orthodox to regard Britain as having one of the most stable and party-orientated political systems in the western world. Party penetration of the state and party identification within society were generally considered to be relatively stable and high, so that it was virtually impossible to conceive of political life in the country without thinking first and foremost of *party* political life.

Since the 1970s, however, the political system in Britain has been under various pressures from which the party system has been far from immune. This rapidly becomes apparent if we start by considering the nature of the 'core' of the traditional British party system. A frequently employed form of shorthand for this was the notion of the 'two-party, two-class' system. This term summarized the way in which the two major parties absorbed approximately 90 per cent of the vote until 1970, and patterns of electoral alignment were overwhelmingly structured by the class cleavage. Moreover, the alternation in power of these parties (Conservative and Labour) as single party governments was underwritten by the effects of the 'first-past-the-post' electoral system; this exaggerated the parliamentary gains of winning parties and generated a fairly regular swing of the electoral pendulum between 1945 and 1979 (see Tables 2.1 and 2.2). Finally, despite a superficial appearance of adversarial conflict between the two major parties, a significant degree of real policy consensus ensured that the party system actually helped foster a relatively homogeneous national political culture.

However, since the middle of the 1970s at least, much of this orthodox account of the post-war system has been challenged by a continuing and multi-dimensional debate about the transformation of British party politics. This challenge is predicated on a number of interconnected developments which have emerged during this period. These developments include a number of high volatility general elections; partisan and class dealignment; the emergence of nationalist cleavages in Scotland and Wales which have

Table 2.1 United Kingdom general election results, 1945–97

Election Year	Con. Vote/Seats		Labour Vote/Seats		Lib/Dem.[1] Vote/Seats		Other Vote/Seats	
1945	39.8	213	48.3	393	9.1	12	2.7	22
1950	43.5	299	46.1	315	9.1	9	1.3	2
1951	48.0	321	48.8	295	2.5	6	0.7	3
1955	49.7	345	46.4	277	2.7	6	1.1	2
1959	49.4	365	43.8	258	5.9	6	0.9	1
1964	43.4	304	44.1	317	11.2	9	1.3	0
1966	41.9	253	47.9	363	8.5	12	1.7	2
1970	46.4	330	43.0	287	7.5	6	3.1	7
1974 Feb.	37.8	297	37.1	301	19.3	14	5.8	23
1974 Oct.	35.8	277	39.2	319	18.3	13	6.7	26
1979	43.9	339	37.0	269	13.8	11	5.3	16
1983	42.4	397	27.6	209	25.4	23	4.6	21
1987	42.3	376	30.8	229	22.6	22	4.4	23
1992	41.9	336	34.4	271	17.8	20	5.8	24
1997	31.4	165	44.4	419	17.2	46	7.0	29

[1] Liberals; Liberal-SDP Alliance, 1983 and 1987; Liberal Democrats.

Table 2.2 Government composition in the UK, 1945–97

Dates	Government Party	Status	Prime Minister
July 1945–Feb. 1950	Labour	Majority	Attlee
Feb. 1950–Oct. 1951	Labour	Majority	Attlee
Oct. 1951–May 1955	Conservative	Majority	Churchill; Eden (1955)
May 1955–Oct. 1959	Conservative	Majority	Eden; Macmillan (1957)
Oct. 1959–Oct. 1964	Conservative	Majority	Macmillan; Douglas-Home (1963)
Oct. 1964–Mar. 1966	Labour	Majority	Wilson
Apr. 1966–June 1970	Labour	Majority	Wilson
June 1970–Feb. 1974	Conservative	Majority	Heath
Mar. 1974–Oct. 1974	Labour	Minority	Wilson
Oct. 1974–Nov. 1976	Labour	Majority	Wilson; Callaghan (1976)
Nov. 1976–May 1979	Labour	Minority[1]	Callaghan
May 1979–June 1983	Conservative	Majority	Thatcher
June 1983–June 1987	Conservative	Majority	Thatcher
June 1987–Apr. 1992	Conservative	Majority	Thatcher; Major (1990)
Apr. 1992–May 1997	Conservative	Majority	Major
May 1997–	Labour	Majority	Blair

[1] Between March 1977 and August 1978, the Labour Government's majority in the House of Commons was only maintained by the support of Liberal MPs. This was only an agreement on parliamentary support; the Liberals did not participate directly in government.

threatened to fragment the national political culture; the erosion of two-party electoral domination (by 1983 only 70 per cent of the popular vote was accounted for by Labour and the Conservatives); the apparent fracturing of the post-war policy consensus by the early 1980s; and the growing chorus of criticism levelled at the damaging iniquities of the electoral system and the adversarial 'winner-takes-all' political mentality that was, for many commentators, closely associated with it.

As a result of these various indications of change, we need to ask how stable the core model of the party system is – does it manage to retain its essential qualities despite the widespread evidence of apparent decay, or is it, in some senses at least, fundamentally transformed? For instance, and notwithstanding the appearance of continuing predominance by Labour and the Conservatives, is it still even appropriate to describe the contemporary British model as an authentic 'two-party system'?

Historical background

Throughout most of the twentieth century, the primary cleavage in the British party system has been that of social class, though it was not yet indisputably sovereign in 1900. Indeed, evidence that class was the predominant factor only became important as the party system changed during the period preceding the Second World War (Wald, 1983).

In 1900, there were two principal parliamentary parties, the Conservatives and the Liberals. Both were bourgeois, in that they supported capitalism, and neither sought radical change in the distribution of power and resources in British society. However, there were key differences, and their respective electoral appeals reflected this. The party system by this time was based upon three principal cleavages: class, religion and imperialism. Class manifested itself as a cleavage in two ways. First, it was apparent in the support offered to the Liberals by elements of the trade union movement (notably the miners). There remained, however, a significant minority of the working class that voted Conservative; this was particularly noticeable in rural areas (Pugh, 1982: 82) and among those deferentially disposed towards social elites. The class cleavage was also apparent in the growth of petty bourgeois support for the Liberals. Victorian Britain had seen a growth in the number of artisans and small businessmen, yet they remained 'outsiders' within British society in many ways. The Liberals offered a home for these aspiring capitalists which the Conservative Party did not, since the latter appealed far more to those content with the existing social hierarchy.

Religion was the second principal cleavage. While Anglicans (adherents of the established state church) predominantly voted Conservative, Nonconformist Protestants tended to support the Liberals. This reflected the fact that Nonconformists had experienced discrimination and prejudice well into the nineteenth century (for instance, legal disqualification from the right to vote or hold public office), while the Liberal Party had inherited the radical mantle of support for the values of religious toleration.

The third principal cleavage on which the party system was based was that of imperialism. As a device of mass political mobilization, this was invented by the great Conservative leader Benjamin Disraeli, and proved a key source of working-class Conservative support (Barnes, 1994: 336). In this context the question of Anglo-Irish relations deserves particular attention. The proposals for Irish Home Rule in 1886, made by Liberal Prime Minister W.E. Gladstone, had a significant impact on the party system. Home rule divided the Liberal Party, creating a group of Liberal Unionists who eventually realigned themselves with the Conservatives, the latter being staunch defenders of the union between Britain and Ireland. More than this, the Irish question divided the country, and especially the working class, by resuscitating long-standing social and political prejudices.

Two developments which jointly transformed the party system during the first three decades of the twentieth century merit particular attention: first, class came to replace religion as the predominant cleavage structuring the party system (Wald, 1983); second, and contingent upon this, the Labour Party replaced the Liberals as one of the two great parties in the system. The Labour Representation Committee (LRC) was originally established in 1900 as frustration about achieving effective co-operation with the Liberals grew within the organized working class. There had been isolated successes, but by the 1880s, the trade unions were dividing into two groups: those who favoured working with the Liberals, and those who desired the formation of a new party as the chief expression of working-class politics. The LRC was set up as an umbrella organization federating the TUC, the co-operative movement, and various socialist societies (such as the Social Democratic Federation [SDF], the Independent Labour Party [ILP] and the Fabian Society), the trade unions having 94 per cent of the affiliated membership. The LRC formally became the Labour Party in 1906.

The replacement of the Liberals by Labour as the main political opposition to the Conservatives in the 1920s was sudden and resulted from a variety of factors. Important among these were the Representation of the People Act of 1918, which further extended the suffrage; splits in the Liberal leadership during and after the First World War; the removal from the political agenda of a Liberal *cause célèbre*, Ireland; and, of course, the growing significance of industrial class issues. With Labour in the ascendant, the Liberals were comprehensively defeated in the 1924 election. Though Liberal decline varied from region to region, it was apparent by the end of the 1920s that Britain's essentially two-party system had realigned itself about the new dualism of social class.[1]

The period of the new two-party system was initially short-lived. Economic collapse in the late 1920s resulted in the formation of the national coalition government in 1931 which effectively governed Britain until the end of the Second World War. Though formally a coalition which included the former Labour leader, Ramsay MacDonald, the National Government was nevertheless dominated by the Conservatives. It was only after the war that full party competition resumed.

Contextual factors

A variety of contextual variables has influenced the development of the British party system. We should not overlook the impact of the electoral franchise, at least in historical context. The suffrage was extended to all adult males and women aged 30 and over in 1918. These changes clearly benefited Labour and contributed to its emergence as one of the leading two parties in the system. While the extension of the franchise to include all adult women (in 1928) does not appear to have greatly affected the party system, the reduction of the age of majority (from 21 to 18) in 1969 may be said to have had some impact. First, unadjusted figures suggest a significant drop in general election turnouts following this move. Second, and more significantly from the point of view of the party system itself, the rise in the centre party vote may be partially explained by an influx of younger voters (Heath *et al.*, 1991: 220).

It should also be noted that the Labour Party in particular has expressed mounting concern about the impact upon electoral registration of recent government policies – most notably the short-lived and highly controversial local government tax known colloquially as the poll tax. Seen as highly regressive in its economic effects, this levy (properly called the Community Charge) was widely regarded as having fostered a reluctance on the part of many citizens – especially those within Labour's natural constituency of the poorer classes – to register with the local authorities that maintain the electoral rolls. The Labour and Liberal Democrat Parties now fear that, notwithstanding the demise of the ill-fated poll tax, this has had a lasting and damaging impact on the electoral register from their point of view. Research indicates that these fears are not unfounded; Smith and McLean estimate that the poll tax may have cost Labour up to seven seats and the Liberal Democrats up to three seats in 1992. Moreover, despite the repeal of the poll tax, its effect on registration and constituency boundary reviews seemed destined to persist into the next century (Smith and McLean, 1994: 241).

Undoubtedly the strongest contextual influence upon the party system, however, remains the electoral system. For national elections, Britain uses a Single Member Simple Plurality (SMSP) – often known as first-past-the-post

– electoral system (Crewe, 1993: 93). This system has a number of well-known biases. First, in terms of seats won, it tends to over-reward the single most popular party. Second, it favours parties with geographical concentrations of electoral support. Thus, while it ensures the representation of strong regional parties like Plaid Cymru and the Scottish National Party, the Liberal Democrats (and their predecessors) suffer(ed), largely because they have had few concentrations of support. To put it crudely, they come second in far too many constituencies for their own good, which may give them the gratification of knowing that they are an authentically national phenomenon, but provides them with few representational advantages. The clearest example of this problem was provided by the result of the 1983 General Election, when the Liberal Democrats' predecessors, the SDP/Liberal Alliance, polled 25.4 per cent of the popular vote, just behind Labour with 27.6 per cent. Yet, whereas Labour received 32.2 per cent of the seats in the House of Commons, the Alliance parties had to satisfy themselves with a paltry 3.5 per cent of the seats. Moreover, there is evidence to suggest that this stark deviation from proportionality in terms of parliamentary representation is even greater when regarded on a regional basis (Dunleavy *et al.*, 1994). Of course, proportionality is by no means the sole normative criterion by which to evaluate an electoral system; many have argued that despite the proportional anomalies, the electoral system does at least foster 'strong and stable government'. The SMSP electoral system is a key factor in the maintenance of the British party system because it militates against the breakthrough of a third party. To confirm this point, simulations of the 1992 and 1997 elections using a variety of alternative electoral systems indicate that both the Additional Member System and the Single Transferable Vote would have given the Liberal Democrats at least 100 seats (Dunleavy *et al.*, 1992; 1997).

Furthermore, it is often overlooked that the electoral system generates cumulative biases beyond the immediate domain of parliamentary representation itself, for it helps determine party access to the resources of the state. For instance, access to free television and radio broadcasting time is related to the current state of party representation in parliament. Similarly, the major parties – and especially one which has been in government for an extended period of time – are well placed to dominate the nomination of non-elected appointments to the welter of state-funded agencies known as 'quangos' (quasi autonomous non-governmental organizations) (Heywood, 1994: 18). It might also be added that the relative dearth of state financial subsidies to political parties reflected, until recently at least, the representational domination of the major parties. While it should not be overlooked that both have often suffered periods of financial difficulty, Labour and the Conservatives have nevertheless enjoyed a considerable relative advantage over third party rivals in financial terms; both major parties have been able to rely on regular sources of corporate support (derived from business in the case of the Conservatives and the trade unions in Labour's case), whereas other parties have generally been able only to look to the personal generosity of sympathetic individuals (Fisher, 1992; 1994a; 1994b; 1995; 1996a; 1996b). Again, then, the fact that the electoral system worked to permanently exclude third parties from power enabled the major parties to operate a kind of informal cartel which maintained their relative advantage over other challengers. In the early 1990s, this 'cartel' showed signs of crumbling, with Labour endorsing the extension of state funding of parties, and giving serious consideration to the case for electoral reform (Plant, 1993).

A final contextual factor worth noting is the fact that Britain became an increasingly centralized unitary state, at least until 1997, 'in which there are no autonomous centres of political power apart from national government' (King, 1992: 224). Local government is weak; there is no Bill of Rights; no Freedom of Information Act; considerable power of party patronage; relatively strong party discipline inside Parliament; and a 'winner-takes-all' adversarial elite political culture, which displays little inclination for bipartisan consensus building. In terms of the party system, the significance of all this is twofold: first, it creates the conditions within which the power of the party controlling the state (and the singular form of the noun is entirely appropriate in the post-war context) can become remarkably pervasive. Thus, party penetration of the state can remain high even if party penetration of society may be decreasing. Second, this undispersed pattern of power may well have fostered the regional resentments which first generated the emergence of Scottish and Welsh nationalism after the 1960s.

The post-war party system

Until the 1970s the post-war British party system was strongly two-party in character. The Liberal Party was reduced to such small representation in the immediate aftermath of the war that serious consideration was given to the idea of merger with the Conservatives (Cook, 1989: 134). Leader Clement Davies rejected Churchill's overtures in 1951, however, and the Liberals survived as a small rump in the House of Commons for much of the 1950s. From the early 1960s, the party enjoyed spectacular by-election successes and, fuelled by these performances, an increasing number of Liberal candidates were fielded. By and large, however, political life was dominated by the Conservatives and Labour, whose combined share of general election votes did not dip below 87.5 per cent until February 1974.

This party system was in some ways rather different to its pre-war counterpart. Whereas the Conservatives had clearly dominated political life during the inter-war years, there was now a credible contender for government in the form of the Labour Party. Labour's enhanced strength can, in a variety of ways, be attributed to the wartime experience. First, the exigencies of war had meant that economic interventionism and state ownership seemed far more acceptable. Second, the war had not only generated a feeling of national unity in the face of a clear enemy, but had also fostered a desire not to return to the far more divided society and severe unemployment of the 1930s. Third, co-operation with Stalin's Soviet Union had helped create greater sympathy for the left in general, and finally, senior Labour politicians such as Clement Attlee and Ernest Bevin had shown themselves to be highly capable members of the government in wartime. There was, in short, a sea change in British politics and in citizens' expectations of government, as exemplified by the Beveridge Report of 1942, which promised widespread welfare reforms once the war was over.

In 1945, then, Labour was well placed to capitalize upon the new mood, although many still believed that the Conservatives, led by wartime leader Winston Churchill, would win the election. In the event, Labour won a landslide majority, the first it had ever enjoyed. Consequently, the pre-war pattern of Conservative dominance gave way to an authentic two-party system, and the high levels of electoral volatility that characterized the era of realignment in the 1920s and 1930s came to be replaced by far more stable patterns of party–voter linkage which overwhelmingly reflected the structural influence of the class cleavage (Bartolini and Mair, 1990: Appendix 2).

A number of key features characterized the operation of this party system up until the 1970s. First, elections produced single-party majorities. This was true of all general elections during the period 1945–70, though majorities did vary in size, and the narrow victories achieved in 1950 and 1964 prompted further elections shortly after the original polls.

Second, there was alternation in government. Between 1945 and 1970, the Conservatives and Labour each won four elections. Moreover, the Conservatives were in power for thirteen years and Labour for twelve. This is not to say that the swing of the electoral pendulum was precisely metronomic: the Conservatives' thirteen years in power comprised a single unbroken incumbency, 1951–64, while Labour's experiences in government occurred either side of this period. Nevertheless, the changes of government occurred regularly enough to constitute a pattern of genuine alternation.

Third, the reasonably lengthy periods in office enjoyed by both parties also contributed an element of stability to the development of public policy. It has been widely acknowledged that this period saw a broad consensus on economic and welfare policy. In economic terms this consensus expressed itself in at least three areas. First, macro-economic management was essentially Keynesian in approach. Second, there was general agreement on the relative size of the public and private sectors. The 1945–51 Labour Government embarked upon a policy of widespread nationalization of public utilities, and subsequent governments largely maintained this level of state ownership (with the notable exception of the steel industry, which was subject to de-nationalization and re-nationalization). Finally, there were attempts to introduce elements of a consensual and corporatist approach into the formulation and implementation of industrial policy (witness the birth of the tripartite National Economic Development Council in 1961). This consensus on economic policy prompted many a reference to 'Butskellism', or the nearly bipartisan approach espoused by the Conservative Chancellor of the Exchequer, R.A.B. Butler, and his Labour counterpart in the 1950s, Hugh Gaitskell. The convergence of economic policy was echoed in the development of welfare and social policy.

With overwhelming public approbation of this Keynesian–welfarist consensus, it is unsurprising that the two-party system of this period was highly stable and impenetrable for minor parties. This cemented the increasingly 'frozen' aspect that the two-party, two-class British system showed to the world, in contrast to the fluid and unpredictable model of pre-war (re)alignment. Admiring commentators of the time were apt to speak as if this state of affairs could endure indefinitely, yet by the middle of the 1970s there was increasing cause to question such an assumption.

Change and adaptation since the 1960s

The impression of a frozen party system that successfully expressed and channelled all significant political demands was undermined after 1970 as a series of new social and political challenges beset the major parties. These challenges were either based on issues and lines of political conflict which potentially cut across existing patterns of electoral alignment, or had the effect of generally undermining the electorate's trust in both major parties. The first challenge which presented itself for consideration was of the latter variety. This was the perennial question of relative national economic decline which became increasingly vexed during the 1970s. Until then, Britain had shared in the growth and modernization that characterized most industrial economies during the 30 years following the war. This changed rapidly in the early 1970s. A number of factors combined to produce this change, including the collapse of the Bretton Woods system which exposed Britain to greater economic uncertainty, and the oil shocks of 1973 which torpedoed the economic aspirations of governments at the time. By 1976,

Britain was facing a severe foreign exchange crisis and was obliged to apply for a loan from the International Monetary Fund (IMF). The result was a shift in economic policy away from Keynesianism, and the establishment of a more market-oriented economic strategy, prosecuted with particular enthusiasm by the post-1979 Thatcher governments.

The widespread perception of weak economic performance undermined the confidence of large parts of the electorate in both major parties. Growing economic frailties interacted with new levels of antagonism and instability in industrial relations. The first manifestation of this problem occurred in the late 1960s when Harold Wilson's Labour Government was beset by an alarming increase in industrial militancy. In response, it attempted to introduce measures to curb the activities of trade unions, but these measures failed to become law after sustained opposition from the unions and elements of the Labour Party itself. Edward Heath's new Conservative Government also attempted to deal with the problem, introducing the Industrial Relations Act in 1971. The Act was far-reaching but proved to be unworkable in the face of trade union non-compliance. Indeed, government–union conflicts played a decisive role in the outcome of at least two general elections in the 1970s – those of February 1974 (when Heath had called a snap election on the issue of union power) and May 1979 (when Callaghan's Labour Government suffered the consequences of the collapse of its corporatist strategy). The longer-term consequences for party system development of the industrial relations issue have been at least twofold: in the first place, the collective recollection of the breakdown in party–union relations in the late 1970s contributed significantly to Labour's prolonged exclusion from power thereafter; and second, it contributed to the SDP schism from the party in 1981. This division of the main party of opposition was a vital factor in explaining Labour's inability to oust the Conservatives during the 1980s.

The period since 1970 has given rise to further issues which have tested the established two-class, two-party system. The first is the *sectoral cleavage*. The development of the activities and responsibilities of the state since 1945 has generated a number of interconnected lines of differentiation between public and private sectors. Specifically, it has been suggested that such public–private tensions express themselves in the form of at least two distinctive types of sectoral conflict – the *consumption* and *production* variants. The former model offers an account of how the expansion of a variety of public and welfare services (especially in housing, health and transport) can differentiate citizens as consumers of these services and benefits, while the production sector model contends that those who work in the public and private sectors, respectively, have diametrically opposed interests. In essence, those who work and/or consume predominantly in the private sector might well be expected to favour cuts in public services and taxes, whereas those more dependent, in one way or another, on the public sector should be far keener to see jobs and services sustained, even at the cost of higher taxes. This public–private dualism cuts across traditional patterns of class alignment, as illustrated, for example, by the presence in the electorate of groups such as manual workers who own their own homes and middle-class professionals employed within the public sector (Dunleavy, 1979; Dunleavy, 1980; Dunleavy and Husbands, 1985). Of the two versions of the sectoral argument, the more empirically persuasive has generally been the consumption variant. In particular, there is much evidence to suggest that public–private housing distinctions have been increasingly significant in structuring patterns of party support since the 1960s (Rose and McAllister, 1985: 61; Heath *et al.*, 1991: 106).

A second cleavage which has (re)emerged since the 1960s to affect patterns of alignment in Britain has been ethnic in orientation. In terms of Rokkan and Lipset's classic scheme of cleavage development, it may be best understood as a centre–periphery cleavage which appeared largely dormant, if not extinct, at the time they wrote in the 1960s. However, during the 1970s it became very apparent that Scottish and Welsh nationalism retained a growing capacity to mobilize electoral support in ways which cut completely across the two-class, two-party model of party competition. We can think of this revival of atavistic conflicts within Britain as resting partly on problems of uneven economic performance (especially in the Scottish case), and partly on cultural resentments of the dominant English component of the British state. This 'denationalization' of the British electorate (Miller, 1983) quite clearly signifies a partial thaw of the apparently frozen party system of the 1960s – especially in the case of Scotland where the two-party pattern of party competition has been replaced by one of Labour predominance in a context of four-party competition; that is to say, by 1992, Labour's average Scottish constituency vote amounted to 40.0 per cent, while the Conservatives, SNP and Liberal Democrats, respectively, averaged 24.4 per cent, 21.2 per cent and 13.2 per cent – all significant levels of response by the Scottish electorate to the overtures of the parties. However, given the vagaries of the electoral system, Labour swept 49 of the 72 seats north of the border, while the Conservatives managed eleven, the Liberal Democrats nine and the SNP just three (Butler and Kavanagh, 1992: 310–12).[2]

Thus, relative economic decline has been the chief issue threatening to undermine popular faith in the major parties *en bloc*, while sectoral and nationalist pressures have proved most likely to generate lines of conflict which cut across class alignments within the electorate. In addition to these factors, however, parties have faced at least one other significant type of challenge: the growth of internal party conflict.

It should be emphasized that an important element of the orthodox account of British two-party politics from 1945–70 stressed – or more accurately, perhaps, simply took for granted – the high levels of internal party discipline and cohesion which existed. Yet since 1970, and even more obviously since 1980, the major parties have begun to come unstuck. Philip Norton's studies of the growth of cross-party voting in the House of Commons have been of central importance in demonstrating this (Norton, 1975; 1980), and they have been confirmed by Jack Brand's equally detailed research in which he asserts that the number of discernible factions in British parliamentary parties has grown (Brand, 1989; 1992). The problem, as Anthony King sees it, lies in the fact that: 'The old boxes are still there, but the new issues do not fit into them. There is now a considerable disjuncture between real politics and traditional two-party politics' (King, 1992: 229). In other words, it is increasingly the case that significant policy divisions in British public life lie *within* parties as much as *between* them, as the parties struggle to come to terms with the complexities of a changing political agenda.

King argues that a number of issues test the internal cohesion of parties in this way, including the environment, women's issues, defence, agriculture, constitutional reform and, above all, the question of European integration. Indeed, King is surely not exaggerating in suggesting that the latter is the 'paradigm case of the breakdown of the traditional two-party pattern' (ibid.), and this has been true ever since Edward Heath guided the country into the EEC in 1973. Until the passage of the Single European Act was complete, intra-party tensions on the issue were probably most apparent within the Labour Party, though by the turn of the 1990s the prospect of 'ever closer union' which inhered in the Treaty of Maastricht was beginning to provoke serious unrest within the governing Conservative Party. The dwindling capacity of the parliamentary whips to assert their authority over recalcitrant backbench MPs was cruelly exposed by the almost triumphant defiance of a hard core of Europhobic Conservatives who were deprived of the party whip in 1995, only to be re-embraced by the Party a few months later despite little or no evidence of contrition on their collective part.

Not every issue inspires internecine conflict in the way that the question of Europe does. Nevertheless, the multiple challenges that the major parties have had to contend with since 1970 have wrought significant changes in the working of the party system. The effect of such changes is well summed up by King who argues that, in the context of growing one-party dominance (a theme to which we shall return), the reality of political life is substantially different to that suggested by the classic Westminster model:

in the 1990s, the voters choose between two political parties, neither of which

has clearly stated views on a wide range of issues, and the normally victorious
Conservative Party then proceeds, within itself, to try to work out policy on the
most contentious issues.

(King, 1992: 230).

In short, the party system has faced a number of interconnected challenges
since 1970 which have jointly served to stretch the credibility of the notion
that it has remained 'frozen'. This is not to suggest that transformation has
been so great as to sweep away all components of the traditional core system;
social class, for instance, clearly retains real importance for British social and
political life (Marshall *et al.,* 1988: 266-8), and Labour and the Conservatives are undoubtedly the most popular national parties, albeit this
popularity may well be contingent upon the workings of the electoral
system. Nevertheless, the effects of the various challenges have been notable
at the levels of electoral behaviour, policy development and party organizational adaptation.

Electoral change

The February 1974 general election provided a new scenario for the post-
war British party system and seemed to many observers to signify, among
other things, the onset of new levels of electoral instability. It was characterized by the return of a minority Labour Government and a surge in third
party support. The Liberals in particular made progress, achieving 19.3 per
cent of the vote, a post-war high and a considerable leap from the 7.5 per
cent they won in 1970. As a result, the Conservatives and Labour together
only managed to score 75 per cent of the popular vote, a notable fall from the
levels achieved at previous elections. Labour called a further general election
in October of that year, managing to achieve a slim majority. Nevertheless,
the two main parties could only increase their share of the vote overall by 0.1
per cent and whilst the Liberals slipped back a little, gains were made by the
nationalist parties. In short, the party system started to take on a more
fragmented appearance as the actual number of parties represented in
parliament increased from four to nine, and the 'effective' number from 2.5
during the late 1960s to 3.1 twenty years later (Laakso and Taagepera,
1979).

There are further indicators we can consult to gauge levels of electoral
instability in the 1970s. The two-party swing, the parties' opinion poll
ratings, overall volatility levels and Pedersen's index of net volatility all tend
to suggest a growth of instability during this decade (though not necessarily
all at the same elections). The most widely employed of these measures in a
comparative context is probably the Pedersen Index, which does not present
any kind of secular trend since 1945 as a whole, but does show how the

elections of February 1974, 1983, 1992 and 1997 were relatively high volatility affairs compared to the post-war norm (Webb, 1992b: 91).

An alternative way of judging underlying patterns of alignment within the electorate is through measuring levels of partisan commitment. While the proportion of partisan identifiers did not alter radically after 1964, the strength with which partisanship was expressed certainly appeared to shrink considerably. Thus, the period from 1964–70 saw the proportion of 'very strong' partisans in the electorate stable at around 44 per cent, but this fell to 30 per cent in February 1974 and 27 per cent in October. Moreover, this downward trend continued so that by 1987 barely one-fifth of the electorate claimed a strong partisan allegiance (Norris, 1990: 127).

In short, the most compelling indication of growing electoral instability after 1970 is the erosion of partisan commitment. A variety of theses have been advanced to help explain this phenomenon, including the expansion of higher educational provision and mass access to television, the twin elements of a new 'cognitive mobilization' which is deemed by some to facilitate the political independence of electors (Barnes and Kaase, 1979). That is, voters become more able to assess information about public affairs without having to rely on party cues (thanks to the role education plays in developing their intellectual skills) at precisely the time that they have far greater access to independent sources of non-partisan information (from the broadcasting media). If true, this may go a long way towards explaining the growing difficulty that parties have in controlling the changing issue agenda of politics.

Then again, the cleavage changes we discussed above could in themselves, of course, constitute an important source of electoral instability. For instance, some commentators have argued that partisan dealignment is a direct corollary of class dealignment in voting patterns; given that partisan and class identities were so closely bound together in the two-party, two-class system, it is inevitable that the weakening of one must affect the other. Quite why class dealignment has occurred – and, indeed, whether it has occurred at all – has been a vexed question in British political science since the 1970s. The emergence of new centre–periphery and sectoral cleavages can in themselves go some of the way towards explaining class dealignment since they cut directly across class identities. In addition, a number of other factors have been suggested, from the embourgeoisement of the increasingly affluent working class after 1960 (Abrams *et al.*, 1960; Goldthorpe *et al.*, 1968), to the growth of mixed-class households (Marshall *et al.*, 1988: 134) and the physical decomposition of class-typical communities (Hobsbawm, 1981).

But is social class really a weaker influence on electoral choice in Britain than hitherto? Since the 1970s a sometimes very intense debate on the question has been waged by a number of well-known protagonists (Franklin, 1985; Heath *et al.*, 1985; Crewe, 1986; Heath *et al.*, 1987; Dunleavy, 1987). The debate has ranged over more than one type of question, including sociological ones (how do you define class?) and (often arcanely) methodological ones (how do you measure class voting?). Our view is that those asserting the decline of class voting have generally had the better of the argument.

Adaptation of policy and ideology

Perhaps the most widely held view of party ideological development in contemporary Britain is that the relatively high degree of policy consensus which existed between the system's major adversaries until the 1970s, was fractured as Labour and the Conservatives both became more extreme in the early 1980s, only for a period of reconvergence – albeit further to the right along the ideological spectrum – to occur after 1990. Moreover, Labour's renewed pursuit of the median voter has brought the party even closer to the left-of-centre Liberal Democrats on many issues, a situation which creates possibilities of enhanced competition and/or co-operation between the two.

British Conservatism has proved unusually resilient and adaptable when viewed from a comparative European perspective; while its philosophical roots probably lie in the irrationalism of the counter-enlightenment, it has proved flexible enough to adapt itself to the changing political and social agendas of the past 200 years. The essence of British Conservatism lies in the twin desire to occupy power and to maintain some system of unequal property relations in society. The modern party is, very crudely, a coalition of traditional 'One-Nation' Tories and economic liberals, in which the latter have increasingly come to predominate since the time of Margaret Thatcher's accession to the leadership in 1975. This is not to say that such changes have not been wrought without significant internal opposition, but the emphasis on 'rolling back the state' in the sphere of economic intervention, privatization of public sector industry, the removal of public subsidies to industry, weakening the power of trade unions, reducing public spending and direct taxation, and curbing state welfare provision tended to prevail within governing circles after 1979. Add to this a public rhetoric of moral traditionalism and popular authoritarianism on social issues, plus a nationalistic resentment of the European Union, and we have in essence the most striking features of Conservative government policy under Margaret Thatcher and John Major.

Yet the price of this New Right predominance proved high. The tensions within the Conservative Party over a diverse range of controversial policies, from Europe to sentencing and prison reform, from the treatment of immigrants claiming asylum to the public lambasting of single-parent families, and from welfare provision to privatization were not resolved while the party remained in government, not even by John Major's more conciliatory leadership style. As Anthony Giddens has pointed out, the source of these tensions may well lie in the fact that the Conservative Party became too radical for its own good: 'For nothing is more corrosive of established traditions, habits and forms of social cohesion, just as Marx pointed out, than the wholesale cultivation of market relations' (Giddens, 1994: 37).

The Labour Party has experienced an ideological odyssey of its own since 1979. In the aftermath of electoral defeat in that year the party leadership lurched notably leftwards and ended up issuing a lengthy and highly radical manifesto for the 1983 general election. This promised withdrawal from the European Community, the imposition of import controls, reflation of the economy, extensive nationalization of industry, new forms of industrial planning and state support, more generous welfare provision and unilateral nuclear disarmament. After Neil Kinnock was elected party leader in the autumn of that year, however, the party embarked on a decade-long process of ideological and organizational 'modernization' which has succeeded in overturning much of this radical charter for 'socialism in one country'. Indeed, by 1992, the party felt able to assert that 'at the core of our convictions is belief in individual liberty' (Labour Party, 1992: 7), and it was made very plain that the proper economic role of the state was to facilitate the smooth working of the market, rather than to replace it. It followed, among other things, that a notably cautious approach to renationalization of public utilities was promised, while the stark anti-Europeanism of 1983 gave way to an unprecedented enthusiasm for the European project (Webb, 1993: 113). Since then a willingness to countenance new forms of thinking that break the mould of Labour Party tradition has also been apparent in the domains of educational and social policy.

As in the case of the Conservative Party, such ideological revision was not possible without signs of internal dissent (most notably over the issue of rewriting the party's constitutional commitment to public ownership of industry in 1995). It provoked, moreover, a debate within party, journalistic and academic circles about the ideological identity of New Labour; clearly, Labour seemed to have moved to the right since 1983 (though for an unusual counter-argument, see Topf, 1994: 164), but did this amount to a simple modernization of its traditional social democratic location, or was a more insidious 'accommodation' (and by implication 'sell-out') to the New Right's agenda taking place (Elliott, 1993; Hay, 1994; Smith, 1994; Wickham-Jones, 1995)?

Since their foundation as a party, the Liberal Democrats have maintained the old Liberal Party's identity within the tradition of radical or social liberalism (Curtice, 1988). In particular, they have laid great emphasis on issues of constitutional reform (including electoral reform, devolution, reform of the House of Lords, the need for Freedom of Information legislation and a Bill of Rights). In addition, their left-of-centre stance on economic, educational and social issues, and their steadfast commitment to the cause of Europe have left many commentators voicing the opinion that they currently share virtually the same ideological space as Tony Blair's New Labour Party. Certainly, the two parties shared many of the same criticisms of the Conservatives in office until the 1997 general election. In view of the prolonged nature of Labour's exclusion from power, this inevitably generated interest in the possibility of greater co-operation, perhaps even a formal coalition, between the two parties in the future. Despite Labour's overwhelming victory in the 1997 election, there are those who recognize that the electoral pendulum could swing back in favour of the Conservatives again all too quickly without some kind of co-operation with the Liberal Democrats (Hugill, 1995: 1). For instance, Peter Mandelson, one of Labour's most influential strategists over the past decade, and a Minister without Portfolio in the new Blair government, has acknowledged that:

> a government with its sights on the long term needs to have the broadest possible political base from which to obtain consent for change that will last . . . this requires a lot of hard thought, inevitably including consideration of Labour's relations with the Liberal Democrats.
>
> (Mandelson and Liddle, 1996: 206)

Adaptation of party organization

The main national parties in Britain have been obliged to adapt to the various challenges they face at the level of organization as well as that of policy. This has been most obvious in the case of Labour, for whom organizational reform has been almost as significant a component of the party's 'modernization' process as programmatic change itself. Indeed, it could be argued that modernization is tantamount to nothing less than the transformation of the party into an 'electoral-professional' organization (Panebianco, 1988). There are a number of organizational strands to this transformation.

First, Labour's leaders since Neil Kinnock (1983–92) have sought to exercise maximum autonomy within the party in order to extend their capacity to manoeuvre according to the demands of party competition. In part this has been effected through decisive actions designed to emphasize their authority on issues of great symbolic significance (Kinnock's battle to expel Trotskyites in the 1980s; John Smith's campaign to reform the role of affiliated trade unions in the party in 1993; Tony Blair's rebellion against the traditional constitutional commitment to public ownership of industry); and in part it has been achieved through the creation of new party organs and agencies which serve as powerful devices of strong leadership. These agencies have been most obvious in the field of election campaign strategy and management (Hughes and Wintour, 1990; Webb, 1992a). However, the creation of a new system of policy commissions and a National Policy Forum in the 1990s could well prove to be important in further reducing the real policy role of the (formally sovereign) annual party conference.

Second, a growing professionalization of the way that the party markets itself has been apparent, and this has increasingly been perceived to be critical to Labour's electoral prospects (Shaw, 1994, chapters 3, 6). Third, there have been a number of moves to enhance the rights of individual party members since the late 1980s (for instance, in candidate selection and leadership election). Though these moves clearly constitute significant steps towards party democratization, we should not overlook the fact that they were almost certainly designed in part as a method by which the parliamentary leadership could dilute the influence of constituency activists who were perceived to be radical – which brings us back to the theme of leadership control once again. In short, one recent commentator has summarized Labour's organizational transformation since the middle of the 1980s in these terms:

> By 1992 the structure of power in the Labour Party had undergone a profound change. The highly pluralistic, deeply polarized Party characterized by institutionalized dispersal of powers and weak central authority had been replaced by a powerful central authority exercising tight control over all aspects of organizational life. Not only was this a crucial aspect of the transformation process, it was the necessary condition for the radical overhaul of its programme and strategy, and one that will not be easily reversed.
>
> (Shaw, 1994: 123)

It has long been an orthodoxy about the Conservative Party that it is essentially an oligarchy – if not a monarchy – with few formal pretensions to internal democracy. Consequently, the leader is often referred to as the fount of policy and authority within the party. This would seem to befit a party with cadre–caucus origins and a long history of defending a non-egalitarian social and political order. For example, many have regarded the annual conference of the National Union of Conservative and Unionist Associations as little more than a (highly stage-managed) consultation and publicity exercise, with little or no real significance for the policy-making process.

Interestingly, however, a detailed and unusual study of Conservative Party conferences in the 1980s produced a reappraisal of this standard view of the party. Kelly (1989) contends that Conservative conferences do in fact play a significant role in influencing policy and that they provide a means by which the grass-roots membership (or at least its activist component) may exercise such influence, albeit in a less than obvious way. The members have a 'hidden' policy influence in so far as 'senior party figures attend these conferences not only to speak but to listen' (ibid.: 182). There are, he points out, a number of examples of grass-roots contributions to conferences working their way into subsequent ministerial speeches, and even into government policy (the influence of the Conservative Trade Unionists' conference upon industrial relations legislation since 1979 is cited as a notable instance).

Kelly concedes that it is difficult to demonstrate this sort of process directly, but insists that this does not make it any less tangible:

> A very low priority is given at these conferences to ballots, majorities and so on; most of the motions at the . . . conferences were passed 'overwhelmingly' and a large section of the audiences could not be bothered to vote at all . . . ministers and senior party officials are interested not so much in the outcome of the debate or even in the wording of the motion as in the 'mood' and 'atmosphere' conveyed by the conference.
>
> (ibid.: 182-3)

Thus, it is too simplistic to regard the Conservative annual conference as nothing more than a stage-managed publicity exercise. The 'mood' of conferences is something which, in Kelly's account, the parliamentary leadership is keen to monitor, and is central to the goal of winning elections. Were the leadership to try and 'stage-manage' the conference system too tightly, it would almost be a 'negation' of its very purpose (ibid.: 185).

Kelly's is a thoughtful and persuasive account which serves to remind us that the modern Conservative Party is not an unconstrained tyranny; indeed, the removal from power of its most autocratic post-war leader in 1990, and the often uncertain grip on power that her successor demonstrated thereafter, should serve as a powerful illustration of this. It may be significant also that recent research suggests that a majority of party members believe themselves to be influential (Whiteley *et al.*, 1994: 38). Notwithstanding this valuable corrective, however, the Conservative Party remains well adapted to the requirements of the modern electoral-professional era, with a strong, relatively autonomous leadership and a highly developed willingness to invest heavily in marketing expertise.

Formed out of the merger between the old Liberal and Social Democratic parties in 1988, the Liberal Democrats are something of an amalgam of these predecessors in organizational terms in that they display the federal structure of the Liberals and some of the more elitist devices of the SDP (such as the Federal Policy Committee). Overall, the Liberal Democratic organization can probably be regarded as a more membership-oriented phenomenon than those of either major party, which is unsurprising for a party which has few

Members of Parliament and relatively little corporate or state financial backing; its members are its lifeblood and need to be offered incentives to maintain their enthusiasm. The benefits of this became obvious by the time of the 1992 election when the members succeeded – 'almost incredibly' in the words of one observer – in expunging the party's serious financial debt (Ingle, 1994: 104).

In short, the historic tensions between leaders and members continue to exist in British parties; while the desire for greater influence on the part of rank and file members and activists has to some extent been met in all of the main parties since 1980, leaders have also responded to the growing pressures of party competition by seeking new ways of centralizing their parties, and enhancing their own autonomy (Webb, 1994).

Conclusion: the emergence of moderate pluralism?

The core of the British party system has long been considered to consist of two-partyism, and few would have disputed this description until the 1970s at least. To adopt Blondel's criteria (1968), we can see that this two-partyism consisted of the high proportion of votes absorbed by Labour and the Conservatives until 1970 (90 per cent plus) and the degree of electoral balance between them (the average difference between the two in terms of the percentage of the national vote won was 3.5 per cent between 1945 and 1974). To these we can add other key features of the system derived from Sartori's scheme of analysis (1976), such as a centripetal pattern of competition for the support of the median voter, single party government and regular alternation in power.

However, in the course of the decade or so following the elections of 1974 there were a number of signs that the essential two-party nature of the system was breaking down under the impact of the multiple challenges it encountered. The average share of the vote taken by the major parties was less than 75 per cent between 1974 and 1987, while electoral imbalance between Labour and the Conservatives emerged (the average difference was now 10.3 per cent). Furthermore, the emergence of the Liberals as a significant 'small' party (with an average Liberal/Alliance vote for 1974–87 of virtually 20 per cent) meant that Britain now exhibited most of the criteria that Blondel designated as belonging to a 'two-and-a-half' party system; only the grossly disproportionate effects of the electoral system restricted the third party to a low level of parliamentary representation. In this sense it is appropriate to speak of a *suppressed* two-and-a-half party system; that is, at the level of the electorate two major parties and one minor party were well supported across Britain as a whole, but at the level of representation, the core of the old two-party model seemed intact. This appeared to hold out the prospect of transition to what Sartori calls 'moderate pluralism'; that is to say, a system which gravitates around three to five relevant parties, in which there is alternation in power between competing parties or blocs of parties, but in which ideological polarization is limited enough for the main dynamic of party competition to be centripetal.

Notwithstanding the evident major party polarization of 1983, the success of the centrist Alliance at the general election held that year emphasized the limits of ideological competition in the British context. Even though the subsequent re-convergence of Labour and the Conservatives undoubtedly squeezed the Liberal Democrats in succeeding elections, they have not been reduced to anywhere near pre-1974 levels; moreover, in 1997, the party succeeded in targeting its campaign efforts so effectively that it virtually doubled its representation in the Commons. In short, the crucial elements of moderate pluralism appear to remain a serious prospect – or they would do so but for the influence of the electoral system.

That said, in the aftermath of the 1992 election a further systemic possibility presented itself. In the wake of the Conservatives' stunning victory – their fourth consecutive one – many observed that two-partyism was not giving way to moderate pluralism so much as to one-party dominance (see, for instance, King, 1992; Heywood, 1994); certainly, this would appear a plausible assertion if we accept Sartori's view that dominance (or predominance, as he calls it) occurs when the major party generally obtains the absolute majority of the seats. He suggests that 'three consecutive absolute majorities can be a sufficient indication [of predominance], provided that the electorate seems stabilized, that the absolute majority threshold is clearly surpassed, and/or that the interval is wide' (Sartori, 1976: 196). Add to this the Conservatives' unprecedented exploitation of the quangocracy, Britain's unitary state and the unwritten constitution's lack of freedom of information provisions, and it is obvious that the growth of predominance was a persuasive rationalization of the party system between 1979 and 1997.

From a post-1997 election vantage point, however, we can see how unwise it was to be seduced too readily by the scenario of growing Conservative dominance. In particular, Sartori's definition prompts the obvious reflection that the electorate never was 'stabilized' into the mould of single-party dominance. The electoral pendulum having finally swung once again, it is clear that the dominance perspective cannot apply. But neither should we be too sure that the 1997 election necessarily heralds the long-term re-emergence of two-partyism. Moshe Maor has spoken of 'restabilization', or 'tendency of a party system to bounce back after a restricted change to its original mode', and argues that 'a change in the two-party format as the expression of the central feature of party government and competition could only come from within' (Maor, 1997: 64). This is fair comment in so far as it goes, and all the weightier for having been made before the 1997 election result was known. But the point is that we should not assume that such 'change from within' (the existing party system) is out of the question.

As we have already seen, Labour's leaders have shown that they regard co-operation with the Liberal Democrats as important if they are to establish a basis for long-term occupation of power; moreover, it is equally clear that some leading Labour politicians (such as Foreign Secretary Robin Cook) openly advocate electoral reform, and Tony Blair himself (though insisting he remains to be persuaded of its merits) has spoken of the need for a referendum on the topic. A groundswell in favour of electoral reform developed within the Labour Party during the course of its long years in opposition, particularly in the southern constituency parties which did so well in the 1997 election.[3] Moreover, this profile of opinion is reflected in the new PLP, with some 48 per cent of surveyed Labour MPs supporting PR, while 39 per cent oppose it (Kellner, 1997: 24), and one can easily imagine that an unpopular mid-term Labour government would find the notion of electoral reform especially alluring if it promised to stave off the threat of a resurgent Conservative Party in 2002.

Electoral reform and even closer co-operation with the Liberal Democrats might then become something more than a distant prospect in the strategic machinations of government politicians. In short, the apparent Conservative dominance of the 1980s and 1990s was never more than a transient state of affairs, and the British party system has restabilized at its old two-party equilibrium for the time being; nevertheless, the suppressed two-and-a-half partyism that also characterizes the system may yet emerge as the new orthodoxy of British politics as it enters the twenty-first century.

Notes

1. It should be noted that while the number of seats won by parties indicated a two-party system, the Liberals still won a significant share of the vote (23.4 per cent) at the 1929 general election.
2. Note, however, that in 1997 Labour's Scottish predominance grew while the context of that predominance, temporarily at least, became *three*-party competition. Labour took 54 seats, whilst the Conservatives lost all theirs, the remaining 18 seats being divided between the Liberal Democrats (12) and the SNP (6). Note too, that the Conservative Party also failed to gain any representation in Wales.
3. The Labour Party membership survey data gathered by Patrick Seyd and Paul Whiteley in the late 1980s revealed that some 57.6 per cent of members favoured the introduction of proportional representation (n = 4946). The party regions with the greatest levels of support for this reform were Eastern, Southern, London and the South-West (all over 60 per cent). The lowest level of support came in the North-West (51.7 per cent). We gratefully acknowledge the Data Archive at Essex University for supplying us with these data.

3

Ireland: A Party System Transformed?

DAVID M. FARRELL

Introduction

In 1921, the Irish Free State was established with the signing of the Anglo-Irish Treaty. This granted Commonwealth status to 26 of the island's 32 counties. In the preceding year, partition of the island had been officially recognized when the northern six counties were given their own governmental system, devolved from Westminster, which subsequently was to be referred to as Stormont, after the location of the custom-built parliament building in a suburb of Belfast.

Partition was the 'solution' adopted by the British government to meet the conflicting desires of the nationalist (largely Catholic) majority who wanted independence and the unionist (largely Protestant) minority, concentrated in the north-east, who wanted to retain the link with Britain at all costs. It was partition and the limited nature of the Irish Free State's independence (the British Crown still had sovereign control) which were to be the cause of a brief, but bloody, civil war in 1922–23, a war which served to crystallize the divisions between the two sides – those supporting and those opposing the Treaty – forming the basis of the party system ever since. The remaining limitations on Ireland's independence from Britain were gradually eroded during the course of the 1930s, the changes being formalized in the new Constitution of 1937. Ultimately, in 1948, Ireland left the Commonwealth and the Republic was declared.

At the time of independence, in 1921, there were two main political parties: Labour, which was formed in 1912 as essentially a trade union party, following the pattern of socialist parties elsewhere, and Sinn Féin ('we ourselves'), set up in 1905, which by 1918 had become the most significant political force striving for secession from the United Kingdom. Sinn Féin split in two over the Treaty, those against seeing it as a sell-out to Republicanism. In 1926, the more pragmatic elements of the anti-Treaty side dropped their policy of abstention (provoking yet another split in Sinn Féin) and, as the new Fianna Fáil party ('the warriors of destiny'), took their seats in Dáil

Éireann (the Irish parliament). By 1932, Fianna Fáil was in office. The pro-Treaty side (Cumann na nGaedheal, 'the club of the Gaels'), which had been in office from 1922–32, merged with other small parties and in 1933 adopted the title, Fine Gael ('family-group of the Gaels'). Apart from a brief decade of multi-party activity in the post-war years, from the 1930s through to the early 1980s, the Irish party system consisted almost exclusively of these three parties: Fianna Fáil, Fine Gael and Labour.

The 1980s and 1990s have seen the rise of a number of new parties, notably on the left, the Workers' Party, and later the Democratic Left; on the right, the Progressive Democrats; and in 'the middle', the Greens. *Prima facie*, the trajectory of Irish party politics today looks more crowded and complex than ten or twenty years ago. In many respects, it has the feel of a party system which has been transformed. The extent to which this is, in fact, the case is the subject of this chapter. Before we consider this question, however, we first need a sound idea of the nature of the traditional party system and the circumstances in which it has operated. We start with a brief overview of the context of Irish party politics.

The context of Irish party politics

For the most part, the environment in which Irish parties operate bears close resemblance to the British Westminster model. In this context, there is little by way of constitutional 'rules of the game' which aid or hinder specific parties. About the only points of any significance are access to the airwaves, which until relatively recently was denied to Sinn Féin (due to its connections with the IRA, a proscribed organization), and some access to state funding (e.g. in some cases, a party has to have a minimum number of TDs (MPs); see Farrell, 1992).

There are two features of the Irish political system which merit special mention. The first of these is the nature of Irish parliamentary representation. For some time, academics have paid close attention to how the TDs represent the interests of their voters. Political relationships have been shown to be clientelistic in nature, with the politician playing a broker role between the constituent and (usually) the relevant civil service department. Originally it was argued that this was a phenomenon of a rural, under-developed society; that as economic and social development occurred, there should be a reduction in the politicians' brokerage role as they involved themselves more in 'conventional' legislative activities. However, research in the 1980s produced little evidence to support this. Dublin-based TDs were found to pay just as much attention to their constituency work as their rural counterparts. If anything, the evidence suggested a widespread increase in the local workload of the average TD (for an overview, see Gallagher and Komito, 1993).

Second, the Irish electoral system of proportional representation by the single transferable vote (STV) feeds the localist emphasis in Irish political culture. STV is a candidate-based system operating within multi-member constituencies, in which voters are expected to rank the candidates in order of preference. Constituency candidates are in competition not only with candidates from other parties, but also with candidates from their own party. It is argued that this promotes a greater emphasis on constituency work (Farrell, 1985; though for alternative perspectives, see Gallagher, 1987; Farrell *et al.*, 1996), and has implications for the style of party organization and the nature of electioneering in Ireland (Farrell, 1994; and below). Of course, being a PR system, STV also influences the number of parties in the system, so that, from time to time, smaller parties have broken through, notably in the 1940s and 1950s, and more particularly since the early 1980s.

The traditional picture of Irish party politics

If we talk, first, in 'numerical' terms, the traditional picture of the Irish party system is easy enough to summarize. For instance, in terms of Blondel's analysis, for much of its history, Ireland can be characterized as having a 'two-and-a-half' party system (Farrell, 1970; O'Leary, 1979), with Labour representing the 'half' party. According to a Sartorian framework, the predominant party in the system has always been Fianna Fáil, with choices of government generally being between Fianna Fáil, on the one hand, and some combination of the other parties on the other. In short, the traditional Irish party system could be characterized as a 'predominant party system' (Mair, 1979; but see Sinnott, 1984).

Underpinning these summary descriptions of the Irish party system is an impression that it has been inherently stable, with few changes of government, and long periods of uninterrupted rule by Fianna Fáil. Of course, such a picture is over-simplified, as it disguises the fact that Ireland has gone through phases of multi-party politics, notably in the 1940s and 1950s when several new parties enjoyed brief electoral success. During this period two separate multi-party administrations were formed, briefly interrupting Fianna Fáil's long-standing grip on power (see Table 3.1). Such exceptions aside, the inherent stability of the party system cannot be gainsaid, at least until the 1980s.

It is common in the comparative literature to refer to the Irish party system as unique, reflected in the weakness of the Left, the absence of class politics, and the inherent similarity between the parties in terms of their policies and

Table 3.1 Government composition in the Republic of Ireland, 1948–97

Year	Party/parties in government	*Taoiseach* (Prime Minister)
1948	Fine Gael, Labour, Others[1]	John A. Costello
1951	Fianna Fáil	Eamon de Valera
1954	Fine Gael, Labour, Others[2]	John A. Costello
1957	Fianna Fáil	Eamon de Valera; Seán Lemass (1959)
1961	Fianna Fáil	Seán Lemass
1965	Fianna Fáil	Seán Lemass; Jack Lynch (1966)
1969	Fianna Fáil	Jack Lynch
1973	Fine Gael, Labour	Liam Cosgrave
1977	Fianna Fáil	J. Lynch; Charles Haughey (1979)
1981	Fine Gael, Labour	Garret FitzGerald
Feb. 82	Fianna Fáil	Charles Haughey
Nov. 82	Fine Gael, Labour	Garret FitzGerald
1987	Fianna Fáil	Charles Haughey
1989	Fianna Fáil, Progressive Democrats	C. Haughey; Albert Reynolds (1992)
1992	Fianna Fáil, Labour	Albert Reynolds
1994[3]	Fine Gael, Labour, Dem. Left	John Bruton
1997	Fianna Fáil, Progressive Democrats	Bertie Ahern

[1] Others = Clann na Poblachta, Clann na Talmhan, National Labour, independent
[2] Others = Clann na Talmhan
[3] The Reynolds government was replaced mid-term by the Bruton government.

Source: Coakley and Gallagher (1993), appendix 3c. Updated by the author and editors.

standpoints. Historically, the explanation for the absence of class politics is straightforward. In Ireland, still part of the UK, the key election was 1918, when as Sinnott (1995: 25) points out, as a result of suffrage extension, the size of the Irish electorate increased from 26 per cent of the population aged twenty and over to 75 per cent. The issue in that election, as the first since the 1916 Easter Rising, was secession from the UK. In recognition of that reality, the Irish Labour Party decided not to field any candidates, not wanting to distract attention from the National Question (Farrell, 1970).

Therefore, at this crucial 'crystallizing' election, the voters were not given the option of voting on the class issue. By the early 1920s, the death knell of class politics had been sounded, since, as a result of partition, the Irish Free State effectively lost its industrial base which was located primarily in Belfast and its hinterlands. That part of the island that ceded from Britain was predominantly a rural, agricultural, peasant-based economy. This same fact also explains why Lipset and Rokkan's urban–rural cleavage is seen not to apply. Given that the new state was also predominantly Catholic (this was, after all, the basis for partition), the religious cleavage was also absent. Whyte (1974) has suggested that the centre–periphery cleavage could be explained away in similar fashion, with the secession of the 26 counties effectively removing any basis for a centre–periphery split based around the Irish Question within the party politics of the United Kingdom. This leads

Whyte to conclude that Ireland is characterized by 'politics without social bases'. From then on, there was a tendency to leave Ireland out of the comparative studies of party systems, on the grounds that it was *sui generis*.

Inevitably, there has been some disagreement over the issue of whether the Irish party system can be fitted into the comparative frameworks. Here most attention has focused on the centre–periphery cleavage. Garvin (1974) has suggested that within the new state there was the basis for such a cleavage, with Fianna Fáil, as the peripheral party having its support base in the west of the island, and Fine Gael, as the establishment party, rooted more in the urban areas of the east. The problem with this perspective, as Sinnott (1995) has shown most effectively, is that the evidence of a geographical split between the support bases of the two major parties is quite tenuous. Sinnott's alternative explanation of how to fit the Irish case into the Lipset–Rokkan framework is based on the significance of the Treaty split. He argues that, in effect, the party of the periphery (Sinn Féin) split in two, between strong peripheralists (Fianna Fáil) and moderate peripheralists (Fine Gael).

Regardless of whether or not we can fit the frameworks of comparativists such as Lipset and Rokkan to the Irish case, there remains the fact that, as outlined by Whyte in the early 1970s, the Irish party system appears quite different from the standard pattern of party politics elsewhere in Western Europe. As Whyte shows, the support base of the Labour Party is not that unusual, that is in terms of the relative differences between the different class categories. In essence, its support base is firmly rooted in the Irish working class. However, this is not the same thing as saying it is *the* party of the Irish working class. The party which best fits that description is Fianna Fáil (for an excellent account of why the Irish Left is traditionally so weak, see Mair, 1992). In fact, with the exception of larger farmers and the partial exception of professional and managerial categories (both of which have traditionally tended to support Fine Gael), Fianna Fáil attracts the plurality of support among most social groups, so earning it the title of 'catch-all party *par excellence*'. Fine Gael is not so easy to tie down in terms of social categories, apart, that is, from its strong base of support among larger farmers. In short, the traditional picture of party politics in Ireland is of a small Labour Party which attracts a loyal, if small, working-class vote; Fine Gael as the party of larger farmers and, to an extent, the better off; and Fianna Fáil, whose support base crosses the different classes, making it the predominant party in the system. The extent to which this picture still applies in the 1990s is explored later.

Another factor which has tended to lie behind the argument of Ireland's uniqueness is the supposition that its parties are 'programmatically indistinguishable, each commanding heterogeneous electoral support' (Carty,

1983: 85). In this sense, therefore, at least part of the blame for why Irish voters traditionally vote cross-class is because there is not much distinguishing the parties from each other. In fact, however, there is quite a deal of evidence of important distinctions between the ideological locations of Irish parties. Three studies following three different approaches have all come to strikingly similar conclusions (for a review, see Sinnott, 1995: Chapter 3).

Peter Mair's content analysis of Irish party manifestos (covering 1948–82, and therefore focusing on the three traditional parties) finds clear evidence 'that there is more of a policy divide in the Irish party system than is normally acknowledged . . . cast[ing] doubt on the notion that the parties are programmatically indistinguishable' (Mair, 1987: 169). Mair uses factor analysis to group the various manifesto themes, producing seven main dimensions. The most important of these is a distinction between, on the one hand, a corporatist emphasis, characterized by three specific policy themes – strong government, social solidarity and the national interest – and, on the other hand, a social democratic emphasis, which stresses such themes as social justice and the need for government control of the economy. In terms of average positions over time, Fianna Fáil tends to lie on the corporatist side of the spectrum, with Labour on the social democratic side, and Fine Gael more in the centre but closer to Labour than to Fianna Fáil. Of course, a major strength of Mair's analysis is that he can plot movements in the parties' positions over time, which he does for the period 1961–82 (Mair, 1987: 189 ff.). This reveals that the most dramatic shifts in policy have been by Fine Gael. All three parties start the period on the corporatist side (though roughly in the same position with respect to each other). From 1961–82, while Labour moves fairly consistently over to the social democratic side, Fine Gael goes through some sharp policy shifts: between 1965–73 it is more social democratic than Labour and briefly, in early 1982, it is more corporatist than Fianna Fáil.

Richard Sinnott's dimensional analysis (1986; 1995), making use of data gathered from interviews with a cross-section of the Irish political elite in the 1970s (and again focused only on the three traditional parties), identifies three main areas of partisan division: a Left–Right axis, which separates Labour from the two larger parties; and two others, based on nationalism and confessionalism, which separate Fianna Fáil from the other two.

A third approach to exploring differences between the parties relies on expert assessment, where political scientists were asked to plot the differences between the parties. Given the relatively easy access to data, this has facilitated some important cross-national research (Castles and Mair, 1984; Laver and Hunt, 1992; Huber and Inglehart, 1995). The most comprehensive study is by Laver and Hunt (1992) whose analysis of the Irish case reveals a very similar set of dimensions to those suggested by Sinnott: taxes and spending (Sinnott's Left–Right dimension); social policy (relating to abortion and homosexuality issues, and therefore similar to Sinnott's confessional dimension); and Northern Ireland (Sinnott's nationalism dimension). For all the potential methodological problems associated with this approach – notably that 'experts talk to experts, read one another's books and academic articles' (Sinnott, 1995: 70) – it has a major advantage that it facilitates relatively cheap and easy comparative analysis, and therefore allows a good opportunity to test the extent to which Irish parties are different from their counterparts elsewhere.

In a recent essay, Laver (1992) set out to test the extent to which Irish parties are 'peculiar' cross-nationally, comparing the relative positions of parties on two dimensions, Left–Right and social, and looking for possible patterns, or constellations, of party systems. He finds that the Irish case best fits the Mediterranean constellation, and illustrates this by superimposing the Irish system over that of France:

> The relative locations of the socialist parties are similar in both systems, though the French parties are at a somewhat greater distance from their rivals on the right. Fianna Fáil fulfils the same role in the Irish party constellation as the Gaullists (RPR) do in the French; Fine Gael fulfils the same role as the French conservatives (UDF).
>
> (Laver, 1992: 373–4)

Change and adaptation

Trends in and among the Irish parties inevitably have been influenced by wider social and economic trends in Ireland. From when exactly to date the start of the process of socio-economic change in Ireland may be debatable, but one significant landmark, it is generally accepted, is the start of national planning at the end of the 1950s (Breen *et al.*, 1990). Planning brought with it the industrialization of society; an accelerated move from the land as people entered the industrial and service sectors, and increased expenditure on education. Concomitantly, and in line with international developments, there was a shift away from protectionism as the country gradually opened up to free trade. This culminated in Ireland's accession to the EC in 1973, and the economic benefits which were reaped, particularly during the 1970s.

As Rottman and O'Connell point out (1982: 76): '[t]he demographic consequences of Irish economic expansion were soon evident'. For the first time since the Famine of the 1850s, the population entered into a period of sustained net growth, reflecting declining emigration rates and an acceleration in the rate of natural increase. By the mid-1970s, net immigration had reached such a rate as to cancel out any apparent benefits from a government strategy of job creation. It was only with the debt crisis – the result of considerable government over-spending from 1977 onwards – and the economic problems of the 1980s that the country was to enter another phase of net population decline (Breen *et al.*, 1990: 68–9).

The point is, however, that the period of the early 1960s up until the present is characterized as one of dramatic demographic change, evident in two main developments. First, there has been a net growth in population, with, in particular, a major increase in the younger population (causing Ireland to have the highest dependency ratio in Europe), made all the more significant by the 1972 decision to lower the minimum voting age to 18. Second, there has been a shift in the occupational structure both in terms of a move from agriculture to industry and the tertiary sector, as well as in terms of distinct shifts within the industrial and tertiary sectors (ibid., 1990). This has had consequences for the class structure in Ireland.

These structural changes have occurred in a period of fast social development, marked for instance by the introduction of television at the start of the 1960s (Farrell, 1984), and more generally, by a trend suggesting a declining role of the Catholic Church, and a rise of secularization. The theme of Ireland as a Catholic nation (even a theocracy) has been much rehearsed, not least by Unionist politicians in Northern Ireland. For long, the country's constitution, its conservative 'social' legislation, and the instances of interference by the Catholic hierarchy in the activities of elected politicians, made such claims difficult to dispute (Whyte, 1980).

From the late 1960s onwards, however, a coincidence of factors started to loosen the hold of the Catholic Church. Among these were the demographic and economic changes outlined above, a more assertive role in constitutional review by the courts (Chubb, 1991), and Ireland's entry into the EC which required changes to existing social legislation to bring the country into line with other EC states (Keatinge, 1991). Gradually, very gradually, reforms were introduced in such areas as women's rights, adoption, and contraception, while in other areas, such as censorship, existing laws were applied less rigorously. The process has not been smooth, however, as evidenced, first, by the failed attempt to introduce divorce in 1986 and the subsequent passing of a referendum on the issue a decade later, but only by the skin of its teeth, and, second, by the debacle over abortion (the subject of referendums in 1983 and 1992, see Sinnott, 1995).

It is inconceivable that these structural and social changes would not have had some effect on Irish voter behaviour and the party system. But the first impressions are not encouraging. Despite the absence to date of an Irish election study, the political science community has been resourceful in accumulating data to examine the issue of social class support for Irish parties, allowing them to test to what extent Whyte's original conclusions (based on the first ever political survey of Irish voters in 1969) have held up over time.

The high point of interest came in the 1987 election (see Table 3.2) when three events coincided to cause a brief flurry of excitement in the political science community. The first of these was the entry of the Progressive Democrats (PDs) onto the scene (see below), which was avowedly right-of-centre in its economic policies, and which succeeded in attracting the votes of middle-class voters. The second development was a clear sign of some bleeding away of Fianna Fáil's cross-class support, as voters started to show signs of voting in more familiar social class terms. The third event was the success of the political scientists in persuading a market research agency to use more complex sociological scales of class voting in its newspaper polls, thus revealing even more dramatically the social class divisions in party support. The trends in 1987 could hardly have been clearer: Fianna Fáil showed signs of a slight shift towards a more working-class support base; Fine Gael shifted more in the opposite direction and continued to enjoy high levels of support among larger farmers; the PDs attracted predominantly a middle-class vote; Labour and Workers' Party support were skewed towards the working class. The researchers concluded: 'the class basis of Irish politics is more evident now than at any time in the previous twenty years' (Laver *et al.*, 1987: 112).

We know with hindsight that the 1987 result was (so far, at any rate) a one-off outcome. In the 1989 election the voters reverted to type, to the extent that the social class voting trends in that election bore a striking similarity to those of 1969 (Marsh and Sinnott, 1990: 125). Even in 1992, when (as Table 3.2 shows) Labour won one of its highest votes ever (19.3 per cent), there was no evidence of opening class divisions. On the contrary, the gain in Labour votes was across the board, from professional and managerial workers right through to the unskilled, so that

> [f]ar from indicating a polarization of Irish politics or the emergence of Labour
> as a distinctive or exclusive party of the working class, the 1992 election
> suggests that Labour had a catch-all appeal that was equivalent, albeit at a
> lower level, to that achieved at any stage by Fianna Fáil.
>
> (Marsh and Sinnott, 1993: 108)

Viewed from an exclusively Irish perspective, the account given in the previous few paragraphs would tend to the conclusion that, having started out as unique, and showing a glimmer of change in 1987, the Irish voters have ended the period remaining unique. This is in the sense that there is little sign of social class patterning the vote. However, viewed from a comparative perspective, it is possible to put quite a different gloss on this evidence. As the vast, and ever-growing, comparative literature on electoral

Table 3.2 Irish national election results, 1948–97

Election Year	Fianna Fáil	Fine Gael	Labour	Progressive Democrats	Workers' Party/ Dem. Left	Others
1948	41.9	19.8	8.7			29.6
1951	46.3	25.8	11.4			16.5
1954	43.4	32.0	12.1			12.5
1957	48.3	26.6	9.1			16.0
1961	43.8	32.0	11.7			12.5
1965	47.7	34.1	15.4			2.8
1969	44.6	33.3	16.6			5.5
1973	46.2	35.1	13.7		1.1	3.9
1977	50.6	30.6	11.6		1.7	5.5
1981	45.3	36.5	9.9		1.7	6.6
Feb. 82	47.3	37.3	9.1		2.2	4.1
Nov. 82	45.2	39.2	9.4		3.3	2.9
1987	44.2	27.1	6.5	11.9	3.8	6.5
1989	44.2	29.3	9.5	5.5	5.0	6.5
1992	39.1	24.5	19.3	4.7	2.8[1]	9.6
1997	39.3	27.9	10.4	4.7	2.5	14.7

[1] This is the vote for the new Democratic Left Party in 1992. In that election the remnants of the Workers' Party received just 0.7 per cent of the vote.

Source: Sinnott (1995: appendix 2). Updated by the editors.

change shows (for a prominent example, see Franklin *et al.*, 1992), there has been a distinct and steady decline in the social class attachment of voters to parties. In other words, it is becoming less and less easy to predict how people will vote from looking at their social class membership, or, to put it another way, there has been a decline in the social basis of voting behaviour cross-nationally. In this sense, therefore, not only does Ireland appear to fit quite well into this international pattern, it could even be suggested that, if anything, the other countries have been catching up with Irish trends!

Ireland fits in well with comparative trends in another sense, and that is in the way the system has been undergoing quite significant electoral and party system change, evident at a number of levels. For instance, there was a change of government in every election between 1973 and 1987, a total of five changes of government in less than fifteen years. This compares with a mere three changes of government between 1948 and 1969 (see Table 3.1). In fact, across the entire period of 1932–69, there were just four changes of government.

In 1989, Fianna Fáil managed to buck the trend of government mortality and remain in office, but only by crossing the rubicon of antipathy within the party towards coalition of any colour or persuasion. In that year Fianna Fáil formed a short-lived administration with the PDs. This was followed, in 1992, by a new coalition government, this time between Fianna Fáil and

Labour. In 1994 a further rubicon was crossed, when the government changed mid-term, Fianna Fáil being replaced by Fine Gael and the Democratic Left, thereby confirming the latter's entry into the 'cartel' of Irish party politics (on 'cartel parties' see Katz and Mair, 1995).

If nothing else, these electoral trends reflect a growing detachment of Irish voters over the period, as shown quite clearly by a steady downward trend in party identification. In his detailed examination of the evidence, Sinnott (1995: 153–4) concludes that, between 1980–92, 'there has been a 20 to 25 percentage point drop in the number of respondents reporting that they are "close to a party" ... The drop seems to have occurred in particular in 1980-81 and between 1983 and 1986.'

As Table 3.3 shows, this growing 'availability' of Irish voters has had at least three main consequences for electoral politics. First, elections have become more frequent (five during the 1980s as opposed to just two in the 1970s), providing one indicator of how governments have become less stable. As Table 3.1 reveals, there is a much greater tendency for coalitions to be formed in recent years. Second, there has been a steady increase in aggregate voter volatility (also confirmed by individual data, see Sinnott, 1995: 145 ff.). In the 1970s, the Pedersen Index averaged only 5.7 per cent, as against a Western European average of 8.2 per cent (Gallagher *et al.*, 1995: 233). In the 1980s, while the European average dropped to 8 per cent, the Irish figure increased to 8.1 per cent. The results in the 1992 Irish election (with aggregate volatility of over 12 per cent) suggests that voter volatility in Ireland continued to be on an upward trajectory. Third, the developments of the past decade have witnessed the rise of new parties (as indicated, in Table 3.3, by trends in the index of effective number of parties). The next few paragraphs provide some background on these new parties, starting with a party which in fact was not all that new.

Coinciding with the outbreak of 'the troubles' in Northern Ireland, Sinn Féin split in the late 1960s–early 1970s. Official Sinn Féin entered electoral politics, eventually changing its name to the Workers' Party (Sinnott, 1995). As Table 3.2 shows, throughout the 1980s, the party made steady gains (albeit on a tiny base), and by 1987, with just under 4 per cent of the national vote, it appeared to be threatening the Labour Party (whose vote had plummeted to 6.5 per cent) as the principal party of the Left. The threat receded in 1989 when, even though the Workers' Party vote increased again (to 5 per cent), Labour's vote increased for the first time in over a decade, to 9.5 per cent.

The second party to make a breakthrough, in much more dramatic fashion, was the Progressive Democrats (PD), winning 14 seats at its first election in 1987. The PDs emerged out of a rift within Fianna Fáil (Lyne, 1987). The prominent Fianna Fáil deputy, Desmond O'Malley, an arch-rival

Table 3.3 Party system volatility and fragmentation,
Republic of Ireland, 1950s–97

	Number of elections	Aggregate volatility[1]	Effective number of parties[2]
1950s	3	10.3	3.26
1960s	3	7.0	2.93
1970s	2	5.7	2.78
1980s	5	8.1	3.03
1992	1	12.0	3.94
1997	1	7.6	3.74

[1] The Pedersen Index, derived as follows: the sum of each party's change in percentage vote from one election to the next, divided by two.
[2] See glossary for definition. For details, see Laakso and Taagepera (1979).

Sources: Gallagher *et al.* (1995: Table 9.8); data on effective number of parties overtime provided by Arend Lijphart; official returns; updated for 1997 by the editors.

to the then leader, Charles Haughey, was expelled from the party in 1985 over policy differences. He acted quickly to take advantage of a strong degree of personal support and an evident dissatisfaction among the general public with 'civil war' politics. In 1986, O'Malley succeeded in enticing a number of national and local politicians from both Fianna Fáil and Fine Gael and between them they set up the PDs. Much as with the Social Democratic Party in Britain in the early 1980s, the talk was of 'mould-breaking' and the media were transfixed. Despite the PDs' impressive results in the 1987 election, sceptics warned of the dangers of being overly-excited by overnight success, pointing to the problems the new, high-profile parties of the 1940s and 1950s had had in their subsequent elections. The scepticism appeared well founded in the light of the electoral performance of the PDs in 1989, when the party's vote plummeted by more than half to just over 5 per cent, a vote which it just about held onto in the subsequent 1992 and 1997 elections (Table 3.2).

The third party to emerge was the Green Party which, after contesting elections unsuccessfully from the mid-1980s, appeared more surprised than most at the success of one of its Dublin candidates in 1989 (Farrell, 1989; Whiteman, 1990). In 1992 that particular Green TD lost his seat, but the party managed to win another seat elsewhere in the capital.

The most recent development in Irish party politics came in 1992, when six of the Workers' Party's seven TDs (including the party leader) left to form a new party, Democratic Left, taking most of the membership with them (Holmes, 1994). The split was provoked by the failure of the party leader to push through organizational reforms to move the party away from demo-

cratic centralism. He was anxious to respond to an internal crisis caused by
the collapse of Communism in Eastern Europe, intense media speculation
about the Workers' Party's alleged links with the Official IRA, and also with
the Communist Party of the Soviet Union, and a party debt of IR £500,000.
When he did not get his way (by a whisker) at a special delegate conference
in January 1992, he opted for 'exit'. In the subsequent 1992 election,
Democratic Left retained four seats in the Dáil, while the Workers' Party was
left without any parliamentary representation.

Change in the number of parties is only one way of examining the issue of
party change. Arguably, even more significant has been organizational
transformation within parties, which has been taking place over the past two
decades. The comparative study of party organizations is currently enjoying
its heyday. As the focus of debate has shifted from one of parties 'under
threat', to one of parties 'adapting and surviving', we have seen over this
period the accumulation of data on the internal dynamics of party organizations, revealing how the parties are becoming more professional, with
greater attention being paid to acquiring a specialized staff, the greater use of
consultants and their marketing skills in election campaigns, and higher
levels of financial expenditure overall. Concomitant with these developments
has been a gradual decline in the role of the party member, and a greater
reliance by parties on state funding. It is these latter two trends which
perhaps most of all give clues to the potential problems of legitimacy which
parties now face, problems which may portend still more organizational
transformation, such as in the areas of leadership election or candidate
selection, and the degree of 'democratic' input into such processes.

The Irish case fits in well with the general trend across Western Europe.
We can see this in a number of key areas. First, campaign strategies have
changed dramatically. The traditional election campaign of bygone days was
essentially a series of constituency campaigns. There was little co-ordination
from the centre and little role for national campaign strategies (Farrell,
forthcoming). From the late 1970s onwards, Fianna Fáil and Fine Gael
began to change all that, and by the mid-1980s the changes had percolated
through to all the parties, so that the campaigns of today are characterized
by the following main features: greater attention to campaign preparation
and planning; the extensive use of consultants and agencies; and the
supplementing of traditional forms of campaign 'feedback' with the more
modern methods of market research (Farrell, 1986; 1993).

Underlying these strategic developments are a number of significant
organizational changes over the past two decades or so. An examination of
party and state records, and interviews with senior party figures have
produced evidence of party organizational developments in at least four
main areas (Farrell, 1992; 1994).

First, the numbers of party staff have increased, particularly in the larger parties. While the overall number remains very small by international standards, it is interesting to note that the rate of increase has been one of the fastest (Mair, 1994a: 7). There is also some evidence of a greater propensity to appoint senior, professional staff, though to an extent this has been somewhat constrained by the tendency of the parties to 'buy-in' expertise as required on a short-term basis during election campaigns.

Second, there has been a decline in the role and significance of the party member. Since the latter part of the 1980s, branch and membership numbers have been in decline. This trend is evident whether looked at in terms of raw numbers or when membership is taken as a proportion of either the electorate or voters. Cross-national comparisons indicate that in the late 1980s, despite the strong localist tradition in Ireland, Irish political parties have one of the lowest proportions of members as a percentage of the electorate (Katz *et al.*, 1992). Furthermore, a decline in the significance of the individual member is revealed by the party accounts which indicate that from about the mid-1980s onwards, there was a drop in the proportion of party income derived from membership dues.

Third, and related, party statutes have been changing. Consistent with the desire of the party elite to professionalize their operations, there have been moves to centralize control around the parliamentary party leadership. This is evident in two main areas: the process of candidate selection, and rules on membership obligations. Taken together with the trends in party staffing, which predominantly have been to the benefit of the parliamentary party, the statute changes have contributed to a clear shift in the locus of power within Irish parties towards the parliamentary leadership, consolidating the stratarchic nature of Irish party organization. Taken to an extreme, these tendencies are suggestive of a future role for party organization which is as little more than an appendage of the parliamentary party, perhaps a 'campaign machine' based on the US model (Herrnson, 1988; Katz and Kolodny, 1992).

Fourth, party politics has become big business. The parties' published accounts reveal a sharp rise in income and expenditure by both Fianna Fáil and Fine Gael from the early 1980s onwards. The trend for the smaller parties is also upwards, though more modestly. However, it is what the accounts do not reveal that is of even more interest. The parties are not obliged to publish accounts. Those that do tend to be selective in what information they provide. The gaps have to be filled by journalistic investigation, revealing in the early 1990s a high level of debt by all parties, but particularly by Fianna Fáil, Fine Gael and the Workers' Party (before the split). In 1992, a major public tribunal into alleged corruption in the agricultural sector unearthed evidence of a high dependency by the right-of-centre parties on financial contributions from that sector, fuelling speculation of possible political corruption. Public disquiet was strengthened in 1997. First Charles Haughey, the former leader (1979–92) of Fianna Fáil and ex-Prime Minister, was accused of receiving cash gifts worth IR£1.3 million. Then, in October, the new Foreign Minister, Ray Burke, resigned amidst another financial scandal.

The intense interest in party finances has led to calls for the introduction of public funding of parties and financial disclosure rules, seen by commentators as a way of reducing the parties' dependence on corporate donations. A curious feature of this debate is that it appears ignorant of the fact that the State already provides Irish parties and politicians with generous financial support. A high proportion of the staff employed by the parties receive their salary from the State; each year the party leaders receive an allowance to support their political activities; the State provides each TD with a secretary, a personal computer, a customized database to help with constituency work, and an allowance. The total amount of money involved is substantial. In 1989, for instance, the combined total income of all the parties was less than IR£3 million. In that same year, an estimated IR£4 million was provided by the State for parties and their parliamentary representatives (Farrell, 1992; 1994).

The combination of these four main areas of organizational change (relating to staffing, membership, statutes and finance) has culminated in a convergence in the style of party organization in Ireland, showing evidence of a trend of party professionalization and centralization which bears close correspondence to trends in other countries (Katz and Mair, 1994). This is despite the fact that, as we saw above, Irish parties are operating in an electoral environment which places great emphasis on local, constituency-level contact between individual politicians and their personal electorates.

Conclusion: a party system transformed?

We have seen in this chapter how the Irish case has matched the comparative trends in Western Europe quite closely: the electoral environment is one of increasing flux, with voters showing an ever-greater willingness to switch votes and with new parties emerging; the established parties have adapted successfully to these more uncertain times and have thereby held their dominant position in the 'cartel' of party politics. In this respect, therefore, we can talk of a successful transformation of the existing party system.

But there are signs of pressure for yet more change, and there are indications that the parties are taking these very seriously. Indicators of the former include the rise of new parties and opinion poll trends which suggest a growing detachment of voters. Perhaps one of the most significant signs has been the growing prominence of single-issue politics, most especially with regard to the demands of right-wing Catholic groups, both in terms of their fielding of candidates in elections and in terms of their role in influencing the calling of referendums.[1] Half of the 18 referendums which have been called since 1937 have taken place in the last twenty years, five in the 1990s. Of the nine referendums held in the past twenty years, six have been about moral issues (Sinnott, 1995). On the face of it, such a development indicates a growing politicization of the 'confessional' dimension and the increasing mobilization of groups active in this area. In this sense, one can talk of a 'threat to party'. Against this, however, there is the fact that groups organized around single issues such as 'pro-life' have yet to make a breakthrough in general elections, causing Sinnott (1995: 295) to posit 'the existence of an alternative channel for the resolution of the most contentious problems in this area ... insulat[ing] the party system from the full brunt of secular-confessional issues by providing an alternative channel for the expression of this cleavage'. This view was confirmed by the failure of such candidates in the 1997 election.

But despite Sinnott's proposal of a pressure-valve role for Ireland's referendum instrument, one can scarcely demur from the conclusion to a recent study of political partisanship in Ireland, that there exists 'a powerfully felt if rather inchoate sense of the need for a change in the dominant priorities in political life' which, the authors' suggest, might be thought of as the 'Mary Robinson effect'. Mary Robinson, a respected civil rights reformer, senior lawyer and member of the Irish Senate was elected President of Ireland in 1990, a result of great significance not only because of the political symbolism of electing a female president and one not representing Fianna Fáil (the first since 1945 – Robinson was nominated by the Labour Party, though officially she campaigned as an independent),[2] but also because of what her vote represented in terms of the underlying seismic shifts in Irish electoral politics. As Sinnott's painstaking analysis of the data shows, Robinson's vote revealed a combination of both the liberal–conservative and urban–rural cleavages which worked to her advantage, suggesting that the election 'did indeed touch a quite fundamental division in Irish society' (Sinnott, 1995: 278). This is consistent with Hardiman and Whelan's contention (1994: 185–6) that the 'Mary Robinson effect' is 'a value orientation that crosses the boundaries of party support'.

There is a sense of impending 'crisis' in the established party system, and this is something which is far from unique to the Irish case. In a number of countries it has prompted parties to 'democratize' their structures in at least two main areas. In some parties (notably in Belgium, Britain and Canada) the focus has been on the rules relating to leadership election, while in other

parties (in most Scandinavian countries, the Netherlands and Germany) it
has been far more on the process of candidate selection (Courtney, 1995;
MacIvor, 1995; Mair, 1994a). All this represents a general trend of trying to
involve the members in the internal workings of the party – although an
alternative gloss can be put on this, and that is that much of this effort to
increase the role of the members is merely cosmetic (Mair, 1994a).

Irish parties have been going through precisely the same sort of angst over
the need to increase the role of the party members. In 1989, the Labour
Party changed its statutes to give members of at least two years' standing the
right to vote for the party leader. Fine Gael has shown signs of a potential
move in this direction. In the light of the party's 1992 election result, the
worst since 1948 (see Table 3.2), a 'Commission of Renewal' was established
with a brief to 'report and advise on the overhaul and renewal of Fine Gael as
a party, in all its aspects' (Fine Gael, 1993: 9). Its report, published in late
1993, proposed a series of organizational and policy changes (Mockler,
1994). Among the former was a proposal to institute direct membership
elections at all levels within the party. In the case of the election of party
leader it was suggested that an electoral college should be established, which
would give 50 per cent of the votes to parliamentary party members, 10 per
cent to local councillors, and the remaining 40 per cent to the members on
an individual basis (Fine Gael, 1993: 37–48). At the subsequent party
conference, in 1994, the party's national executive was mandated to bring
forward specific proposals.

Fianna Fáil's proposals for internal party change were far more muted. It
also established a commission (on the 'Aims and Structures of Fianna Fáil')
in the light of the party's poor showing in 1992, but unlike the more
ambitious plans of Fine Gael, in its 1993 report, the Fianna Fáil commission
ended up placing more emphasis on the need to streamline the role of local
and national officers in the party rather than on any major organizational
restructuring (Fianna Fáil, 1993). Despite the limited objectives of the
Fianna Fáil commission and, indeed, the fact that Fine Gael did not hurry to
implement changes in the light of its commission's recommendations, '[t]he
very commissioning of the . . . reports seems to indicate that both Fianna Fáil
and Fine Gael believe that their existing organizations are no longer appropriate in a political environment that is in a state of flux' (Mockler, 1994:
170).

In conclusion, party politics in Ireland in the 1990s is very different from
that of the 1960s, in a number of respects. The party system has shifted from
being a two-and-a-half party system to a more conventional multi-party
system. It has also shifted from being a 'predominant' party system to one
which can more accurately be described, in terms of Sartori's framework
(1976), as a 'moderate pluralist' party system. The system has changed from

being one of the most stable and unchanging of Western Europe to one which is far less stable, where government survival is now far from guaranteed and where voters show every willingness to shift and change at will. Thus, government alternation has become a prominent feature of the party system since 1973, while the coalition formed after the 1997 election confirmed that Fianna Fáil could no longer claim a right to govern alone. Its minority government with the PDs was dependent on the good will of a number of independents nominally including the first member of Sinn Féin ever to be elected to the Dáil.

The established parties have so far successfully adapted to this changed environment, and are showing signs of still further organizational change to meet the challenges, if not of a more active membership, then certainly of a more 'participatory' electorate. The Irish party system is, therefore, not so much a transformed party system but rather one that is still transforming.

Notes

1. Given Ireland's written constitution, referendums are required to change, insert or delete any of its articles, and these referendums must be initiated via Dáil bills. There is no right of public initiative. However, this has not prevented the increasingly vociferous interest groups from bringing pressure to bear on the politicians and thereby influencing the calling of referendums.
2. Mary Robinson was succeeded by Mary McAleese in 1997. While nominated once more by Fianna Fáil, she too was noteworthy for being a Northern Irish UK citizen.

4

France: Living with Instability

DAVID HANLEY

Introduction

The student of parties and party systems will find France a rich terrain, offering a complex and shifting system to which all the main typologies of party systems can be, and have been, applied. Sartori's classic study charted a systemic evolution from strongly polarized multi-partism to a model with a predominant party (1976). Among recent commentators, Charlot sees the French party system as hovering between straight bipolarism and multi-partism with a dominant party (1989). Writing in the early 1980s, Wilson saw a 'dualist party system ... of two coherent and durable coalitions' (1982: 21). Bartolini, writing just as the *Front National* was about to take off in French politics, saw a two-bloc system but with three ideological poles (1984). Machin saw a predominant party, the Socialists (this was before the 1993 elections) but prudently took refuge in a more general characterization of the system as 'schizophrenic' (1989). At times, it seems that the only abiding characteristic of the French party system is its fluidity. Such a picture conceals as much as it reveals, however. The French party system has very deep roots, the study of which suggests much continuity beneath the high degree of apparent fluctuation.

The genesis of the French party system

Conventional wisdom tends to date the modern French party system from the birth of the first official party in modern France, the Radical party, which was formally registered in 1901. To accept this is, however, to turn one's back on several decades of activity prior to this date which were decisive for the emergence of parties as we know them today.

The emergence of constitutional monarchy early in the nineteenth century saw the beginnings of a vigorous parliamentary life in France (Rémond, 1969). Politics remained the preserve of a small landowning minority (a quarter of a million in a population one hundred times that size), and partisan organization was rudimentary. Nevertheless, sharp and sophist-icated struggles were conducted between the elites as power shifted from the monarch towards the elected assembly. These elites, whilst united in defence of their privileges, disagreed on most other areas of policy, sometimes to the point of paralysing the régime (Tudesq, 1964). The coming of male manhood suffrage in 1848 (very early in comparison with most of Europe) increased the development of partisan consciousness. Even the authoritarian Second Empire (1852–70) was unable to delay the march of parliamentary politics (Zeldin, 1958).

Thus, when republican government became firmly established after 1870, the seeds of modern partisan life were already firmly sown. Contemporaries usually understood it in terms of a Left–Right split or, as Goguel expressed it, in terms of a party of *movement* versus a party of *order* (Goguel, 1946). We should note that movement ranged over those seeking change in the political, economic and cultural spheres, while order included conservative republicans as well as those who sought reversion to less democratic modes of power. Long before 1900, groups of deputies formed and reformed along these lines, with many nuances inside both camps; formal organization within parliament and the country was vestigial, but by 1914, this polarized type of politics had found expression in a number of formal parties, so much so that we may speak meaningfully of a party system.

If we are to trace the genesis of parties from the classic cleavages defined by Lipset and Rokkan (1967a), we must nevertheless start from the split between democrats and authoritarians. This is structurally linked to, but by no means coterminous with, societal cleavages. It is possible to state in general terms that ever since the Revolution, authoritarians tended to be drawn from the ranks of the possessing classes, and democrats from the dispossessed or at least the 'rising' elements within society.

It is true that the aristocrats who lost property and status during the Revolution remained implacable enemies of the Republic until well into the twentieth century; it is also true, on the other hand, that Republicanism was always carried by an alliance of urban intellectuals, artisans, workers and later, parts of the poorer peasantry. This schema, however, omits the two most important social groups in nineteenth-century France, the *grands bourgeois* and the peasantry.

The *grands bourgeois* or *notables* (Lhomme, 1960), essentially men who had gained economic power in the Revolutionary period, were the major arbiters of French political life for most of the nineteenth century; relatively few in number, their economic, cultural and political influence was immense. While their favoured régime option was probably a constitutional monarchy with restricted suffrage where power lay in parliament, they were ready to endorse both authoritarianism when economically threatened, as after 1848, and, later on, to recognize the inevitability of universal suffrage and republican government. They backed the latter firmly provided it remained socially and economically conservative.

The peasantry was powerful by inertia and mass, not by its control of political resources like the *notables*, still accounting for 46 per cent of the workforce in 1906. Largely indifferent to politics, it wanted only a régime that would guarantee its land rights. Any system prepared to do so obtained its support.

The anti-clericalism of the Revolution divided France durably. Militant secularism became an early and unquestioned part of the republican–democratic canon. In the minds of republicans, Catholicism was equated with political subservience and ideological confusion. The Church, however, continued to command the loyalty not just of the aristocratic losers of 1789 but of large parts of rural France, particularly the East, the West and areas south of the Massif Central, where even today it is possible to speak of a 'Catholic vote'. Not even the emergence of an industrialized working class challenged this. With the complicity of the Church hierarchy, such areas became virtual no-go areas for republican politics until after the Second World War. The replacement of cultural differences by socio-economic cleavages never really took effect. A partisan split on religious lines existed clearly alongside one based on societal and régime-related divisions. In Catholic areas, the predominant vote for one or other of the right-wing groups was usually as much cultural as class-based.

Of the remaining cleavages typical of the emergence of modern party systems, the centre–periphery cleavage played less of a role. The Revolution had seen the victory of Jacobins over Girondins or centralizers over decentralizers. Throughout the nineteenth century, decentralization came to be identified with those parts of the Right that had never accepted the Revolution. All the Republican groups, including the later working-class left, were Jacobins with a vengeance.

In a sense, the centre–periphery cleavage was partly subsumed into the religious one. Those peripheral parts of France with the strongest regional identities, hence objects of deep suspicion to the Jacobin republicans, were precisely areas such as Alsace, Brittany or the Basque country, where Catholicism was the dominant culture. This is probably the main reason why regional parties were never more than of marginal importance.

Finally, the urban–rural cleavage did not lead to separate party formation. Despite their numerical weight, French farmers never set up more than ephemeral party groupings. Their needs were addressed either by Catholic politicians or by republicans.

By 1914, a recognizable party system existed, though in organizational terms the parties were but pale versions of those of today. The best structured parties were those of the Left. The industrial working class gave birth not to one party but to two. The socialist SFIO (*Section Française de l'Internationale Ouvrière*), formed by Guesde and Jaurès out of competing minorities in 1905, had a simple but effective revolutionary doctrine of marxism (Kergoat, 1983; Portelli, 1980). By 1914, it had a mass membership, was active in most of the country, had a stable electorate of workers, public employees and poorer peasants, and was an established force in local government.

The PCF (*Parti Communiste Français*) was set up in 1920. Aiming to apply Leninist principles to the making of the revolution it was soon locked in combat for the votes of the working class with the SFIO which it despised as reformist. After many years of sectarian detours, the PCF burst into mainstream politics, becoming a major actor in 1936 via the Popular Front electoral alliance.

The pivotal party of the system was the Radical party (*Parti Républicain Radical et Radical-Socialiste*). Founded in 1901 and dedicated to the preservation of parliamentary government and the cause of secularism, especially in education, it spoke for the middle classes of provincial France – shopkeepers, craftsmen and professionals – and for many rural voters who feared the rich and the powerful. In Birnbaum's terminology, it spoke for *les petits* against *les gros* (1979). It was probably the purest carrier of the ideology of republicanism and can be seen as a direct product of the religious–secularist cleavage.

The picture on the Right is more complex, a plethora of party and group names often concealing a distinct lack of organization. The pattern was one of groups of broadly conservative politicians (believers in a free market and a minimal state), confident of their voters' support and free to negotiate deals and alliances on a pragmatic basis (Anderson, 1974). It is usual to distinguish two very broad tendencies. A more republican group with secularist sympathies, firmly attached to the régime, usually followed the flag of the *Alliance Démocratique*. To their right, the *Fédération Républicaine* grouped deputies often of Catholic persuasion, often more aggressively nationalist and generally less disposed to policies of social accommodation. A further nuance is provided by the presence of the small Popular Democrats, an embryonic Christian Democratic party, the first attempt at a political organization of Catholics independent of the established Right.

The final element in the system was a semi-peripheral one, the Leagues (Passmore, 1993; Rémond, 1968; Machefer, 1974; Plumyene and Lasierra, 1963). These extra-parliamentary bodies were often formed by middle-class activists, usually on fixed incomes squeezed by government austerity policies and exasperated with their inability to influence policy via traditional parties. They devoted much activity to demonstrations and campaigns against 'corrupt politicians' and 'the system', famously laying siege to parliament and bringing down two governments in February 1934. Their very existence put pressure on the established parties, maintaining a tradition of robust anti-parliamentary activism that persists to this day. The *Front National* (FN) is the grandson of this type of politics.

These were the political forces which made up the inter-war system. The system was endemically multi-party, reflecting the depth and number of cleavages in French society. A 25 per cent share of the vote was the most that any party could aspire to. The system was also ideologically polarized in Sartori's terms, with the PCF notionally dedicated to the overthrow of capitalist democracy, and the Leagues (and some of the parliamentary Right) equally critical of republicanism from their different standpoint. Yet, the pre-war French party system showed remarkable flexibility despite this ideological polarization. The electoral arithmetic made coalition the rule. What is remarkable is the range and variety of the coalitions and the speed with which they formed and dissolved.

The inter-war period was dominated by the moderate right of *Alliance Démocratique* (Goguel, 1946) which often governed with the Radicals. Sometimes, this coalition was extended to include some independent socialists (a formula known as *concentration républicaine*) or even wider to include some of the *Fédération Républicaine* (this formula was reserved for moments of crisis and known as *union nationale*). The effects of the economic depression and the threat posed by the Leagues led to a new type of coalition, the Popular Front, where the SFIO, Radicals and independent socialists formed an all-Left government, which the PCF supported in parliament but did not join (Rémond, 1981; Jackson, 1988).

The variety of coalitions was equalled by their fluidity. Changes within one parliament were frequent. Thus the 1924 elections saw the victory of the *cartel des gauches* (a Socialist–Radical alliance) but long before the next elections, France was being governed by centre–right combinations led by Poincaré. Similarly, the Popular Front's electoral triumph of 1936 soon gave way to governments led by Radicals but which went back to the orthodox economic policies of the Right which voters had just rejected. This flexibility undoubtedly did much to preserve democracy in the difficult times of the 1930s. It also demonstrates the highly absorptive characteristics of the French party system.

Long before 1936, the SFIO had become a system party. Its decision to enter government that year, thereby breaking a hallowed shibboleth, merely confirmed that this self-proclaimed Marxist revolutionary party had become, in fact, a major actor within the system. With an electorate to satisfy in terms of policy output and a cadre of experienced MPs eager for office, it could no longer sit on the sidelines waiting for capitalism to collapse under the weight of its own contradictions. The SFIO's discourse remained extreme, but its practice confirmed it as a member of the parliamentary club. It had been painlessly digested by the system. Much the same had happened to the Radicals a generation previously, though their goals were less far-reaching than those of SFIO. This absorptive, incorporative character of the party system merits further examination.

The foundations of the French party system

Among those factors which might be thought to lie at the base of modern party systems, analysts often assign particular importance to electoral systems. Whether this is important in the French case must be a matter of some doubt (Cole and Campbell, 1989: 33).

Throughout the Third Republic (1870–1940), the mode of election of deputies varied considerably, swinging between PR (usually on a departmental basis) and the single-member constituency with two ballots which seemed to have become the norm in the 1930s (ibid.). The latter system certainly increased the saliency of the deputy among his voters. Constituencies were small, with 5,000 votes often securing a seat. The deputy was not, by and large, under pressure from local militants to implement a national party programme (except to a limited extent for SFIO and PCF representatives). Parties of the Right and Radicalism were characterized by deliberate organizational weakness, being mainly electoral committees at grass-roots level. These were cadre parties, and within them the deputy and his friends were all-powerful.

The key to this system of interest mediation, which began with the constitutional monarchies and matured under the Second Empire (1852–70), was the peculiar link between local and national politics. The majority of deputies were (and still are) local office holders as well, typically mayors or *conseillers généraux* (councillors). Unlike in Britain, a political career in France had to be pursued at both levels. In short, the peculiar position of deputies as essentially local representatives gave them a good deal in common and predisposed them to accommodation.

This professional solidarity was reinforced by a cultural factor, namely, the strong Jacobinism of all party elites. All, from the PCF to the far end of the moderate right, accepted the French version of the centralized state. Centralization was seen as essential to the constitution and the enhancement of nationhood. The only serious decentralizers left by 1900 were those who were ultimately not Republicans. Part and parcel of Jacobinism was also secularism, which again was shared by all from the PCF to just short of the *Fédération Républicaine*.

A final consideration is the deep fear of authoritarianism, bred of the knowledge that both previous Republics had been overthrown by a strong man. This led deputies to mistrust any outstanding individual, especially if he had ideas about strengthening the executive or reducing the influence of parties. Deputies shared a feeling that democracy involved, by its very essence, compromise and bargaining.

Such factors explain the fluidity of the party system and the role played by its pivot, the Radical party. Scarcely absent from government during the latter half of the Republic, this party shared power alternately with Right and Left, varying its programmes and policies. It acted as a sort of thermostat, preventing a meltdown of the party system. It was able to do so thanks to its ideological proximity to the forces of the Left (secularism and also a populist discourse in favour of *les petits*), which co-existed with a readiness to adopt policies congenial to the Right (essentially fiscal conservatism and mistrust of anything resembling big government).

Radicalism was able to make masterful use of the alliance possibilities of the second ballot, drawing from voters of the Left or moderate Right, according to the tactical needs of the moment. These ambiguities were, however, more easily tolerated in a milieu of mainly educated, middle-aged males with a distinct career pattern.

The product of a largely agricultural, pre-modern society in which socio-economic change proceeded slowly, the pre-war French party system was much derided at the time. Since then, it has usually been given a major share of the blame for France's unpreparedness for the Second World War and consequent defeat. The argument has been that such a system could not produce governments with enough authority to cope both with the domestic convulsions resulting from the depression and the foreign policy challenges stemming from the rise of fascism. The above account suggests that this verdict is harsh and that the suppleness of the party system in fact helped a still divided society to retain democratic politics during a difficult period.

The Fourth Republic: recomposition or consolidation?

It is generally accepted that the French political class missed the opportunity accorded by the Liberation in 1944 to devise a new political system that would avoid the weaknesses of its predecessor (Williams, 1964). The institutional structure of the Fourth Republic (1946–58) exhibited the familiar features of a weak executive derived from coalitions made obligatory by a fragmented party system. This fragmentation was not helped by the adoption of PR at departmental level for electing deputies. Thus the party system retained most of its pre-war characteristics although there were also some innovations.

On the left, the PCF and SFIO remained vigorous, especially the former which, thanks to its Resistance record and diligent penetration of the trade union movement, was now the biggest party in France, winning a quarter of the popular vote (Bell and Criddle 1994a). Radicalism could still draw more than 10 per cent. The Right remained as loosely structured as ever. The formal organizations of the *Alliance Démocratique* and *Fédération Républicaine* soon disappeared, discredited by the pro-Vichy behaviour of many of their elites during the Occupation. They were replaced by formations such as the PRL (*Parti Républicain de la Liberté*) which aggregated the interests of the Right's traditional clientele (Vinen, 1993; 1995).

The most spectacular innovation in the system was the appearance in 1944 of the MRP (*Mouvement Républicain Populaire*). This explicitly Christian Democratic party was born of Resistance activists socialized into politics through the Catholic action movements of the inter-war period. The MRP at last provided Catholics, especially those interested in reform, with a vehicle whose democratic credentials were impeccable. Its appeal extended from progressive Christians through to supporters of the old reactionary Right, and this ambiguity was its major problem. Electorally, it peaked at some 28 per cent and it never went below 12 per cent, making it an almost compulsory coalition partner, similar to the Radicals before 1939.

Two 'surge' parties also deserve mention. In 1946, de Gaulle retired from the headship of the post-Liberation provisional government in disgust at 'the return of the parties'. In 1947, he launched his own political vehicle, the RPF (*Rassemblement du Peuple Français*). It soon reached 20 per cent of the vote, taking support from the MRP, socialists and traditional Right. It was more than a variant of the latter, combining a 'Bonapartist' advocacy of strong, presidential leadership, an unflinching nationalism and a social programme cleverly dosed with welfarism. Best seen as a variant of the populist right, it showed organized Gaullism to be a force to be reckoned with, as became clear after 1958.

Alongside it, the short-lived Poujadist movement of the mid-1950s showed that extra-parliamentary politics of the pre-war League style were still attractive to the provincial middle classes losing out to economic modernization (Hoffmann, 1956). The Poujadists' brief and chaotic foray into the 1956 parliament served mainly as a reminder that neither the traditional nor the Gaullist Right could take their grip on some of their natural supporters for granted.

These newcomers changed the dynamics of the system. The MRP became the key player, sharing in government alternately with the Left (the 'tripartite' governments of 1944–47 which achieved much by way of economic and social reconstruction) and later, after the removal of the PCF, with combinations of the SFIO, Radicals and moderate Right in 'third force' governments. Every major group had a share in government except the Poujadists. The PCF was a regular coalition partner until 1947. Even the

RPF, set up explicitly to fight the 'Republic of parties' was joining governments by 1954.

As in 1940, it took external pressure to disaggregate the party system: the crisis of decolonization, mediated to a degree through the effects of the Cold War, was decisive in bringing down the régime. Thus, the crisis of 1947, when the PCF was evicted from government, clearly reflected the acceptance by the French elite that the PCF would have to be subjected to 'containment' within France. This removed at a stroke the biggest party in France as a possible coalition partner, a party which had generally behaved responsibly within a democratic framework. It is obviously impossible to know if increasing involvement in government would have continued to lead the PCF away from the Soviet model, gradually allowing its incorporation as a system party as had happened with the SFIO. What is certain, however, is that the PCF had little incentive to play other than a wrecking role once it had been placed into a ghetto and its repeated attempts to escape ignored. Sitting on a quarter of the vote that was to all intents and purposes 'sterilized', the PCF cynically helped bring down a number of governments. When, in 1958, its help was needed to save the régime, unsurprisingly it did not oblige.

With governments drawn from the 'third force' parties at the centre of the system often representing a bare half of the electorate (Gaullism as well as the PCF was regarded as being inimical to the system), it is scarcely surprising that these coalitions found it increasingly hard to deal with the war in Algeria which dominated all else from 1954.

These governments were in an impossible situation. Algerian nationalism was too strong to be overcome by the 'military solution' (the official doctrine). No mainstream figure dared advocate the other option, independence, for fear of upsetting the settlers, the colonial bureaucracy and the army. These powerful interests were well represented in parliament, particularly through the Radical party and the moderate Right. The result was a policy vacuum, filled in practice by the army and settlers, who increasingly behaved autonomously from government and whose actions went unchecked.

When Algerian interests staged an insurrection in May 1958, threatening to invade Paris, the elites felt so isolated that they could only turn to the providential rescuer de Gaulle, who persuaded them that he alone could save democracy. He also managed the feat of persuading the insurrectionists that he could keep Algeria French. Riding to power on this tide of ambiguity, he put through a new constitution that changed the party system.

The Fourth Republic party system displayed continuity with the past. Despite historic disagreements, the elites were united by the same republican beliefs and by the same party structures, and their attitudes were co-operative and consensual. There was also considerable voter fidelity, although the advent of the MRP and organized Gaullism did somewhat rejig that pattern.

The Fifth Republic: a definitive solution?

Seen from the vantage point of the late 1990s, the Fifth Republic has clearly operated a party system distinct from that of its predecessor (Frears, 1991; Wilson, 1982). By the end of 1962, when de Gaulle won his referendum on the election of the President by universal suffrage and his UNR party led the field in parliamentary elections, it was clear that the General was reshaping the party system. His indispensability in office as the only man who could solve the Algerian problem without a civil war enabled him to swing a large part of the old Right behind his new party while extending the latter's appeal leftwards thanks to the popularity of his institutional changes and the onset of an economic boom.

From then until the death of Pompidou in 1974, the Gaullist party under its various names, together with allies from the moderate Right (organized mainly as the Independent Republicans of Giscard d'Estaing) enjoyed parliamentary majorities loyally supporting a president who increasingly became the powerhouse of policy-making. The opposition of the PCF and SFIO was ineffectual, as was that of the so-called Opposition Centrists (the remains of the MRP and Radicals). Gaullism clearly deserved the name of a predominant party during this period.

The presidency of Giscard d'Estaing (1974–81) saw a more delicate balance. On the right, Giscard's *Union pour la Démocratie Française* (UDF), composed of his Independent Republicans and the Opposition Centrists who had by now gone over to him, enjoyed an often tense parity with Gaullism, revamped as the *Rassemblement pour la République* (RPR) by Jacques Chirac after he fell out with Giscard. Against them were pitted the united left, the PCF and the new Socialist party (PS), born out of a merger of the SFIO and smaller groups in 1972. Armed with a common programme of government, it was catching the Right up rapidly through the 1970s. Commentators thus saw the party system as a *quadrille bipolaire*, using an analogy from the dance floor. This signified a reasonably symmetrical polarization between a left bloc and a right bloc, within both of which two roughly equal partners cohabited.

Mitterrand's presidential victory of 1981 and the PS landslide in the parliamentary elections signalled a move back to the dominant party mode of the 1960s, except that now the PS was dominant, not Gaullism. Just as Gaullism had only had a rather weak partner in the shape of Giscardism, so the PS now had to deal with a rapidly weakening PCF. This situation did not last long, however. The Right's electoral victory of 1986 ensured it a bare parliamentary majority, ushering in the period of cohabitation between a socialist president and a prime minister from the right.

The system was further complicated by the emergence of the *Front National* as a major player with over 10 per cent of the vote and some 30 deputies (the Socialists having changed the electoral system back to departmental PR as before 1958). The PCF had meanwhile regained its autonomy, leaving government and officially breaking with left unity, although it generally continued to ally with the PS on second ballots.

It would be hard to characterize the French party system at this point as being anything other then a multi-party one. Although Mitterrand was easily re-elected president in 1988, the PS never won enough votes to form a majority on its own. In 1993, it was humiliatingly routed in the National Assembly elections, although the durability and capacity for recovery of the PS under Jospin were demonstrated by the early National Assembly elections of 1997 when the PS emerged as the overwhelming winner, taking 253 seats, up from only 63 seats in 1993. This outcome made Jospin's nomination as prime minister and a new period of cohabitation this time with Chirac, inevitable.

None of the components of the Right enjoy dominance over the other as in the 1960s, though the RPR is currently ahead. Even though Chirac won the 1995 presidential contest, his narrow victory (given the extremely favourable circumstances for the Right) and the strong rally of the Left behind Jospin at the second ballot suggest that talk of a new dominant party is misplaced. This was confirmed by the subsequent difficulties experienced by Chirac's government and in particular by Chirac's gamble in calling the 1997 National Assembly elections in order to strengthen his position in advance of delicate EMU negotiations in 1998. This gamble misfired spectacularly as French voters expressed their anger at policy failures, notably on unemployment, and at a patent attempt to bounce them into support for a struggling president.

The French party system today

Compared to the Fourth Republic, the present party system shows several structural changes (see Table 4.1). Gaullism has achieved organizational permanency as a party of the Right. The 'Orleanist' or independent Right has been organized more tightly into the Republican Party which, under the umbrella of the UDF, adopted a permanent relationship, albeit of very loose character, with a number of other parties. These latter include the remains of the Radical party and the rump of Christian Democracy (the CDS, recently renamed *Force Démocratique*, FD). It would seem that none of these forces still believes that it can prosper as a fully autonomous party.

The picture is further complicated by the apparently permanent decline of the PCF (from above 20 per cent to about 7 per cent in fifteen years) and the rise of the FN from nowhere to a steady 10–12 per cent over the past dozen years. While there is still a socialist party, it is in many ways very different from the old SFIO of 1958, having won more than 35 per cent of the vote and, in 1981 and 1988, two presidential elections. A final point is that green politics is lively, still attempting to capitalize on a favourable disposition among voters.

Table 4.1 French National Assembly elections, 1958–97

	1958	1962	1967	1968	1973	1978	1981	1986	1988	1993	1997
Abstentions[1]	24.8	33.3	20.7	21.4	20.4	18.4	30.1	24.9	35.3	34.4	35.0
Far Left	–	2.0	2.2	4.0	2.2	3.3	1.2	1.5	0.4	1.8	2.5
PCF	18.9	21.9	22.5	20.0	21.4	20.6	16.1	9.7	11.3	9.2	10.0
Socialist	15.5	12.4	18.9	16.5	20.8	25.0	39.5	31.6	37.6	20.3	27.7
Ecologists	–	–	–	–	–	1.4	1.1	–	0.4	7.6	6.9
Other Left	10.9	7.4	–	–	–	–	–	–	–	–	–
Centre	11.1	7.9	17.4	12.4	16.7	(See UDF)					
Other Right	20.0	11.5	(with centre)		UDF	2.7	2.7	2.9	4.7	6.5	–
UDF + allies	–	–	–	–	–	23.9	19.7	42.1[2]	18.5	19.1	14.3
Gaullists	20.6	36.0	38.5	46.4	37.0	22.8	21.2	42.1[2]	19.2	20.4	15.6
Far Right	2.6	0.8	0.6	0.1	0.5	0.8	0.6	10.1	9.7	12.7	15.2

[1] This figure includes spoilt ballots.
[2] RPR/UDF joint result. For details of parties, see Cole, 1998.

Source: Cole, 1998: 266.

French voters thus remain as dispersed as ever in their electoral preferences; indeed, a system offering choices running from the authoritarian saloon-bar xenophobia of the FN to the trenchant workerism of the PCF or the ideological variants of Green politics would probably have to be called strongly polarized. The French people have, however, been forced to express their preferences in a tighter party framework than before, and the key to this is usually seen as the electoral system (Cole and Campbell, 1989).

For the election of deputies, the Fifth Republic reverted to the single-member constituency system with two ballots operational before the Second World War. At the same time, it imposed a threshold for qualifying for the second round, eventually ratcheted up to 12.5 per cent of registered voters, equivalent to about 20 per cent of the first round vote. This high figure has been crucial in concentrating party minds on alliances (Bartolini, 1984). It makes sense for candidacies not to be too widely dispersed on either the Left or Right, as the best-placed candidate on either side is clearly going to need the voters of less successful candidates from that camp in the second ballot.

This has led smaller parties to combine in advance so as to maximize their presence even on the first ballot (the *raison d'être* of the UDF), as well as leading to ever closer collaboration between the main parties in either camp. Latterly, the RPR and UDF have usually been able to carve up the overwhelming majority of constituencies by national agreement, leaving only one candidate from the mainstream Right on the first ballot.

Rules for other contests have helped this 'bipolarizing' tendency whereby Left faces Right on the decisive ballot. Since the presidency has been decided by universal suffrage (from 1962) (see Table 4.2), the second round of this contest has been open solely to the two best-placed candidates from the first. Again, the pressure is on parties to strike deals for the second ballot which, to some extent, moderates or distorts the competition on the first.

Table 4.2 French presidential elections, 1965–95

	1965	1969	1974	1981	1988	1995
de Gaulle	55.2					
Mitterrand	44.8		49.2	51.8	54.0	
Pompidou		57.6				
Poher		42.4				
Giscard d'Estaing			50.8	48.2		
Chirac					46.0	52.6
Jospin						47.4

Source: Cole, 1998: 268.

All these bipolar electoral pressures encourage parties to ally within their own camp; but they do not imply mergers or absorptions of one party by another. What they do is intensify the competition within the fields of Left and Right. It is here that we must seek further keys to the party system changes that have occurred.

Whereas the PS has become clearly hegemonic on the Left, the picture on the Right is more complicated, with the UDF and RPR in constant, albeit diluted, competition and both threatened equally of late by the rise of the FN. Much of the explanation for this is related to the ways in which the parties of Left and Right have responded to the opportunities opened up by the electoral system, as well as to a number of other extraneous challenges. Pierce (1992) insists on the active roles played by parties, particularly the PS, in responding to the opportunities created by the new institutions so as to raise voter identification with *party* (as opposed to vaguer Left or Right sympathies) to unprecedented levels, fragile though much of this identification might prove to be.

On the Left, the whole enterprise of creating the successful post-1972 PS stemmed from realizing what the new electoral system involved. Left-wing elites as different as the big city master of clientelism Defferre, the nationalist neo-Marxist Chevènement, and the professional Centre–Left politician Mitterrand, realized that the Left had to ally to have any chance of winning office. This would only come about, they reasoned, if the Communists were clearly not the dominant alliance partner. Thus a new-look socialist party had to be put together quickly out of the SFIO and the various oddments of 'the non-communist Left'. This operation was carried out with boldness and speed, and within a year a joint manifesto with the PCF was signed. Soon after, the PS was forging ahead of the latter in the polls. Thereafter, the PS won two presidencies and three elections, one, in 1981, by a landslide. Its strong performance in the 1995 presidential election and the 1997 Assembly election shows that it is still hegemonic on the Left and a viable government party.

The PCF, on the other hand, has declined steadily, now representing only inner city ghettos and some old mining seats. Members and voters tend to be older and from declining social groups, and the future looks bleak (Bell and Criddle, 1994b). Yet clearly when the PCF leaders accepted the PS's challenge they must have been confident of coming out on top. Their failure tells us much about how parties react to opportunities.

The PS became the major party of France in the late 1970s and 1980s because it recognized that profound socio-economic and cultural changes were taking place, and it found a discourse and programmes to give expression to the new types of voter demand.

The party's sociological analyses detected a France that was at the peak of industrialization and urbanization, but where already an increasing proportion of the workforce belonged not to manual categories but to the salaried middle classes. Educated and articulate, their demands were less for the traditional panaceas of public ownership than for involvement in decision-making. The PS, with its talk of decentralization and self-management, served them an enticing mix. At the same time, its more traditional socialist economics appealed to working-class voters often loyal to the PCF.

Culturally, the PS had long lived on a stiff diet of republicanism, in which anti-clericalism figured strongly. While the general decline of religious practice is considered to have helped the Left, the PS was aware that many reform-minded Catholics could be won over from Gaullism or the CDS if the traditional ideological hardness towards them was mitigated. Although this process was not always easy (cf. the hole into which the party dug itself over Catholic schools with the 1984 Bill), the change of tone and the recruitment of Rocard sympathizers and CFDT activists showed the broader approach of the party. It has since been translated into considerable electoral strength in areas like Brittany, considered virtually out of bounds to the old SFIO. Willingness to dump sacred cows extended to other areas of ideology. The party's overnight about-face on nuclear weapons in 1978 showed its ability both to recognize electorally damaging policies and to change them.

Above all, the party succeeded in keeping a leftward profile but remaining distinct from the PCF. There were several aspects to this. Its vague image of self-managing socialism was attractive precisely because it was not the Soviet model. The way in which the party was led was different too. It had a clear leader, Mitterrand, experienced, obstinate, articulate and possessing consummate political skill. The PS also conducted its business in an argumentative way, with highly sophisticated factionalism that never reached the point of civil war; it was democratic but in the last analysis, it also had enough discipline to appear capable of governing (Hanley, 1986).

All these features mark positive attempts by the PS to identify changes within the electorate and to respond to them. However, the party's strategy also rested on another fundamental assumption, namely, the structural limitations of the PCF. To put it simply, the socialists knew that one day the pendulum would swing to the Left but that within the Left, the PCF was bound to lose the internal battle.

From being well ahead of the socialists in terms of votes, members, resources and support organizations, the PCF has shrunk to a position approaching marginality. It is suggested that its decline owes much to the collapse of communism in Eastern Europe. While this is true to the extent that the end of the communist party states discredited a model with which the PCF was closely associated, this begs the question as to why the PCF was well advanced towards marginality some way *before* 1989.

The party proved incapable of addressing social change. Workerist by instinct and practice, it could never come to terms with the decline of heavy industry and consequently of the importance of those skilled, unionized manual workers who comprised its backbone. The new salaried middle classes (or 'layers' as the party unflatteringly called them) could only fit into party schemas as largely passive allies of the working class. Their demands for participation were met by late and empty slogans about self-management (mainly during the short-lived 'Eurocommunist' phase of the mid-1970s) which were flatly contradicted by the 'top-down' way in which the party itself operated.

Leadership remained centralized in the hands of a small group of ex-workers turned bureaucrats, long trained in habits of instinctive loyalty and refusal to question any decision once taken. Admiration for the USSR was part and parcel of their culture. The party's internal selection and disciplinary procedures were excellent for isolating and forcing out dissenters, but they also forced out any new ideas or approaches, guaranteeing the continuity of the same type of leadership, ever more remote from reality. Only very recently does the PCF seem to have woken up to this, with the change of leadership from Marchais to Hue in 1994.

Rivalry on the Right has taken its own forms. The Gaullist party achieved hegemony after 1958 with remarkable speed. Built rapidly by Pompidou and the Gaullist 'barons' who profited from the fear of political instability which made de Gaulle indispensable until the Algerian problem was solved, the party was associated from the start with the new institutions which seemed to guarantee stability. It was also able to claim credit for the surge of economic growth of the 1960s and to bask in the glory of new, assertive foreign and security policies. Most of this highly popular set of policies doubtless owed little to the party *per se*, but as the supporter of de Gaulle, and with his endorsement, the party was bound to do well. As such, it took votes from the old Right, the MRP and even partly from the Left (Ysmal, 1989). By 1968, its electorate was a mirror image of French society, with a big, popular and working-class component. It behaved like a natural party of government.

In short, the UNR, as it was called by 1968, had shown that it was possible to give lasting organizational effect to the vague current of rightist populism which had but flickered under the Fourth Republic. This was achieved by understanding and exploiting the new opportunities afforded by the institutional changes of 1958. Moreover, although de Gaulle's initial role was crucial, this success cannot be ascribed to the charisma of a great man. After the 1968 riots, the party was able to survive the departure of the General and carry on governing under the leadership of its new leader, Pompidou. The Gaullists were in no great difficulty even when Pompidou's sudden death produced a dramatic effect on the dynamics of the French Right. Faced with a presidential election against a rampant Left led by Mitterrand, part of the Gaullist apparatus, led by Chirac, abandoned as a likely loser the Gaullist candidate, Chaban Delmas, and threw their weight behind Giscard. He scraped home by the barest margin. Although Chirac was appointed prime minister, he was removed by Giscard after two years and hurled all his energy into revamping the Gaullist machine as the *Rassemblement pour la République* (RPR).

Giscard's own rump liberal party, soon to be relaunched as the *Parti Républicain* (PR), could never rival the RPR in terms of members, money or seats. One possibility would have been to hold early elections and to try to create a president's party, which might have won over large numbers of Gaullist deputies and broken the RPR; this would have been emulating what de Gaulle did between 1958 and 1962. Giscard opted for a less confrontational strategy by waiting until the 1978 elections before creating an electoral cartel, the *Union pour la Démocratie Française* (UDF), which allied his own party to the remains of Radicalism, some dissident socialists frightened by the deal with the PCF and, most importantly, the Christian Democrats who had recognised the bipolar pull of the electoral system and were ready to deal with the pro-European right.

This motley collection was no substitute for a structured political party and continues to this day to have difficulty in developing greater unity (Cole, 1990). It could only hope to succeed against the RPR if the presidency were spectacularly successful but the economic conditions of the later 1970s put paid to such hopes. The *rapports de force* between the two rightist partners remained roughly equal in terms of votes and seats until Giscard's defeat in 1981. By then, the chance of supplanting RPR hegemony on the Right had gone.

The RPR steadily recovered its hegemony. The 1986 National Assembly elections were won by the RPR–UDF together on a neo-liberal manifesto directly in the lineage of the Orleanist Right. However, the coalition leader and eventual prime minister was Chirac who did not hesitate to abandon the classic statist discourse of Gaullist populism for market-friendly liberalism.

Even a second socialist presidency did not delay the RPR's relentless clawback of ascendancy within the Right. The 1993 elections brought it the biggest share of deputies, and in 1995, the UDF was unable or too timid to have its own presidential candidate. Chirac had to beat a UDF proxy from within his own ranks in the shape of Balladur. This time, the manifesto was much more critical of liberalism, talking a language of Keynesian economics and social compassion.

Just as for the Left, this account demonstrates the need for both unity and adaptability. The RPR regained its ascendancy over its rival (albeit the amount of compensation which it has to pay is greater than 30 years ago) because, despite stresses, it kept its unity. Unity enabled it to make the ideological and programmatic changes described above with surgical ruthlessness, doing exactly what it had diagnosed as necessary to win votes.

By contrast, the UDF's divisions remain evident and to some extent insurmountable. Liberals and Christian Democrats are not obvious bedfellows despite the dilutions undergone by Christian Democracy (Hanley, 1994). When compounded by personal rivalries, often with a territorial base, these fissures are likely to widen and remain a source of weakness. As the UDF and RPR are competing for broadly the same type of voter, the RPR is always likely to have the edge. The parties of the UDF have settled for a comfortable second place without a project of their own.

In sum, bipolarization has created competition within both the Left and the Right, but in each camp, one party has better seized the various opportunities.

Multipartism with a difference?

Institutional change and the response by party actors have, to some extent, reshaped the French party system. It retains, however, most of its abiding historical characteristics. It is still multi-party, by any definition. The main forces are still in business, even though name changes have been frequent (as with the Gaullists) and some historic parties (Liberals, Christian Democrats and remaining Radicals) prefer to hide within the larger confines of a semi-party (UDF) for tactical reasons. The Socialists have changed from the days of the SFIO, but are still recognizably the same party. The Greens and FN have brought lasting diversity from other directions.

Second, the system remains polarized, though some qualification is necessary here. Sartori's notion of strong ideological polarization reflected the tensions of the Cold War and the weight of strong communist parties within western systems. Today, we may still speak of a Left–Right polarity as the main divide, but it is a weaker one. The collapse of the communist states, the apparent exhaustion of European social democracy and the trimming of ultra-liberal policies which did not fulfil their promise by right-wing governments have led to a narrowing of the ideological space.

The Left seeks a number of economic and social guarantees from the state, and is generally in favour of what the French call 'cultural liberalism' (protection of individual and collective expression and rejection of repressive or traditionalist moral codes). The Right stands for economic individualism, sterner repression and for getting government off the citizen's back. These alternative cultures still tend to structure voting behaviour and tend to be reflected through recognizable social groups. The aged, the rich, the religious and the rural tend to vote on the Right, whereas the irreligious, the urban and the lower classes vote on the Left. Such classic syndromes have been important since the study of electoral behaviour began in France (Dupoirier and Grunberg, 1986: 165). The 'new voters' who were discovered during the 1988 elections and who appeared to be voting on rational choice, 'shopping basket' criteria, with no reference to sociological or cultural variables, were even then admitted to be few in number (Habert and Ysmal, 1988).

Continuing but moderate polarization helps explain a third characteristic of the French party system which we can term its core–periphery dimension. In effect, only those parties which are close to the notional dividing line between Left and Right have any prospect of forming a government (see Table 4.3). This means the RPR–UDF and the PS. Outside this core lie the others who have become pure repositories of protest, free to argue maximalist cases precisely because they are never likely to be in a position to turn their theses into policy. These parties are well aware of the fact, as are the

Table 4.3 Government composition in the French Fifth Republic, 1959–97

Dates	Prime Minister	Party support
Jan. 1959–Apr. 1962	M. Debré (G)	G+MRP+Ind
Apr. 1962–Nov. 1962	G. Pompidou (G)	G+MRP+Ind
Nov. 1962–Jan. 1966	G. Pompidou	G+RI
Jan. 1966–Apr. 1967	G. Pompidou	G+RI
Apr. 1967–May 1968	G. Pompidou	G+RI
May 1968–July 1968	G. Pompidou	G+RI
July 1968–June 1969	M. Couve de Murville (G)	G+RI
June 1969–July 1972	J. Chaban-Delmas (G)	G+RI+CDP
July 1972–Mar. 1973	P. Messmer (G)	G+RI+CDP
Mar. 1973–Feb. 1974	P. Messmer	G+RI+CDP
Feb. 1974–May 1974	P. Messmer	G+RI+CDP
May 1974–Aug. 1976	J. Chirac (G)	G+RI+Ref
Aug. 1976–Mar. 1977	R. Barre (non-party)	RI+G+CDS+Rad
Mar. 1977–Apr. 1978	R. Barre	RI+G+CDS
Apr. 1978–May 1981	R. Barre (UDF)	UDF+G
May 1981–June 1981	P. Mauroy (PS)	PS+MRG
June 1981–Mar. 1983	P. Mauroy	PS+PCF+MRG
Mar. 1983–Jan. 1984	P. Mauroy	PS+PCF+MRG+PSU
Jan. 1984–Mar. 1986	L. Fabius (PS)	PS+MRG
Mar. 1986–May 1988	J. Chirac (G)	G+UDF
May 1988–June 1988	M. Rocard (PS)	PS+MRG
June 1988–May 1991	M. Rocard	PS+MRG
May 1991–Apr. 1992	E. Cresson (PS)	PS+MRG
Apr. 1992–Mar. 1993	P. Bérégovoy (PS)	PS+MRG
Mar. 1993–May 1995	E. Balladur (G)	RPR+UDF
May 1995–Nov. 1995	A. Juppé (G)	RPR+UDF
Nov. 1995–June 1997	A. Juppé (G)	RPR+UDF
June 1997–	L. Jospin (PS)	PS+PCF+Greens+MDC

Key to party abbreviations

CD   see UDF
CPD   *Centre Progrès et Démocratie* (Christian Democrat rump willing to support Gaullism after 1969)
G   Gaullist[1]
Ind   Independants (conservatives)[2]
MDC   *Mouvement des Citoyens*
MRG   *Mouvement des Radicaux de Gauche* (left-wing split from Radical party after 1972)
MRP   *Mouvement Républicain Populaire* (Christian Democrat)
PCF   *Parti Communiste Français*
PS   *Parti Socialiste*
PSU   *Parti Socialiste Unifié*
Rad   Radical party
Ref   *Réformateurs* (ephemeral Radical–Christian Democrat alliance of early 1970s)
RI   *Républicains Indépendants* (liberal conservatives loyal to Giscard, later to become PR – see UDF)
SFIO   *Section Française de l'Internationale Ouvrière* (socialist pre-1969)
UDF   *Union pour la Démocratie Française* (includes liberal *Parti Républicain*, Christian Democrat *Centre des Démocrates Sociaux* and Radical party)

Table 4.3 *contd.*

UDSR   *Union démocratique et socialiste de la Résistance* (Centre–Left group of Fourth
Republic, allied with Radicals)

This list does not include non-party members of governments.

[1] Gaullist subsumes the different names of the Gaullist movement at various times in
its history (RPF, ARS, UNR, UDR, RPR).
[2] Independents includes all subgroups of moderate, liberal conservatism (e.g. Peas-
ant Party).

core parties. So are about 80 per cent of the electorate. This explains why the
PCF, Greens and FN are able to concentrate on the fraction of the electorate
who feel left behind by economic change, especially in the context of
Europeanization and globalization, and to argue for solutions equally radical
in their different ways. The leaders of the core parties know, however, that
brutal solutions such as mass expulsion of immigrants, closing down all
nuclear power stations or extensive *dirgisme* are unworkable and cannot be
sold to most voters.

Moreover, they know that whether it is the moderate right or the PS in
power, both will have to work within very tight parameters. The core parties
are loath to admit this openly but French voters have seen them all in power
more than once within the present generation and they are able to judge the
parties by results. The parties have in fact 'interiorized' their status, accepting their own ascription to the core or the periphery, or to put it more
brutally, to relevance or irrelevance.

Conclusion: coping with moderate polarization

This moderately polarized, multi-party system is likely to persist. Although it
faces a number of challenges, its inner resilience is such that it should easily
overcome them. We shall identify its strengths before considering these
challenges.

First, French parties are now on a sounder logistical footing than ever
before. They were long used to surviving by a mixture of private subsidy and
extortion of monies from firms seeking public contracts by means of 'classic'
mechanisms known to all. The wave of scandals of the late 1980s led the
government to pass laws outlawing private donations and instituting state
funding on a generous, vote-related basis which benefits small parties in
particular (Rieken, 1995).

Second, the range of electoral opportunity is remarkably flexible. The
discussion in this chapter has centred on national contests and has thus paid

much attention to bipolarization. Other arenas, however, operate proportional systems where parties can secure rewards approximating to their electoral weight (Machin, 1989). Municipal elections offer one such opportunity but we must not forget the elected regional councils with their big budgets and growing powers.

At a higher level, France elects its MEPs by PR, leaving a party only a 5 per cent threshold to clear to secure seats. In short, 'second order' elections provide great opportunities for forces like the FN and Greens which tend to be squeezed in the bipolar national contests. Even the much maligned two-ballot system provides, at the first ballot, a chance both for voters to protest before voting for real and for parties to show their weight. This amounts to a system of 'second prizes', a sort of semi-visible irrigation system of the French party system and a huge source of strength.

What of the challenges levelled at this system? The Maastricht referendum of September 1992 split the country down the middle. However, this cleavage was rapidly subsumed (Guyomarch, 1995). All the core parties are integrationist in outlook while all the peripheral parties were nationalist. This caused difficulties for some of the core parties, especially the RPR, in managing their electorates. However, the 1995 presidential contest between Chirac and Jospin, whose positions on Europe were virtually indistinguishable, suggested that the core parties had made the integrationist view widely shared. Europe is thus an addition to existing stress factors, but it is not a new factor.

Another problem cited is the 'crisis of representation' (Mayer and Perrineau, 1992; Mossuz-Lavau, 1994). Analysts cite the growing number of abstentions (over 30 per cent in 1993 and 1997) and spoiled ballots (5 per cent in 1997 – see Table 4.1) and, more seriously, the growing vote for peripheral parties or candidates (36 per cent in 1993, 37 per cent in 1995 and fully 47 per cent in 1997). These trends have gone hand in hand with mounting distrust of professional politicians. Politicians rarely enjoy high esteem anywhere. Their dip in popularity in France coincided with a heavy wave of politico-financial scandals and some recovery could be expected as parties no longer have to rely on cheating to survive.

While the vote for peripheral parties is impressive, one might ask how many of their representatives get elected in national contests – the answer is a bare 20 Communist deputies. This is because of the 'filter effect' of the first ballot alluded to above. At the decisive ballot, the French continue to vote for mainstream parties.

What is more interesting is to speculate about the development of the peripheral forces. It is certainly not inevitable that they will continue to reside on the margins. It is possible to envisage a reformed PCF under Hue inching its way back towards some sort of national pact with the PS. The evidence for this was significantly strengthened in 1997 when Jospin, before the National Assembly vote, negotiated a joint statement and a second ballot deal with the PCF, desperate under Hue to halt its decline and gain credibility as a government party. The PCF achieved both aims, holding its share of the vote, but increasing its tally of MPs and obtaining two medium-sized ministries.

An even more significant deal in 1997 was struck with the realistic fraction of the Greens, led by Dominique Voynet, which gave the Greens a free run in a number of winnable seats. They ended up with eight MPs and a seat in the government – a rare instance of a party passing the legislative and executive thresholds in one attempt.

A third part of the Jospin coalition was the *Mouvement des Citoyens*, recognizable to all as the ex-CERES of Jean-Pierre Chevènement. Now an autonomous party after its split from the PS, local deals with the PS and PCF secured it seven seats plus the office of Interior Minister for its leader.

In systemic terms, therefore, the National Assembly in 1997 saw two entirely new entrants. They immediately became, moreover, part of a governing alliance and could thus be said to have core status. The same is true of the PCF. In that sense, the greater numerical diversity of the system, which *a priori* might seem a source of instability, could well prove the opposite in that the fragments are becoming more integrated. Obviously all depends on the success of the new government in handling the issue of European integration and the social and economic policy inseparable from it.

This consideration brings us to the last consequence of the 1997 election. The FN raised its vote to its presidential level (15.1 per cent), but still only won one MP (significantly, the Mayor of Toulon, a known supporter of alliances with the moderate Right). Having done well enough in the first ballot to be entitled to 133 candidacies in the second, it left most of them in the ring, dividing the Right and handing a number of seats to the Left. Le Pen's confrontational logic reflected his belief that the core parties' vote could collapse next time. The electoral rules and the refusal of the moderate Right to compromise mean, then, that the FN is still held outside the mainstream. While awaiting possible progress in the elections of 2002 (presidential and National Assembly), it will in the meantime concentrate on building up its local base. It should be remembered, however, that a number of moderate Right MPs saw the FN withdraw its challenger on the second ballot, benefiting from what Le Pen called an 'indulgence'. Clearly there is a hint here of future deals which might prove hard to resist; the logic is not entirely confrontational.

The 1997 elections showed the flexibility of the party system, particularly in the swift revamping which took place on the Left. The system was still able to exclude the FN, while not entirely closing the door to it. The major problems remain for the moderate Right, the UDF and RPR, squeezed between a radical Right and a revived social democratic Left. However, even a moderate swing of the pendulum could restore its fortunes relatively quickly.

In the late 1990s, the French party system has settled into a kind of stability or at least it seems able to manage the demands of a varied society without enormous difficulty. It provides governments which function, even if voters do not always like the results. The system allows the voters to enforce change easily enough, and of late, they have made full use of that facility.

The French system has always proved remarkably sensitive to external pressure and it has usually found the means of diverting or absorbing it. This absorptive capacity has been a theme of this chapter and, when speculating about the future, it has to be suggested that this capacity could well come into operation again.

What determines the capacity of parties to adapt, absorb challenges or ultimately to fail is the quality of party elites. They are the ones who have to recognize changes, from within and without, to frame a response and to implement it. If the French party system has worked well up to now, it speaks volumes for the quality of these elites. There are no real grounds for pessimism in looking at the future since the French party system remains finely poised but also highly functional.

5

Italy: Rupture and Regeneration?

PHILIP DANIELS

Introduction

The post-1945 Italian party system has differed markedly from the party systems of the other large Western European democracies. The key distinguishing feature of the Italian party system was the pre-eminent position of the Christian Democratic Party (DC) which dominated government without interruption from the early post-war years until 1992. Italy was commonly described as a 'blocked system', signifying the lack of alternation in government between competing parties or political alignments.

In descriptive terms at least, observers of the Italian party system painted a largely consensual picture. The proliferation of parties, the polarization of political competition and the ideological fragmentation of the system were seen as root causes of Italy's characteristic problems of coalition instability and ineffective government. The descriptive consensus on many of the key features of the Italian party system was not matched, however, by agreement on interpretative models. Three of the most influential models, Sartori's (1976) 'polarized pluralism', Galli's (1966) 'imperfect bipartyism' and Farneti's (1983) 'centripetal pluralism' offered significantly different interpretations of the Italian party system's format and dynamics.

The continuity in key elements of the Italian party system and the emphasis on its immobility tended to obscure its dynamic features. In common with other Western European democracies, electoral change did occur in Italy although it typically had only a limited impact on the relative strengths of the parties. Nevertheless, the competitive dynamics of the system *did* change over time and the ideological polarization attenuated, particularly from the mid-1970s onwards as the communist Left sought to transform itself into a party of government.

The picture of continuity and immobility changed dramatically in the 1990s with the rapid and fundamental transformation of the entire Italian party system. Some traditional parties have disappeared entirely or fragmented; others have changed their names and identities; new parties and political formations have entered the political arena; national elections have produced unprecedented levels of electoral volatility; and new electoral rules at both national and local levels have altered the pattern of party competition. While the old post-war party system has been swept away, the format and dynamics of the new system are not yet clearly established.

The post-war party system, 1945–92

Following more than twenty years of fascism and wartime occupation, a competitive party system was re-established in Italy in the post-1945 period. The political parties quickly assumed a central role in the consolidation of a new democratic regime. The parties' influence became so pervasive and all-encompassing that the post-war Italian political system was defined largely by the nature of its party system. The label *partitocrazia* (literally, party-ocracy) described not only the parties' dominance of state structures but also their penetration into all areas of civil society. At the heart of this 'republic of the parties' (Scoppola, 1991) stood the DC, ever present in national government from 1945 until the early 1990s. This remarkable longevity in office, always as the largest coalition partner, is testimony to the party's flexibility and adaptability – 'a party for all seasons' (Pasquino, 1980).

The DC's initial post-war success owed much to the political and organizational support of the Catholic Church. In the critical election of 1948, which set the tone for subsequent Left–Right political competition, the DC and Church portrayed the election as a 'choice of civilizations'. The Left, and in particular the communist PCI, was deemed to be a threat both to Italy's position in the western camp and to the country's democratic system. The Left–Right polarization in domestic politics was reinforced by the East–West dispute in international politics. In the early post-war years, the PCI identified strongly with the Soviet Union while the DC aligned with the West. The delegitimization of the PCI, the principal party of opposition, was a deliberate structuring of political competition by the DC and it became an enduring feature of post-war Italian politics.

Over the years the DC employed a variety of means to consolidate its hold on government. Most importantly, the party used its access to state resources to build up a vast network of patronage and clientelism which underpinned its base of support. In addition, the DC enlarged the party base of government coalitions through selective integration, bringing first the smaller Centre and Centre–Right parties (PLI, PRI and PSDI) and later the Socialist Party (PSI) into government (see Table 5.1). This successful alliance strategy effectively precluded any other coalition formulae and left the PCI, the only viable alternative to the DC, bereft of potential party allies. The neo-fascist MSI was also excluded from participation as a coalition partner in national govern-

Table 5.1 Italian election results, Chamber of Deputies, 1946–92

	1946[1]	1948	1953	1958	1963	1968	1972	1976	1979	1983	1987	1992
DC	35.2	48.5	40.1	42.3	38.3	39.1	38.7	38.7	38.3	32.9	34.3	29.7
PCI	18.9)	31.0	22.6	22.7	25.3	26.9	27.1	34.4	30.4	29.9	26.6	16.1[3]
PSI	20.7)		12.7	14.2	13.8)	14.5[2]	9.6	9.6	9.8	11.4	14.3	13.6
PSDI	–	7.1	4.5	4.6	6.1)		5.1	3.4	3.8	4.1	2.9	2.7
PSIUP	–	–	–	–	–	4.4	1.9	–	–	–	–	–
Manifesto/ DP/PRC	–	–	–	–	–	–	0.7	1.5	1.4	1.5	1.7	5.6[4]
PRI	4.4	2.5	1.6	1.4	1.4	2.0	2.9	3.1	3.0	5.1	3.7	4.4
PLI	6.8	3.8	3.0	3.5	7.0	5.8	3.9	1.3	1.9	2.9	2.1	2.9
UQ	5.3	–	–	–	–	–	–	–	–	–	–	–
PSdA	0.3	0.2	0.1	–	–	0.1	–	–	–	0.3	0.4	0.3
Monarchists	2.8	2.8	6.9	4.8	1.7	1.3	–	–	–	–	–	–
MSI/AN	–	2.0	5.8	4.8	5.1	4.5	8.7	6.1	5.3	6.8	5.9	5.4
PdA	1.5	–	–	–	–	–	–	–	–	–	–	–
SVP	–	0.5	0.5	0.5	0.4	0.5	0.5	0.5	0.5	0.5	0.5	0.5
PR	–	–	–	–	–	–	–	1.1	3.5	2.2	2.6	1.2
Greens	–	–	–	–	–	–	–	–	–	–	2.5	2.8
Rete	–	–	–	–	–	–	–	–	–	–	–	1.9
Northern Leagues	–	–	–	–	–	–	–	–	–	0.3	1.3	8.6
Others	4.1	1.6	2.2	1.2	0.9	0.9	0.9	0.3	2.1	2.1	1.2	4.3
Turnout	89.1	92.2	93.8	93.8	92.9	92.8	93.2	93.4	90.6	89.0	88.7	87.2

[1] Election to Constituent Assembly
[2] Stood as PSU (Unified Socialist Party)
[3] Result for PDS (Democratic Party of the Left)
[4] Result for PRC (Communist Refoundation Party)

Key to Party Names and Abbreviations

AD	Democratic Alliance
AN	National Alliance
CCD	Christian Democratic Centre
CDU	United Christian Democrats
CS	Social Christians
DC	Christian Democracy
DP	Proletarian Democracy
FDLI	Federation of Italian Liberals
FDV	Federation of the Greens
FI	Forza Italia
Ind Sin	Left Independents
LAL	Lombardy Alpine League
L d'AM	Southern Action League
LD	Dini List
LN	Northern League
LP	Pannella List
LVD'A	Aosta Valley List
MDCU	Unitary Communists' Movement
MS-FT	Social Movement–Tricolour Flame
MSI	Italian Social Movement

Table 5.1 *contd.*

PCI	Italian Communist Party
PdA	Action Party
PDS	Democratic Party of the Left
PLD	Liberal–Democratic Pole
PLI	Italian Liberal Party
PPI	Italian People's Party
PR	Radical Party
PRC	Communist Refoundation Party
PRI	Italian Republican Party
PS	Socialist Party
PS d'A	Sardinian Action Party
PSDI	Italian Social Democratic Party
PSI	Italian Socialist Party
PSIUP	Socialist Party of Proletarian Unity
PSU	Unified Socialist Party
Rete	Network
RI	Italian Renewal
RS	Socialist Renewal
SVP	South Tyrol People's Party
UD	Democratic Union
UDC	Centre Union
UQ	Everyman's Party

ment. With the exclusion of the extreme Left and Right parties from government, the arithmetic of the seats in the multi-party parliament meant that the smaller parties of the Centre and Centre–Right were virtually indispensable coalition allies alongside the DC.

In structural terms, post-war Italy has had a multi-party system with the DC and PCI as the largest parties until the early 1990s. The multi-party format of the system reflected the enduring importance of a series of political cleavages and traditions and it was sustained by a system of proportional representation which offered a low threshold for electoral breakthrough and enabled small parties to preserve representation in parliament.

Academic interest in the Italian party system has generated a number of alternative models. The most influential model described Italy as a case of 'polarized pluralism' (Sartori, 1976). The principal features of this model were the radicalization of the electorate reflecting the deep cleavages in society and the actions of the parties themselves; the high number of parties which, in competition for political space, projected sharply differentiated images to the electorate; the existence of two extreme, anti-system poles on the Left and Right (PCI and MSI) which monopolized opposition and produced strong centrifugal and destabilizing tensions; and the crowded centre of the party spectrum, dominated by the DC, which meant that opposition parties had little incentive to moderate their appeals and compete for that centre space. According to Sartori, this 'polarized pluralism' produced coalition instability, an incapacity to govern and jeopardized Italian democracy itself.

Galli's (1966) model of an 'imperfect two-party system' offered an alternative interpretation. According to Galli, this system was dominated by two parties (the DC and PCI), both with deep subcultural roots in distinctive geo-political zones and sectors of society. Together the two parties accounted for two-thirds of the electorate and in this respect the Italian party system resembled the bipolar format of many other democracies. The crucial difference, however, was that in Italy there was no cohesive, homogeneous governing coalition and no effective alternation in government. Italy was a limited competitive party regime, with the DC a permanent party of government and the PCI relegated to a role of permanent opposition.

More recently, Farneti has described Italy as a case of 'centripetal pluralism' (1983). Farneti acknowledged that Sartori's 'polarized pluralism' was an accurate description of the Italian party system until the early 1960s but thereafter the system was characterized by growing centripetal dynamics. In spite of the ideological fragmentation and the projection of sharply differentiated images to the electorate, pragmatic party elites were attracted to the centre in order to get access to the resources available to parties of government. Rather than an alternation of competing party alignments, the dynamics of 'centripetal pluralism' were characterized by a competition to forge an alliance with the centre.

The competitive dynamics and configuration of the system changed significantly over time, however, undermining the interpretative schema of these three time-bound models. While the party system remained static in some of its essential features, important changes occurred from around the mid-1970s. The DC's position of pre-eminence was gradually weakened, the result primarily of electoral change and increasing public dissatisfaction with the consistently poor performance of government. At the same time, the PSI, fully exploiting its pivotal role in coalition formation, increasingly challenged the DC's control of government throughout the 1980s. Nevertheless, despite this shift in the internal balance of power within the governing coalition, there appeared to be little prospect of an alternative party alignment, based around the PCI, entering government.

Change and adaptation: the 1990s transformation

Since the early 1990s the Italian party system has been fundamentally transformed. A system renowned for its immutability and apparent capacity to withstand repeated political crises has undergone a rapid and unprecedented restructuring. The parties which make up the system have changed markedly. The three national elections of 1992, 1994 and 1996, the last two contested under a new quasi-majoritarian electoral system, have significantly altered the party system. The party system is now highly fluid with parties and electoral alliances still undergoing change and with an electorate characterized by unprecedented levels of volatility.

The sources of this fundamental transformation of the party system may be divided into two broad categories of *long-term* and *short-term* factors. The long-term factors, whose impact pre-dates the 1990s, refer primarily to changes in electoral behaviour and weakening links between voters and traditional political parties. In common with other Western European democracies, Italy has experienced rising levels of electoral volatility, growing anti-party sentiment and increasing rates of abstention since the mid-1970s. The loosening of electoral attachments and the growing disenchantment with the performance of governing parties opened up the prospect of significant party change (Bardi, 1996; Morlino and Tarchi, 1996). This did not occur, however, until the early 1990s and was brought about by a series of short-term exogenous factors. The most important of these were the widespread judicial investigations into party corruption (*tangentopoli*) and the introduction of a new electoral system. The corruption scandals deeply implicated the regime parties, particularly the DC and the PSI, and seriously damaged their standing with the electorate. The resulting party dealignment created a vacuum in the party system which, coupled with the impact of the quasi-majoritarian electoral system, gave a potential opening to new party formations and electoral alliances.

In order to understand the process and contours of party system change in Italy, it is necessary to analyse the interplay of three factors: first, the rise of new parties and the transformation of existing parties which has significantly altered the range of choices offered to voters; second, changes in electoral behaviour, the social implantation of parties and the structure of political cleavages; and third, the introduction of a quasi-majoritarian electoral system which has altered the dynamics and logic of party competition. Each of these elements will be examined in turn but it should be noted that while they are analytically distinct they cannot be strictly separated in terms of their impact on the evolution of party system change: for example, the rise of new parties and the recomposition of existing parties is a response both to the new political space created by electoral dealignment and to the different structure of incentives offered by the new electoral system.

The changing party landscape

By the mid-1990s the Italian parties bore little resemblance to those which had contested elections in the late 1980s. The 1994 national elections marked a significant transformation of the party landscape but many of the changes, affecting parties across the political spectrum, were well under way before this date.

The initial phase of fundamental change commenced in the late 1980s. On the left of the political spectrum, the PCI undertook a long process of self-reform to its culture and identity in an attempt to project itself as an acceptable party of government. The fall of the Berlin Wall in 1989 and the disintegration of the Eastern Bloc regimes had a profound effect on Italian domestic politics and acted as a catalyst in the transformation of the PCI. The party secretary, Achille Occhetto, had already embarked upon a 'new course' of reform for the PCI and he argued that the failures and collapse of the Eastern bloc regimes made it essential for the party to go further and abandon its communist identity.

Following a bitter internal debate, a new party, the Democratic Party of the Left (PDS), was created in 1991 (Ignazi, 1992b; Daniels and Bull, 1994). Many of the opponents of the change, primarily from the orthodox communist wing of the PCI, split away to create a new party, Communist Refoundation (PRC). The split weakened the new PDS in organizational and membership terms, but at the same time the loss of the orthodox communist element added credibility to the party's transformation and renewal. The transformation of the PCI prompted further changes on the left of the political spectrum. Proletarian Democracy (DP), located to the left of the PCI, disbanded and many of the elements of the party were absorbed into the PRC. Since its formation, the PRC has consolidated its electoral base, winning 5.6 per cent of the vote in 1992, 6 per cent in 1994 and 8.6 per cent in 1996. In early 1995, the PRC lost a small element of its parliamentary representation when the so-called Unitary Communists broke away to give support to the non-party Dini government.

The other significant development during this initial phase of party change was the formation and electoral breakthrough of a new formation, the Lega Nord (LN) (Northern League). The LN, formed from a variety of regional leagues and local lists principally from Lombardy, Piedmont and the Veneto, articulated a populist protest against what it saw as a profligate, corrupt, centralized state based in Rome. The LN successfully tapped a reservoir of popular discontent and protests and posed a particular electoral challenge to the DC which was held to be primarily responsible for the corruption, waste and mismanagement which characterized national government. The DC was increasingly vulnerable to this regionalist challenge in the post-1989 period, when the 'glue' of anti-communism, which had bonded voters to the DC, lost much of its political relevance.

The DC, the dominant party in post-war Italian politics, entered into deep crisis in the period 1992 to 1994. In electoral terms, the party had experienced a gradual erosion over a number of years (Giovagnoli, 1996). The process of secularization, the erosion of the Catholic subculture, dissatisfaction with government policy failures particularly in the economic sphere, and the declining resonance of the party's anti-communist appeal even before the fall of the Berlin Wall in 1989, all contributed to the DC's electoral and political difficulties. The party's long-term difficulties were compounded by two developments in the 1990s: first, the *mani pulite* ('clean hands') investigations, which showed the DC to be deeply implicated in a pervasive system of corruption, seriously damaged the party's legitimacy; second, the DC, already internally divided, fragmented in anticipation of a Left–Right bipolar competition resulting from the new quasi-majoritarian electoral law introduced in 1993.

In an attempt to project a new image and limit electoral damage the DC transformed itself into the Partito Popolare Italiano (PPI) in January 1994. The bipolar logic of the new electoral system compounded deep divisions in the PPI over alliance strategy, however, and a number of elements broke away from the party: some right-wing leaders joined the National Alliance which was essentially the neo-fascist MSI (Italian Social Movement); others joined Silvio Berlusconi's Forza Italia launched in January 1994; the *Centro Cristiano Democratico* (CCD) became part of the right-wing coalition, the Freedom Pole, in the 1994 elections; the *Cristiano Sociali* (Social Christians) formed part of the left-wing Progressive alliance in the 1994 elections; Mario Segni, at the forefront of the 1991–93 referendum campaigns for electoral reform, formed his own centrist political movement, the Pact for Italy; others joined *La Rete* (the Network), the Centre–Left movement formed by Leoluca Orlando, the former DC mayor of Palermo. The PPI, the largest remnant of the old DC, split again over alliance strategy in the spring of 1995: the newly-formed CDU (United Christian Democrats), led by Rocco Buttiglione, favoured an electoral alliance with the right-wing Freedom Pole while the PPI, led by Gerardo Bianco, sought to align with the Centre–Left Olive Tree alliance under Romano Prodi's leadership.

The Socialist Party (PSI), pivotal to government coalitions throughout the 1980s, suffered a similarly dramatic and rapid collapse. The 1992 election demonstrated the failure of the 'long-wave' strategy, the PSI's attempt to attract disaffected communist voters and supplant the PDS as the leading party of the Left. The party's political and moral bankruptcy was demonstrated in the rapid unfolding of corruption scandals in the post-1992 election period. The leader, Craxi, was replaced in 1993 and the party lost elements of its leadership to two new formations, Alleanza Democratica (AD) and Forza Italia (FI). After the 1994 election the party splintered into a number of small formations.

Two historic parties of the lay centre, the Liberals (PLI) and the Republicans (PRI), have suffered similar crises and disappeared from the political scene. Fragments of both parties have dispersed across the political spectrum: in the 1994 election, there were elements in the left-wing Progressive Alliance, the centrist coalition Pact for Italy and in the Freedom Pole. The Social Democratic Party (PSDI), like the Republicans and Liberals a regular party in post-war coalition governments, was similarly affected by the *mani pulite* investigations. After a series of leadership changes and a formal split, the party disappeared.

On the right of the political spectrum, the MSI (Italian Social Movement) has undergone an important process of self-reform. Following the party's success in local elections in late 1993, the leader, Gianfranco Fini, formed the AN composed of the MSI and right-wing elements from the former DC. Fini attempted to distance the party from its fascist inheritance and to project an image as a mainstream conservative party. He saw the opportunity for a reformed MSI to occupy the political space which had been opened up as a result of the collapse of the DC and other regime parties. In addition, the bipolar logic of the new electoral system gave the reformed MSI the potential to be a rallying point for forces of the Right, particularly in southern Italy. The AN recruited intellectuals from the democratic Right to bolster the party's more moderate image but the continued presence of unreformed fascists in the party and Fini's gaffes about the virtues of Mussolini's regime demonstrated that the party still had some way to go before it could be accepted as a mainstream conservative party (Ignazi, 1994). Nevertheless, as part of the victorious Freedom Pole in the 1994 election, AN entered the Berlusconi government. In early 1995, a party congress formally adopted AN as the party's new name. The new formation included a small right-wing element of the former DC but hardline elements of the MSI rejected the more moderate identity of the AN and broke away to form a new party, the Social Movement-Tricolour Flame (MS-FT).

The most significant change on the right of the political spectrum was the formation and electoral breakthrough of Forza Italia (FI) in early 1994. This new political movement was the creation of Sivio Berlusconi who used personnel, organizational resources and television networks of his Fininvest business empire to mobilize political support. Berlusconi saw an opportunity to occupy the political space opened up by the demise of the DC and the PSI, creating a new movement able to appeal to conservative voters reluctant to support the essentially anti-system LN or MSI. Forza Italia made a spectacular impact, emerging as the largest party in the March 1994 elections.

The changing electorate

For much of the post-war period, the stability of Italian voting behaviour was seen as a key underlying reason for the crystallized party system. The stability of electoral choice was rooted in the distinctive Catholic and socialist subcultural traditions. These two subcultures reflected an enduring clerical–secular cleavage and underpinned the electoral ascendancy of the two major parties, the DC and the PCI. The subcultural contexts encapsulated voters in a network of auxiliary and flanking organizations and the political values and orientations of the tradition were sustained through processes of inter-generational socialization. The two subcultures were strongest in two distinct geo-political zones: the 'white' north-east of Italy, where a strong Catholic subculture sustained the DC, and the 'red belt' of central Italy where a strong anti-clerical tradition had evolved into a socialist subculture and provided the principal bastion of PCI electoral strength. By its very nature, the subcultural vote tended to be very stable.

The picture of the stable, immobile electorate was seriously challenged from the mid-1970s onwards when Italy experienced rising levels of electoral volatility and partisan dealignment. This reflects, in part, the erosion of the Catholic and socialist subcultures which had been at the base of the relatively stable voting patterns. The subcultures have been weakened by long-term processes of economic and social change, including occupa-tional and spatial mobility, urbanization, rising levels of education and the growing influence of the mass media. In addition, the Catholic subculture has been eroded by the process of secularization (Cartocci, 1994) and the weakening of church organization. The decline in the political salience of anti-communism, following the post-1989 transformation of the Eastern bloc regimes, also undermined a key element in the electoral appeal of the DC.

The loosening of social ties and declining attachments to traditional political subcultures has opened up 'the electoral market' (Mannheimer and Sani, 1987) with more voters ready to shift their allegiance from one party to another; as a general trend, there has been a shift towards issue voting and away from voting on the basis of ideological affiliation or subcultural belonging. These more transient links to parties, which have been very pronounced in the 1990s, have provided the new political movements and parties with a potential pool of voters (Calvi and Vannucci, 1995). At the same time, the weakening of traditional cleavages, such as class and religion, has created the opportunity for other bases of political division, such as regional demands, to become more salient in electoral choice.

Social changes have also undermined the traditional organizational struc-tures of the established parties over a number of years. Levels of membership and party activism have declined consistently, the party apparatuses have been increasingly bypassed by direct recourse to the mass media and territorial units have lost significance (Scalisi, 1996). In addition, the organizational structures of the regime parties have been fundamentally weakened by the *mani pulite* investigations. The new political movements which have emerged since the late 1980s have deliberately avoided the label 'party' and have adopted a variety of new, non-traditional organizational models.

The new electoral system

The introduction of a quasi-majoritarian electoral system, first used in the national elections of 1994, has had a significant impact on party system change. For more than a decade, electoral reform had been a key theme in Italian debate on institutional reform since the system of proportional representation was viewed as a primary reason for the fragmented party system and the unstable, multi-party governing coalitions. Advocates of reform saw it as a way of producing clear election winners with secure parliamentary majorities, more durable governments and greater governmental accountability to voters. Reform proved elusive, however, since there was no consensus on the need for change and even among those that favoured reform there was little agreement on the shape a new electoral system should take. This deadlock was finally broken as a result of a popular referendum in April 1993 which designated a quasi-majoritarian electoral law for the Senate. This popular endorsement of electoral reform compelled parliament to act and resulted in the redrafting of the entire parliamentary electoral system. The final reform established a quasi-majoritarian principle for both the Chamber of Deputies and the Senate, with three-quarters of the seats allocated by a first-past-the-post electoral formula in single-member districts and one-quarter by proportional representation in both cases, but with significant differences in detail between the two sets of regulations (Donovan, 1995; Fusaro, 1995; Katz, 1996). These reforms have played an important part in the restructuring of political competition and in the transformation of the party system.

The party system after the 1994 and 1996 elections: format, dynamics and competition

The national elections of 1994 and 1996, contested under the quasi-majoritarian electoral law, confirmed significant changes to the Italian party system. The parties making up the system had already altered radically during the first half of the 1990s: some transformed their image and identity (PCI to PDS and MSI to AN), others collapsed and fragmented (DC, PSI, PSDI,

Table 5.2 Italian election results, Chamber of Deputies, 1994*

Electoral Alliances and Parties	Single–Member Seats	Proportional Seats		Total Seats
		Vote (%)	Seats	
Freedom Pole/Pole of Good Government				
Forza Italia	74	21.0	30	104
AN	87	13.5	23	110
LN	107	8.4	11	118
Lista Pannella	0	3.5	0	0
CCD	22	–	–	22
Pannella Riformatori	6	–	–	6
UDC	4	–	–	4
PLD	2	–	–	2
Total	302	46.4	64	366
Pact for Italy				
PPI	4	11.1	29	33
Segni Pact	0	4.6	13	13
Total	4	15.7	42	46
Progressive Alliance				
PDS	72	20.4	38	110
RC	27	6.0	11	38
Greens	11	2.7	0	11
PSI	14	2.2	0	14
Rete	6	1.9	0	6
AD	18	1.2	0	18
CS	5	–	–	5
RS	1	–	–	1
Ind Sin	10	–	–	10
Total	164	34.4	49	213
SVP	3	0.6	0	3
Lista Valle d'Aosta	1	–	–	1
L d'AM	1	0.2	0	1
Other Lists	0	2.7	0	0
Total Others	5	3.5	0	5
Total	475	100.0	155	630

* Turnout 86.1 per cent.

PLI, PRI) and new formations entered the political arena (LN and FI). In terms of party actors, then, the new party system bore little resemblance to that which had been in place from the early post-war years through until 1992 (see Tables 5.2 and 5.3).

The 1994 election

The transformation of traditional parties and the entry of new political formations produced a highly fragmented party configuration in the run-up to the 1994 national elections. Nevertheless, in response to the structure of incentives offered by the new electoral system, the major parties grouped together into four competing electoral cartels. These alliances aimed to field a common candidate in each of the single-member constituencies. They did

Table 5.3 Italian election results, Chamber of Deputies, 1996*

Electoral Alliances and Parties	Single-Member Seats	Proportional Seats		Total Seats
		Vote %	Seats	
Freedom Pole				
Forza Italia		20.6	37	
AN		15.7	28	
CCD-CDU	169	5.8	12	
Pannella-Sgarbi		1.9	0	
Total	169	44.0	77	246
LN	39	10.1	20	59
Olive Tree				
PDS		21.1	26	
For Prodi		6.8	4	
Dini List	246	4.3	8	284
Greens		2.5	0	
Others		0.5	0	
RC[1]	15	8.6	20	35
Total	261	43.8	58	319
Other Lists	6	2.1	0	6
Total	475	100.0	155	630

* Turnout 82.9 per cent.

[1] Communist Refoundation was not a formal part of the Olive Tree alliance but reached an electoral accord with it for the single-member seats.

not operate in the PR seats where most of the parties presented their own lists of candidates. The four electoral alliances in 1994 were, from left to right, the Progressives, the Pact for Italy, the Freedom Pole and the Pole of Good Government.

The Progressives, the electoral alliance of the Left, included eight parties or movements. The Pact for Italy, the centrist alliance, brought together the Segni Pact and the PPI. The Freedom Pole and the Pole of Good Government alliances were put together by Berlusconi, the leader of FI, who sought to construct a unified Centre–Right coalition to compete with the Left. The PPI, however, refused to join an alliance which included the LN and the MSI-AN. At the same time, the LN refused to join an electoral coalition with the MSI-AN. Berlusconi overcame this antagonism between the LN and the MSI-AN by creating two different Centre–Right coalitions with FI present in both. In the north and centre, the Freedom Pole was the alliance of FI and LN with a number of other small parties. In the South, where the LN was not present and clearly had little prospect of an electoral breakthrough, the Pole of Good Government was made up of FI and MSI-AN along with a number of other small parties and formations. This was the new pattern of political competition which voters and parties faced in the March 1994 elections: in the single-member districts the basic pattern was tripolar, with most contests effectively a 'three-horse' race among the candidates from the Progressive alliance, the Pact for Italy and the Freedom Pole (in the North and Centre) or the Pole of Good Government (in the South).

The right-wing coalition emerged as the winner of the elections, but it was not an unequivocal victory. The election produced a divided parliament, with the Right coalition having a clear majority in the Chamber of Deputies but just short of an overall majority in the hung Senate. The electoral performance of the individual parties and movements is shown in the PR element of the elections. The most significant features of these PR results were:

1   FI emerged as the largest single party only two months after its foundation.
2   The MSI-AN increased its share of the vote from 5.4 per cent in 1992 to 13.5 per cent in 1994.
3   The Centre performed badly: the PPI and the Segni Pact polled a combined vote of 15.7 per cent, little more than a half of the DC's share of the vote in 1992.
4   The Left, represented by the PDS and PRC, recovered from the setback of 1992 and the combined vote of 26.4 per cent in 1994 was approximately the same as the vote of the PCI in 1987.

In the proportional component of the election, the combined strength of the Right electoral alignment (LN, FI, MSI-AN and Lista Pannella) was 46.4 per cent, compared to 34.4 per cent for the Left (PRC, PDS, La Rete, Greens, AD and PSI) and 15.7 per cent for the Centre (PPI and Segni Pact). This tripolar structure of electoral competition in the PR results was not repeated, however, in the outcomes of the plurality contests in single-member districts. In these contests, the outcome was essentially bipolar with the centrist alliance, the Pact for Italy, winning only four seats in the Chamber of Deputies and three in the Senate. The right-wing coalitions were the clear winners in the single-member districts, taking 63.6 per cent (302) of the seats in the Chamber of Deputies and 55.2 per cent (128) in the Senate. The Progressive alliance achieved a disappointing result, winning 34.5 per cent (164) of the seats in the Chamber of Deputies and 41.4 per cent (96) in the Senate.

Thus, the 1994 elections produced a predominantly Left–Right pattern of competition and an essentially bipolar outcome. This bipolarism at the level of electoral alliances did not, however, signify a reduction in the fragmentation of the party system. The PR element of the electoral system helped a number of parties to gain parliamentary seats, compensating for poor performances in the plurality contests. In addition, candidatures in the single-member districts were shared out among many of the parties and movements which made up the electoral alliances.

The 1994 elections produced significant regional variations in the distribution of electoral support. Electoral analysis in Italy traditionally distinguishes between the Northern, Central and Southern geo-political divisions. Using the single-member districts for the Chamber of Deputies as an indicator, the Right achieved an exceptional result in the North, winning 162 of the 180 seats, while the Progressive alliance secured only 14. In the Centre, the pattern was reversed with the Progressives taking 77 seats and the right-wing coalition only three. Only the South emerged as highly competitive both in terms of the distribution of seats among the electoral alliances (Right 137, Progressives 73 and Centre 4) and in terms of the typically lower margins of victory compared to the plurality contests in the North and Centre. Thus, the electoral reforms did not produce a competitive bipolar system at national level; rather, the outcome of the elections showed the country divided into three areas, with the North and Centre essentially non-competitive and the South highly competitive.

The 1994 election was also notable for the exceptionally high levels of volatility. The changes and discontinuities in the party system, including the splits in the DC, the collapse of other traditional parties and the emergence of new formations, make it difficult to draw comparisons with the results of the 1992 election. Nevertheless, indices of total volatility show that more than one-third of the electorate changed party preference between 1992 and 1994, clearly indicating a destructuration of the party system and a more competitive electoral market. Figures for the level of total volatility vary from 37.2 per cent (D'Alimonte and Bartolini, 1995) to 41.4 per cent (Morlino, 1996).

The 1996 election

The fluid state of Italian party politics in the period 1994 to 1996 was clearly demonstrated by the continued changes in parties and by the significant alterations in the pattern of electoral alliances for the 1996 elections. The most significant development was the creation of the broad Centre–Left Olive Tree electoral alliance, under the leadership of Romano Prodi, which grouped together most of the elements of the Progressives with centrist formations including the PPI and the Dini List-Italian Renewal. The PRC, unwilling to align with the Centre, was not a formal part of the Olive Tree coalition but, in order to avoid splitting the Left's vote, it made an electoral accord with it for the plurality contests in the single-member districts.

On the right of the party spectrum, there were also significant changes in the pattern of alliances compared to 1994. The LN, which had resigned from the Berlusconi government in December 1994 (although 40 of its 162 parliamentarians switched to the Freedom Pole in January 1995), did not join an electoral alliance. In contrast to 1994, the Freedom Pole became a nationwide electoral alliance composed principally of FI and AN and joined by the CDU which reached an electoral accord with the CCD. The Right alliance was potentially weaker than in 1994, however, for in addition to the loss of the LN, it faced competition from the extreme-Right Social Movement-Tricolour Flame.

Much of the change to the pattern of electoral alliances represented a direct response to the structure of incentives and constraints produced by the new electoral system: for example, the broadening of the left alliance to embrace elements of the Centre was an attempt to maximize electoral appeal, particularly in the plurality contests in single-member districts; the electoral accord between the Olive Tree alliance and the PRC was crucial to the Centre–Left's success in the single-member districts; and the formal Left–Right split in the centrist PPI in the spring of 1995, with the new CDU gravitating towards the right pole and the remainder of the PPI towards the left pole, was in part a response to the 'squeezing' of the Centre in the emerging bipolar logic of competition.

The structure of party competition in 1996 differed significantly from 1994: in the single-member districts in the South and Centre, the competition was basically bipolar, with the Olive Tree alliance and the Freedom Pole the principal contestants, although the MS-FT also fielded candidates in many districts. In the North, competition in the single-member districts was typically tripolar involving the LN, the Freedom Pole and the Olive Tree. This bipolar tendency can be seen in the reduction in the number of candidates standing in single-member districts for the Chamber of Deputies: the average number of candidates in each constituency dropped from 4.5 in 1994 to 3.3 in 1996 and in around two-thirds of single-member districts no more than three candidates were standing (Sani, 1996).

The election brought a victory for the Centre–Left and the long-awaited alternation in government. The Olive Tree government was dependent, however, on the support of the PRC to achieve a majority in the Chamber of Deputies; and in the Senate, it fell one seat short of an overall majority. The most significant features of the results for the Chamber of Deputies were:

1 The unexpectedly strong performance of the LN in northern Italy, particularly in Lombardy (24.6 per cent of the vote) and the North-East (27.6 per cent).

2 The setback for the Freedom Pole which won 120 seats fewer in the Chamber of Deputies (from 366 to 246) compared to 1994.

3 The Centre–Left's strong showing with the Olive Tree and the PRC winning a combined total of 319 seats in the Chamber of Deputies compared to 213 for the Progressive alliance in 1994. The Olive Tree

won 118 single-member districts from the right-wing alliance and lost only 26 seats to it.

4   In the PR component of the election, the PDS emerged as the largest party (21.1 per cent), marginally ahead of FI (20.6 per cent). The combined vote for the PDS and the PRC, 29.7 per cent, represented a continuation of the Left's recovery and was on a par with the PCI's performance in 1983.

5   The elections confirmed the political fragmentation of the Centre: the two principal inheritors of the Catholic political tradition, the PPI (actually the list Popolari con Prodi which included the PRI, the South Tyrol People's Party and Democratic Union) and the CCD/CDU, polled 6.8 per cent and 5.8 per cent, respectively, in the proportional element of the elections.

In the PR component of the elections, the combined vote of the right-wing lists was 44 per cent: the 10.1 per cent won by the Lega Nord and the 0.9 per cent of the MS-FT give an indication of just how costly the splits in 1994 and 1995 were for the Right. The Centre–Left lists won a combined total of 43.8 per cent, leading some commentators to suggest that the Right was still in the ascendancy in the country but had lost the elections as a result of the capricious mechanics of the electoral system.

In fact, the results in the plurality single-member contests showed that the Olive Tree candidates were typically more popular than the combined strength of the constituent parties and movements which made up the alliance. Thus, while in the proportional component of the election the Right won 16,481,785 votes compared to the Olive Tree's 16,270,935, in the plurality contests the Olive Tree won 16,712,249 votes compared to the right's 15,081,410. The reasons for this are not certain but it may be partly explained as a vote for a government led by Romano Prodi and an endorsement of the parliamentary coalition which had largely sustained the Dini government from early 1995 to 1996.

In the single-member districts for the Chamber of Deputies, the Olive Tree Alliance and Progressives (actually only the PRC) won 54.9 per cent (261) of the seats (compared to 34.5 per cent for the Progressives in 1994); the Freedom Pole won 35.6 per cent (169) of the seats (compared to 63.7 per cent for the Freedom Pole and Pole of Good Government in 1994); and the LN 8.2 per cent (39 seats). The pattern of alliances in the single-member contests was crucial: the electoral accord with the PRC was vital to the Olive Tree's victory, while the Right lost potential votes to splinter parties and the LN. For example, had voters for the MS-FT voted for the Freedom Pole, this alliance would have won 34 more seats in the Centre–South and two more in the North (Sani, 1996).

The outcome of the elections in the single-member districts revealed important variations in the pattern of competition: in the Centre and South the pattern was essentially one of Left–Right bipolar contests; in much of the North, in contrast, competition was tripolar involving the Left alliance, the Right alliance and the LN. This picture is confirmed by the heavy concentration of the vote on the three major contestants in the single-member districts – the Right and Centre–Left electoral alliances along with the LN in many northern districts. Nevertheless, as in 1994, the bipolarism at the level of electoral coalitions did not disguise the fact that the party system remained fragmented in terms of parties represented in parliament.

The territorial variations in the distribution of electoral support were once again evident in the 1996 elections but with significant differences compared to the results of 1994. Most significantly, the North became much more competitive in terms of the distribution of seats as a result both of the LN's decision to stand alone and the formation of the Olive Tree alliance; of the 180 seats, the Freedom Pole won 61 (compared to 162 in 1994), the Olive Tree and Progressives won 76, and the LN, benefiting from the territorial concentration of its vote, won 39. In the Centre, the Olive Tree and Progressives emulated the performance of the Left in 1994, winning 77 of the 80 single-member districts. As in 1994, the South was again highly competitive; of the 215 seats, the Freedom Pole won 105 and the Olive Tree 108. Thus, while the Centre remained a bastion of Left electoral strength, the North and South were competitive both in terms of the distribution of seats and the typically narrow margins of victory for the winning candidates. The increased competitiveness of the system in 1996 could be seen clearly in the reduction in the average margins of victory in the single-member districts; in 1994 the average gap between the first and second-placed candidates was more than 17 per cent but this fell to 11 per cent in 1996 (Sani, 1996). The growing competitiveness of the party system was also indicated by the increased number of marginal districts; for example, in 1996, in 120 single-member districts the percentage gap between the elected candidate and the runner-up was 3 per cent or less.

The victory for the Olive Tree alliance in the 1996 election did *not* come about as the result of a major shift in votes from the Right to the Centre–Left in the 1994–96 period. In terms of the structure of the vote, there was a marked underlying continuity, clearly visible in the similar patterns of the territorial distribution of party support in the two elections. The percentage shares of the votes for the major parties were relatively stable over the two elections, and in 1996 rates of electoral volatility returned to levels characteristic of the pre-1994 period. The volatility which did occur in 1996 tended to be *intra-bloc* rather than *cross-bloc*, a consistent feature of electoral mobility in Italy since the mid-1970s. Rather than any significant movement of votes, the crucial factors in producing a victory for the Olive Tree alliance in 1996 were the changes to the electoral alliances and the impact of the mechanics of the electoral system. The choices of alliance strategy made by party elites in the 1994–96 period significantly altered the pattern of competition and the alternatives offered to electors in the plurality contests.

Most significantly, the construction of the Olive Tree alliance created a broad Centre–Left alignment of parties, while on the right the LN's decision to contest the elections on its own seriously damaged the Freedom Pole's performance in the north. The mechanics of the electoral system translated the Olive Tree's relatively small lead over the Freedom Pole in terms of votes into a clear victory in the distribution of parliamentary seats. The electoral system tends to magnify victories, producing a premium in terms of seats to the winning electoral alliance in the plurality single-member districts; thus, in 1996 for the Chamber of Deputies election the Olive Tree alliance and the PRC won 45.3 per cent of the vote but 54.9 per cent of the seats in the single-member districts. The PR component of the election to some extent attenuates this effect but does not remove it. The capacity of the electoral system to produce clear winners is not, however, inherent in its mechanics; in both 1994 and 1996 a fortuitous combination of circumstances based on the territorial distribution of the vote and the construction of electoral alliances produced clear winners but a small shift in votes or changes to one or more electoral alliances could produce a stalemate.

The shape of the new party system

The 1994 and 1996 elections produced markedly different outcomes, reflecting the highly fluid state of Italian party politics. Parties and electoral alliances have continued to change, the electorate remains mobile, and both parties and voters are adapting to the structural incentives of the new electoral system. With so much in a state of flux, the precise configuration and dynamics of the evolving party system remain unclear. As with all systems in transition, a number of divergent and often contradictory trends are evident; for example, the plurality single-member contests have encouraged the formation of electoral alliances and a tendency towards bipolar competition but at parliamentary level the party system is still multi-party and the alliances remain fluid and fragmented (Verzichelli, 1996). As we have seen, the party landscape has been transformed in the 1990s but this does not in itself constitute party system change: in other words, the party units might change but in a number of key structural features the party system might correspond to or be equivalent to the previous system. This section analyses three key structural dimensions of the party system: the number of parties, ideological distance and the dynamics of party competition.

The number of parties

Notwithstanding the electoral reforms, the number of parties represented in parliament increased in 1994, with twenty parties securing seats in the Chamber of Deputies; in 1996, sixteen parties gained representation. The quasi-majoritarian electoral system has not produced a reduction in the number of parties for a combination of three reasons: first, the compensatory effect of the proportional element of the electoral system partially counteracts the reductive impact of the plurality element; second, the electoral accords among the various electoral alliances on the sharing out of single-member districts enables smaller parties to win seats; and third, the plurality component does not penalize small parties with a territorial concentration of support (Katz, 1996; Morlino, 1996).

In the parliamentary arena, the 1994 elections did not produce a stable realignment of the parties. The significant splits and realignments in many of the parliamentary party groups during the course of the twelfth legislature (1994 to 1996) reflected the fluidity in the party system. At the same time, the unprecedented number of individual parliamentarians moving from one group to another showed the organizational weaknesses and the lack of parliamentary discipline of some parties. Following the 1996 elections, nine parliamentary groups were formed in the Chamber of Deputies and eleven in the Senate. The disjuncture between the party system in the electoral arena and that in the parliamentary arena was once again evident; for example, deputies elected as part of the Olive Tree alliance joined four separate parliamentary groups in the Chamber of Deputies – the Democratic Left–Olive Tree, the Popolari and Democrats–Olive Tree, Italian Renewal and the Mixed Group.

The electoral alliances show no signs of developing into more permanent common party structures and, for some parties and movements, the alliances are viewed primarily as a means of maximizing parliamentary representation under the new electoral system. The continued multi-party character of parliament has prompted some commentators to suggest that in at least one of its essential features the current party system resembles closely the format of the post-war system which existed until 1992–93. In both 1994 and 1996, the winning electoral coalitions have not translated smoothly into cohesive parliamentary majorities and the multi-party composition of both chambers continues to create potential problems for governmental stability. In one sense, the governmental majorities are now potentially more unstable since there is no longer a dominant or pivotal larger party comparable to the DC; in the governing Olive Tree coalition only the PDS has percentage electoral support in double figures.

Thus, fragmentation of the party system has become more pronounced since 1992 following the breakdown of the DC and the split in the Left: in the present system, the three largest parties (PDS, FI and AN) are approximately equal in terms of electoral support and the fourth party, the LN, has a significant share of both the vote and parliamentary seats. Measured in terms of electoral and parliamentary fragmentation, the party system remains a case of 'extreme pluralism' (Morlino, 1996). The systemic relevance of these small parties has been questioned (Pappalardo, 1996): a number of them are small elite groups with weak institutionalization, a tenuous electoral hold and a dependency on one or other of the electoral cartels. Nevertheless, in a highly fragmented parliament, their influence is potentially significant.

Ideological distance

In Sartori's classic description of the Italian party system as a case of 'polarized pluralism', it was not simply the number of parties but also their ideological orientation and the extended ideological distance along the Left–Right dimension which defined the system. This feature of the party system, which began changing significantly in the mid-1970s with the PCI's 'historic compromise' strategy, has been fundamentally altered in the 1990s. The principal anti-system parties, a permanent feature of the post-war Italian party system, have been transformed into parties of government. The transformation of the PCI into the PDS in February 1991 and the formal change of the MSI into the AN in January 1995 marked significant points in the full integration of these parties into the system. The MSI-AN entered the Berlusconi government in spring 1994 and the PDS secured office as the principal element of the Olive Tree alliance in 1996. In addition, while the PRC is not a formal part of the Olive Tree government, it has given parliamentary support to the government of Romano Prodi. At the same time, the system is no longer characterized by significant bilateral opposition identified in Sartori's model of polarized pluralism since the extreme parties of Left and Right (the PRC and the MS-FT) are significantly smaller than the PCI and MSI and they do not monopolize opposition in the way that the PCI did for much of the post-war period.

The dynamics of party competition

While the new electoral system and the breakdown of the traditional centrist bloc have produced a bipolarization effect, the competitive dynamics of the new party system are not yet settled. In both the 1994 and 1996 elections the outcomes were a pronounced Left–Right bipolar competition at the level of electoral alliances. At the level of parliamentary representation, however, the system remains multi-party.

Both centripetal and centrifugal trends have been in evidence since 1994. The significant weakening of anti-system parties, the democratic integration of former anti-system parties, the end of bilateral opposition and the electoral competition for the centre ground opened up by the fragmentation of the DC are all indicative of the ideological depolarization and centripetal drives in the system. At the same time, centrifugal tendencies are also clearly in evidence. First, since the 1994 election campaign Left–Right political competition has often been highly polarized and characterized by highly emotive political appeals and discourse; the Right's use of anti-communist rhetoric in both the 1994 and 1996 elections is the clearest example. Second, in the 1996 election to the Chamber of Deputies the most radical elements of both the Left and Right electoral alliances increased their support (the AN from 13.5 per cent in 1994 to 15.7 per cent in 1996 and the PRC from 6 per cent in 1994 to 8.6 per cent in 1996). Third, among the parties not in electoral alliances, the MS-FT polled a small vote but damaged the Freedom Pole alliance, particularly in the South, and the LN consolidated its position in northern Italy.

The LN poses a particular challenge to the nascent party system for it has succeeded in politicizing a regionalist cleavage which cuts across the Left–Right political axis and runs counter to the emergent bipolarization in the party system. With a relatively secure electoral constituency based on a community of interests and clear socio-economic and territorial identities, the LN has no immediate need to forge electoral alliances nor any incentive to moderate its policies. Since the 1996 election the League's extremist posturing has intensified, culminating in the unilateral declaration of independence for the state of 'Padania' in September 1996.

There is no prevailing logic, inherent in the existing politico–institutional structure, which will lead the party system unequivocally towards either a centripetal or centrifugal pattern of competition. Institutional structures and electoral mechanisms provide constraints and incentives but parties and leaders choose which political space they occupy, their ideological orientations and alliance strategy. If a centrifugal logic were to prevail in the new system, with a polarization of the Left and Right electoral alliances, then a potential political space could open up for a pivotal centre party or centrist electoral coalition. Proposals to reconstitute a 'great Centre' have made no progress, however, and the centre remains highly fragmented in both electoral and party terms.

The elections of 1994 and 1996 saw electoral support concentrated on the parties of Left and Right, an outcome consistent with indices of voter self-placement which show that the numbers identifying with the traditional Centre have declined while the majority of voters locate themselves in a Centre-Left or Centre–Right political space. In addition, the Catholic vote, which underpinned the centrism of the DC, had scattered across the party spectrum (Garelli, 1996; Rovati, 1996). Since 1994 the new bipolar logic of the system has limited the electoral potential of the Centre parties and forced them to ally with either the Right or Left electoral coalitions. The political space and electoral prospects for the Centre will be further reduced if a centripetal or moderate bipolar competition characterizes the new system. This trend is already evident with the PDS and its left-wing allies moving towards the centre ground in the construction of the Olive Tree electoral alliance. This centripetal tendency is less evident on the right of the political spectrum, where the Freedom Pole electoral alliance, composed principally of FI and the ex-fascist AN, has occupied a clearly defined rightist political space and has made little attempt to move towards the centre ground. Indeed, the Freedom Pole's failure to appeal to the centre was seen as an important factor in its defeat in the 1996 elections. Nevertheless, the dividing line between the Centre–Left and right-wing alliances is fluid and gives leaders of both electoral blocs scope to appeal to parties and voters located in the centre political space.

Conclusion: rupture and regeneration?

The Italian party system has undergone a rapid and fundamental trans- formation in the 1990s. It is still in a highly fluid state and its future format and competitive dynamics are therefore inevitably uncertain. The introduc- tion of a new electoral system and the demise of the traditional regime parties have had a bipolarizing effect on the system: in both the 1994 and 1996 elections, and especially so in the latter, the outcomes have produced a predominantly Left-Right patterning of party competition. Notwithstanding this bipolarization effect in the electoral arena, at the parliamentary level the party system remains fragmented and multi-party, reproducing all the familiar problems of governmental instability which have afflicted post-war Italy. The new electoral system and party alliances have so far failed to produce secure parliamentary majorities and cohesive and durable govern- ing coalitions. In 1994, the right-wing coalition secured a parliamentary majority but this evaporated after eight months following the LN's exit from Berlusconi's government. Following the 1996 election, the Olive Tree alli- ance was dependent on parliamentary support from the PRC and thus faced difficulties in steering unpopular policies through parliament. This was confirmed when the government was brought down in late 1997 over the

1998 budget proposals. Nevertheless, the Prodi government was rapidly reformed and an election avoided.

The co-existence of two different types of party system, one in the electoral arena and one in the parliamentary arena, demonstrates that a change to the electoral system alone is not sufficient to transform the nature of Italian party politics and party government. Such a transformation would require more extensive reforms to include, *inter alia*, the organization of party groups in parliament and the rules on the formation of governments.

In some crucial respects, however, party government in Italy has changed fundamentally since 1994. The system is no longer 'blocked' and, as the 1996 election demonstrated, relatively small electoral swings can produce alternation in the party alliances in government. In this sense, the system has become more competitive and open. In addition, the current multi-party character of government differs from that which prevailed for most of the post-war period: the electoral alliances are now elected on a common platform and the fates of the individual parties in government are more closely linked. The effect of these changes is to produce a clearer choice for voters and a closer connection between the act of voting and the formation of governments. In short, governing coalitions and the constituent parties, and the opposition too, have become more accountable to the electorate.

The party system has not yet settled into a stable format and there is no clear linear development towards a consolidation of bipolar competition. While the electoral system has altered the pattern of party competition, it cannot be relied upon to produce clear governing majorities. The evolution of the party system will be shaped crucially by institutional choices and the actions of political leaders. Thus, a 70-strong Bicameral Constitutional Committee was established in 1997 to identify an acceptable package of reforms regarding such fundamental matters as the nature and structure of the Italian state, the form of government and the organization and role of the judiciary. Formally, the Committee was not required to address the question of a new parliamentary electoral system. In practice, informal agreement on this critical issue was regarded as essential if adequate cross-party support was to be found for any constitutional reform package. Following the initial deliberations of the Committee, it was considered likely that any new constitution would create a federal Italy with a *directly* elected President of the Republic. In June 1998, however, the committee ceased to meet, with no accord having been reached.

If the current electoral and institutional arrangements, or something very similar, remain in place, then the party system is likely to remain fragmented and characterized by both centripetal and centrifugal dynamics. The role of political leaders is important in this context, since the nature of their political appeals, their ideological positioning and their choice of alliance strategies will have an important impact on the format and competitive dynamics of the nascent party system. Voters, parties and leaders will continue to adapt to the structure of opportunities and constraints that shape electoral arrangements. It is unlikely that the electoral alliances of the Right and Left will be transformed into new, unified parties or federations without institutional and/or political incentives to surrender their separate identities.

Finally, the policy performance of the parties in government and the stability of governing coalitions are crucial to the consolidation of the new party system. In a little more than two years from 1994 to 1996 Italy has had a government of the Right under Berlusconi, a technocratic, non-party government led by Lamberto Dini and a Centre–Left coalition under the premiership of Prodi. Continuing political instability and policy failure are likely to exacerbate the already high levels of anti-party sentiment and provoke new crises and changes in parties. This may explain the survival of the Prodi government and cross-party co-operation on the issue of constitutional change which provided some grounds for limited optimism.

Nevertheless, many of the new parties are particularly vulnerable since they have weak national and local organizations and no strongly developed roots in civil society. If the parties fail to agree on further institutional and electoral reform, then the Italian party system is likely to remain in a highly fluid state characterized by looser ties between parties and voters, a proliferation of parties, tenuous electoral alliances and unstable parliamentary party groups.

Acknowledgement

The author would like to thank the British Academy and the Small Grants Panel of the University of Newcastle upon Tyne for their financial assistance which supported the research upon which this chapter is based.

6

Germany: From Hyperstability to Change?

CHARLIE JEFFERY

Introduction

The parameters for the study of party systems in Western Europe have typically been defined by the classic trade-off between continuity and change. This in part reflects the influence of the seminal work of Lipset and Rokkan (1967a) whose assertions about the 'freezing' of post-war party systems continue to shape debate. The question of continuity versus (or amidst) change is also one logically begged by the course of twentieth-century European history which has seen successive eras of rapid socio-economic change, the caesurae of two world wars and, for the majority of countries, the traumata of regime change. These historical discontinuities provide a fascinatingly fluid backdrop for the study of the development of Western European party systems and would seem to set out a stern and almost unpassable test for any supposition of enduring party system continuity. The sternest such test would ostensibly seem to be provided by Germany.

Twentieth-century Germany has seen unparalleled discontinuity. Following the relative stability of the Wilhelmine era, the Weimar years provided an extreme context for party system development. Buffetted by extraordinary economic and political dislocation, the Weimar party system proved to be deeply flawed and unstable, riven by processes of sectionalization, fragmentation and polarization, and was ultimately swept away – in part because of these flaws – by the National Socialist dictatorship established in 1933.

Following the hiatus of the Third Reich, competitive party politics re-emerged throughout occupied Germany after 1945 only once again to be extinguished, very rapidly, in the one-party state of the emergent German Democratic Republic (GDR). The western Federal Republic of Germany (FRG), by contrast, saw an enduringly successful reconstruction of democratic party politics on a radically different basis to that of the Weimar years. In an initial period of consolidation, party competition gradually concentrated around two major parties, the CDU/CSU (the Christian Democratic

Union in unison with its Bavarian sister, the Christian Social Union) and the SPD (Social Democratic Party), supplemented only by the smaller, liberal Free Democrats (FDP). After this process of concentration was, by the early 1960s, complete, this so-called 'two-and-a-half' party system entered a period of hyperstability characterized by a moderate 'politics of centrality' (Smith, 1976) and consensus.

The emergence of new issues and new parties, most notably the Greens, opened up the prospect of a more fluid, or 'defrosted' (Padgett, 1989), and potentially more polarized party system. However, before any conclusions could be drawn about the significance of this new fluidity, the collapse of Soviet-bloc communism precipitated German unification within the framework of an expanded Federal Republic. Unification saw an electoral 'colonization' of the former GDR by the West German party system, qualified only by a substantial residue of support for the post-communist Party of Democratic Socialism (PDS), the successor to the former state party of the GDR, the Socialist Unity Party (SED). The result of the extension of West German party structures into post-communist Eastern Germany has been to bifurcate party competition across the old inner German border between a western party system consisting of the CDU/CSU, SPD, Greens and a now debilitated FDP and an eastern party system consisting of the CDU, SPD and PDS.

Historical background before 1945

The party system of the Weimar Republic was, as Table 6.1 shows, highly fragmented with five to seven parties possessing a substantial basis of electoral support. Fragmentation reflected a highly sectionalized party system. Parties tended to identify with, draw their support from, and define their ideologies and policies with regard to particular social group interests. This form of sectionalized interest representation is given clear illustration by the parties of the Left: the SPD; in the early years, the Independent Social Democrats, the USPD; and later the Communist Party, the KPD. Taken in combination, and notwithstanding considerable voter exchange between them, these parties collectively had a relatively stable basis of support throughout the Weimar years which was located primarily in the manual working class, and all pursued variations of Marxist ideology intended to address the interests of the manual working class. Much the same applies to the Centre Party (taken together with its Bavarian offshoot, the BVP), which had a stable, almost exclusively Catholic electorate, and which was driven by an ideology of social Catholicism.

The situation becomes less clear-cut, however, when one considers the parties of what Larry Eugene Jones (1979) has called the 'bourgeois centre',

Table 6.1 Weimar Republic, election results, 1919–32

Party	1919	1920	1924a	1924b	1928	1930	1932a	1932b
SPD	37.9	21.6	20.5	26.0	29.8	24.5	21.6	20.4
USPD	7.6	17.9	0.8	0.3	0.1	0.0	–	–
KPD	–	2.0	12.6	9.0	10.6	13.1	14.6	16.8
Centre/BVP	19.7	17.8	16.6	17.3	15.2	14.8	15.7	14.8
DDP	18.6	8.4	5.7	6.3	4.9	3.8	1.0	0.9
DVP	4.4	14.0	9.2	10.1	8.7	4.5	1.2	1.8
DNVP	10.3	15.1	19.5	20.5	14.2	7.0	5.9	8.8
Splinter parties	1.6	3.1	8.5	7.5	13.9	14.0	2.6	3.4
NSDAP	–	–	6.6	3.0	2.6	18.3	37.4	33.1

the DNVP, DVP and DDP (respectively, the German National People's Party, People's Party and Democratic Party). These were what are typically termed 'middle-class' parties, representing some combination of (big and small) business and farming interests, civil servants and white-collar workers, partly tempered also by religious and regional factors. On the whole, these parties proved conspicuously unable, amid the upheavals of the Weimar years, to defend the various 'middle-class' interests they strove to represent and, as a result, they underwent a process of electoral erosion which favoured, particularly in the 1928 and 1930 elections, a burgeoning group of splinter parties (Childers, 1983: 129–91).

These splinter parties presented an image of sectionalization gone mad. They sought to represent the interests of often remarkably small social groups, among them the Party for People's Rights and Revaluation (representing rentiers and small investors), the Saxon Farmers' Party or the League of Farmers and Vineyard Owners in the German South-West. Moreover, given the nearly pure form of proportional representation used in the Weimar years, even such socially marginal parties were able to secure parliamentary representation.

Two points are worth noting about this cacophony of niche parties in the 'bourgeois centre'. First, their profusion and narrowly sectional orientation suggest a society in deep flux which lacked the clearly identifiable cleavage structures on which the Lipset–Rokkan thesis of long-term continuities in the social foundations of party politics is based. There was no *one* 'middle class' as such in the Weimar years, but rather a series of different middle classes which lacked any sense of collective identity and interest (beyond, at best, a shared anti-Leftism).

Second, the tendency to party political sectionalization evident in extreme form in the 'bourgeois centre' but also in the manual worker and Catholic populations, had serious implications for party interaction, coalition formation and governmental stability throughout the Weimar years. It indicated a narrowness of perspective which led parties to be unwilling to subordinate sectional interests or to compromise sectionally based ideologies in pursuit of any wider, shared conception of *national* interest. Consequently, both coalition formation and coalition maintenance were inherently difficult. Unstable, short-lived governments regularly foundered over the unbridgeable differences produced by divergent priorities. This sectional merry-go-round limited governmental effectiveness and fed a growing popular disillusionment with the Weimar system reflected in escalating support, after 1928, for unambiguously anti-system parties on both the left, in the form of the KPD, and, in particular, on the right, in the form of the Nazi NSDAP.

The process of polarization after 1930 paralysed the parliamentary system. The dramatic success of the Nazi Party reflected the breadth and attractiveness of the vision of national community, regeneration and assertion it projected. This was not merely a party of the dislocated (and largely Protestant) 'lower middle class' as many, most notably Lipset (1960: 131–78), have over-simplistically argued. It was a party with an appeal which transcended social cleavages, extending its support also into the *haute bourgeoisie*, manual worker and Catholic electorates (Hamilton, 1982; Childers, 1983, 1986; Hailbronner, 1992).

The NSDAP was, in its mass base, an archetypal *Volkspartei*, or 'catch-all party', with a social breadth of support unparalleled before or since in German party history. It was this very antithesis of Weimar's sectionalized party politics which enabled the NSDAP to gain the momentum to take over government in 1933. The result was, of course, disastrous for Germany. The terroristic, expansionist and ultimately genocidal policies of the Third Reich eventually generated a broad, international, anti-Nazi coalition which secured Germany's unconditional surrender in 1945, and which then partly dismembered the Reich and occupied the remainder of the German territory.

Despite the initial commitment of the occupying powers to rebuild a denazified and democratized united German state, the dynamics of the emerging Cold War led to the creation of two German states divided by the 'iron curtain' and, later, the Berlin Wall. Germany's division snuffed out the attempt made in the emergent East German state to re-establish genuinely competitive party politics, leaving the new, western Federal Republic to take up the baton bequeathed by the party system of the Weimar years.

The Federal Republic: contextual variables

The relaunching of competitive party politics in the FRG was undertaken in a vastly changed context. A range of structural and cultural factors laid out a new environment for party system development.

Two key structural factors arose from the electoral system adopted for the FRG. In *Bundestag* elections, voters cast two votes, one for a constituency candidate, and one for a party list, the latter being decisive in calculating the proportional representation of parties in the *Bundestag*. However, the vote share won by the party list normally has to rise above a 'hurdle' of 5 per cent of the vote before the party qualifies for proportional representation (the only exception being when a party wins three constituency seats outright, which acts as an alternative, though a much rarer and tougher 'hurdle').

The qualifying 'hurdle' was initially applied in 1949 at 5 per cent of the vote in each *Land* (or region), but was revised in 1953 to become a much more stringent hurdle applied at the national level (a stringency only ever relaxed in the 1990 unification election, when separate 5 per cent hurdles were applied in East and West Germany). This modified system of PR has made more or less impossible the 'splinter party phenomenon' and extreme party system fragmentation which dogged the Weimar Republic. Most significantly, this form of modified PR supported the process of party system concentration which transformed a multi-party *Bundestag* in 1949 to a 'two-and-a-half party' *Bundestag* by 1961.

A second important feature of the electoral system is that it allows 'ticket-splitting' between constituency and party list vote. Ticket-splitting allows for widespread tactical voting, normally by casting the constituency vote for one of the major parties, CDU/CSU or SPD, and the party list vote for smaller parties, normally the FDP, or, more recently, the Greens. Tactical vote-splitting allows for highly nuanced electoral judgements. It allows for preliminary expressions of dissatisfaction with particular parties without wholly abandoning past party allegiances, typically by casting a con-stituency vote for one's 'traditional' party, while casting the party list vote for an alternative. This form of ticket-splitting, for example, did much to establish the Greens as a parliamentary party force in and after 1983 as disgruntled SPD supporters cast party list votes for the Green alternative. Ticket-splitting also allows voters to set aside strict party allegiance and vote tactically to support a particular coalition alignment, as happened, for example, in the 1994 *Bundestag* election, when CDU/CSU supporters 'lent' party list votes to an ailing FDP to ensure that it remained in the *Bundestag* and that the CDU/CSU–FDP coalition could be renewed. Finally, ticket-splitting has allowed for the expression of two 'cultural' factors which have done much to shape the development of the FRG party system.

The first of these factors was the aversion to extremism which pervaded post-war (West) German politics. This aversion was conditioned both by the experience of the National Socialist regime and by the practice of communist rule in the GDR after 1949. It found constitutional expression in a provision of the FRG Basic Law which allows for anti-democratic parties to be banned (as happened twice in the 1950s), but, more importantly, *popular* expression in what Gordon Smith (1976: 402) called a 'restricted ideological space' in the FRG, a gravitation towards a non-ideological 'politics of centrality' in reaction to the excesses of Nazism and Communism. Ticket-splitting played a key role in securing this politics of centrality, at least for the 20-year period between the mid-1960s and mid-1980s when the FDP received party list votes from CDU/CSU or SPD supporters in order that it could act as a 'liberal corrective' to any perceived non-centrist tendencies of the larger parties.

In similar vein, ticket-splitting has been used to give expression to an aversion to single party government in the Federal Republic, again as shaped by the experience of Nazism and communist rule in the GDR (Pulzer, 1962: 425–6). Indeed, only once has a single party – the CDU/CSU in 1957 – won an absolute majority in the FRG. Since then, whenever an absolute (and always CDU/CSU) majority has seemed a possibility – as in 1976, 1983 and 1990 – a late trend towards ticket-splitting has ensured continued coalition government.

Two final contextual factors deserve mention. The first concerns the crucial period of party system renewal and consolidation in the first fifteen years of the FRG. This was a period of continual and, at times, spectacular economic growth. It was also a period in which sectional interest politics failed to re-emerge with the intensity which had undermined the stability of the Weimar Republic. Sectional interest politics are, above all, the politics of distributional conflict. In the Weimar years, endemic economic instability meant that distributional questions were always at the forefront and had accentuated the trend towards sectionalization. Rapid and continuous economic growth in the formative years of the FRG made distributional questions far less acute and allowed party politics to transcend narrow sectional rivalries and develop a basis for more stable and constructive inter-party interaction.

Finally, consideration should be given to the significance of post-war German federalism for the party system. As a federal state, the pattern of national party politics in the FRG is flanked, and to an extent shaped, by the party systems of the *Länder*. Much has been written, albeit rather inconclusively, about the link between *Länder* and national party systems (Roberts, 1989; Sturm, 1993).

One area where the federal dimension has unquestionably been important, however, is in the expression in *Länder* elections of mid-term dissatisfaction with the sitting national government (much the same function that by-elections perform in the UK) and, taking dissatisfaction a stage further, in the pre-figuring of national-level changes of government by voter 'experimentation' with new patterns of coalition formation in the *Länder* (ibid., 1993: 104–5). This 'experimentation' happened in the second half of the 1960s, again in the early 1980s, and was arguably happening once more in the 1990s when the creation of a number of both SPD–Green and CDU–SPD coalitions has established experience and practice in coalition alignments which provide a potential future alternative to that of the decaying CDU/CSU–FDP coalition which has endured at national level since 1982.

The party system 1949–82: concentration and stabilization

The results of the first *Bundestag* election of 1949 presented a picture of considerable fragmentation, with ten parties securing parliamentary representation. The parties were a mixture of old and new, with the SPD latching directly on to its pre-war, manual worker traditions, with both the far-Left KPD and a post-Nazi far Right (the DRP) also represented, and with a continued tendency to splintering in the 'bourgeois centre', largely on a regional basis. Regional splintering was facilitated by the separated and disjointed re-emergence of party politics in each of the three western occupation zones between 1945 and 1949. It was also supported by the application of the 5 per cent hurdle at *Land* level for the first and last time in 1949.

Alongside this picture of broad continuities between Weimar and the FRG, two new, and extremely important, nationwide parties had emerged by 1949: the FDP and the CDU/CSU. The foundation of the FDP was an attempt to bring together different strands of the hitherto divided German liberal tradition, while the CDU/CSU represented an altogether new type of party. Although descended closely from the inter-war Centre Party (and Bavarian BVP), the CDU/CSU styled itself as a democratic *Volkspartei*, a catch-all 'party of the whole people'. Consequently, it abandoned the dogmatic, social Catholic ideology of its predecessor, adopting instead a moderated ideological profile based on a more open and inter-denominational Christianity, supplemented (after a short flirtation with quasi-socialist economics) by a commitment to the emergent West German 'social market economy' and a western-oriented foreign policy informed by a dogged anti-communism. This was a party platform designed to transcend the sectionalism of the Weimar years and to appeal to, and integrate, broad sections of the non-left electorate.

As Table 6.2 shows, this attempt at electoral integration was remarkably successful, with the CDU/CSU vote rising dramatically throughout the 1950s to an absolute majority by 1957. The losers in the process were the minor parties of the 'bourgeois centre', all of which had effectively been absorbed into the CDU/CSU by 1961, by which point only two other parties – the SPD and FDP – were still represented in the *Bundestag*.

The process of concentration was facilitated by the startling rate of

Table 6.2 Federal Republic of Germany, election results, 1949–94

Party	1949	1953	1957	1961	1965	1969	1972	1976	1980	1983	1987	1990	1994
CDU/CSU	31.0	45.2	50.2	45.3	47.6	46.1	44.9	48.6	44.5	48.8	44.3	43.8	41.5
SPD	29.2	28.8	31.8	36.2	39.3	42.7	45.8	42.6	42.9	38.2	37.0	33.5	36.4
FDP	11.9	9.5	7.7	12.8	9.5	5.8	8.4	7.9	10.6	6.9	9.1	11.0	6.9
Green	–	–	–	–	–	–	–	–	1.5	5.6	8.3	5.1	7.3
PDS	–	–	–	–	–	–	–	–	–	–	–	2.4	4.4
Other	27.8	16.5	10.3	5.7	3.5	5.5	0.9	0.9	0.5	0.5	1.2	4.2	3.6

economic growth over which the CDU/CSU presided during the 1950s which largely marginalized the sectional sensitivities of distributional politics of the Weimar years. It was also accelerated by the application of the 5 per cent hurdle nationwide from 1953, and by the elimination of the parties of the far Left and far Right, which fell both to a stiffening aversion of the electorate to extremist parties and, ultimately, to constitutional bans (the post-Nazi SRP in 1952 and the KPD in 1956).

During the process of concentration, the SPD, however, remained wedded to the sectionalism which had conditioned its politics in the Weimar years. It continued to style itself unequivocally as a working-class party and to pursue a form of democratic Marxist ideology. This 'cloth-cap', Marxist image prevented the SPD from extending its electorate much beyond manual worker groups and condemned it to electoral stagnation at around the 30 per cent mark. The SPD's electoral weakness was confirmed by the party's steadfast opposition to what had become extraordinarily popular CDU/CSU policies in economic management and foreign relations and its inability to produce leaders capable of challenging the authority of Konrad Adenauer, the CDU Chancellor from 1949 to 1963. As a result, government was conducted under CDU/CSU-dominated coalitions into the 1960s (see Table 6.3).

Frustrated by electoral stagnation and enervated by a new, younger generation of party leaders, most notably Willy Brandt, the SPD embarked on radical change in the second half of the 1950s. The signal event here was the Bad Godesberg party conference of 1959. A new party programme was adopted at the conference which attempted to relocate the SPD as a moderate, left-of-centre *Volkspartei*. The remnants of Marxist ideology were more or less expunged from the party programme and, in the following years, this reorientation was confirmed by the acceptance of the guiding principles of CDU/CSU economic policy (the socially responsible market economy as opposed to the SPD's previous adherence to socialist interventionism and large-scale nationalization) and foreign policy (Western European and Atlantic integration as opposed to a previous emphasis on non-alignment in

Table 6.3 Government composition in the Federal
Republic of Germany, 1949–94

Election	Coalition parties	Chancellor
1949	CDU/CSU, FDP, DP	Konrad Adenauer (CDU)
1953	CDU/CSU, FDP (until Oct. 1956), DP, GB/BHE (until July 1955), FVP (from Oct. 1956)	Konrad Adenauer (CDU)
1957	CDU/CSU, DP (until Sept. 1960)	Konrad Adenauer (CDU)
1961	CDU/CSU, FDP	Konrad Adenauer (CDU) (until Oct. 1963) Ludwig Erhard (CDU)
1965	CDU/CSU, FDP (until Dec. 1966) CDU/CSU, SPD (from Dec. 1966)	Ludwig Erhard (CDU) Kurt-Georg Kiesinger (CDU)
1969	SPD, FDP	Willy Brandt (SPD)
1972	SPD, FDP	Willy Brandt (SPD) (until May 1974) Helmut Schmidt (SPD)
1976	SPD, FDP	Helmut Schmidt (SPD)
1980	SPD, FDP (until Oct. 1982) CDU/CSU, FDP (from Oct. 1982)	Helmut Schmidt (SPD) Helmut Kohl (CDU)
1983	CDU/CSU, FDP	Helmut Kohl (CDU)
1987	CDU/CSU, FDP	Helmut Kohl (CDU)
1990	CDU/CSU, FDP	Helmut Kohl (CDU)
1994	CDU/CSU, FDP	Helmut Kohl (CDU)

international politics, which sought to combine both anti-communism and an aversion to the Western European–Atlantic 'capitalist club'). This conscious attempt to break out of the 30 per cent electoral ghetto bore steady fruit in the following *Bundestag* elections, with the SPD moving towards electoral parity with the CDU/CSU by the end of the 1960s.

The transformation of the SPD significantly altered the dynamics of inter-party competition. As early as 1961, a non-CDU/CSU-led government had become numerically (if not yet politically) possible for the first time since 1949. More generally, the emergence of the SPD as a new *Volkspartei* restricted the ideological distance over which the party system was spread and served to concentrate party competition on a moderate and for the most part, consensual middle ground. This was confirmed in 1966 with the first major change of coalition alignment since 1949, when the FDP withdrew from the CDU/CSU's embrace, precipitating the establishment of a grand coalition between the CDU/CSU and SPD.

The grand coalition allowed the SPD to establish its credibility and moderation as a governing party while also allowing the FDP to re-define its image in opposition and to move closer to the SPD. The result was the creation of a novel SPD–FDP coalition in 1969, and the cementing of West German party politics into the ultra-stable 'two-and-a-half' party pattern which endured through to the 1980s.

Before examining this period of ultra-stability in the party system in more depth, however, it is worth discussing the extent to which longer-term stabilities underlay the configuration of the FRG party system which had evolved by the 1960s. The existence of such stabilities is, of course, the core of the claim made by Lipset and Rokkan (1967b: 50) that the party systems of the 1960s were 'frozen' around the social cleavage structures of the 1920s and also, 'in remarkably many cases', around the party organizations of that era.

This is, by any standards, an ambitious claim, and seems doubly extravagant in a German context where the path of party system development between the 1920s and the 1960s was ruptured in succession by dictatorship, military defeat, partial dismemberment, occupation and national division. This ruptured historical path means that any examination of continuities between the 1920s and the 1960s necessarily has to labour under the problem of comparison of vastly different political contexts embedded in territorially incongruent Germanies: the economically and politically unstable, and progressively delegitimized Weimar Republic, which stretched eastwards to Lithuania and far into present-day Poland, and a West German FRG only around half the size, which enjoyed far greater levels of stability and – largely as a result – increasing acceptance as a legitimate political entity. Unsurprisingly, Germany is not one of the 'remarkably many cases' where there is a strong continuity between 1920s and 1960s party organizations: only one party, the SPD, was active in both Germanies in both decades.

Potentially more serious problems exist, moreover, with the more important part of the Lipset–Rokkan claim: that the social cleavages of the 1920s underlay and structured the party system of the 1960s, in the sense that the ideological contours of the party system remained stable whether or not the same party organizations were involved. The problem here lies in the assumption that the social contours of modern, industrial society had been established in 1920s' Germany forming clear-cut social cleavages. This rings true only to a limited extent.

For example, manual workers certainly constituted, at least in urban, industrial centres, an identifiable and demarcated social milieu in the Weimar years, and they formed the social basis of a stable, left-wing vote. The same can be said of Germany's Catholic population, much of which had a strong sense of commonality and shared identity which set it aside from other Germans and formed the basis of a stable, Catholic, Centre Party vote. It is not clear, however, that the sense of social collectivity implied by the term 'cleavage' existed outside the dense social networks which underpinned the manual worker and Catholic milieux and their respective party organizations. There was little coherence in the non-Catholic population nor in the non-manual worker population with the exception of a broad, but non-uniform anti-leftism. There was certainly no sense of positive cohesion, no identifiable middle-class identity, as arguably existed in Britain. Rather, a hotch-potch of dislocated groups existed, often more antagonistic towards one another than to the Left, which are, yet, typically hauled collectively under the unsatisfactory umbrella designation of 'middle class'.

These groups had been buffetted and torn, created and marginalized by the scale and rapidity of Germany's late industrialization in the 40 years or so before the First World War; they had undergone the upheaval of war and uncertainties of defeat; they had been devastated and traumatized by first the post-war hyperinflation and then the great depression. Moreover, they lacked the sense of stability and perspective provided by the fixed points of social and political identification evident within the manual worker and Catholic milieux. These were highly disoriented, anomic social groups whose boundaries and identities were continuously fissured by massive processes of social transformation begun by rapid industrialization, perpetuated into the Weimar years, and later forced on further by the industrial restructuring and social mobilization conducted in service of the Nazi dictatorship. 'Middle-class' Weimar society was, in other words, a fluid world which does not easily lend itself to the assumption of the attainment of relative social stasis on which Lipset and Rokkan's claims are based.

Given the social dynamics of the Weimar era, it is not surprising that clear limits apply to the continuities in social underpinning evident in the party systems of Weimar and the West German FRG. Throughout the pre-unification FRG, manual workers formed the hard core of the SPD electorate, especially where they were unionized and thus further organizationally bound to the traditional left milieu (Padgett and Burkett, 1986: 261–3). Much the same applied to Catholics and the CDU/CSU, especially if they were regular churchgoers, similarly bound to their social milieu (ibid.: 271–3). The same cannot generally be said of the Protestant population or of the 'middle class' (ibid.: 264–7, 271–3). Partial exceptions exist if one dis-aggregates from the Protestant population the regular churchgoers, who tended to vote disproportionately for the CDU/CSU, and, from the umbrella heading of 'middle class', the self-employed 'old middle class', which also emerged as a supplementary core CDU/CSU electorate after 1949 (ibid.: 270, 273).

These exceptions, while testament to the new, integrative capacity of the CDU/CSU *Volkspartei* are, however, both of limited significance in absolute numerical terms, and they can only in part qualify the wider picture of an FRG population in which important social groups lacked stable and long-term social cues for the determination of electoral choices. This is all the more the case given two additional historical factors. First, the 'old middle class' and the Protestant population were among the earliest and hardiest supporters of the NSDAP (Childers, 1983: 50–118). One can therefore hardly see here the broad ideological continuity between Weimar and FRG electoral choices in those social groups which Lipset and Rokkan suggest should exist. Second, the great majority of the Protestant population of the Weimar years was located outside the territory of the West German FRG, either in the territory of what became the GDR or in the former German areas absorbed into Poland and the Soviet Union after 1945. Any Weimar–FRG comparison here is necessarily of limited value.

The wider framework for identifying long-term continuities is further nuanced by the fact that the core voter groups of the SPD and CDU/CSU, organized manual workers and regular, church-going Catholics, were in relative decline as proportions of the electorate. Taking up the slack in a swift rise to social predominance was the 'new middle class' of white-collar workers and public servants which, in terms of size, was incomparable to the 'new middle class' of the Weimar era and which could only look back to an opaque pattern of 'bourgeois centre' fragmentation for long-term electoral cues. Moreover, while little change occurred in the proportions of the population which were nominally Catholic or Protestant, the number of regular churchgoers in both denominations – the real cue for electoral partisanship – was also in steady decline among Catholics, and had already stagnated at a very low level among Protestants by the 1960s.

The electoral 'market' of the FRG was, in other words, increasingly shaped by groups of 'new middle class' and secular voters who lacked strongly rooted loyalties to particular parties or political traditions. This was, of course, one of the key reasons why the CDU/CSU, and later the SPD, adopted the *Volkspartei* strategy: simple socio-electoral arithmetic dictated a need to branch out in the 'market place' and broaden party appeal. The two *Volksparteien* did this very successfully, as can be seen in the high, roughly equal and relatively stable levels of electoral support they secured from the late 1960s to the early 1980s (see Table 6.2 again).

The ability of the CDU/CSU and SPD to supplement the structurally rooted loyalties of their declining core electorates with rising levels of support from new voter groups has typically been explained by the concept of party identification – the development of stable, affective attachments to a party's image, identity and policy profile (Crewe, 1985: 1–20) which led around two-thirds of both CDU/CSU and SPD supporters to express a 'strong' sense of identification with their party by 1980. The ability of the CDU/CSU and SPD thus to secure a broad electoral base and generate high and stable vote shares set the scene for the next phase in the development of the party system, the so-called 'two-and-a-half' party system, which endured from the late 1960s through to 1983.

Unlike in other Western European countries, this was a period of unusual party system stability in the FRG. It was a period in which the CDU/CSU, SPD and FDP – in Gordon Smith's (1989b) terms, the 'core' parties in the FRG party system – almost entirely mopped up the vote, securing together over 99 per cent of the vote in the 1972 and 1976 elections on a turnout of over 90 per cent. A crucial element in this situation was the fact that neither of the *Volksparteien* was able to broaden its appeal sufficiently to generate an absolute majority, and therewith single party government. This invested the FDP with a key role.

The FDP has always been an oddity of the FRG party system. It has never expanded beyond a modest share of the overall vote (between 6 and 12 per cent), and it has never been able to rely on a stable social base of electoral support. Despite this, it has been out of government only between 1957 and 1961, during the years of the CDU/CSU absolute majority, and again during the grand coalition between 1966 and 1969. For the rest of the post-war period, electoral arithmetic has thrust it into the role of '*Mehrheitsschaffer*', or majority-maker. This role took on a particular importance following each of the six successive elections between 1961 and 1980 in the sense that the FDP's support could 'make' *either* a CDU/CSU-led *or* an SPD-led coalition. Despite tactical flirtation with the possibility of an SPD–FDP coalition after the 1961 and 1965 elections, a so-called 'social–liberal' coalition only became politically feasible once the SPD's post-Godesberg reorientation had been confirmed in the period of grand coalition in the late 1960s.

From that point, and until the emergence of the Greens in 1983, the FDP could act as powerbroker between the two *Volksparteien*. Thus, the FDP acted as the indispensable 'linchpin' (Padgett, 1989: 125) of a 'two-and-a-half' party system, facilitating the transition to SPD-led government in 1969, and the re-establishment of CDU/CSU-led government in 1982, when the FDP abandoned the social–liberal alignment in mid-term. The powerbroking role was facilitated by the dual ideological strands of social and market liberalism it had inherited from pre-1933 German liberal politics, the former providing an ideological point of contact with the SPD, and the latter with the CDU/ CSU (Pappi, 1984). Equally, the FDP's market liberal tradition could act as a constraint on the stronger tendencies to economic interventionism inherent in the SPD, and the social liberal tradition as a similar constraint on the stronger social conservatism of the CDU/CSU. The FDP was thus a further centripetal force on the already ideologically moderate *Volksparteien* which served to concentrate party competition firmly on a consensual centre ground. This neatly balanced party system, bounded by what Gordon Smith (1976) aptly called the 'politics of centrality', presented the culmination of a process of party system change away from CDU/CSU dominance towards a hyperstable situation of *Volkspartei* parity and consensual, centrist party competition.

Change and adaptation I: pre-unification

The patterns of instability and volatility which had begun to rock party systems elsewhere in Western Europe in the 1970s (Mair, 1989: 261–2) became apparent in the FRG in the early 1980s, throwing the neatly balanced centrism of the 1970s out of equilibrium. The primary indicator of change was the breakthrough of 'New Left' politics as a parliamentary force after 1983. The emergence of the Greens, mainly at the expense of the SPD, seemed to presage a shift away from centrism and towards a form of more polarized party competition.

As Table 6.2 shows, the inroads made by the Greens into the SPD vote were sufficient in 1983 and 1987 to rule out the possibility of an SPD–FDP coalition. This destroyed the pivotal, linchpin position of the FDP, tying it to a continuation of the coalition formed in 1982 with the Christian Democrats. The loss of votes to the Greens also caused the SPD's partial abandonment of the electoral middle ground in an attempt to recover strength by competing for the New Left vote.

A rudimentary two-bloc party system (Padgett, 1989: 127–30) thus emerged between the SPD and Greens on the left and the CDU/CSU and FDP on the right. The tendency to polarization was seemingly further enhanced in the later 1980s with the emergence of the far Right to electoral prominence (at least in *Land* and European parliament elections), leading some elements of the CDU/CSU themselves to shift rightwards and peddle a more conservative and nationalist message in the hope of warding off the far Right electoral challenge (Clemens, 1991).

Much of the debate about the factors which precipitated the destabilization and unbalancing of the 'two-and-a-half' party system has revolved around the notion of *Parteienverdrossenheit*, a growing sense of popular disillusionment with the FRG party system (Jeffery and Green, 1995). This sense of disillusion had a number of sources. Most fundamentally, the two *Volksparteien* had, in a sense, become victims of their own success at electoral integration. As noted above, the dictates of electoral competition in a changing social context had led the CDU/CSU and SPD to moderate their ideological heritages in the attempt to integrate new social groups. The corollary was what Elmar Wiesendahl (1990) coined the 'modernization trap', a blurring of party identity and direction which disillusioned those supporters still attached to the parties' original or presumed ideological thrust. The problem was revealed in particular after changes of government. When the SPD assumed the role of leading coalition partner in 1969 it was unable to meet the aspirations for far-reaching political reform of parts of its support, in particular the 'new' post-materialist left which had emerged in the 1960s, above all through the student movement.

Equally, when the CDU/CSU returned to government in 1982, it was unable to add policy substance to its rhetoric of the *Wende*, literally a turnaround of emphasis in the direction of neo-liberal market reforms analogous to those in the UK after 1979 and the USA after 1980 (Webber, 1992). Despite promises of clear, ideologically driven policy change, voters were confronted by technocratically driven governmental pragmatism and, at best, incremental policy change. The perception of a lack of genuinely alternative government provoked alienation and withdrawal among those motivated by ideology or principle: why support one of these parties if it offered little that its competitor did not?

The process of alienation sparked by the 'modernization trap' was accelerated by the established parties' organizational structures which were highly bureaucratized and failed to offer opportunities for new groups or ideas to shape or modify the parties' established direction. The problem was exemplified in the SPD when many of those who had joined the party amid the spirit of reform and renewal of the late 1960s left in disillusionment in the 1970s when confronted by the ossified and impenetrable structures of the Social Democratic 'organizational dinosaur' (Wiesendahl, 1990: 13).

This sense of impenetrability had particular implications for the demographic regeneration of the parties. The established parties proved increasingly unable to renew themselves by attracting new cohorts of younger members, 'losing' potential youth input to other, more unconventional and direct forms of political participation. While this problem was a general one, it was felt most acutely by the CDU, whose youth organization membership fell from 260,00 to 196,000 between 1983 and 1991, leaving it increasingly, and reflecting low female membership levels, a party of middle-aged and old men (Conradt, 1993: 74).

The outcome of the petrification of party structures was the creation of a *Machtmonopol*, a monopoly of power of an insulated, self-selecting politician caste widely perceived as remote from the electorate and motivated by self-interest, and seen by some as an unpalatable combination of 'cliques, cabals and careers' (Scheuch and Scheuch, 1992). The corollary of this *Machtmonopol* was, for some critics, the *Entmündigung des Volkes*, a loss of public 'voice' in politics (von Arnim, 1990).

A final nail in the coffin of the reputation of the established parties was their deep involvement in a number of scandals which cast severe public doubt over their probity and confirmed the perception of parties as a self-serving *Machtmonopol* (Jeffery and Green, 1995). Three landmark scandals are worth recalling: the Flick affair, involving illegal donations to party funds between 1969 and 1980 by the Flick industrial conglomerate and suspicions that senior politicians accepted bribes; the Barschel affair of 1987, concerning allegations of electoral 'dirty tricks' by the CDU in Schleswig-Holstein which culminated in the suicide of the local CDU leader, Uwe Barschel; and the voting through of an extravagantly enhanced pay and benefits package by and for the *Land* parliamentarians of Hesse, which generated an impression of politicians using the state as a *'Selbstbedienungsladen'*, a 'self-service shop' for their collective enrichment. The net result was a highly unfavourable climate of opinion for the established parties in Germany in the 1980s and a consequent weakening of party identification and partial dealignment of established voter–party ties.

In similar vein, a growing trend of split-ticket voting was apparent, with the percentage of split votes rising from a low point of 6 per cent in 1976 up to around 14 per cent in 1987 (Dalton, 1989: 105–6). These indices of dealignment and of growing volatility in voting behaviour had an important corollary: that of a growing 'short-termism' in electoral choices, with voters increasingly making, and changing, their choices during the election campaign. This 'short-termism' reflected a growing issue sensitivity in voting behaviour, with party issue positions, party images and the personalities of leading party figures all playing a greater role in electoral decision-making (ibid.: 118–120).

This complex of *Parteienverdrossenheit*, partial dealignment and growing short-termism posed a particularly difficult challenge for the two *Volksparteien*, whose socially diverse electorates were especially vulnerable to erosion in the new electoral environment. Both suffered crises of identity and direction in the 1980s, as memorably captured in Rudolf Wildenmann's (1989) image of the *Volksparteien* as *'ratlose Riesen'*, as baffled giants, reacting with head-scratching perplexity to increased popular disillusionment and associated changes in voting behaviour.

The sense of bafflement was at its most acute in the case of the SPD. At the heart of the problem was the emergence of the Greens who had succeeded in attracting support among younger and well-educated voter groups disillusioned by the inability of the SPD to respond to and articulate the 'new politics' issues which had emerged to prominence since the late 1960s. From 1983, the SPD was caught in the strategic dilemma, never satisfactorily resolved, of trying to recapture 'new' Left, 'new politics' voters from the Greens without alienating its traditional core, 'old' Left electorate among unionized manual workers (Padgett, 1987; Merkl, 1988).

A similar, but less pronounced problem was felt by the CDU/CSU, whose continued electoral success disguised a growing instability in the party's support base, and a vulnerability to electoral erosion both at the centre (from which the FDP and SPD stood to benefit) and on the right, where a new force, the *Republikaner*, had made a mark in European and West Berlin elections in 1989. The CDU/CSU thus also found itself in a strategic dilemma, as manifested in an at times acrimonious intra-party debate between centrist modernizers and right-wing traditionalists (Clemens, 1991).

Change and adaptation II: post-unification

The strategic bafflement of the *Volksparteien* was, of course, a *West* German phenomenon. The process and manifestations of dealignment which caused it do, nevertheless, help to put the questions confronting the FRG party system as a result of unification into perspective. Unification presented a unique challenge – that of the integration of a post-communist electorate – to a party system already under growing strain. The East German electorate emerged on to the battleground of competitive party politics after 45 years of one-party rule and, before that, four years of Soviet occupation and the twelve years of the Third Reich.

The East Germans lacked the usual paraphernalia which help structure voting behaviour: the regular rhythm of competitive elections and party organizations and traditions, buttressed by ties to intermediary organizations like trade unions and churches. The East German electorate was to a large extent a blank sheet, essentially non-aligned, lacking in party identification and highly sensitive to short-term influences.

Unification brought together a dealigning western electorate with an essentially non-aligned eastern one. Moreover, the level of fluidity was increased even further by the special character of the first post-unification election in 1990 which focused on the one, overriding issue of unification. In this situation, the German voter was more likely than ever before in the post-war period to make a short-term, issue-driven voting decision.

Given the short-termism prevalent in 1990, the election result might be seen as something of an anti-climax. It was in many senses a triumph of the 'core' parties of the former West Germany, the CDU/CSU, SPD and FDP. These had helped to establish, and later merged with, sister parties in the East after the collapse of communist rule and together succeeded in mopping up over 75 per cent of the East German vote in 1990 while maintaining their hold on over 90 per cent of the western electorate. This triumph was, however, interpreted divergently. Gordon Smith (1993) saw it as a telling testament to the integrative capacities of the core parties and, by implication, to an enduring stability of a party system robust enough to accommodate even the upheavals of unification.

Smith's commentary is certainly true to the extent that the western parties were able collectively to gather another 9 million or so votes in the East and to retain their core position in the West. However, an alternative view insisted that the triumph of the core parties rested on extremely shaky foundations with Norpoth and Roth (1993: 222) seeing 'massive turbulence' under the 'serene surface' of the 1990 election results, and Padgett (1993: 44) identifying the potential for a new era of unpredictable change in German electoral politics, a *'Wende ohne Ende'*. These commentators lacked confidence in the ability of the core parties to maintain a reliable and enduring basis of support across the new united Germany. To do this, they would not only have to shore up their position in an increasingly disillusioned and capricious western electorate, but also to root themselves in an eastern electorate which, buffetted by the dislocation of post-communist transformation, had priorities and concerns widely divergent from those in the West.

The East also has a rather different social base. Whatever the qualms expressed above about the Lipset–Rokkan 'freezing' hypothesis, social background in the West does still provide at least some electoral cues. The most significant of these – the alignment of manual workers to the SPD, and of practising Christians, especially Catholics, to the CDU/CSU – have proved to be of either less relevance, or even of irrelevance in the East.

While the Christian vote was given disproportionately to the Christian Democrats in the East in both 1990 and 1994, it has little absolute significance. Following decades of state hostility to organized religion in the GDR, 67 per cent of East Germans (compared to just 19 per cent of West Germans) lacked any religious affiliation in 1992 (Gibowski, 1995: 105–8). Moreover, initial expectations (McAdams, 1990: 305) that the SPD would be able to draw on its 'traditional' strength among the manual workers of the East, last displayed in the Weimar years, proved to be an over-optimistic reading of inter-war 'freezing'. In fact, the CDU won over 48 per cent of the manual worker vote in the East in 1990, compared to the SPD's 24.7 per cent and, despite losses among this group – probably the hardest hit by the problems of post-unification transformation – still held a lead of 40.6 per cent to 35.1 per cent over the SPD in the 1994 election (Gibowski, 1995: 108).

The prevalence of secularism and the 'inverted social profile' (Padgett, 1993: 39) of the class vote compounded the problems facing the western parties in generating a stable, cross-German electoral profile. They have not, by any means, risen to that challenge. In fact, evidence has accumulated that when the western party system 'colonized' the East, it took with it the sense of *Parteienverdrossenheit* which had emerged in the West. The level of confidence and 'trust' in political parties fell to an unprecedented level in the early to mid-1990s (Jeffery and Green, 1995). This reflected in part an extraordinary proliferation of 'self-service' scandals which led the then German president, the widely respected Richard von Weizsäcker (1992), to make a blistering attack on the irresponsibility of the parties in their exercise of power.

More broadly, however, it reflected the failure of the CDU/CSU–FDP government and the SPD opposition to offer any real, nationwide sense of direction in political life. This has proved true in particular in the case of the FDP. Christian Søe (1993) summed up the problem by playing on the title of Hans Fallada's famous novel *Little man, what now?*, asking instead 'little party, what now?' Since one of its best ever election results in 1990, when it skilfully traded on the popularity of its then leading figure and Foreign Minister, Hans-Dietrich Genscher, the FDP has shown little sense of purpose beyond being in government, a problem compounded by the lacklustre leadership provided by Genscher's successor, Klaus Kinkel, and the even greyer Wolfgang Gerhardt who replaced him. The result was a disastrous series of elections in the *Länder* and a very real, if unconsummated fear that the FDP would fail to mount the 5 per cent hurdle in the 1994 federal election. Despite surviving that election, the FDP remains very weak at *Länder* level, particularly in the former East Germany. Despite a partial recovery in 1996, the long-term prospects for the FDP remain, however, highly uncertain.

A similar, though less serious situation exists for the SPD and CDU/CSU, neither of which has succeeded in carrying out a genuine programmatic or strategic renewal since unification. The SPD under its recent leaders, Rudolf Scharping and Oskar Lafontaine, has become mired in a '*Vermittlungs-ausschusspolitik*', a rather faceless politics focused on the Mediation Committee of the *Bundestag* and *Bundesrat* (the second chamber in which Germany's *Länder* are represented, and on which the SPD has had a majority for most of the post-unification period).

The CDU/CSU has also failed to offer clear direction, as bluntly admitted by a senior party figure who, in the run-up to the 1994 election, suggested that 'we try and focus on foreign policy, because we have lost our competence in economic policy and we have got nothing of much significance to present in domestic politics' (Hofmann and Perger, 1994: 293). In fact, the major electoral asset of the CDU/CSU in 1994, as in 1990, was the personal authority of Helmut Kohl. This, given Kohl's advancing age and approaching retirement -- probably during the 1998-2002 *Bundestag*, should the CDU/CSU remain in power – presented a dangerous situation for a party which lacked an obvious and authoritative successor as leader (Clemens, 1995). The most likely successor, in 1997, was Wolfgang Schäuble, CDU leader in the *Bundestag*.

Two further factors have compounded the sense of alienation. First, the CDU, SPD and FDP have all failed to establish dynamic East German organizations capable of securing input into strategic programming (Padgett, 1995: 76–9). Beyond the tokenistic appointments of prominent East Germans to senior party positions, like Wolfgang Thierse in the SPD and Angela Merkel in the CDU, the overriding picture is one of continued organizational ossification and unresponsive *Machtmonopol*. Second, the core parties are widely perceived to have failed to deliver in policy terms. The record of economic management since 1990 has been at best undistinguished, dogged by a failure to foresee serious problems and a slowness of reaction when the problems did emerge to full light.

Debates in other policy fields such as asylum issues, abortion, tax reform, the financing of the welfare state and the question of German army contributions to NATO and/or UN missions also tended to drag on for months, even years, without effective resolution, compounding an impression of stagnation and immobilism. This policy stagnation undermined public confidence nationwide in both the CDU/CSU–FDP government and the SPD opposition, which has been firmly bound into the government process via its *Bundesrat* majority and *Vermittlungssauschusspolitik*.

These various factors, 'sleaze', directionlessness, and organizational and policy stagnation, were reflected in a growing sense of voter detachment from the CDU/CSU, FDP and SPD which was amply illustrated in the run of *Land* elections held after the 1990 *Bundestag* elections. These provided graphic illustration of highly volatile voting patterns in both East and West.

A number of broad trends can be identified in this volatility. The first is the evident weakness in most of the *Länder* of voter attachments to one or both of the *Volksparteien*, with especially large swings against the SPD in Hamburg in both 1993 and 1997; and against the CDU in Baden-Württemberg in 1992, and Brandenburg in 1994. Second, it is important to note the destination of the anti-*Volkspartei* swing. In part, the other *Volkspartei* benefited, but more often the swing fell in favour of 'non-core' parties, most notably the Greens, who benefited mainly from disillusionment with the SPD, and for whom the *Länder* provided a basis from which to launch an impressive recovery from the disappointing *Bundestag* result in 1990, but also the parties of the far Right, who made significant inroads into both the SPD and, especially, the CDU vote.

Moreover, the post-communist PDS, capitalizing on the perceived incapacity of the other parties to address the concerns of the East, made significant advances which created a momentum which was to lead it, unexpectedly, to regain *Bundestag* representation in 1994. Third, the FDP, mired in a directionless drift, became deeply unpopular, failing to cross the 5 per cent hurdle in every *Land* election from Baden-Württemberg in 1992 until the next election in Baden-Württemberg in 1996. Fourth, the weakness of the core parties and the success of the non-core parties forced the reconsideration of traditional patterns of coalition-building, notably with the establishment of SPD–Green coalitions in Hessen, Hamburg, Bremen (with the FDP) and Saxony-Anhalt (with the 'toleration' of the PDS), and CDU–

SPD grand coalitions in Baden-Württemberg (1992–96), Mecklenburg-Vorpommern and Thuringia. Finally, and more broadly, the outlines of a party system bifurcated by the former East–West border began to emerge, with a four-party system in the west (CDU/CSU, SPD, Greens and a much weakened FDP) and a three-party system in the East (CDU, SPD and PDS).

These features of the *Länder* elections since 1990 suggested that dealignment in the West and a lack of stable alignments in the East had not been overcome. However, the 1994 federal election results did not, at least on the surface, entirely bear out this wider picture, returning as it did the same CDU/CSU–FDP government and the same opposition parties.

Nevertheless, a number of factors qualify this superficial image of stability. First, the FDP's weakness after 1990 raised severe doubts about whether it would clear the 5 per cent hurdle and re-enter the *Bundestag*. Although it did so quite comfortably, albeit only with the 'loaned' tactical votes of CDU/CSU supporters, the prospect of FDP failure launched intense debates about coalition possibilities without the FDP. These drew on the experiences of the *Länder* after 1990, with some foreseeing a grand coalition of CDU/CSU and SPD, and others a 'Red–Green' coalition of the SPD and Greens, possibly dependent on the support of the PDS.

The 1994 election result did not definitively close these debates. That they were conducted at all indicates that a new, open and rather unpredictable mode of party competition has emerged in the new Germany. The 1994 election was the closest fought election in the FRG since 1949, and the closest ever that a sitting government has come to being voted out of office. It pointed to a potential for governmental turnover unprecedented in a political system used to long periods of coalition government. Moreover, the East–West pattern of results confirmed the tendency to a bifurcation of the party system with just two genuinely national parties, the CDU/CSU and the SPD, and three parties with a limited, regionally based electoral potential: the Greens and FDP in the West, and the PDS in the East. This tendency to bifurcation has the potential severely to complicate the dynamics of coalition formation in the future.

The question posed by Bürklin and Roth (1994: 26) before the 1994 election may prove to be a prescient one for observers of the German party system: 'Are we standing at the end of an era of stable party political majorities and therefore of workable [majority] governments?'

Conclusion: a continuous state of change?

The recollection of Bürklin and Roth's question is not meant to imply any analogy to the instability and unworkability of government which plagued the Weimar Republic. It should be seen rather as a contrast to the hyperstability of both party system and government which prevailed from the mid-1960s to the early 1980s. It is also a reflection of the impact of unification. The peculiar character of German unification, which confronted two different electorates with a party system which, the PDS excepted, had developed in the context of only one of those electorates, presents a challenge unique in the history of the study of party systems.

As Helmut Kohl (1991) put it shortly after unification, the German parties face an immense challenge of social integration, of 'bringing them [east-erners and westerners] together again, bridging the gulf which separates those minds'. The challenge is an especially piquant one given that the western electorate from which this party system had sprung was itself displaying increasing disillusionment with the core parties in the decade before unification. Even in a purely western context, the core parties were increasingly unable to 'bridge the gulfs' which had emerged in the minds of an increasingly detached and sceptical electorate. The experience of the pre-unification West between 1980 and 1990 suggests that the core parties are unlikely wholly to succeed in the task of social integration. As a result, German electoral politics in the coming years may indeed be characterized, as Padgett (1993) suggested, by *Wende ohne Ende*, a continuous state of change.

7

Austria: From Moderate to Polarized Pluralism?

KURT RICHARD LUTHER

Introduction

For many years, the Austrian party system was exceptionally stable (Luther, 1989). There were two mass parties: the SPÖ (*Sozialistische Partei Österreichs* or Socialist Party of Austria) and the ÖVP (*Österreichische Volkspartei* or Austrian People's Party), which could rely on the uncritical support of their respective encapsulated subcultures and between them attracted 90 per cent or more of the vote. They dominated parliament and until 1966 governed together in a series of grand coalitions. Austria was thus widely regarded as an almost archetypal case of consociational democracy (Lijphart, 1968, 1969; Luther, 1992). Moreover, despite the absence of alternation in power, the high degree of concentration meant that the Austrian party system was often classified as an example of two-partism (Blondel, 1968).

Given his emphasis upon the mechanics, as opposed to merely the format of party systems, Sartori (1976: 185, 190) concluded that Austria had, until 1966, been a case of moderate pluralism. Only once single-party government and alternation started did Austria really fit Sartori's two-party type. Yet three consecutive SPÖ absolute majorities in 1971, 1975 and 1979 indicated a period of 'predominance' (ibid.: 192-201) while in 1983 the party system reverted to moderate pluralism (Müller, 1997). Since then, Austria has witnessed growing dealignment, the emergence of new parties and in particular the dramatic rise of Haider's right-wing populist FPÖ (*Freiheitliche Partei Österreichs* or Austrian Freedom Party).

The emergence of the Austrian parties and party system

The genesis of Austria's party system constitutes a classic example of Lipset and Rokkan's proposition that the parties 'able to establish mass organizations and entrench themselves in the local government structure before the final drive towards maximal mobilization have proved the most viable' since the 'narrowing of the "support market" ... left very few openings for new movements' (1967b: 51). The parties which until recently dominated the post-war Austrian party system are the direct descendants of extra-parliamentary movements formed during the last quarter of the nineteenth century. Each was organized around a more-or-less distinct political sub-culture, or *Lager*,[1] based predominantly within the German-speaking area of the Austro-Hungarian Dual Monarchy. The origins of the ÖVP lie in the clerical and originally vehemently anti-capitalist Christian Social Party (CSP) which emerged to represent the Catholic–conservative subculture. After early successes in Vienna, the party's support came predominantly from Austria's conservative rural peasantry and petite-bourgeoisie. By 1914, however, the CSP had successfully forged ties with aristocratic and business elements and had thus largely been transformed from an 'outsider' party to one identified with the status quo (Boyer, 1981; Diamant, 1960).

The forerunner of today's SPÖ was the anti-clerical Social Democratic and Workers Party (SDAP), formed in 1888/1889 (Brügel, 1922-1925; Kule-mann, 1979; Maderthaner and Müller, 1996). Its leadership contained disproportionately large elements of the assimilated Jewish and secular intelligentsia. The transformation of the initially loosely structured SDAP into Europe's most densely organized party was greatly facilitated by the mass mobilization it achieved in connection with its key role in the struggle for universal male suffrage. The gradual development of the primarily 'externally created' SDAP and CSP into almost archetypal mass parties (Duverger, 1964; Neumann, 1956) also owed much to their extensive networks of auxiliary associations. By the 1920s, both had achieved excep-tionally high levels of organizational density with distinct ideological profiles (Duverger, 1964: 40–60; Simon, 1957; Wandruszka, 1954; but see also Jeffery, 1995).

One measure of their success in narrowing the 'support market' is the extent to which they were able to restrict the growth of the so-called 'Third *Lager*'. This was made up of anti-clerical and anti-socialist Austrians employed mainly in white-collar jobs, or the state bureaucracy. It included non-Jewish elements of the intelligentsia and embraced many of those whose German-national orientation had historically been the most pronounced. It achieved significant levels of political mobilization amongst the student body and was quite well supported among Austria's administrative elite, but was never represented by a single, mass party. Third *Lager* parties had relatively small memberships and were ideologically and organizationally less cohesive. They were thus closer to Duverger's 'cadre party' ideal type (Duverger, 1964: 63-71). Further evidence of the major parties' dominance of the early Austrian party system is the negligible impact upon the SDAP's electorate of the emergence in 1919 of the Communist Party of Austria (*Kommunistische Partei Österreichs*, or KPÖ).

The most salient cleavages underpinning the party system at the 'critical junctures' (Lipset and Rokkan, 1967a) of suffrage expansion were largely mutually reinforcing. Austria's successful Counter-Reformation and its 'National Revolution' had left the Catholic Church closely allied with the Habsburg dynasty which, defeated by Prussia in 1866, had lost its previously dominant position among the community of German states. Accordingly, the clerical versus anti-clerical cleavage saw the CSP and its allied Catholic-conservative *Lager* opposed not only by the anti-clerical socialist camp, but also by the Third *Lager*. The latter's criticism of the Habsburg's multi-national Catholic state was predicated upon anti-clericalism and pan-Germanism. The national revolution had of course also generated centre–periphery cleavages between the German-speaking political and administrative elite of the Dual Monarchy and the national minorities, but since our focus is the German-speaking area which went on to form the Austrian republic, we will not consider this ethnic cleavage further. Second, the cleavage between industrial labour, on the one hand, and farming and enterprise, on the other, found the Socialists defending the interests of the former against the Christian Socials and their German-national allies. Both the religious and the class cleavages contained a regional dimension with the CSP representing the majority of the Catholic rural peasantry and land-owners, while the Socialists were supported by the secular, urban proletariat of above all Vienna. The internal division of the German-national camp on the urban–rural dimension was enshrined in the two main party-political expressions of the Third *Lager*: the predominantly urban Greater German People's Party and the Agrarian League.

The Habsburg monarchy's collapse in 1918 left the Empire's German-speaking rump economically unviable and bereft of a distinctive national identity. All the parties supported the incorporation of 'German Austria' into the German Reich. When the Allies ruled this out, the Socialists and Christian Socials grudgingly co-operated in framing the compromise con-stitution of the First Austrian Republic, the 'state nobody wanted' (Andics, 1968; Tálos *et al.*, 1995). From 1918 to 1920, they collaborated in a grand coalition government, of which the Socialists were the largest party. There-after, however, coalitions were formed exclusively between the Catholic–conservatives and German-nationals. Except in their Viennese municipal stronghold, the Socialists were relegated to the role of permanent opposition, a status underscored by the Marxist Linz programme of 1926.

As the economy worsened, the parties became increasingly radical and conflict escalated. In March 1933, the bourgeois government unconstitu-tionally suspended parliament, thereafter banning the KPÖ and then the Austrian National Socialists. Each of the two main *Lager* had for some time been operating their own militias, between which there were increasingly violent confrontations. In February 1934, these culminated in a short civil war after which the victorious Christian Socials outlawed all Socialist organizations. The bourgeois forces then established a one-party authoritarian dictatorship which lasted until the *Anschluß* of March 1938, when the 'Austro-fascist' state was incorporated into Hitler's Third Reich.

The post-war rebirth of the Austrian party system

The background to the post-war re-establishment of Austria's party system was decidedly inauspicious: the country had experienced over three decades of profound regime discontinuity; its people had manifestly failed to develop a shared national identity capable of bridging the gap between the mutually hostile identities of its polarized political camps (*Lager*) and Austria's political parties had proved unwilling, or unable, to maintain a functioning multi-party system in the face of economic crises and anti-democratic threats. Yet the Second Republic fairly quickly established a stable, two-party system and has, for over 50 years, been characterized by domestic peace and economic prosperity. This was not achieved by a fundamental recasting of governmental institutions. Unlike Germany, Austria re-adopted its ill-fated inter-war constitution. Nor were the key political actors replaced. The establishment of the Second Republic was largely undertaken by the same parties and, indeed, by some of the same individuals that had set up the First. Moreover, though their political ideologies were somewhat attenuated, the post-war *Lager* were fundamentally the same as in the First Republic, as were their party organizations (Wandruszka, 1954; Simon, 1957).

The successful rebirth of the party system has much to do with the altered circumstances of 1945. Defeated Austria was once again in a dire economic situation but, in marked contrast to the punitive reparations imposed after the First World War, the Allies now sought to stimulate reconstruction via the Marshall Plan. Second, the experience of incorporation into Nazi Germany had, for the overwhelming majority of Austrians, discredited pan-Germanism, thus helping prepare the ground for the gradual development of an Austrian national identity (Bruckmüller, 1996). Similarly, the Allied occupation of Austria from 1945 to 1955 generated a common desire to get rid of the foreign forces, thereby enhancing aspirations for independent statehood. Third, Nazism and subsequent Allied occupation also facilitated a narrowing of the party system's ideological spectrum. The weak KPÖ was further delegitimized by the Soviet occupation of eastern Austria until 1955 (and subsequently by communist repression in adjacent Hungary and Czechoslovakia), while the Allies' anti-fascist consensus militated against a revival of the anti-democratic Right. Indeed, for the crucial first four post-war years the Allies permitted only the ÖVP, SPÖ and KPÖ to form. It was not until 1949 that they licensed a Third *Lager* party (the *Verband der Unabhängi-gen* (League of Independents, or VdU), formed in part to appeal to liberals and those not incorporated into the socialist and conservative *Lager*, but mainly to attract former Nazis (Riedlsperger, 1978). Yet by then, the two main *Lager* had for four years been re-establishing their subcultural networks and it is not surprising that their parties succeeded in consolidating a long-lasting duopolistic control over Austria's political 'support market'. Accordingly, the VdU enjoyed only a short existence. It was replaced in 1956 by the FPÖ (Stäuber, 1974) which for the next 30 years was rarely able to obtain the support of more than half of the proportion of the Austrian electorate initially mobilized by the VdU (Luther, 1997a).

Institutional variables

Party competition in the Second Republic has been influenced by a number of interrelated contextual variables. Among the most important of the institutional factors is Austria's proportional electoral system (Müller, 1996). The system in force until 1970 inflated the electoral 'price' of minor parties' seats. Since the small Third *Lager* party was deemed uncoalitionable and the electoral system reproduced at parliamentary level the socio-political stalemate between the two major *Lager*, the electoral system militated in favour of oversized coalitions. The 1970 reforms increased proportionality while the 1992 reform slightly reversed this.

Elections to the 183-seat national parliament now operate according to a modified party list system which provides a fairly proportional outcome. Until 1970, there was an 'effective threshold' of 8.5 per cent which was reduced by the 1992 reforms to 2.6 per cent (Lijphart, 1994: 25–9, 39) despite the introduction of a formal 4 per cent threshold. That is not to deny that the new threshold constitutes a constant concern for the Greens, who in 1995 obtained merely 4.8 per cent of the national vote, and for the Liberal Forum (LiF). An 'internally created' party formed in February 1993 by five MPs who broke away from the FPÖ, the LiF's vote declined from nearly 6 per cent in 1994 to 5.5 per cent in 1995. The hurdle proved insurmountable for an anti-EU protest party which, despite obtaining over 53,000 votes, i.e. twice the average 'price' of the parliamentary parties' seats, failed to gain representation.

Federalism is a second institutional factor impinging upon the operation of the party system. First, the constitutions of seven *Länder* require *Land* governments to be grand coalitions.[2] Parties excluded from national govern-ment thus usually continue to share some of the spoils of office at the *Land* level since, notwithstanding their constitutional weakness, the *Länder* offer considerable scope for the *de facto* exercise of political power (Luther, 1997b).

Moreover, given the territorial concentration of SPÖ and ÖVP support, federalism for many years meant that both major parties had *Länder* in which they exercised a virtual political hegemony (Luther, 1989).

A third institutional factor concerns the (paucity of) constitutional and statutory regulation of Austrian political parties. There is no equivalent of Article 21 of the German Basic Law which requires parties' internal organization to be democratic and which permits anti-democratic parties to be banned. The state's powers to act against neo-Nazi activities have until recently been used very sparingly. However, the 1945 *Verbotsgesetz* designed to combat fascism revivals was amended in 1992, *inter alia* by the introduction of the possibility of shorter sentences, to encourage the authorities to use their powers more frequently in light of a rash of neo-Nazi attacks since 1990.

Only in 1975 was a specific 'Party Law' introduced, Article I of which has constitutional status. To obtain party status under the 1975 law, parties merely have to deposit their statutes with the Ministry of the Interior. Since the law imposes no substantive restrictions on parties but entitles them to benefit from the system of state subsidies with the introduction of which it was primarily concerned, the parties have naturally all complied. The system militates against new parties which, unless and until they overcome the hurdle of parliamentary representation, lack the financial muscle of their established, state-subsidized opponents. Accurate figures on party finances are notoriously difficult to obtain but Austria's parties are probably among the most generously financed in Europe (Sickinger, 1995).

'Cultural' variables shaping the Second Republic's party system

The 'format' and 'mechanics' of post-war party competition have been governed less by formal institutional variables than by the following three inter-related 'cultural' factors. First, Austrian society was, until the 1980s, dominated by the pillarization of, in particular, the socialist and Catholic–conservative subcultures. A myriad of *Lager*-specific occupational, educational and cultural associations ensured that the lives of the members of the subculture could be lived 'from womb-to-tomb' within their own milieu (Diamant, 1958; Lorwin, 1974a; Powell, 1970; Stiefbold, 1975; Houska, 1985; Luther, 1992; Müller, 1992a). Rival '*Lager* mentalities' were characterized by deference, strong partisan attachment and distrust of rival *Lager* (Plasser *et al.*, 1992). Yet pillarization should not be regarded as a socio-political given. Rather, it was successfully promoted and further refined by the major parties which consciously used it to structure the electorate, reducing the electoral potential of other parties and thereby consolidating the party system to their advantage.

Pillarization not only facilitated a very high degree of party-political penetration of Austria's socio-economic system, but also helps explain why Austria has had the highest levels of party membership of any country in the western world (von Beyme, 1985; Katz and Mair, 1992). The SPÖ and ÖVP are extraordinarily successful mass membership parties, or parties of mass integration (Neumann, 1956). Their combined membership until 1990 at least, was over a million, in a total population of under 8 million. For many years, these parties' organizational density (membership as a proportion of voters) was between 25 and 30 per cent. The KPÖ's membership density has consistently been even higher than that of the SPÖ and ÖVP though it soon ceased to be a mass membership party. In 1949, its membership density stood at 70 per cent and it was still some 65 per cent in 1970, albeit of an electorate that had fallen by about 80 per cent. By 1990, the KPÖ had only just under 26,000 voters, but given a membership of *circa* 9,000, its membership density still stood at 35 per cent. By contrast, the membership profile of the FPÖ is more akin to Duverger's cadre party ideal type (1964). The size of the major parties' membership has declined by between a quarter and a third since the peak reached in the 1970s. Conversely, the FPÖ's membership has slowly and steadily increased, albeit from a much lower level (with the exception of the period of the change in leadership from Steger to Haider).

A second 'cultural' factor structuring party competition and arguably the most crucial explanation for the successful re-formation of the post-war Austrian party system, is the essentially accommodative culture of the SPÖ and ÖVP party elites. In 1945, the centrist wings of the two main *Lager* assumed a controlling position in their respective parties. They replaced the confrontational orientation that had characterized most of the First Republic with a commitment to overcome the profound mistrust between the *Lager*. Confrontational political rhetoric was of course not abandoned, especially in the electoral arena where it served to confirm rival '*Lager* mentalities' and ossify pillarized structures (Hölzl, 1974). The *prima facie* paradoxical coexistence–existence of a segmented society, on the one hand, and elite accommodation, on the other, is of course the core characteristic of 'consociational democracy' (Lijphart, 1968, 1969; Luther and Müller, 1992) and the elite's changed orientation has been attributed by some (Lijphart, 1968: 21) to elite political behaviour deliberately designed to counteract disintegrative tendencies in the system. In the Austrian case, this is typically understood to imply that the post-war elite were persuaded of the merits of democratic co-operation by their experience of regime collapse in 1934 and in particular by virtue of their shared political persecution during the Nazi period.

The most frequently cited expression of elite accommodation has been

Austria's propensity for oversized, 'grand' coalitions (Dreijmanis, 1982). Much more pervasive, albeit often less visible and more difficult to quantify, has been *Proporz*, according to which the two dominant parties structured the distribution of the majority of public sector posts and state resources (including access to electronic media) in rough proportion to their relative electoral weight. Largely as a consequence of the nationalization of former Nazi enterprises, the state controlled one of the largest nationalized industry sectors of any western country (Müller, 1985). Accordingly, the parties had enormous scope not only for economic intervention to protect their client groups' jobs, but also to exercise influence over individual appointment decisions. In some areas, *Proporz* meant that each *Lager* received an equal share of resources, or employees, while elsewhere, the principle of segmental autonomy permitted the *Lager* to run organizations independently (Luther, 1992: 72–93). *Proporz* greatly extended the 'reach' of the party system (Luther, 1992), which penetrated the socio-economic realm to an extent comparable only with 'partitocracies' such as Belgium and Italy (Deschouwer *et al.*, 1996). As a system of political patronage, *Proporz* further enhanced the competitive advantage of the two main parties and their associated subcultures by allowing them to act as gatekeepers in the distribution of spoils.

The pervasive system of *Proporz* meant that for many Austrians, party membership was regarded as a prerequisite for access to housing, jobs, licences to trade and other benefits. In a 1980 survey which examined Austrians' perceptions of why people join political parties, 79 per cent said they felt the prospect of career advancement was either a very important, or an important factor, while 72 per cent similarly evaluated the possibility of obtaining housing more easily. Just under half the sample felt an affinity with a party's values to be important and 23 per cent considered it either insignificant, or only slightly relevant (Deisler and Winkler, 1982: 94–8, 237).

The major parties' accommodative orientation also shaped the party system's 'style'. The SPÖ and ÖVP came to share in the promotion of various formative 'founding myths' of the Second Republic, including the propositions that Austria had been 'the first victim of Nazi aggression' and that it had in 1955 freely opted for permanent neutrality (Menasse, 1992). The prevalent decision-making style was consensual and reflected in practices such as mutual veto and log-rolling, as well as in the high proportion of laws passed unanimously (Luther, 1992). Over time, co-operation significantly reduced the ideological distance between the major parties, creating bipartisan agreement on major policy areas.

A final key contextual variable is 'social partnership', Austria's extra-constitutional system of corporatist decision making which has both institutional and behaviourial, or cultural dimensions. Its core focus has been economic and social policy (Gerlich *et al.*, 1985; Gerlich, 1992). The five corporatist interest groups are inextricably linked to one or other of the two main *Lager* and together the corporatist actors came to constitute a sort of shadow government with a significant role in policy implementation. The implications of this system for party competition were profound. Through their organic links to the interest groups, the SPÖ and ÖVP have had privileged access to information and to technical expertise in many respects rivalling that of the state bureaucracy. Moreover, obligatory membership, the interest groups' service provision to their members and their quasi-state role in implementing government policy provided the two main *Lager* with additional opportunities to exercise patronage and thus further enhanced membership incentives. Yet the system of social partnership was, in the long run, to have perverse, or unintended, effects for the ÖVP and SPÖ, whose close association with 'their' interest groups had the capacity to make them 'prisoners' of the latter and thus less flexible than parties not entrenched in the corporatist system.

'Core elements' of the post-war party system

The number and relative size of parties

One of the most distinctive features of Austria's post-war party system has been the domination of the national electoral and parliamentary arenas by two very large parties: the ÖVP and SPÖ. As can be seen in Table 7.1, from 1945 to 1983 their average combined shares of the national vote and of National Council seats were 90.2 and 94 per cent, respectively. Once the new party system had stabilized in 1956, fractionalization remained remarkably low for some 30 years. In the *Bundesrat* (Austria's indirectly elected territorial chamber), concentration was even more pronounced. With the minor exception of the years 1949 to 1955, the *Bundesrat* was from 1945 to 1987 the exclusive preserve of the ÖVP and SPÖ.

Since the mid-1980s, however, the electoral arena has witnessed a growth in the number of parties and a significant narrowing in the disparity between their relative strengths. The logical corollary of Austria's weak electoral system has been an analogous trend in the parliamentary arena. Both changes are captured in the measures of party system fractionalization (F_e and F_p), which rose to their highest ever Second Republic values (0.74) in 1994, before dropping back marginally in 1995 (Table 7.1). Though the procedures governing the appointment of members of the *Bundesrat* are such that changes in voter behaviour are both under-represented and delayed, there have nevertheless been tangible alterations here also. Thus the FPÖ's

Table 7.1 Austrian national election results, 1945–95: votes and seats

Party		1945	1949	1953	1956	1959	1962	1966	1970	1971	1975	1979	1983	1986	1990	1994	1995
SPÖ	(vote)	44.6	38.7	42.1	43.0	44.8	44.0	42.6	48.4	50.0	50.4	51.0	47.6	43.1	42.8	34.9	38.1
	(seats)	76	67	73	74	78	76	74	78	93	93	95	90	80	80	65	71
ÖVP	(vote)	49.8	44.0	41.3	46.0	44.2	45.4	48.3	44.7	43.1	42.9	41.9	43.2	41.3	32.1	27.7	28.3[5]
	(seats)	85	77	74	82	79	81	85	81	80	80	77	81	77	60	52	53[5]
FPÖ (VdU)	(vote)		11.7	10.9	6.5	7.7	7.0	5.4	5.5	5.5	5.4	6.1	5.0	9.7	16.6	22.5	21.9
	(seats)		16	14	6	8	8	6	6	10	10	11	12	18	33[1]	42	40[5]
Greens	(vote)													4.8	4.8	7.3	4.8
	(seats)													8	10	13	9
LiF	(vote)															6.0	5.5
	(seats)														(5)[1]	11	10[5]
Others	(vote)	5.6	5.6	5.7	4.5	3.3	3.5	3.7	1.4	1.4	1.2	1.0	4.1	1.0	3.7	1.6	1.4
	(seats)	4	5	4	3												
Turnout		96.8	96.8	95.8	96.0	94.2	93.8	93.8	91.8	92.4	92.9	92.2	92.6	90.5	86.1	81.9	86.0
SPÖ+ÖVP	vote	94.4	82.8	83.4	89.0	89.0	89.4	90.9	93.1	93.2	93.4	92.9	90.9	84.4	74.9	62.6	66.4
SPÖ+ÖVP	seats	97.6	87.3	89.1	94.5	95.2	95.2	96.4	96.4	94.5	94.5	94.0	93.4	85.8	76.5	63.9	67.8
Fractionalisation[2] (Rae index)	F_e	0.55	0.64	0.64	0.60	0.60	0.59	0.58	0.56	0.56	0.56	0.56	0.58	0.63	0.68	0.74	0.72
	F_p	0.52	0.61	0.60	0.55	0.54	0.54	0.53	0.53	0.55	0.55	0.55	0.56	0.62	0.67	0.74	0.72
Effective no. of parties[3]	N_v	2.22	2.78	2.76	2.48	2.48	2.46	2.39	2.29	2.28	2.26	2.27	2.40	2.72	3.16	3.87	3.59
	N_s	2.09	2.54	2.47	2.22	2.20	2.20	2.14	2.15	2.21	2.21	2.22	2.26	2.63	2.99	3.78	3.51
Net volatility[4]			12.17	4.00	5.69	2.97	1.72	6.24	6.65	2.04	0.42	1.31	4.81	9.95	10.09	15.51	3.88

[1] On 4 February 1993, five of the 33 FPÖ MPs elected in 1990 broke away to form the Liberal Forum.

[2] Own calculations of index of electoral (F_e) and parliamentary (F_p) fractionalisation (Rae 1967).

[3] Own calculations of Laakso and Taagepera's (1979) index of effective number of parties at the level of votes (N_v) and of seats (N_s).

[4] Own calculations of Pedersen (1979: 4) index (i.e. cumulated gains for *all* winning parties standing at the election).

[5] Since 1995, the FPÖ has gained 2 seats, 1 via a LiF defection and 1 from the ÖVP as a result of a re-run ballot in Burgenland.

Source: Bundesministerium für Inneres, 1996.

representation had, by late 1996, increased to 14, reducing the SPÖ and ÖVP's combined share of *Bundesrat* seats from 100 to 78 per cent.

The extent of the overall change to Austria's national party system can perhaps be illustrated most clearly by means of the index of the 'effective number of parties' (see Table 7.1). With the exception of the general elections of 1949 and 1953, when the newly licensed Third *Lager* party (the VdU) succeeded in making a considerable electoral impact, the degree of fractionalization of the Austrian party system was, until the mid-1980s, that of a two-party system. The subsequent sharp rise in fractionalization had, by 1994–95, left Austria with a degree of fractionalization approaching that of a four-party system. In sum, Austria no longer exhibits the extremely high level of concentration so characteristic of its post-war party system.

Ideological distance

The failure of the First Republic was in large part due to the inability (or unwillingness) of the political elite to overcome intense ideological polarization. It is thus not surprising that relations between the Second Republic's encapsulated *Lager* subcultures was initially also characterized by a considerable degree of suspicion, or even outright hostility (Stiefbold, 1975: 141–56, 204–12). The high 'ideological temperature' inherited by the Second Republic's party system was deliberately sustained in the electoral arena by 'propaganda wars' (Hölzl, 1974) in which the parties sought to convince their followers that if they failed to vote for their *Lager* party in sufficient numbers, they ran the risk of their opponents obtaining an absolute majority and putting an end to democracy. The ÖVP claimed the Socialists might erect a 'red dictatorship' akin to the 'people's democracies' already installed in nearby eastern Europe. For its part, the SPÖ reminded its voters of the role the bourgeois parties had played in the collapse of democracy during the inter-war years and suggested that without the Socialists' moderating influence, an ÖVP government would, for example, scrap workers' welfare benefits and pensions. Both major parties restricted their stated electoral goal to achieving a balance of power, accusing their opponents of secretly harbouring the dangerous and inherently undemocratic ambition of obtaining an absolute parliamentary majority and forming a single-party government. Meanwhile, the Third *Lager* accused both the SPÖ and ÖVP of abusing power for party-political ends and was in turn dismissed by its opponents as little more than a bunch of inveterate Nazis. Writing of Austrian electoral campaigns from 1945 to 1971, Hölzl (1974: 9–14) concluded that for nearly a quarter of a century, the Second Republic's general elections had constituted 'decisions made in, or partly out of, fear'.

This type of ideological polarization and the profoundly negative campaigning it generated can be regarded as a core element of the first two decades or so of the Second Republic, but its credibility was even then being undermined by political practice. In the first place, despite their many deficiencies, the series of grand coalition governments that ruled Austria from 1945 to 1966 gave a lie to the proposition that the rival *Lager* could not be trusted. Notwithstanding their electoral rhetoric, the two major parties had manifestly not only developed a largely bipartisan approach to a range of key foreign and domestic policies, but had established consensual mechanisms such as social partnership for tackling issues over which they did not agree. In other words, ideological polarization in the electoral arena had not prevented the development of both substantive and procedural consensus in government. Moreover, from 1966 onwards, Austria was ruled by a series of single-party governments (ÖVP from 1966–70 and SPÖ from 1970–83), none of which posed the predicted threat to the maintenance of democracy.

Second, the decline of ideological polarization was also reflected in change to the parties' programmatic profiles. Thus Pelinka and Welan (1971: 285) argued that in respect of the three historically most emotive and divisive issues (clericalism; attitude to democracy; and the socio-economic, or property question), the major parties' programmes were characterized by 'a preponderance of consensus over competition'. That development was later confirmed not only by other qualitative studies, (Kadan and Pelinka, 1979: 62–74), but also by more recent quantitative approaches (Horner, 1987, 1997; Müller *et al.*, 1995). At the risk of oversimplification, one can identify three stages in the development of ideological polarization within the Second Republic's party system.

The first covers the period up to the mid-1960s when the party system was characterized by polarized ideological rhetoric which, with few exceptions, was not, however, reflected in political practice. By the end of this first period, the two major parties' programmes had moved much closer in respect of the traditional socio-economic Left–Right dimension and thereafter continued to shadow each other, whilst the FPÖ's ideological profile meant that it was largely considered to be beyond the pale. During the second stage, from the late 1960s to the early 1980s, emotionally less charged issues related to modernization and value change gradually became the main conflict dimension of the party system. For their part, the leaders of the Third *Lager* initiated a deliberate change in their ideological profile from that of a backward-looking party, emphasizing protest and German-nationalism, towards gradual liberalization, albeit of a distinctly conservative variety (Luther, 1987, 1996a, 1996b). The third stage covers the period since the Greens' entry into parliament in 1983 and Haider's assumption of the leadership of the FPÖ in 1986. It has witnessed the emergence onto the political agenda of new and in part very divisive issues, including immigration, internal and external security, European integration, privatization and deregulation as well as issues connected with the financial viability of the existing welfare state arrangements. Many of these issues challenge core elements of the major parties' policy consensus and thus help explain why governing capacity has become a key conflict dimension (Müller, Philipp and Jenny 1995: 146–61). Second, the Greens' 'postmaterialist' agenda has not only enhanced the salience of issues such as the environment, gender and democratization, but also often makes it difficult to locate parties on a simple Left–Right ideological continuum. Third, much of the ideological conflict between the electorally now much weaker 'major' parties and the opposition parties relates to what Dahl (1966: 341–4) would term structural as opposed to policy-oriented opposition. Many of the established parameters of party competition (e.g. mutual veto, social partnership and *Proporz*) are being subjected to radical attack, especially from Haider's FPÖ, but also – albeit from a different perspective and in different language – from the Greens. Finally, the nature of political discourse in the electoral and parliamentary arenas has again become much more polarized.

Movements in party support

As a subculturally encapsulated polity with a pronounced '*Lager* mentality', Austria for many years constituted a classic example of 'frozen' cleavages. We lack survey data from the first two post-war decades, but other evidence (Simon, 1957; Blecha *et al.*, 1964; Engelmann and Schwartz, 1974; Haerpfer, 1985; Haerpfer and Gehmacher, 1984) strongly suggests that until the early 1980s the overwhelming majority of Austrian voters were extremely loyal, with their voting behaviour to a very large extent predicated upon the traditional cleavages of class and religion. In 1969, for example, these still accounted for 46 and 36 per cent, respectively, of variation in voter behaviour (Haerpfer, 1983: 134).

Since the 1970s, however, Austria has experienced a process of depillarization, caused variously by socio-economic factors such as Austria's changing occupational structure; urbanization; increasing geographical and social mobility; secularization and rising levels of education. Together, these have significantly reduced subcultural encapsulation. Between 1972 and 1990, the proportion of SPÖ and ÖVP adherents living in party-politically consonant social networks declined from 86 to 57 and from 78 to 48 per cent, respectively (Plasser, Ulram and Grausgruber, 1992: 23). Changes to the structure of political communication also fostered depillarization as the growing salience of electronic media was accompanied by a dramatic fall in the combined share of total Austrian newspaper circulation held by SPÖ and ÖVP party newspapers, from 39 per cent in 1952 to only 9 per cent in 1988 (Müller, 1992a: 54–7).

The political consequences of depillarization were initially confined mainly to attitudinal change. For example, between 1954 and 1990, partisanship among SPÖ and ÖVP adherents fell from 81 to 43 per cent and 82 to 47 per cent, respectively, while from 1969 to 1990, uncritical party support in the population as a whole declined from 65 to 34 per cent (Plasser *et al.*, 1992: 25–8). The proportion of party identifiers dropped from 73 per cent in 1954 to 44 per cent in 1994 (Ulram, 1997: 517). Meanwhile, dissatisfaction with political parties increased and has in part been reflected in the growth in both postmaterialist and more chauvinistic, or authoritarian, orientations (Plasser and Ulram, 1982; Deisler and Winkler, 1982; Ulram, 1990; Plasser and Ulram, 1991; Müller *et al.*, 1995). In due course, depillarization reduced the efficacy of the major *Lager* parties' two traditional mobilizing techniques. In 1972, 59 per cent of respondents had agreed that 'if you have a particular ideology, there is only one party you can vote for and you must stick with it'. By 1990, after two decades of de-ideologization by the SPÖ and ÖVP, only 37 per cent did so (Plasser *et al.*, 1992: 24). Material incentives based upon individual and group patronage continued to work for some time, but by the mid-1980s at the latest, they too were considerably weakened. On the one hand, public sector contraction and the state's gradual withdrawal from the socio-economic sphere reduced patronage opportunities. On the other hand, patronage was increasingly regarded as illegitimate, in part because of a series of corruption cases, but also because of value change and critical reporting in the more independent print and electronic media. Accordingly, the major parties are often caught in a cleft stick: using patronage to mobilize their traditional supporters frequently results in alienating the electorally increasingly significant proportion of the population which lacks *Lager* partisanship.

Though depillarization gradually expanded the previously extremely small pool of floating voters, for most of the 1970s there was not only little change in parties' electoral fortunes, but also the unprecedented sight of a party obtaining a plurality of votes and seats. This apparent contradiction is not as great as it seems. The SPÖ's electoral majority was possible only because of the willingness of the predominantly middle-class, non-aligned, personality- and issue-oriented voters to vote SPÖ. The unifying elements of the SPÖ's 'electoral coalition' during the 1970s were the personality of Kreisky and the appeal of a social-liberal consensus based upon 'economic growth, full employment and its guarantee of stable prices and a tightening of the social welfare net' (Birk and Traar, 1987: 55). In short, the electoral impact of depillarization was merely postponed by the success of the Kreisky-led SPÖ in more than compensating for the decline in its core vote by attracting and retaining the floating voters. From 1971 to 1979, the SPÖ thus enjoyed three consecutive absolute majorities and there was little net volatility, since individual volatility flows largely tended to cancel each other out.

Accordingly, until the early 1980s, the Second Republic's party system remained characterized by very low levels of net movement in party support. Average net electoral volatility between 1953 and 1979 was merely 3.49 per cent and in 1975 dropped as low as 0.42 per cent (see Table 7.1). Even the relatively high 1966 and 1970 levels (which presaged single-party ÖVP and SPÖ governments, respectively) are low by international standards (Pedersen, 1979; Bartolini and Mair, 1990). Significant change at the aggregate level only really started in 1983, with the entry of the Greens onto the political scene, and grew especially from 1986 when, under the leadership of Jörg Haider, the revitalised FPÖ experienced the first of three dramatic electoral victories (Table 7.1). Though volatility declined again in 1995, it is too early to assume that the period of high volatility is at an end.

Even if it were, depillarization and three consecutive elections with unusually high levels of aggregate volatility have left their mark upon party support.[3] First, even comparing the 1995 election results with 1986 rather than with earlier elections, it is clear that there have been fundamental changes in the party-political profile of different social groups. Some of the ÖVP's greatest losses have been among its traditional core voters: the self-employed (−21 per cent); farmers (−19 per cent); and unemployed women (−18 per cent). The only social group among which it still retains majority support is farmers, who account for only 7 per cent of the working population. The SPÖ too has suffered especially badly in its socio-economic heartland. For many years, it had obtained over two-thirds of the blue-collar vote and even in 1986, its support amongst skilled workers lay at 56 per cent and amongst the unskilled or semi-skilled at 59 per cent. In 1995, however, the SPÖ was only able to muster the votes of 40 and 43 per cent, respectively. For its part, the FPÖ has increased its support the most among blue-collar voters of both categories and among the youngest age cohort. A very worrying development for both the SPÖ and ÖVP is the ageing of their electorates.

The capacity of socio-structural variables to predict voter choice has been much reduced. To be sure, religiosity is still important, with 59 per cent of all religiously active Austrians voting for the ÖVP. Similarly, union membership predisposes voters to support the SPÖ, as does living in a blue-collar household (Plasser et al., 1995: 45). Yet between 1969 and 1995, the Alford index of class voting declined from 26 to a mere 9 points. Applied to the FPÖ, the index registers 12 (Plasser, Ulram and Seeber, 1996: 183). Indeed, if one looks not at the political profile of socio-demographic groups, but at the socio-demographic profile of party support, one finds a very interesting picture. Blue-collar voters now comprise only 21 per cent of the SPÖ's electorate, while they make up 35 per cent of the Austrians who cast their vote for the FPÖ. In other words, the SPÖ now shares with the FPÖ its traditional role as *the* party of the working class. Though Green voters tend to be slightly younger than Liberal Forum voters, there are significant similarities in the profile of the electorate of the Greens and the LiF. Both parties recruit especially well among younger age cohorts, women, persons with low levels of religiosity, higher levels of education and white-collar employees, who make up a third of each party's electorate.

To focus exclusively on changes to the sociology and volatility of the Austrian electorate would be to neglect another indicator of dealignment: the increase in non-voting and in spoilt ballots. Until the late 1980s, turnout remained high by international standards, never falling below 90.5 per cent. Since then, non-voting has increased, reaching over 18 per cent in 1994. If one adds the voters who spoiled their ballots, one finds that approximately 20 per cent of the Austrian electorate failed to cast a valid vote.

To conclude, the significant shifts in party support outlined in this section have had important effects on the structure of party competition. The previously small FPÖ has attained a level of electoral support not much lower than that enjoyed by the SPÖ and ÖVP and party system concentration has thus declined greatly. Second, new parties have emerged and though they are fishing in the same relatively small (albeit growing) segment of the electoral pool, both the Greens and the LiF appear to have established themselves in the party system. Third, as electoral outcomes have become less predictable, the parties have invested more resources in campaigning which has tended to become increasingly candidate-centred. Fourth, substantial changes have occurred in the socio-demographic composition of the three traditional parties' electorates which is already having a significant knock-on effect on their programmatic profile. For example, the FPÖ has, in the 1990s, repeatedly sought to re-define its ideology to reflect its changed electorate. The most recent change, in 1997, and for a traditionally anti-clerical party perhaps the most surprising, has been the FPÖ's assertion that it is now a party not only of the workers, but also of Christian values. Fifth, even if volatility were to revert to its previously very low level, three successive elections with unusually high levels of volatility (1986–94) mean Austria is unlikely to resume the pattern of party support typical of the period up to the 1970s. For a start, the SPÖ and ÖVP's electoral dominance is unlikely to return. Moreover, the parties' support is likely to remain precarious since the cumulative effect of a succession of highly volatile elections has been an electorate that is accustomed to changing its vote and is therefore less predictable. Finally, there has been a dealignment in party support and some factors (e.g. public versus private sector employment (Plasser, Ulram and Ogris, 1996: 190–2) seem to have become more important as determinants of voting behaviour. It is, however, premature to speak of a realigned party system since it has not yet proved possible to identify a model that adequately explains contemporary voting behaviour (Plasser and Seeber, 1995).

Government opposition relations

Government office is arguably the prime goal pursued by political parties, so an assessment of the structure of competition for office should offer valuable insights into the nature of a party system. Table 7.2 details the duration and party composition of all post-war Austrian governments. It also contains information on the three aspects of the government formation process which Mair (1996) has argued together offer a useful indication of the extent to which the structure of party competition is open or closed, namely, alternation, innovation and access.

The only example of wholesale alternation is the replacement of single-party ÖVP rule by a single-party SPÖ government in 1970. Leaving aside the KPÖ's departure from Figl's first cabinet in 1947, there have been only three cases of partial alternation: 1966, when the ÖVP–SPÖ Grand Coalition was replaced by a one-party ÖVP government; 1983, when the SPÖ government was extended to include the FPÖ; and finally 1987 when, in response to Haider's election as leader of the FPÖ, the SPÖ called a snap election which led to the current sequence of SPÖ–ÖVP coalitions. Overall, the degree of alternation in the post-war party system has thus been low.

The same can be said in respect of innovation. For over 29 of the 50 years since November 1947, when the first ÖVP–SPÖ Grand Coalition government was sworn in, Austria has been ruled by this formula. The elections of 1966 and 1970 produced two consecutive innovative governmental formulae: ÖVP and SPÖ single-party governments, respectively. In view of the legacy of mutual suspicion inherited from the First Republic, these were important innovations, demonstrating that both parties could be trusted to rule alone. The only other innovation has been the SPÖ–FPÖ coalition of 1983–86. Though short-lived, it may well prove to have (had) a greater long-term influence upon the party system than has hitherto been assumed, in that, as Mair (1996: 104) has argued, 'a shift in the range of governing options' may act to 'undermine established preferences and promote instability' in the party system.

If one considers the question of access to government, one finds a very uneven picture. The most impressive record is that of the SPÖ which has

Table 7.2 Government composition in Austria, 1945–97[1]

Cabinet	Date in	Duration (years)	Party composition (chancellor party named first)	Structure of competition[2]		
				Alt	Invtn	Access
Renner	27.04.45	0.6	SPÖ-ÖVP-KPÖ			
Figl (I)	**20.12.45**	**1.9**	**ÖVP-SPÖ-KPÖ**			**0**
Figl (II)	20.11.47	2.0	ÖVP-SPÖ	p	I	3
Figl (III)	**08.11.49**	**3.4**	**ÖVP-SPÖ**	N		**3, 4**
Raab (I)	02.04.53	3.2	ÖVP-SPÖ	n		3, 4
Raab (II)	**29.06.56**	**3.0**	**ÖVP-SPÖ**	N		**3, 4**
Raab (III)	**16.07.59**	**1.7**	**ÖVP-SPÖ**	N		**4**
Gorbach (I)	11.04.61	2.0	ÖVP-SPÖ	n		4
Gorbach (II)	**27.03.63**	**1.0**	**ÖVP-SPÖ**	N		**4**
Klaus (I)	02.04.64	2.0	ÖVP-SPÖ	n		4
Klaus (II)	**19.04.66**	**4.0**	**ÖVP**	P	I	**1, 4**
Kreisky (I)	**21.04.70**	**1.5**	**SPÖ**	W	I	**2,**
Kreisky (II)	**04.11.71**	**4.0**	**SPÖ**	N		**2, 4**
Kreisky (III)	**28.10.75**	**3.6**	**SPÖ**	N		**2, 4**
Kreisky (IV)	**05.06.79**	**4.0**	**SPÖ**	N		**2, 4**
Sinowatz	**24.05.83**	**3.0**	**SPÖ-FPÖ**	P	I	**2**
Vranitzky (I)	16.06.86	0.6	SPÖ-FPÖ	n		2
Vranitzky (II)	**21.01.87**	**4.0**	**SPÖ-ÖVP**	P		**4, 5**
Vranitzky (III)	**17.12.90**	**4.0**	**SPÖ-ÖVP**	N		**4, 5**[3]
Vranitzky (IV)	**29.11.94**	**1.3**	**SPÖ-ÖVP**	N		**4, 5, 6**
Vranitzky (V)	**12.03.96**	**0.9**	**SPÖ-ÖVP**	N		**4, 5, 6**
Klima	28.01.97		SPÖ-ÖVP	n		4, 5, 6

[1] To define a cabinet, the criteria 'same chancellor', 'same party composition' and 'between parliamentary elections' were used. Information for parliamentary election years are in bold.

[2] Own application of Mair's (1996) criteria to all governments except Renner's Provisional Government, which preceded the first parliamentary elections of November 1945. Alternation (Alt) relates to change in the party composition of governments. There can be wholesale (w), partial (p), or no (n) alternation. Alternation following parliamentary elections is indicated in upper case. Innovation (Invtn) denotes governments comprising previously unknown party combinations. Access relates to opportunity to participate in government and is indicated here by its obverse: existing parliamentary parties *excluded* from government. (1 = SPÖ; 2 = ÖVP; 3 = KPÖ; 4 = VdU/FPÖ; 5 = Greens; 6 = LiF).

[3] From 4.2.1993, when 5 FPÖ MPs broke away to form the LiF, the excluded parties were 4, 5 and 6.

been in government for over 90 per cent of the post-war period and in terms of office-holding is thus one of Western Europe's most successful parties. Its only experience in opposition was from 1966 to 1970, since when it has continuously held the chancellorship, ruling alone from 1970 to 1983. The ÖVP's record is more modest, though still good: the party has been in government for over two-thirds of the post-war period. Between December 1945 and April 1966, it held the chancellorship and was the dominant Grand Coalition party. From 1966 to 1970, it even succeeded in forming

Austria's first single-party government. Since 1970, however, its position has been less exalted. It languished in opposition for 17 years and since 1987 has had to content itself with the role of junior government party.

The other parties have had little or no government experience. The KPÖ was in parliament from 1945 to 1959, but only held government seats during the rather unusual period up to November 1947. For their part, Third *Lager* parties have been excluded from government for all but 3.6 of the 48 years since the VdU's admission to the party system in 1949. The FPÖ has been an excluded, or isolated party for most of its existence. Since 1986, the number of parliamentary parties has increased from three to five, while the SPÖ and ÖVP's combined share of parliamentary seats dropped from 91 per cent in 1983 to as low as 63 per cent in 1994. Accordingly, since 1986, the 'Grand Coalition' has not been nearly as grand as it was before 1966. Its relationship to the opposition has changed in other significant ways also. It now faces not one, but three opposition parties: two are new and the parliamentary strength of the third is not far behind that of the junior governing party. Moreover, as mentioned above, the opposition parties devote considerable attention to 'structural' opposition. Finally, the government is faced with bilateral opposition, the implications of which will be returned to below.

To summarize, with the exception of the 1983–86 SPÖ–FPÖ coalition, the Second Republic's governmental arena has, since 1947, remained the exclusive preserve of the SPÖ and ÖVP. With one exception, alternation has been at best partial, but usually non-existent, whilst innovation too has been limited. In short, a relatively closed structure of competition for office has been and remains a 'core element' of the post-war party system. In view of the partial but profound changes Austria has of late experienced in the number and relative size of parties, in ideological polarization and in its traditionally hyperstable pattern of party support, it is perhaps surprising that the number of parties enjoying access to government has not increased. To be sure, the Liberal Forum has from its inception been regarded as a potential governing party and the Greens have, since the early 1990s, also emphasized their willingness to assume government responsibility. Yet, both have to date remained in opposition, as has Haider's FPÖ. Though this may be regarded as a measure of the success of the SPÖ and ÖVP in resisting pressure for change, it is unclear how long it will prove possible for them to keep a lid on the head of steam that has been building up since the mid-1980s.

The site of decisive encounters

As Dahl (1966: 338–41) has pointed out, parties can compete in a number of different arenas, or 'sites'. In some party systems, there may be sites that are 'decisive', in that 'victory in that encounter entails a rather high probability of victory in the rest' (ibid.: 338). Austria's electoral arena has of course always been an important site of encounters between parties, but during the period of Grand Coalition government (1945–66) it was not decisive. Far more important was the government arena where the two dominant parties competed to determine government policy. Indeed, Engelmann (1966) concluded of this period that the government arena was not only the site of government policy-making ('the pooling of government'), but also the main location for opposition to government policy ('the pooling of opposition').

Yet many of the key encounters determining government policy were made not in the cabinet itself, but in extra-constitutional fora. One was the coalition committee, made up of the ten or so most powerful members of the political elite of both *Lager*, only a few of whom held seats in cabinet (Rudzio, 1971). A second was the corporate arena, where the principle of mutual veto had traditionally obtained (Gerlich, Grande and Müller, 1985). It became increasingly important from the late 1950s and in respect of at least economic and social policy, it constituted the 'site of decisive encounters'. Through 'their' interest groups, the consent of the two main *Lager* parties thus continued to be indispensable for decision-making, regardless of whether they were in government. A fifth site in which the two major parties competed for power and influence was the bureaucratic arena. Since 1967, elections have regularly been held for civil servants' representatives and they clearly demonstrate both the extent of party-political activity within the state bureaucracy and the party-political orientation of the different sections of the state apparatus (Luther, 1992: 88–91). Through their influence in the bureaucratic arena and their 'osmotic relationship' to the main interest groups which transferred 'to themselves the regulatory functions of the welfare state' (Secher, 1960: 901), the SPÖ and ÖVP acted as gatekeepers for a wide range of other state resources. The two major Austrian parties thus exercised influence not only in all areas of public life, but also penetrated deeply into 'civil society'.

The logical corollary of this system was that constitutional structures such as cabinet and parliament became 'merely formal instrumentalities of party and group power' (Secher, 1960: 906). The National Council was largely relegated to the role of a rubber stamp for decisions formally approved in cabinet but in reality hammered out in the coalition committee, or in the structures of social partnership. The role of MPs was to be disciplined lobby-fodder, dutifully passing Acts handed down to them. Indeed, until as recently as the 1983–86 parliament which faced an SPÖ–FPÖ government controlling merely 55 per cent of parliamentary seats, 70 to 80 per cent of legislation was passed unanimously.

Since the late 1960s, however, there have been significant changes in the scope of political parties and in the relative salience of the various sites of party competition. At the risk of oversimplification, one can identify two phases. The first lasted until the late 1980s and covers the period of one-party government and the SPÖ–FPÖ coalition. This is a period when the electoral arena became more decisive, since electoral outcomes determined the party composition of government. On the other hand, the influence of the corporate arena also grew, which led to the somewhat paradoxical result that while grand coalition government came to an end, policy-making was still determined by accommodation between the two major *Lager* parties and their associated interest groups. Consequently, in many ways, grand coalition government was transferred from the government to the corporate arena.

The salience of Austria's corporate arena has declined since the late 1980s (Gerlich, 1992). Moreover, though Austria has been ruled by SPÖ–ÖVP grand coalition governments since 1987, the role of the coalition committee is much less influential than it once was. There has been a relative strengthening of the government arena, where the cabinet has 'increasingly become a force in its own right' (Müller, 1992b: 111). On the other hand, parliament has also reasserted itself. Not only has unanimous voting dramatically declined, but parliament is now far more active. MPs make much more frequent use of procedures such as question time, written questions and committees of investigation. This is in part a consequence of the growing strength of the opposition parties which, until the mid-1980s, rarely accounted for more than about 5 per cent of parliamentary seats, but now hold about a third (see Table 7.1). There has also been a sharp decline, even within the governing parties' parliamentary caucuses, in the hitherto exceptionally high levels of party discipline. In short, there has been a reassertion of formal constitutional structures. Yet since both the electoral and parliamentary arenas have become less predictable, party government has become more vulnerable.

Conclusion: polarization and normalization?

By the late 1980s, the Austrian party system had experienced change in many of its core features, but as yet these amounted only to 'restricted', rather than to 'general' change or 'transformation' (Luther, 1989: 24). This chapter has documented significant further change in all the core features of

Austria's post-war party system. With the exception of the national governmental arena, the SPÖ and ÖVP have lost their long-standing predominance. Instead, there are three nearly equal-sized parties and two minor parties. Indeed, the FPÖ's rapid growth continues to pose a significant threat to the ÖVP's position as the second-largest party, whilst Haider's structural opposition challenges Austria's traditionally consensual style of party interaction. It therefore now seems appropriate to conclude that the Austrian party system has undergone 'general change', even if a 'new equilibrium' (Smith, 1989a: 354) has still not been established.

Sartori's typology (1976: 131–216) was useful in classifying the party system up to 1966, not least because it highlighted the fact that, despite its two-party format, the mechanics of party competition were those of moderate pluralism. It also permitted one to see how, after a period of SPÖ predominance from 1971 to 1983, the installation of the SPÖ–FPÖ coalition and the subsequent readoption of SPÖ–ÖVP 'grand coalition' government in 1987 marked a return to moderate pluralism (Luther, 1992; Müller, 1997). However, the changes identified in this chapter suggest the Austrian party system has since entered a period of transition. It has moved away from moderate pluralism, but its current type and trajectory are not yet clear. It exhibits many of the characteristics of Sartori's 'polarized pluralism' type (1976: 131–45). First, with the entry onto the political stage of the LiF in 1993, Austria's party system at least reached (if not crossed) Sartori's numerical threshold for polarized pluralism of '*around* five (or six)' parties (ibid.: 131ff.). Second, the FPÖ has considerable 'blackmail potential', contributes significantly to polarizing political debate and greatly influences the strategy of the other parties. Since it undeniably articulates 'opposition of principle' and has a '*delegitimizing impact*' on the regime, it clearly meets Sartori's (1976: 132ff.) general criterion of an 'anti-system' party. Third, the governing parties are faced with 'bilateral opposition' from the Greens on the left and the FPÖ on the right. Fourth, the centre of the political spectrum is occupied and competition is thus arguably no longer bipolar, but multipolar. Finally, from the mid-1980s, Austria witnessed a 'persistent loss of *votes* to the extremes' and thus an 'enfeeblement of the centre' (1976: 136).

Admittedly, there are respects in which the Austrian party system does not fit the polarized pluralism type. The governing parties may well be faced by bilateral opposition, but Austria cannot be said to have 'a maximum spread of opinion' (Sartori, 1976: 135); there is no 'politics of outbidding', nor is there evidence for the existence of both an 'irresponsible opposition' and 'semi-responsible' governing-oriented parties (Sartori, 1976: 138f). The emergence in 1993 of the centre-oriented LiF and the slight decline in 1995 in the vote for the 'extremes' of FPÖ and Greens suggest that centrifugal competition may be weakening. Indeed, the Greens are hardly an anti-system party, but are on the contrary increasingly regarded as a potential governing party. Notwithstanding these caveats, however, there is much to be said for the proposition that the Austrian party system has at least made significant moves in the direction of polarized pluralism.

When considering the factors that cause (or prevent) party system change, it is important, however, to emphasize not only variables exogenous to the party system (e.g. institutional factors, socio-cultural and economic change and changes in the international environment), but also endogenous factors such as the role of the parties and political actors themselves. For they can and do (at least in part) shape their own environment and effect their own futures through their behaviour and the strategic choices they make. Thus the decline of the major parties can to some extent be regarded as a consequence of the behaviour of their own elites. There has been a funda- mental change in the degree of popular acceptance of the traditional methods used by parties to structure and mobilize their support, as well as of the traditional style of political decision-making. Some of the parties' strat- egies and behaviours have thus had a perverse, or unintended effect and are in part responsible for the predicament in which the traditional parties find themselves. Conversely, the success of, in particular, the FPÖ has much to do with Haider's not inconsiderable political skills.

Since the 1970s, there have also been significant changes in the character of the party-political elites, among whom traditional ideological orientations have largely given way to a more technocratic approach. In part, this is a consequence of generational change, as politicians with personal experience of Austro-fascism and Nazi occupation were gradually replaced. In the case of the ÖVP and in particular the SPÖ, it is also related to the fact that these parties have been in government so long. The resulting 'governmentness' of the two major parties has contributed to alienating the party elite from their grass roots, which has further undermined already weakening *Lager* loy- alties. It is among the political elites of the opposition parties that the greatest changes are apparent, however. The Greens (at least initially) brought an unconventional approach to the political process; they emphasized matters such as the environment and gender equality rather than *Lager* politics; engaged in direct action and included within their ranks a relatively large proportion of women. The political elite of the LiF is certainly much more conventional in its background and style. However, the LiF's location on the political spectrum opens up a hitherto inconceivable range of coalition permutations that offer the opportunity for Haider's political isolation to be extended (Luther, 1995). The greatest change in Austria's party-political elite has of course been in the FPÖ. Since the period of Steger's leadership (1980–86), when technocracy and careerist ambitions greatly shaped the behaviour of the party elite (Luther, 1996a, 1996b), Haider has eschewed consensual conventions and pursued an aggressive style that challenges most of the fundamental features of the post-war party system. Moreover, the loyalty of the FPÖ party elite is oriented less to the party as such than to Haider himself, to whom most directly owe their positions.

Electorally, the FPÖ has been by far the most successful of Europe's new breed of right-wing protest parties. It has exercised a not inconsiderable indirect influence upon the policy of the governing parties which have sought to steal its thunder on issues such as immigration. However, electoral success does not necessarily translate into government participation, at least not unless a party wins an absolute majority. Since the FPÖ is highly unlikely to be able to do so, its prospects of entering government are dependent upon it finding other parties willing and able to enter into coalition with it.

The SPÖ and ÖVP's deliberate strategy of isolating the FPÖ from the national governmental arena well illustrates the extent to which political actors can influence the nature of the party system. Though the two parties have become more vulnerable in the electoral and parliamentary arenas where competition has taken on a new significance and a new edge, they have so far succeeded in excluding Haider from national government. This may be regarded as refusing to accommodate the electorate's expressed preference for change and thus as merely increasing public resentment at the traditional elite's unresponsiveness. However, if we accept Mair's (1996) proposition that change in the structure of competition for government may well serve to further destabilize a party system, then the strategy of exclusion may well prove to be the SPÖ and ÖVP's best hope of avoiding even more radical change to the party system.

Whichever interpretation proves to be correct, it is important to stress that the changes the Austrian party system has undergone since the mid-1980s (and in particular the rise of Haider's populist FPÖ) should not necessarily be regarded as pathological. Indeed, they can in some respects be regarded as a 'normalization' of the party system, inasmuch as some of the Austrian exceptionalism (shared in part with other 'consociational' countries (Luther and Deschouwer, 1998)) has receded. Austria has undergone a gradual process of depillarization and depoliticization of civil society. New party actors have emerged in the electoral and parliamentary arenas and there has been a significant strengthening of opposition parties not based on seg- mented subcultures. In turn, the 'site of decisive encounters' has started to shift from extra-constitutional structures such as Austria's corporate system of Social Partnership towards formal institutions such as government and parliament where party interaction is both more competitive and less predictable.

However, as is clear from the other contributions to this volume, analo- gous developments are to be found in a range of West European democracies.

Accordingly, though there has since the mid-1980s without doubt been considerable change in respect of the format and mechanics of many arenas of the Austrian party system, other West European party systems have themselves not remained still. Put another way, the notional West European 'norm' to which Austria has apparently been moving has itself shifted, with the result that, notwithstanding the change that has occurred during this period, the Austrian party system remains in many respects quite distinctive.

Notes

1. The term *Lager* denotes an (armed) camp, a not altogether inappropriate term, given the parties' inter-war establishment of armed para-military organizations. The originator of the '*Lager* theory' is Wandruszka, who argued one could justifiably speak of a 'natural or divinely-ordained tripartite division of Austria' into three *Lager* (1954: 291).
2. Since this chapter was written, one of the seven (Salzburg) has started the process necessary to end this requirement and other *Länder* may well follow suit. It is speculated that this change may be motivated in large measure by a desire to exclude the FPÖ from *Land* governments, in each of which it is currently still represented.
3. Unless indicated otherwise, the data on the voting profile of selected socio-demographic groups and on the social structure of the parties' electorates provided in this paragraph and the next derive from Plasser and Ulram (1988: 85) and Plasser *et al.* (1995: 41). See also Luther and Deschouwer (1998) for fuller details.

8

Sweden: A Mild Case of 'Electoral Instability Syndrome'?

DAVID ARTER

Introduction

The Swedish five-party system succumbed only gradually to the symptoms of 'electoral instability syndrome'. For a long time, the patient appeared relatively healthy and did not run the sort of electoral fever which had led in Denmark and Norway, in 1973, to the fragmentation of existing parties and the creation of entirely new ones. What was striking was the apparently *high volatility containment threshold* of the Swedish party system. The basic configuration of two left-wing parties comprising a large social democratic party and a small communist grouping, plus three non-socialist parties, the Agrarian-Centre, Liberals and Moderates (conservatives), on the Centre–Right, had remained unchanged for 70 years. It was not until 1988 that a new party, the Greens, appeared on the parliamentary scene. Three years later, two other newcomers, the Christian Democrats and New Democrats, cleared the 4 per cent electoral threshold and gained *Riksdag* (parliamentary) representation.

However, having fought the 'virus' for so long, a resistance was apparently built up and the Swedish party system developed relatively mild symptoms of the disease. By 1994, one of the new parties had disintegrated and the other returned to parliament by the merest whisker. Moreover, having sunk, in 1991, to its lowest point since 1928, the social democratic party returned to near its post-war average with 45.2 per cent of the vote three years later.

From when to when? A time frame for analysing party system change

According to Gordon Smith, there are no ready ways of establishing criteria for assessing change in party systems. The heart of the problem is to resolve the question of 'from what to what', to decide what the essential features of the system are in the first place before proceeding to see what has changed and by how much (Smith, 1989b: 167). Given the preponderance of analyses with conclusions (or at least speculations) based on developments at the most recent general election, the prior question would appear to be '*from when to when?*' Clearly, there is the need to set a study of party system change in an appropriate time-frame. The focus of this chapter will be on developments in the eight *Riksdag* elections between 1973–94. There are several reasons for the choice of 1973.

First, it facilitates comparisons with developments in the other Nordic states since the 'earthquake elections' in that year in Norway and Denmark appeared to signal the breaking of the party system mould, with splits in existing parties and the emergence of wholly new ones. Second, although the shift to unicameralism in Sweden in 1970 did not significantly weaken the social democrats' electoral supremacy or disturb its hegemony of governmental power (stretching continuously back to 1932), the 1973 poll generated a strong undercurrent of electoral volatility, albeit not on the scale of that in Denmark and Norway. In particular, the Centre (formerly Agrarian) Party became the first (and so far last) of the three non-socialist parties to achieve over one-quarter of the voting electorate. The only party to benefit from the electoral volatility of the early 1970s, the significance of its gains appeared to many to have lasting implications. For two political scientists, indeed, the advent of the Centre Party as the leading bourgeois party could be seen as 'a function of the decreased incidence of class voting in Sweden' and they noted that by 1973 the proportion of the working class voting for the two left-wing parties had dropped to 75 per cent (Berglund and Lindström, 1978: 189).

Before reverting to the basic question of 'from what to what' and a delineation of the core structures of the Swedish party system, it is worth noting that between 1973 and 1994 there were significant *prima facie* changes to both the *overall dynamics* of the party system and the *electoral balance* between the individual parties. On the former point, the Social Democrats (SAP) forfeited their monopoly of office in 1976 – there were non-socialist governments between 1976–82 and 1991–94 – and a rudimentary alternation of power vested the party system with increased bipolarity. On the latter, it may be said, with the advantage of hindsight, that 1973 represented a further stage in a cycle of electoral volatility which resulted in a marked shift in the centre of gravity within the non-socialist bloc. The Centre replaced the Liberals as the leading non-socialist party in the early 1970s and then lost that status to the Conservatives in 1979.

The relatively belated appearance, by Nordic standards, of three new parliamentary parties in the period 1988–94 appeared to represent a significant developmental phase in the Swedish party system. As Steven Wolinetz has observed, the most obvious distinction is not between 'people's parties' [like the SAP] with [over] 35 per cent of the vote and medium-sized parties with 15–20 per cent [one or more of the non-socialists], but between the older more established parties and the newer parties which have squeezed themselves into several West European party systems.

(1991: 126)

Yet none of the three new parties, the Greens, Christian Democrats or New Democrats maintained a parliamentary footing throughout the period 1988–94 (see Table 8.1). Interestingly, following the turbulence of the post-1973 scene in Denmark and Norway, the established parties have also reasserted themselves there, a fact prompting Smith to comment that the Danish party system appears to have undergone no more than a 'restricted change', not 'general change' let alone 'transformation' (1989b: 166–7). In Sweden, too, while the SAP in 1991 plunged to its worst performance since 1928, it bounced back only three years later with 45.2 per cent, twice as much as the second largest party, the Moderates.

Table 8.1 Swedish general election results, 1970–94[1]

PARTY	1970	1973	1976	1979	1982	1985	1988	1991	1994
Left–Communists[2]	4.8	5.3	4.8	5.6	5.6	5.4	5.9	4.5	6.2
Social Democrats	45.3	43.6	42.7	43.2	45.6	44.7	43.7	37.6	45.2
Liberals	16.2	9.4	11.1	10.6	5.9	14.2	12.2	9.1	7.2
Moderates	11.5	14.3	15.6	20.3	23.6	21.3	18.3	21.9	22.3
Centre Party	19.9	25.1	24.1	18.1	15.5	12.4[3]	11.4	8.5	7.7
Christian Democrats	1.8	1.8	1.4	1.4	1.9	–[3]	3.0	7.1	4.0
New Democrats	–	–	–	–	–	–	–	6.7	1.2
Greens	–	–	–	–	1.7	1.5	5.5	3.4	5.0

[1] Following the 1994 election, the *Riksdag* (parliamentary) term was extended from three years, the shortest in Western Europe, to four.
[2] The Left–Communists became simply the Leftist Party (*Vänsterpartiet*) in 1990.
[3] The Centre Party and Christian Democrats formed an electoral alliance for the 1985 election.

'From what to what?': The essential features of the Swedish party system

Traditionally, Sweden has approximated most closely to the five-party Scandinavian party system model described by Sten Berglund and Ulf Lindström in the late 1970s. It has been characterized by a bifurcated parliamentary Left – a powerful social democratic party flanked by a relatively weak but stable radical Left – and a fragmented bourgeois camp comprising essentially town-based liberal and conservative parties and, distinctively in Scandinavia, a farm-based Centre Party – with a capital 'C'. In the Swedish case three features warrant emphasis.

First, the Swedish party system has comprised essentially class-based parties which has facilitated an orthodox Left–Right placement of parties. The Swedish party system has lacked the evident multi-dimensionality manifest in the existence, in Norway, of a confessional party (the Christian People's Party) and, in Finland, of an ethno-regionalist party (the Swedish People's Party). As Berglund and Lindström insist, 'In the five-party system, parties fall along one dimension, left–right, defined in economic terms' (1978: 18). Hans Bergström makes the same point in stronger terms when insisting that the Swedish party system has been 'the simplest in any of the democracies' in that in no other country has the basic Left–Right scale accounted for so much electoral behaviour (1991: 8). It might be added that the one dimension cross-cutting the Left–Right scale has been the rural–urban axis, although the Agrarians' change of name to Centre Party in 1957 simplified matters.

Second, the dominance of the social democratic SAP has been unique in combining three elements: electoral strength, the length of its participation in cabinets, and its monopoly of governmental power. The extent of its voter support can be seen from the fact that between 1944–85 the SAP polled an average 45.7 per cent of the vote and in five of the contests held between 1938 and 1968, it won over half the votes cast. Its longevity of governmental tenure can be seen in that at the time of the 1991 election the SAP had governed for 56 of the 70 years since the first *Riksdag* election conducted on the basis of universal suffrage in 1921. The SAP's exclusive hold over the reins of power is reflected in the way the party has governed Sweden single-handedly for over four decades. Following the 1994 election, Ingvar Carlsson returned to lead a social democratic (minority) cabinet precisely as he had done between 1988 and 1991 (Arter, 1994) before handing over, in 1996, to Göran Persson (see Table 8.2).

Finally, the Swedish party system has been one of the most 'frozen' in Lipset and Rokkan's terms. From the advent of universal suffrage until 1988 (when the Greens made a parliamentary breakthrough), the same five parties were represented in the *Riksdag*. Indeed, it was not until 1991 that Sweden experienced an 'earthquake election' and then the tremors registered significantly less on the Richter scale, so to speak, than those in Norway and Denmark in 1973. In Norway, in the wake of the rejection of EEC membership, the main system parties dropped from a combined 95 per cent of the vote in 1969 to 76 per cent in 1973; in Denmark, which favoured joining the EEC, the share of the 'old parties' plummeted from 84 per cent in 1971 to 58 per cent in 1973. In Sweden's 'mini-quake' the share of the vote

Table 8.2 Government composition in Sweden, 1970–98

Years	Prime Minister	Party	Government	Support
1970–73	Olof Palme	SAP	SAP	163
1973–76	Olof Palme	SAP	SAP	156
1976–78	Thorbjörn Fälldin	Centre	C, Libs, Mods	180[1]
1978–79	Ola Ullsten	Liberals	Liberals	39
1979–81	Thorbjörn Fälldin	Centre	C, Libs, Mods	175
1981–82	Thorbjörn Fälldin	Centre	C, Libs	102
1982–85	Olof Palme	SAP	SAP	166
1985–86	Olof Palme	SAP	SAP	159
1986–88	Ingvar Carlsson	SAP	SAP	159
1988–91	Ingvar Carlsson	SAP	SAP	156
1991–94	Carl Bildt	Moderates	Mods, C, Libs, CD[2]	170
1994–96	Ingvar Carlsson	SAP	SAP	161
1996–98	Göran Persson	SAP	SAP	161

[1] In 1970 the unicameral *Riksdag* comprised 350 parliamentarians, but following the so-called 'lottery *Riksdag*' experience between 1973–76, when both the socialist and non-socialist blocs had 175 members apiece and the Speaker had to draw lots to resolve deadlocked votes, the number was reduced to 349.
[2] Christian Democrats.

polled by the five 'old parties' fell from 90.8 per cent in 1988 to 81.6 per cent in 1991.

Sartori characterized Sweden as a predominant (one-party dominant) party system although, despite its stranglehold on government, the SAP only won an absolute majority of seats in the 1940–44 and 1968–70 *Riksdags* (Sartori, 1976). However, while in the nine parliamentary elections since the shift to unicameralism the two left-wing parties have won over half the popular vote on four occasions (1970, 1982, 1985 and 1994) compared with the non-socialists' once, in 1976, the SAP has not been able to monopolize office, and Sweden can no longer be regarded as a predominant party system.

The pre-1973 Swedish party system: a low volatility system

Before tackling the question 'to what?', the distinctive electoral aspects of the traditional five-party Swedish model should be sketched. First and foremost, there was the historical level of *electoral stability*. Thus, Gösta Esping-Andersen comments that the conventional theory of competitive democracy is difficult to reconcile with the unique degree of electoral stability that marks Swedish social democracy (1990: 33). This uniqueness applies not only to social democracy, since it has been estimated that between 1921 and 1940 over 80 per cent of Swedish voters supported the same party at two consecutive elections (Berglund and Lindström, 1978: 88). A more comparative perspective on electoral stability can be gained from Mogens Pedersen's calculus of the volatility of 13 Western European party systems between 1948 and 1977 based on the cumulative gains of all the winning parties in the system (1985: 39). Sweden emerged with an average electoral volatility of 5.2 per cent, the lowest of the four mainland Nordic states and lower than all the other countries surveyed except Switzerland and Austria (see Table 8.3). Sweden, in short, belonged to a group of party systems with a notably stable distribution of party strength.

Table 8.3 Average electoral volatility in the Nordic countries, 1948–77

Country	1948–59	1960–69	1970–77	National average
Sweden	4.8	4.3	6.6	5.2
Finland	4.4	6.9	9.1	6.8
Norway	3.4	5.2	17.1	8.1
Denmark	5.5	8.9	18.7	11.0

Related to electoral stability has been a second feature of voting behaviour, namely the substantial degree of political cohesion of the main socio-economic groupings. The party-building process in Sweden was bound up with the representation of economic cleavages and the basic five-party model has been sustained by a high level of solidly class-based voting. The farmers vote in force for the Agrarian–Centre Party; the workers for one of the parties of the Left; and the middle classes for either the liberals or conservatives. A more detailed picture can be gained from Petersson and Särlvik's 1964 survey data. In that year, 84 per cent of the blue-collar workforce voted for one of the two left-wing parties – 78 per cent for the SAP; 93 per cent of farmers voted for one of the non-socialist parties – over two-thirds for the Agrarian Party; and 83 per cent of professional persons and the larger entrepreneurs (the 'old middle class') supported one of the non-socialist parties, mainly the conservatives and liberals. Of the small-firm owners, moreover, 72 per cent voted for a non-socialist party, principally the liberals. However, among the lower white-collar workers and rural workers (farm labourers and lumberjacks, for example), political loyalty was roughly evenly divided between the socialist and non-socialist parties (Petersson and Särlvik, 1975: 88).

The exception to the class base of the parties was the electoral support for social democracy which involved a cross-class alliance between the workers and elements of the salaried strata. From its accession to power in 1932, the SAP sought to be a 'people's party' (*Volkspartei*) stressing, according to Per Albin Hansson, a famous Social Democratic Prime Minister of the 1920s, the importance of the 'people's home' (*folkhemmet*) and adopting a pragmatic rather than dogmatic ideological approach. Esping-Andersen notes that the

SAP's rise to power in the 1930s and 1940s was based not so much on the working class, in the sense of an urban factory proletariat, as the rural classes. This was because heavy industry (iron-ore mining, hydro-electric power and timber) was located in small and isolated rural localities (1990: 38). He also argues that the controversial supplementary pensions issue between 1957–59 enabled the SAP to transform itself from a 'people's party' to a new 'wage earners' party, directed towards the so-called 'new middle class' (ibid.: 46–7). The SAP's electoral success in the 1960s bears witness, he claims, to its enhanced ability to attract white-collar voters. This is noteworthy since Smith deploys the notion of the *Volkspartei* as one of his benchmarks for assessing changes in the essential features of party systems. It was partly on the basis of the strength of middle-class support for the SAP, coupled with the sizeable (although as it turned out short-lived) backing for the Centre Party from non-farming groups, that Torben Worre felt able to describe the Swedish party system in the early 1970s as 'the least class oriented' in the Scandinavian region. He also notes that the Alford index of class voting in Sweden fell from +53 in 1956 to +36 in 1976 (Worre, 1980: 314–15). The Swedish party system, in short, was being affected by electoral instability syndrome.

Post-1973: the onset of electoral instability

There was a clear increase in aggregate electoral volatility (AEV) in Sweden in the 1970s. It stood at 6.6 per cent for the period 1970–77 compared with 4.3 per cent for 1960–69 (see Table 8.3). Both the level and rate of increase remained relatively modest compared with Denmark and Norway, however, in both of which AEV in the 1970s was nearly three times higher than in Sweden. In Norway, moreover, the average AEV more than tripled and in Denmark, it more than doubled, compared with the 1960s. During the 1980s, AEV in Sweden rose further to 7.4 per cent (1979–90), again a moderately small rise which, because it was based on the cumulative gains of the winning parties, concealed to a degree the real extent of electoral instability. In 1985, for example, as many as 20 per cent of voters made up their minds in the final week of the campaign (Arter, 1989: 95) and three years later twice that proportion was undecided how (and if) to vote when the election campaign began (Bergström, 1991: 22). The level of electoral volatility in Sweden rose steeply in the 1990s. The AEV for 1991–96 stands at 13.2 per cent, reaching a record 15 per cent in 1991, a classic case of a 'high volatility election'. Some 30 per cent of voters changed parties, a statistic which prompted Gilljam and Holmberg to comment that 'the Swedish electorate is no longer one of the most stable in the world' (1992: 31). Three years later the figure was only marginally lower at 29.2 per cent, with 13.8 per cent of voters switching to or from the three new parties. As much as 10 per cent of the electorate decided only on polling day itself which way to vote, with the Christian Democrats in particular appearing to profit from 'eleventh-hour' support (*Nordisk Kontakt*, 1994: 90–1).

The rise in AEV averages in Sweden from about 1973 gives an indication of the scale of increased electoral volatility without permitting an insight into its distribution across the political spectrum. Indeed, it needs emphasizing, as Table 8.4 demonstrates, that throughout the first decade and a half of unicameralism 1970–85, that is before the parliamentary breakthrough of the Greens in 1988, the level of *cross-bloc volatility*, i.e. the total gains of the two old blocs (the SAP and Left Communists, on the one hand, and the non-socialist *troika* of Centre, Liberals and Moderates, on the other), at just under 2 per cent was significantly lower than the overall AEV (Mair, 1985: 410). A feature of Swedish electoral volatility in the 1970s and 1980s (up to 1988), in short, was the extent of *intra-bloc mobility* and, above all, the extent of voter shifts between the established bourgeois parties. Thus, the Centre gained 5.2 per cent in 1973 to achieve over a quarter of the electorate, but lost 6 per cent in 1979. In 1973 only 21 per cent of Centre Party supporters felt a strong identification with the party – even less than the Left Communists' hard core of supporters (Berglund and Lindström, 1978: 188). The Liberals lost 6.8 per cent in 1973, but gained 8.3 per cent in 1985; the Conservatives gained 4.7 per cent in 1979 and 3.3 per cent in 1982, but lost 2.3 per cent in 1985.

Table 8.4 The level of cross-bloc volatility in Sweden, 1970–94

Election year	Left bloc	Percentage non-socialist	Winning percentage
1970	50.1	47.6	–
1973	48.9	48.8	1.2
1976	47.5	50.8	2.0
1979	48.8	49.0	1.3
1982	51.2	45.0	2.4
1985	50.1	47.9	2.9
			Average 2.0
1988	49.6	41.9	
1991	42.1	39.5	
1994	51.4	37.3	

It is almost tautological to assert that increased electoral volatility has been bound up with decreased partisan allegiance. The proportion of voters reporting any degree of party identification fell from 65 per cent in 1968 to 48 per cent in 1991 and, not surprisingly, in 1988 only 30 per cent of Green supporters possessed any form of identification (strong or weak) with their party. The figures for the SAP and Moderates were 69 and 58 per cent, respectively. Many Green voters patently belonged to the most volatile groups in the Swedish electorate (Bennulf and Holmberg, 1990: 181). The increased electoral volatility may also be connected with the decreased confidence in parties and politicians. In 1991 and 1994 approximately two-thirds of voters expressed 'not much' or 'very little' confidence in politicians (Gilljam and Holmberg, 1995: 86–7). It has also been argued that in the scramble to attract the growing body of volatile voters and achieve short-term electoral gains, the political parties have behaved in a way that has reinforced political mistrust and to a degree eroded their own 'core electorates'. Thus, referring to the 'shrinking ideas market' during election campaigns, Åsard and Bennett contend (albeit with little empirical corroboration) that parties have put symbols before substance, opaque rhetoric before the reality of clearly articulated policy alternatives and that the SAP in particular has sought to depoliticize the debate and keep controversial issues off the electoral agenda (1995). Such a strategy, they insist, will prove counter-productive by feeding political mistrust and voter volatility and ensnaring the parties in the vicious circle of devising anodyne solutions in search of short-term electoral gain.

If electoral volatility is integrally tied up with weakened partisanship and possibly also the declining legitimacy of the older parties, it is not clearly correlated with a significant downward trend in voter turnout. In both the Nordic and wider Western European perspective, turnout in Sweden has been generally high. It has averaged 89.2 per cent in the nine elections since the advent of unicameralism in 1970. Voter volatility, even when motivated by negative sentiments towards the available options, has entailed an active transfer between existing parties rather than passive support for the 'sofa party'. Significantly, the highest turnout of 91.8 per cent in 1976 was the watershed year when the non-socialists finally dislodged the SAP from power, while the second highest of 91.4 per cent in 1982 was the year the SAP returned to government following six years in the wilderness. Two caveats on the consistently high electoral participation rate in Sweden are none the less in order.

First, turnout dropped in 1988 to a record low of 86.0 per cent. In an election dominated as never before by a single issue, the environment, and which witnessed the parliamentary breakthrough of the first new party since 1918, turnout fell to a Swedish nadir! Yet the 1988 turnout was only just over 3 per cent below the average for elections to the single-chamber *Riksdag* and electoral participation *rose* marginally in the 'high volatility elections' of 1991 and 1994, albeit not to the 90 per cent plus of the mid-1970s and early 1980s.

Second, there is evidence of limited demobilization among young and first-time voters. For example, in 1988, the national average of 86 per cent was exceeded by all age-groups between 35–74 years, but among first-time voters it was almost 10 percentage points lower at 75.6 per cent and for 20-year olds turnout was lower still at 72 per cent. Three years later the differential between the national turnout of 86.7 per cent and that of young voters was greatest in the 21-year-old category which registered a 75.5 per cent participation rate. In 1994 turnout among first-time voters was 81.7 per cent, 5 percentage points below the average for the electorate as a whole.

Any discussion of electoral instability in Sweden must take account of an apparent decline in class voting and *prima facie* evidence of a weakening in the class-based profile of the established political parties. It seemed that amid the electoral turbulence of 1991 only 16 per cent of the Centre Party's support derived from farmers, and that the working class proportion of the SAP's overall poll was down to 52 per cent compared with 74 per cent in 1956. Equally, even the most cursory evaluation of the changed relationship between class and party must acknowledge the salience of several inter-vening variables. In other words, the relationship between class and party has become attenuated not least because neither side of the equation has remained constant.

On the one side there has been the impact of social structural change on the relative size of the 'classes'. As late as 1950, over 20 per cent of the economically active population was engaged in agriculture compared with about 15 per cent in the tertiary sector (Berglund and Lindström, 1978: 23). By the 1990s, in contrast, well over two-thirds of the labour force was employed in the service sector which also contained a high proportion of female employees from the professional level downwards (Boje and Nielsen, 1993). The high Alford index of class voting in Sweden (as elsewhere in Scandinavia) was inflated as a result of the simple dichotomization of the social structure into working class and middle class, a methodology which artificially incorporated the numerically significant farming population into the middle class. But even a simplified three-way schema dividing the economically active population into working class, middle class and farmers, which bore some resemblance to reality in the immediate post-war years, has been rendered obsolete by the advent of an economy dominated by the service sector.

At the same time, the political parties responded to social structural change, pursued adaptive strategies and sought to modernize their appeal. The SAP, as noted, having abandoned Marxism (namely, a policy of com-pulsory collective ownership) in 1932 in preference for a broad-based 'people's party model', began, in the late 1950s (ironically at precisely the time the West German SPD at Bad Godesberg adopted a reformist, non-Marxist line) to present itself as a 'wage-earners' party' with a view to targetting the growing body of the so-called 'new middle classes'. The Agrarians for their part, seeking an urban–industrial string to their bow, became the first of the farmers' parties in Scandinavia to adopt the designation 'Centre Party' (the Norwegian party followed suit in 1959 and the Finnish in 1965). More modestly, in 1969, the Rightist Party (*Högerpartiet*) abandoned a name with nineteenth-century overtones for the more 'voter-friendly' title, Moderate Coalition Party (Moderates). While it is essential to acknowledge the impact of social structural change and the parties' response to it, nevertheless Berglund and Lindström felt able to assert in the late 1970s that 'class is still the most important determinant of voting behaviour in Scandinavia' (1978: 16).

It is true that amid the tremors of the 1991 'mini-quake' election, nearly two-thirds of industrial workers (those in manufacturing, mining and construction) voted for the SAP, although 10 per cent voted for the Moderates, compared with a mere 2 per cent in 1964, and 17 per cent opted for one of the three new parties, the Christian Democrats, New Democrats and Greens. Among the 'rest of the workers' category, moreover, that is, transport workers, print workers, caretakers and firemen for example, less than half (48 per cent) voted for the SAP, 14 per cent favoured the Moderates, 11 per cent the Centre and 16 per cent one of the new parties. Similarly, while 45 per cent of farmers voted for the Centre Party in 1991, this was 20 percentage points down on its average for the period 1960–88, and 23 per cent supported the Moderates and 27 per cent one of the new parties. The same phenomenon of the increased vote dispersal or decreased political cohesion of social groups is evident among the 'old middle class' of professionals. Two-fifths of them backed the Moderates in 1991, one fifth the SAP (compared with only 8 per cent in 1964) and 22 per cent the 'middle parties' (Liberals and Centre) (Gilljam and Holmberg, 1992: 200). Even adjusting at the margins for a 'campaign effect' and perhaps, too, a 'period effect' (the growing appeal of 'new right' thinking during the late 1980s), it seems fair to assert the case for a greater electoral instability among the traditional 'core classes' of the political parties.

The point should not be exaggerated. Class remains a fair predictor of voting behaviour and it must remain an open question whether the arrival of the Greens, Christian Democrats and New Democrats, in providing fresh options, contributed to a decline in class voting (in the sense of prompting deviations from established voting patterns) or rather whether the emergence of these new parties is best perceived as simply representing a further stage in the long-term decline in class voting. That is, were the new parties more cause or effect of the diminished importance of class? The two inter-pretations are not, of course, mutually exclusive.

New conflict dimensions and new political parties

Parties and party systems change, according to Peter Mair, to the extent that they lose control of their agenda-setting role (1985: 420). In the Swedish case one could envisage this involving, for example, the dominant SAP surrendering control of the political agenda to one or more of the opposition parties, a trade union such as the peak blue-collar federation LO or, indeed, some other organized interest. To an extent this may be said to have happened in the 1970s, since the SAP's radical policy on socialism and democracy was adopted unenthusiastically by the party leadership in response to external circumstances. Partly it was a response to a series of election defeats: during the aforementioned decade the SAP lost ground in three consecutive elections and ended up in 1979 with 43.2 per cent of the parliamentary vote compared with an average of 46 per cent between 1945–69. As Bo Särlvik commented: 'something had gone wrong with the Social Democrats' electoral appeal in the 1970s and it had still not been put right at the end of the decade' (1980: 254). Partly, too, it was a response to the way the Centre Party had hijacked the 'new left' agenda with its emphasis on environmental protection and the decentralization of decision-making.

It could also be argued that, outflanked by the Centre, the SAP leadership yielded to a controversial democratic socialist agenda – particularly in respect of the contentious wage-earner funds scheme effectively foisted on it by leading LO economists. Certainly, the wage-earner funds provided an invaluable 'cause' around which the non-socialist parties (divided over the nuclear power issue) could unite; the funds were unloved by the average SAP voter and brought the business lobby on to the streets to demonstrate its opposition. The proposal, moreover, went through several mutations and dilutions before the joint SAP–LO version was finally announced in 1981 (when the SAP was an opposition party). It provided for the creation of 24 regional funds to be financed by a 1 per cent charge on the total cost of employees' salaries and a 20 per cent appropriation on the profits of enterprises in so far as these could be classed as 'excessive profits'. Faced with the sitting target of six years of fractious and unstable non-socialist govern-ment (the coalition parties were divided over taxation policy as well as the environment), it was clear that the SAP won a narrow victory in 1982 *in spite of* the unpopularity of the wage-earner funds scheme. The latter was anathema, particularly to middle-class SAP supporters for whom it appeared to represent a device for achieving socialism by the backdoor. Although the party political polarization sparked by the wage-earner funds issue revived the classical Left–Right, socialism versus capitalism cleavage, the political agenda also reflected new cross-cutting conflict dimensions with the potential to generate significant party system change.

From the early 1970s, several issue-based cleavages emerged which, although not immediately spawning new parties, vested the Swedish party system with a multi-dimensionality it had previously lacked. The highly charged question of nuclear power created an *environment versus the economy* cleavage and, simplistically stated, aligned those persons principally concerned with the quality of life (a nuclear-free environment) against those corporate sector elements for whom the quantity of life, i.e sustained economic growth, was of paramount importance. Indeed, the energy issue may be said to have ushered in an era of post-materialist politics which saw the emergence of green parties with a small, and ultimately a capital, 'G'. In 1973 the Centre Party, profiting from an unequivocally anti-nuclear stance, polled over one-quarter of the electorate and this was almost three times its performance as an Agrarian Party on the eve of its change of name. The Centre Party's leader, Thorbjörn Fälldin, went on in 1976 to head a three-party non-socialist cabinet (breaking the SAP's 44-year stranglehold on power), but this collapsed in autumn 1978 on the very issue of the future of nuclear power, which the Liberals and Moderates favoured. Even before the Harrisburg nuclear power accident in the United States, the SAP was divided on the question and at its instigation the matter was delegated for resolution by the people at a referendum in 1980. The result was open to some interpretation, but a majority of voters seemed to favour a gradual phase-out of nuclear power by the year 2010. Significantly, however, the anti-nuclear alternative gained the support of 40 per cent of voters and this encouraged a core of activists to found the Green Party in 1981.

By the 1985 general election, all the parties – except the Moderates – campaigned on environmental protection and the 1988 election saw the Greens become the first new parliamentary party in 70 years. They had gained seats on more than half the county councils in 1985, to be sure, and the public subsidies they received for this performance (on the basis of the number of elected councillors) were transferred to the coffers of the national party and used to fund the 1988 campaign. Interestingly, in that year, the three 'greenest' parties, the Greens, Centre and Left–Communists (against capitalist exploitation of the environment) gained a combined 6 per cent of the vote – and all three advanced individually – whereas the three 'growth-oriented' parties, the SAP, Liberals and Moderates, lost a combined 6.4 per cent.

Writing on the 1988 election, Bennulf and Holmberg emphasize the elite character of the green dimension and conclude that 'the green breakthrough in Sweden has not yet created a coherent green dimension in the mass public' (1990: 176). It is not at all clear what this statement means. If it is probably fair to assert that ordinary voters lacked a green *Weltanschauung*, that is, a cohesive green ideology informing their views, it is fair to counter that the same could equally be said of ordinary voters in respect of a coherent liberal or even social democratic dimension. Green issues influenced voters in a way other issues – pensions, sickness benefits, annual holidays – influenced voters and, quite undeniably, green issues aligned parties and voters (Greens, Centre and Left–Communists versus the SAP, Liberals and Moderates) in a way that cut across the traditional Left–Right divide.

Of course, it is also true that the Greens served as a channel for diffuse protest, especially in the wake of such scandals as Ebbe Carlsson's private investigation into the death of Olof Palme, the former prime minister. When, in 1991, the Green vote dropped to 3.4 per cent and they forfeited their parliamentary toehold, environmental questions were less prominent and there was a new populist party on the scene. Over one-third of Green voters switched to one of the four non-socialist parties (Moderates, Liberals, Centre and Christian Democrats) that formed a coalition under the Moderate Carl Bildt between 1991–94 whereas 11 per cent abstained and 9 per cent defected to the protest-based New Democrats. Yet although the number of strong identifiers among their supporters was only 29 per cent in 1991, the Greens returned to the *Riksdag* three years later.

Unlike in Norway, a Christian party had not established itself in Sweden in connection with the prohibition issue in the 1930s. However, the 'psyche-delic, hippy, Beatles-dominant mood' of the 1960s and the attendant liberal amendments proposed to the legislation on abortion and pornography animated a *morality versus secular* cleavage which led to the formation of a religious-specific party as early as 1964. The Christian Democrats (Kds) were committed to protecting Christian ethics and standards against the pervasive licentiousness and were in a real sense the first 'post-materialist' or, perhaps more exactly, anti-materialist party in Sweden. Faced with a 4 per cent national electoral threshold and a 12 per cent regional barrier which it came close to surmounting in its stronghold of Jönköping province, Kds's modest 1 to 2 per cent of the total vote at general elections looked likely to condemn the party to a perpetual extra-parliamentary fate. However, an electoral alliance with the Centre Party in 1985 (the legality of which was strongly challenged by the SAP) propelled the Kds leader, Alf Svensson, into the *Riksdag*. From a Centre Party viewpoint, the manoeuvre probably repre-sented an error of judgment since Kds supporters tend to be located in the very type of rural community and small town where the Centre Party has its greatest appeal (Sainsbury, 1986).

The electoral alliance was not renewed in 1988, but three years later the Christian Democrats achieved 7.2 per cent of the national vote, the highest poll of any of the three new parties that gained parliamentary representation between 1988–91. The Kds made gains at the expense of all the other parties, principally the Liberals (who made up 17.6 per cent of the Kds's electorate in 1991) and the Centre Party (which comprised 15 per cent). Clearly, those persons who earlier had sympathized with the party but felt that supporting it would be a 'wasted vote' were fewer in number than at previous elections. Significantly, in 1991 the Kds became the leading party among regular churchgoers, 36 per cent of whom backed it, compared with 21 per cent in 1988. However, the extent of the Kds's electoral advance, and the concomitant secularized nature of its total electorate also meant that regular churchgoers no longer comprised a majority of Kds voters. They made up 46 per cent in 1991 compared with 68 per cent in 1988. In terms of voter perceptions, as Gilljam and Holmberg noted (1992: 222), the Kds in 1991 could be described as a 'one man, two issue party': family policy, religion and Alf Svensson catapulted the Kds into parliament. In 1994, the Kds, polling exactly 4 per cent of the national vote, hung on to its parliamentary status by a whisker. Both the Greens and New Democrats had failed to be returned to the *Riksdag* at the election following their breakthrough, and although both Svensson (Minister for Overseas Development) and a second Kds cabinet member Mats Odell (Communications) had performed creditably, the Kds was split on a third issue which cut across the Left–Right placement of voters and parties. This was the question of Swedish membership of the European Community, the application for which was lodged in July 1991.

The period leading up to the EU referendum in November 1994, at which Swedes voted by a margin of 53–47 per cent to join, opened up a *centre–periphery* cleavage. The European issue was, of course, multifaceted and an inter-party consensus prevailed on matters such as the defence of popular democratic control and (at least the fiction of) national sovereignty against the imperatives of supra-national decision-making in Brussels. This was a valence issue in that all the parties expressed concern to minimize the so-called 'democratic deficit' and to maximize *Riksdag* scrutiny of EU directives.

More divisive, particularly during a recession and rising unemployment, was the postulate of the free movement of labour inherent in the single market and popular fears of an influx of foreigners and immigrants which could be exploited by the radical Right. By 1994, New Democracy was explicitly racist. However, the central EU cleavage was a conflict between a defence of the interests of the rural periphery, the small farmers in the outlying regions, against those of the cosmopolitan urban centres which strongly favoured EU accession. The periphery found allies in the Greens and

Left–Communists, partly on the grounds, among other things, that Sweden had higher environmental standards than the EU, but also, it was inferred, because a primary rationale of the EU was an unacceptable 'growth at all costs' wealth generation in ever wider markets. Grass-roots opinion in the Centre Party, the traditional organ of the farmers, was strongly opposed to the EU (the larger farmers in the southern region of Skåne were the exception), but the Centre leadership, in government with the pro-EU Liberals and Moderates, did not wish to rock the boat.

With four established parties either in favour of EU membership (Liberals and Moderates) or divided and therefore equivocal on the issue (Centre and Social Democrats), the two solidly anti-EU groupings, the Greens and Left–Communists (renamed simply Leftist Party in 1990) not surprisingly profited. While the Greens returned to the *Riksdag*, two months before the EU referendum, the Leftist Party under their new leader, Gudrun Schyman, fared better than at any time since 1944. Moreover, at the first Swedish elections to the European Parliament in September 1995, the Greens and Leftists together polled nearly one-third of the vote.

By then, the third new party (perhaps more anti-party), the New Democrats, had departed the parliamentary stage. Formed, like Mogens Glistrup's Progress Party in Denmark, only months before the 1991 general election by a Count, Ian Wachtmeister, and a fairground owner, Bert Karlsson, the New Democrats' diffuse anti-establishment protest appealed widely. Karlsson's dismissive reference to the 'crocodile politicians' in the other parties – 'all mouth and no ears'! – was typical of the populist rhetoric of a radical rightist party reminiscent (in addition to Glistrup's) of Carl I. Hagen's Progress Party in Norway (15.3 per cent in the general elections in September 1997) and the Finnish Rural Party (mark 2) under Pekka Vennamo in the early 1980s. It gained most of its votes from SAP electors (24 per cent) and, indeed, two-fifths of its support comprised blue-collar workers, second only to the SAP with 53 per cent. Its next largest vote sector consisted of former supporters of the Moderates (20 per cent) and previous abstainers (18 per cent) and it gained least from the Kds (3 per cent) and Leftists (1 per cent). It also appealed to young voters, presumably as an unknown, albeit highly irreverent quantity, and 14 per cent of first-time voters and 10 per cent of persons under 30 backed it in 1991. As to the reasons for voting New Democrat, every fifth supporter referred to the party's hard line on immigrants and asylum-seekers; every tenth mentioned taxes, the economy and the bloated public sector; and over half cited such things as the need for 'a fresh start', 'the party understands how the people think', and the like. The New Democrats' support was stronger in the countryside and small towns than in the cities and it also polled well among small entrepreneurs (Gilljam and Holmberg, 1992: 223).

In theory, the New Democrats held the balance of power in the 1991-94 *Riksdag*, but despite rumblings and threats they did not vote against the non-socialist coalition and, in any event, division in their ranks became endemic. Karlsson fell out with Wachtmeister and withdrew from politics; Wachtmeister was accused by rank-and-file parliamentarians of being unduly authoritarian and defections followed. By 1994, there was a new leader and the New Democrats were in disarray. The New Democrats have been described as a 'flash party' (Taggart and Widfeldt, 1993); they turned out to be a flash in the pan and although at the time their breakthrough was sensational in the context of the essentially consensual character of Swedish political culture, their importance should not be overestimated. Indeed, they were outperformed in 1991 by the Christian Democrats.

Conclusion: to what? so what?

Viewing the period 1973–97, what conclusions can be drawn about the nature and extent of party system change in Sweden? Moreover, what about the question 'so what?' What is the value of an analysis of party system change for understanding the wider workings of the political process? How far have changes to the basic configuration of parties and their relative electoral strengths affected patterns of elite interaction and co-operation?

In the absence of a generally accepted checklist of criteria for assessing change in party systems, Smith's emphasis on the importance of delineating the essential features, as a means of resolving the question 'from what to what', seems a reasonable point of departure. In this context, it will be recalled that Sweden constituted by far the closest fit to Berglund and Lindström's five-party 'Scandinavian party system' model with a large social democratic and smaller radical leftist party and three non-socialist parties, Agrarians, Liberals and Conservatives, all five situated along a unidimensional Left–Right continuum. In Worre's terms, the Swedish party system, as elsewhere in Scandinavia, was dominated by 'three big class parties': social democrats, Agrarians and Moderates. There were no deviations along ethnic lines (such as the Swedish People's Party in Finland) and non-functional cleavages were of minor importance during the crucial stages of the party-building process. In sum, as multiparty systems go, to paraphrase Bergström, Sweden, with its '2+3 formula', has been one of, if not the simplest, in Western Europe.

Seen in such a light, recent developments in the Swedish party system have represented at best a case of 'restricted change' in Smith's terms, since following the 1994 election the essential features appeared very much intact. The five historic parties gained 88.7 per cent of the vote and the SAP returned to government with over 45 per cent of the vote, a figure close to its post-war average. The radical Left gained its best result since 1944 (when it managed 10.3 per cent) and probably profited from the late defections of SAP 'anti-marketeers' (the SAP was badly divided on the EU membership issue). Equally, the leading government party and pro-EU Moderates under Carl Bildt gained fractionally. The losers were the so-called 'middle parties'. The Swedish Centre is presently the 'poor relation' of the Nordic Centre parties, failing to attract the protest support the Finnish party contrived in March 1991 or the Norwegian party mustered in September 1993 on a vigorously anti-EU platform. The Liberals fell back further and their leader Bengt Westerberg resigned.

The five-party vote increased in part because support for the New Democrats collapsed amid acrimony and recrimination. The Christian Democrats, however, narrowly survived and the Greens returned to the *Riksdag* after an electoral term away. Indeed, since 1988 more than five parties have been represented in the *Riksdag* and there are presently seven. Clearly, as Berglund and Lindström point out, 'the presence of more than five parties constitutes a deviation from the [Scandinavian party system] model', although they add that this is 'to a lesser degree as long as the parties compete on the same left-right dimension' (1978: 18). Obviously, since 1988 then, Sweden has deviated from the Scandinavian party system model not only because there have been more than five parties represented in the *Riksdag*, but more importantly because the Greens and Christian Democrats cannot easily be located on a classical Left–Right party spectrum. The Swedish party system, therefore, may be said to have witnessed a modestly increased pluralization and experienced a modestly increased multi-dimensionality.

Although the historical configuration of Swedish parties remains essentially unchanged, the electoral bases of the five 'old' parties have become less stable over the last quarter of a century. Class voting has declined and issue voting increased. Gilljam and Holmberg, in fact, interpret the decline in class voting (questionably perhaps in view of the appeal of the 'new right' radicalism of the Moderates) as evidence of the diminished salience of the traditional Left–Right cleavage in Swedish politics and a growing convergence of parties and voters on a left-right continuum (1992: 233). In the context of the rising level of electoral volatility, it could be argued that the five-party system was bolstered by the adoption, in 1970, along with the shift to unicameralism, of a 4 per cent electoral threshold – the highest in the Nordic region until Norway's adoption of a similar provision in 1987. This point should not be laboured, however, since high-impact populism – such as the Danish Progress Party's 15 per cent in 1973 and the Finnish Rural Party's 9.8 per cent three years earlier – would, of course, have broken through as, indeed, New Democracy did at its first attempt with 6.7 per cent in 1991.

In any event, a feature of Swedish developments appears to be not so much party system change as *party system resilience*. A twofold increase in electoral volatility in the 1970s and 1980s compared with the 1950s and 1960s, demonstrates in particular that the high level of instability among non-socialist voters, and the advent of new conflict dimensions (the divisive nuclear power issue, for example) were contained within the framework of the existing party system. It was only when volatility reached 30 per cent in 1991 that two new *Riksdag* parties, the Christian Democrats and New Democrats, made a parliamentary breakthrough. Even then, it was in part at the expense of a third, the Greens, which in 1988 had been the first new *Riksdag* party in 70 years but three years later lost its parliamentary footing altogether. In 1994, the Greens returned, the New Democrats splintered and disappeared, whilst the Christian Democrats held on only by the skin of their teeth.

In terms of alterations to the basic contours, the 'from what to what' question, the extent of party system change in Sweden appears limited. Increased electoral volatility was principally reflected in the fluctuating fortunes of the bourgeois parties; there was some erosion in support for the SAP, though not until 1991 did it experience the scale of reversal encountered in turn by the Liberal and Centre parties; and compared with elsewhere in Scandinavia, new parties were fewer, smaller and belated. The New Democrats, moreover, imploded within the lifetime of a single *Riksdag*. This was in sharp contrast to the Danish Progress Party and Finnish Rural Party.

In terms of significant changes in the patterns of interaction and co-operation between the five old parties, the Swedish party system *has*, nevertheless, been transformed in the last two decades. The turning point was 1976. It was then that the social democratic stranglehold on power was broken, and the Centre, Liberals and Moderates combined in coalition under Fälldin. Non-socialist cabinets have in fact governed Sweden for nine of the last 20 years. It is of course true that necessity (i.e. an overriding desire to dislodge the SAP) has in large part been the mother of non-socialist co-operation and that the low level of governing cohesion among them was affected by the impact of new conflict lines, particularly 'green issues'. The first Fälldin coalition between 1976–78 collapsed on the nuclear power issue. The only non-socialist cabinet to serve the full three-year electoral term was the Bildt government of 1991–94 (which also included the Christian Democrats) and even then the Centre leader, Olof Johansson, resigned over the controversial Öresund bridge linking Sweden and Denmark.

The critical point is that from 1976 Sweden acquired the bipolar dynamics of Sartori's moderate multipartism and the shift from a predominant party system occurred within the existing framework of the five-party Scandinavian model underpinned by relatively minor electoral shifts between the competing party blocs. The crucial perspective on party system change in Sweden, therefore, is *not* that of Denmark and Norway, i.e. a proliferation of new parties, a dramatic decline in the combined vote share of the five 'old' parties or even the heightened multi-dimensionality of the cleavage structure (the impact of 'new politics'). Rather, the novel element has been that in a competitive multi-party market place the three non-socialist parties have contrived a sufficient measure of co-operation, despite their divisions, to create an alternation of power. Mutual suspicions have, of course, remained rife: the Liberals angled after a coalition with the SAP during the 1994 election campaign and the minority SAP cabinet is sustained in office by a legislative deal with the Centre. But it is possible to speak of 'crunch co-operation' between the non-socialist parties: when it has come to the crunch, the non-socialists have combined forces against the SAP and broken its monopoly of power. In sum, in any analysis of party system change in Sweden, the importance of *elite inter-party relationships* as an independent variable must be acknowledged. For the three leading non-socialist parties in Sweden a *ménage à trois* has been essential to divorcing the social democrats from power.

9

The Netherlands: Resilience Amidst Change

HANS-MARTIEN TEN NAPEL

Introduction

Almost fifteen years ago, the Dutch-American political scientist Arend Lijphart published a book entitled *Democracies: Patterns of Majoritarian and Consensus Government in Twenty-One Countries* (1984). Lijphart argued that there are two main models of democracy: Westminster or majoritarian democracy and consensus democracy. The majoritarian elements of the Westminster model include: the concentration of executive power in single-party and bare-majority cabinets; executive domination of the legislature; a two-party system; a one-dimensional party system and a plurality system of elections. On the other hand, the elements of the consensus model which act to restrain the majority include: executive power-sharing in grand coalitions; a balanced executive–legislative relationship; a multi-party system; a multi-dimensional party system and proportional representation.

According to Lijphart, majoritarian democracy works best in relatively homogeneous societies like the United Kingdom. The consensus model, in contrast, is especially appropriate for plural societies. Since the single most important characteristic of Dutch politics is without doubt that the Netherlands is a plural society, a country of political and religious minorities (Daalder, 1966; Andeweg and Irwin, 1993: 23), it is hardly surprising that, at least as far as the five variables mentioned above are concerned, the Netherlands can be considered to be the prototype of a consensus democracy.

The Netherlands has not only had a multi-party system but also a *multi-dimensional* party system ever since the first attempt at a 'breakthrough' of the existing party system finally became successful in the 1870s. Both before and after the Second World War, moreover, at least five political parties have been 'relevant' (Sartori, 1976). Although at first sight therefore the model of extreme, or polarized, pluralism seems to apply, Sartori himself has more than once indicated that the Netherlands belonged in the category of moderate pluralism (Sartori, 1976; Sani and Sartori, 1983; see also Daalder,

1987: 266). As will be argued below, the Netherlands has retained its multi-party and multi-dimensional character. However, the partial success of the second major attempt at a 'breakthrough' of the party system, launched by the Socialists immediately after the Second World War, has led to recent speculation about a possible 're-dichotomization' of Dutch politics. The comparison between a first and a second attempt at a 'breakthrough' in the party system was made by Bruins Slot (1952: 154–79) among others.

This chapter will deal with the historical development of the Dutch party system before 1945, the contextual variables of most relevance, the post-1945 party system and then the processes of change and adaptation up until the present day.

Historical background before 1945

As was noted above, the single most important characteristic of Dutch politics is, and has always been, that the Netherlands is a plural society. Two cleavages have traditionally been of particular importance: religion and social class. The oldest, and in many respects the most important, of the two is religion. As a result of this cleavage, Dutch society has, since the origins of the Dutch state in the sixteenth century, consisted of three main religious groups: Roman Catholics (the oldest group), orthodox Protestants and a secular or humanist minority.

Although the size of the different groups, as well as the relations between them, has naturally varied over the centuries, these three groups, with their distinctive identities and histories, have always been important. The existence of these three distinct groups has contributed to the fact that it has proven extremely difficult, if not impossible, to write a truly comprehensive political and social history of the Netherlands. Each of the three groups has brought forth its own gifted, sometimes excellent, historians (Puchinger, 1979). However, the first real 'synthesis' of Dutch social and political history has yet to be written, despite occasional claims to the contrary (see, however, Israel, 1995).

Industrialization in the Netherlands took place later than in other Western European countries. Therefore, the second cleavage mentioned above – social class – did not become important until around 1880. Moreover, because of the binding force that religion constituted within both the Catholic and the orthodox Protestant segments of the population, only the secular or humanist group was actually divided into two parts as a result of this cleavage. Thus, from about the end of the nineteenth century, it has been possible to speak of four minorities in Dutch society: the Catholics, the orthodox Protestants, the secular working class or the socialists and the secular middle class or the liberals.

What makes the Dutch case interesting from a comparative point of view is that for most of the twentieth century, the first three groups (Catholics, Protestants and secular working class) have in effect been tightly organized subcultures that structured most, if not all, aspects of political, social and personal life in the Netherlands. In Dutch, these subcultures are usually known as *zuilen* or pillars. The segmentation of Dutch society into these different subcultures is called *verzuiling* or pillarization. The idea behind this metaphor is that the four separate pillars were – like those of a Greek temple – kept apart, only being joined at the top by the political elites, thus supporting the 'roof' of the Dutch state (Lijphart, 1975; Van Schendelen, 1984). A caveat is needed here, however.

For at least some social scientists and historians, the term 'pillarization' has a largely negative meaning. The period of pillarization between 1870–1960 is, possibly partly as a result of personal experiences and frustrations, regarded by them as a culturally 'dark' period of Dutch history, in which the political and religious elites of the day succeeded in controlling their rank and file adherents on an unprecedented scale. Others, however, are more positive about the same period in Dutch history, and they are even inclined to regard it as a kind of second 'Golden Age' in which religious and political life flourished once more (see, for example, Puchinger, 1993b). The same caveat applies to the 1960s and 1970s. As a result of processes of secularization and individualization and a number of other factors like the impact of television and the effects of generational change, the pillars started to crumble in the 1960s. Pillarization has become de-pillarization.

To many social scientists and historians, this marks a kind of liberation from a 'medieval' past, and the dawning of a new era of 'enlightenment'. Others, however, are increasingly worried about the effects that the secularization and individualization processes may have on the cohesion of Dutch society. They regard the present situation as being a culturally 'dark' era because relatively few people and organizations are still trying to maintain an explicit relation between their religious and other beliefs and social and political action. This might even be an explanation for the widening 'confidence gap' between Dutch citizens and the Dutch political system about which a number of Dutch politicians and political commentators have become increasingly concerned over the last few years (Van Gunsteren and Andeweg, 1994). Because of the de-pillarization process, Dutch people are finding it increasingly difficult to relate to parties and politicians that in their eyes have become too technocratic.

No matter to which 'school' one belongs in this respect, however, there can be no doubt that, despite the organizational and quantitative changes that have taken place during the last twenty years, the Netherlands remains a country of religious and political minorities. Roman Catholicism, the

Reformation, and Humanism still constitute the three main foundation stones on which Dutch society and civilization are built, although – like most of its neighbours – the Netherlands has gradually become more multi-cultural in the post-1945 period because of immigration.

Since the subcultures structured almost every aspect of social and political life, it is only natural that the birth of Dutch political parties was very much tied to the development of the pillars. Yet, it is not possible to fully compre-hend the process of party formation, without first paying attention to the fact that in the first half of the nineteenth century one could already speak of a conservative–liberal dichotomy in parliament. The liberals were clearly the dominant group. Among other things they were, with J.R. Thorbecke as their renowned leader, the driving force behind the amendments to the Dutch constitution of 1840 and 1848 by which modern parliamentary government was introduced. In the latter stages of the nineteenth century, however, liberalism gradually became dominant in many other sectors of society as well, including the economy and the churches. Despite, or maybe partly because of, their dominant position, the Liberals have traditionally remained less organized than the three other groups in Dutch society (Taal, 1980; Daalder and Koole, 1988).

Thus, the first liberal party was formed only in 1885, and that was mainly in reaction to the formation of the religious parties. In addition, until the Second World War, and again after 1966, there have been at least two separate liberal parties because of differences of opinion with regard to universal suffrage and the role of the state in social and economic life among other things. The most important of these were the conservative–liberal Liberal Union (LU, since 1921 called Liberal State Party or LSP) and the progressive–liberal Radical Democratic League (VDB, founded in 1901).

Meanwhile, around 1850 an orthodox Protestant historian and states-man named G. Groen van Prinsterer began to free himself ideologically and politically from the rival political group, the conservatives. In this process, that had already started in the 1830s and that can only be explained against the background of the complex religious and theological climate of those years, the lectures he gave for friends during the winter of 1845–46 on the topic of 'Unbelief and Revolution' played an important role (Groen van Prinsterer, 1922 [1847]). Although Groen van Prinsterer would sit prac-tically alone in parliament for another two decades, he indirectly laid the foundations for what, in 1879, became the first national party organization in Holland, the orthodox Protestant Anti-Revolutionary Party (ARP) (De Wilde and Smeenk, 1949). By then, the conservative group in parliament had virtually disappeared (Lucardie, 1988).

The name Anti-Revolutionary Party referred to the French Revolution, which because of the principle of *ni Dieu, ni maître*, was interpreted as a revolt against God. Its first leader was the charismatic A. Kuyper, who had also authored the party's first programme.

By 1894, De Savornin Lohman, the parliamentary leader, and several other more conservative members had left the Anti-Revolutionary Party, with universal suffrage, as in the case of the liberals, being one of the main divisive issues. In 1908, this group joined with two other small religious parties to form a second orthodox Protestant party: the more theocratic Christian-Historical Union (CHU) (Van Spanning, 1988). While most adherents of the Christian-Historical Union belonged to the Dutch Reformed Church, the Anti-Revolutionary Party drew its support largely from the Calvinist churches that had been founded by Kuyper in 1892.

Although a Roman Catholic State Party (RKSP) was not formally established until 1926, the Catholics were the second group within the Dutch population to begin to organize itself politically (Rogier and De Rooy, 1953). Originally, the Catholic members of parliament had worked closely with the liberals. The main reason for this was that the Catholics had been discriminated against in the time of the Republic (1579–1795), when the orthodox Protestants had, despite their minority status culturally and economically, been the dominant group and had acted very much as if the Netherlands was a Protestant country. The Catholics expected, not without reason, to benefit from their political co-operation with the liberals as the latter were preparing the constitutional amendments of 1840 and 1848 which not only paved the way for modern parliamentary government but also included the introduction of a bill of religious and other rights.

As a result, despite an emotional appeal from a number of orthodox Protestants to the king, the episcopal hierarchy was reintroduced in the Netherlands in 1853. During the 1860s, however, Catholics and liberals gradually grew apart. One reason for this was that the Vatican, as well as the Dutch bishops, began to seek the establishment of Catholic schools, something which the liberals opposed. Another reason was that the liberals successfully tried to end the official diplomatic ties that existed between the Netherlands and the Vatican. Also more generally, the liberals became increasingly anti-clerical. Following the example of Kuyper, in 1883 a poet and priest by the name of H.J.A.M. Schaepman devised the first Catholic political programme. Yet, as mentioned above, it would take until 1926 before the first Catholic party was formally founded.

One explanation for this was that the Catholics long remained hesitant about involving themselves directly in politics after they had been discriminated against for centuries. A second reason is that, for the Catholics, political action was and has always remained, less central than activities in other sectors of society. In this, they differed from the orthodox Protestants and, to a lesser extent, the socialists.

Not only did the orthodox Protestants and Catholics start to organize themselves politically in the second half of the nineteenth century but they also began to co-operate closely in parliament and the cabinet in the so-called Coalition. This was a remarkable development because it occurred in a country in which orthodox Protestants and Catholics had gone their separate ways for centuries and in a period when no ecumenical contacts whatsoever between their respective churches existed. The fact that the Coalition was formed can to a large extent be attributed to the common goal of the provision of public subsidies for religious schools that the two groups shared, but as so often the good personal relations between Kuyper and De Savornin Lohman, on the one hand, and Schaepman, on the other hand, were instrumental as well.

The Coalition of orthodox Protestants and Catholics resulted in a number of cabinets especially those after the First World War, and it did not break up definitively until 1939. Before that, during the 1930s, the Anti-Revolutionary Prime Minister, H. Colijn, had occasionally broadened the Coalition by including the liberals, something he had been in favour of since at least 1913 (Puchinger, 1969; 1980; 1993a).

The secular working class finally organized itself in the Social Democratic Workers' Party (SDAP, founded in 1894), with P.J. Troelstra as its first leader (Perry *et al.*, 1994). A socialist party had already existed before 1894 (the SDB, founded in 1882) but under the leadership of F. Domela Nieuwenhuis, however, this party had developed more and more in an anarchist direction. Until the Second World War, the socialists remained in opposition at the national level because they were generally considered to be too radical and too anti-monarchist to participate in government. Immediately after the First World War, in 1918, they were even accused, wrongly, of staging a revolutionary uprising.

This situation changed in the 1930s, when the Social Democratic Workers' Party officially abandoned Marxism and turned more towards personalism and socialist planning. In 1937, it adopted a reformist programme of basic principles that finally made the party acceptable as a coalition partner for the Roman Catholic State Party in particular as well as the Christian-Historical Union whose relationship with the Anti-Revolutionary Party had deteriorated during the 1930s.

The Anti-Revolutionary Party had developed in a more conservative direction, whereas the Roman Catholic State Party as well as the Christian-Historical Union had gradually advocated more progressive policies in order to combat the international economic recession. There had, however, been a growing number of differences of opinion between the religious parties already since 1917, when the common goal of public subsidies for religious schools had been achieved. In 1939, a cabinet of Christian Historicals and

Roman Catholics was formed, a cabinet that also contained two socialists for the first time. In addition, there was one minister with an Anti-Revolutionary background in this cabinet against the will of the leadership of the ARP.

On the basis of the above, then, we can conclude that between 1879 and 1940 the Netherlands had a multi-party system and a multi-dimensional party system. This is particularly the case since only the major political parties have been mentioned above. *Within* all three pillars, in addition, there were also several smaller parties (Lucardie, 1991). The most important of these within the orthodox Protestant pillar were the Political Reformed Party (SGP, founded in 1918 and currently the oldest political party in the Netherlands), and after 1945, the Reformed Political League (GPV) and the Reformed Political Federation (RPF).

Within the socialist pillar, there were the Communist Party of the Netherlands (CPH, later CPN) and, after 1945, the Pacifist Socialist Party (PSP). Although from time to time there have also been smaller parties within both the Catholic and the liberal pillars, these parties have generally been more short-lived. At the parliamentary elections of 1933, a record number of 54 party lists was submitted, 14 of which eventually proved successful.

If we count the liberal parties as being one, however, only five parties were strictly 'relevant'. Of the two traditional cleavages in Dutch society until 1940, religion was politically the most important although, especially during the economic recession of the 1930s, it became increasingly clear that important changes were under way (Koole and ten Napel, 1991).

Contextual variables

As is clear from the above section on history, the multi-party system and the multi-dimensional party system that the Netherlands has known since the second half of the nineteenth century, were mainly the result of the plural character of Dutch society. This is perhaps best illustrated by the fact that between 1848 and 1917 the Netherlands had a single member district system. Of course, the introduction of a system of proportional representation in which the country was treated as a single electoral district and universal suffrage in the latter year (universal suffrage for men was introduced in 1917 and for women in 1919) made it easier for new political parties to gain seats, especially since the Dutch electoral system is one of the most proportional systems in the world (Daalder, 1975). Yet, it should nevertheless be emphasized that around eight different political groups were already represented in the Dutch parliament at the turn of the century.

The introduction of proportional representation and universal suffrage had a noticeable impact on the relative strengths of the parties. More specifically, the liberals were reduced in size after 1917, whereas the three major religious parties together acquired an absolute majority of the seats in the second chamber which they did not relinquish again until 1967. Just as the nineteenth century can be characterized as the liberal century in Dutch politics in many ways, the twentieth century was to become the century in which the Christian parties played a pivotal role.

Before 1917, cabinets had comprised either the liberal parties (which together with the socialists constituted the Left in Dutch politics) or the religious parties that represented the Right. Between 1917 and 1994 in particular, the Catholics participated in every cabinet, except in the short-lived Colijn V cabinet in 1939, initially together with the two major orthodox Protestant parties but increasingly also with either the liberals, or the socialists, or both.

It is interesting to note that, despite repeated attempts at political and administrative reform, the electoral system as well as other contextual variables (Müller, 1993) have remained largely unchanged since 1917. Compared with several other Western European countries, the Netherlands can therefore said to be characterized by a relatively high degree of institutional conservatism (Andeweg, 1989). Only very recently, after the formation of the first coalition without the Christian Democrats since 1917 (see later), modest proposals have been put forward by the present Kok cabinet for a reform of the electoral system (with the German electoral system acting as the main source for inspiration) and, more importantly, the introduction of a corrective referendum at national level. According to some authors, it is likely that in the near future elements of direct democracy such as referendums and initiatives but also new techniques like 'deliberative' polling will either be introduced or gain in importance (see, for example, Beedham, 1993). One of the interesting things about such a development would be that, as Lijphart himself has argued (1984), referendums and other elements of direct democracy are not specifically related to the characteristics of either model of democracy that we set out at the start of this chapter.

Therefore, the distinction between majoritarian and consensus democracies in Western Europe might well become more and more diffuse if this were to happen. Such convergence is, of course, also likely to occur as a result of the continuing process of European integration. For the time being, however, it remains to be seen whether there will in fact be a parliamentary majority even for the modest proposals for institutional reform of the Kok cabinet. There is a general feeling that, in order to achieve such support, any proposals will have to be limited. Therefore, even if adopted, the reforms are not likely to have a significant impact on the political system in general and the party system in particular.

As far as the individual political parties are concerned, over the past decades, there has been a significant drop in the membership figures for almost all parties. At present, only about 3 per cent of the Dutch population is a member of a political party, compared to approximately 10 per cent in the early 1960s. It should be emphasized, however, that this apparent 'decline' of parties does not necessarily imply 'the end of party'.

Given the fact that some form of representation will remain necessary in the future, it is more likely that what we are really witnessing is a transformation from the traditional 'mass bureaucratic party' to what Ruud Koole has called the 'modern cadre party' (1992; 1994). At present, nobody seems to long for the 'electoral-professional party' (Panebianco, 1988). On the contrary, a sharper, instead of a more diffuse ideological profile for the traditional political parties, might be one of the potential remedies when it comes to closing the widely perceived confidence gap between Dutch citizens and the political system.

The post-war party system

Following the Second World War, a second major attempt at a 'breakthrough' in the Dutch party system was launched by the Social Democrats. The main reason for this was that, as a result of pillarization, they could only appeal to non-religious voters. Therefore, unlike in neighbouring countries, they were not able to attract more than 20 to 25 per cent of the national vote. More specifically, the Social Democrats tried to reintroduce the two party system and the one-dimensional party system that the Netherlands had known in the first part of the nineteenth century. Like the earlier attempt undertaken by Groen van Prinsterer around 1850, however, this second 'breakthrough' initially remained unsuccessful.

Before long, after the possibility of forming a unified, Protestant People's Party had briefly been discussed, the two major orthodox Protestant parties re-emerged as separate parties, whereas the Roman Catholic State Party merely changed its name to the Catholic People's Party (KVP). As a result, although an ideologically somewhat broader formation, the Labour Party (PvdA) which was founded in 1946 closely resembled its immediate predecessor, the Social Democratic Workers' Party.

This was even more the case, after P.J. Oud together with a small group of other progressive Liberals, who had formerly belonged to the Radical Democratic League but had joined the Labour Party after 1945, became disenchanted and left the party again in 1947. A year later, this group of progressive Liberals joined with the conservative Party of Freedom (PvdV, founded in 1945 as the successor to the Liberal State Party) to form the People's Party for Freedom and Democracy (VVD).

Thus, after 1945, the Netherlands retained its multi-party system as well as its multi-dimensionality. At this point, the major parties of the Catholic, the orthodox Protestant, the socialist, and the liberal pillars were, respectively, the Catholic People's Party; the Anti-Revolutionary Party and the Christian-Historical Union; the Labour Party and the People's Party for Freedom and Democracy. Together, these five system parties used to win between 86 and 92 per cent of the national vote during the first two decades after 1945 (see Table 9.1).

As far as the importance of the two traditional cleavages in Dutch society are concerned, however, there was a change in that after the Second World War social class became the most important cleavage for a while as the central issues of this period included the reconstruction of the country after the war and the establishment of the welfare state. That social class had become the most important cleavage was illustrated by the fact that the terms 'right' and 'left' that had earlier stood for, respectively, the 'religious' and the 'non-religious' parties, now came to mean 'conservative' and 'progressive' in socio-economic terms.

Partly as a result, there was once again, as in 1917, a significant change as far as the composition of the cabinets was concerned (see Table 9.2). The Social Democrats, who had entered government for the first time in 1939, continued to take part in a series of broad 'Roman-Red' coalitions in the years immediately following the war. From 1948 to 1958, these cabinets were headed by a socialist prime minister, W. Drees. Between 1959 and 1989, however, the three religious parties mostly worked together (24 out of 30 years) with the liberals.

Some have argued that this was only natural since the Catholic Party in particular was not so much a centre party but a party of the right (in the socio-economic meaning of the term) and they were thus ideologically closer to the liberals than to the socialists (Daudt, 1980). Others, however, have correctly pointed out that this relatively long period of isolation between 1959 and 1989 was at least partly the socialists' own fault. More specifically, the relationship between the religious parties and the Labour Party inevitably suffered from the polarization strategy adopted by the latter party in the 1960s and 1970s. This will be dealt with in more detail later on.

Because of the importance of the socio-economic cleavage, the Labour Party and (conservative) liberals worked together in only two cabinets, Drees I (1948–51) and Drees II (1951–52). From 1959 onwards, they more or less explicitly excluded the possibility of their co-operating within the cabinet, thus making it much easier for the Catholic People's Party to play its pivotal role in Dutch politics than would otherwise have been the case.

With the advantage of hindsight, it is possible to argue that a first indication of the changes that were to come in the 1960s and 1970s was the

Table 9.1 Dutch election results, 1946–98

Party	1946	1948	1952	1956	1959	1963	1967	1971	1972	1977	1981	1982	1986	1989	1994	1998
KVP	30.8	31.0	28.7	31.7	31.6	31.9	26.5	21.8	17.7							
ARP	12.9	13.2	11.3	9.9	9.4	8.7	9.9	8.6	8.8							
CHU	7.8	9.2	8.9	8.4	8.1	8.6	8.1	6.3	4.8							
CDA										31.9	30.8	29.4	34.6	35.3	22.2	
SGP	2.1	2.4	2.4	2.3	2.2	2.3	2.0	2.3	2.2	2.1	2.0	1.9	1.7	1.9	1.7	1.8
PvdA	28.3	25.6	29.0	32.7	30.4	28.0	23.6	24.6	27.3	33.8	28.3	30.4	33.3	31.9	24.0	29.0
CPN	10.6	7.7	6.2	4.7	2.4	2.8	3.6	3.9	4.7	1.7	2.1	1.8	0.6	–	–	–
PvdV	6.4	–														
VVD	–	7.9	8.8	8.8	12.2	10.3	10.7	10.3	14.4	17.9	17.3	23.1	17.4	14.6	20.0	24.7
KNP	–	1.3	2.7													
GPV	–	–	0.7	0.6	0.7	0.7	0.9	1.6	1.8	1.0	0.8	0.8	1.0	1.2	1.3	1.3
PSP	–	–			1.8	3.0	2.9	1.4	1.5	0.9	2.1	2.3	1.2			
BP	–	–			0.7	2.1	4.8	1.1	1.9	0.8	–					
D66							4.5	6.8	4.2	5.4	11.1	4.3	6.1	7.9	15.5	9.0
PPR										1.7	2.0	1.7	1.3	–	–	–
DS'70										0.7						
RKPN										0.4						
RPF											1.2	1.5	0.9	1.0	1.8	2.0
EVP											0.5	0.7	0.2			
Centre											0.1	0.8	0.4	0.9	2.5	0.6
GL														4.1	3.5	7.3
AOV															3.6	0.5
Unie 55+															0.9	0.5
SP												0.5	0.4	0.4	1.3	3.5

Table 9.1 *contd.*

Source: Andeweg and Irwin, 1993: 105; Daalder and Schuyt, 1986: A1300-27 (supplemented for 1998).

Key to party abbreviations

AOV	Aged League
ARP	Anti-Revolutionary Party
BP	Farmer's Party
CDA	Christian Democratic Appeal
Centre	Centre Party/Centre Democrats
CHU	Christian-Historical Union
CPN	Communist Party
D'66	Democrats '66
DS'70	Democratic Socialists '70
EVP	Evangelical People's Party
GL	Green Left
GPV	Reformed Political League
KNP	Catholic National Party
KVP	Catholic People's Party
NMP	Dutch Middle Class Party
PPR	Radical Party
PSP	Pacifist Socialist Party
PvdA	Labour Party
PvdV	Party of Freedom
RKPN	Roman Catholic Party of the Netherlands
RPF	Reformed Political Federation
SGP	Political Reformed Party
SP	Socialist Party
Unie 55+	Union of those 55 or older
VVD	People's Party for Freedom and Democracy

Table 9.2 Government composition in the Netherlands, 1945–94

Date installed	Prime Minister	Composition[1]
24 June 1945	Schermerhorn	*PvdA*/KVP/ARP/np
3 July 1946	Beel I	PvdA/*KVP*/np
7 August 1948	Drees I	*PvdA*/KVP/CHU/VVD/np
15 March 1951	Drees II	*PvdA*/KVP/CHU/VVD/np
2 September 1952	Drees III	*PvdA*/KVP/ARP/CHU/np
13 October 1956	Drees IV	*PvdA*/KVP/ARP/CHU
22 December 1958	Beel II	*KVP*/ARP/CHU
19 May 1959	De Quay	KVP/ARP/CHU/VVD
24 July 1963	Marijnen	*KVP*/ARP/CHU/VVD
14 April 1965	Cals	PvdA/*KVP*/ARP
22 November 1966	Zijlstra	KVP/*ARP*
5 April 1967	De Jong	*KVP*/ARP/CHU/VVD
6 July 1971	Biesheuvel I	KVP/*ARP*/CHU/VVD/DS70
20 July 1972	Biesheuvel II	KVP/*ARP*/CHU/VVD
11 May 1973	Den Uyl	PPR/*PvdA*/D66/KVP/ARP
19 December 1977	Van Agt I	*CDA*/VVD
11 September 1981	Van Agt II	PvdA/D66/*CDA*
29 May 1982	Van Agt III	D66/*CDA*
4 November 1982	Lubbers I	*CDA*/VVD
14 July 1986	Lubbers II	*CDA*/VVD
7 November 1989	Lubbers III	PvdA/*CDA*
22 August 1994	Kok	*PvdA*/D66/VVD

[1] Party of the Prime Minister in *italics*; np = non-partisan.

Source: Andeweg and Irwin, 1993: 119 (supplemented for 1994)

formation of the Farmers' Party (BP), a rightist protest party in the late 1950s. More importantly, in 1966 a party called Democrats '66 (D'66) was founded. Over the years, this party has developed into a progressive–liberal system party not unlike the pre-War Radical Democratic League, as opposed to the conservative–liberal People's Party for Freedom and Democracy. The original purpose of D'66, however, was to 'explode' the pillarized party system.

Apart from the Farmers' Party and Democrats '66, several other 'new' parties were to enter the Dutch parliament during the 1960s and the 1970s such as the Pacifist Socialist Party (PSP), which had gained two seats in 1959 already, the Radical Party (PPR) and the Democratic Socialists '70 (DS'70).

As in other Western European countries and the United States, new 'post-materialist' issues such as the environment, peace, and the need for individual self-expression suddenly appeared on the political agenda. As will become clear later on, however, in the end, these issues would not replace religion and social class as the two most important cleavages in Dutch politics.

Change and adaptation

By the time Democrats '66 was founded, the traditional pillars in Dutch society had already started to crumble (Blom and Van der Plaat, 1986; Irwin and Van Holsteyn, 1989a; 1989b). As far as political life is concerned, the parliamentary election of 1967 marked a turning point. Until 1994, the election of 1967 was the only really 'historic' national election the Netherlands had experienced since the introduction of the system of proportional representation and universal suffrage in 1917.

The election of 1967 was important for a number of reasons, particularly because the three religious parties lost their combined parliamentary majority which they had enjoyed continuously for 50 years. Second, the Catholic People's Party especially lost votes dramatically. In just nine years, between 1963 and 1972, the party lost almost half its seats in parliament. Third, the Labour Party also reached a historic low point of 23.6 per cent of the vote. Fourth, the liberals, who had always opposed the principle of pillarization because of their conviction that religion was and had to remain essentially a private matter, gained one seat. Fifth, both the new Farmers' Party and Democrats '66 were highly successful in 1967.

Partly because of the heavy vote losses of the religious parties, in particular the progressive parties, but to a certain extent also the liberals, adopted the so-called 'polarization strategy' (Daalder, 1986; Tromp, 1989). By doing away with the 'accommodationist' political style of the 1940s and 1950s, it was hoped by the progressive parties that the electorate would be forced into two opposing camps. The religious parties would then either have to choose co-operation with the left-wing parties or with the right-wing parties. In either case, they would split and, as a result, disappear. The main purpose of this strategy was therefore to achieve the 'breakthrough' in the party system which had ultimately failed immediately after the Second World War.

Once again, these efforts turned out to be in vain, however, and eventually even counter-productive. They were counter-productive because the relatively hostile political environment proved to be an extra stimulus for the merger of the two major orthodox Protestant parties and the Catholic People's Party into the Christian Democratic Appeal (CDA) in 1980. Other incentives for co-operation between the three parties that had formerly belonged to two different pillars included the clearly decreasing hold which the Anti-Revolutionary Party, the Christian-Historical Union and the Catholic People's Party had upon their respective Protestant and Catholic electorates and the wish of important portions of the Catholic and orthodox Protestant subcultures to nevertheless maintain an explicit relation between the Christian faith and political action.

In addition, the fact that the leaders of the three parties had come to know each other in the *Nouvelles Equipes Internationales* (the European Christian Democratic Movement) and the strong desire within all three parties for co-operation at the municipal and provincial levels were significant (ten Napel, 1992; see also Lucardie and ten Napel, 1994). This merger of the three religious parties into the Christian Democratic Appeal can be regarded as the single most important party political renewal in the Netherlands since the Second World War.

Although the Christian Democrats have no longer occupied a majority position in parliament but only about one third of the seats since 1967, they have been able to maintain their strong position in the centre of Dutch politics and even strengthen their crucial role during cabinet formations by merging. As a result, until 1994, it proved to be impossible to form a national coalition without the Christian Democrats. A similar attempt by Democrats '66, the Labour Party and the Radical Party to form a progressive people's party failed in the early 1970s.

After a brief *intermezzo*, the Den Uyl cabinet of 1973–77 in which the Socialists worked together with representatives from the Catholic People's Party and the Anti-Revolutionary Party, the Christian Democrats between 1977 and 1989 largely maintained their co-operation with the liberals that had started in 1959, with the main issue now being the crisis of the welfare state.

In 1986, the Christian Democrats even openly announced before the elections that they wanted to continue the prevailing coalition for the first time in Dutch parliamentary history. Paradoxically, this polarization strategy of the right, as it has been called, did not lead to a split within the Christian Democratic party, but instead to a 'landslide' victory of nine seats. Moreover, for the first time, the Christian Democratic Appeal proved able to attract a substantial number of non-religious voters. At least in part, this was made possible by the popularity of the then prime minister and leader of the CDA, Ruud Lubbers (ten Napel, 1995).

In 1989, however, the parliamentary caucus of the People's Party for Freedom and Democracy (VVD) withdrew its support from the second Lubbers cabinet. After the liberals had been defeated in the elections that were subsequently held, a third Lubbers cabinet was formed which consisted of Christian Democrats and Labour. By that time, the Labour Party had distanced itself through a series of programmatic and organizational reviews from the style and postures adopted in the late 1960s and the 1970s, notably and in particular the polarization strategy (Wolinetz, 1993). In a sense, this coalition of Christian Democrats and Labour therefore appeared to mark the end of a period of relative turmoil in Dutch politics and the return to the system of consociational or consensus democracy that had existed until the

1960s. Particularly at the start, this cabinet was sometimes compared to the series of broad 'Roman-Red' coalitions headed by Drees between 1948 and 1958.

In 1994, however, the Christian Democratic and Labour system parties performed especially poorly in the second chamber elections. The Christian Democratic Appeal suffered an unprecedented loss of 13 per cent of the national vote, whereas the Labour Party was back at its historic low point of 1967 with a mere 24 per cent of the vote (a loss of 8 per cent). The post-materialist Democrats '66, on the other hand, performed so well that it actually doubled in size. The conservative–liberal People's Party for Freedom and Democracy (VVD) also gained 5.4 per cent of the vote. It had now become clear that the conservative liberals were the main party to gain from the process of de-pillarization.

Although, as we saw above, the People's Party for Freedom and Democracy suffered electoral losses during the second half of the 1980s as a result of leadership problems (after having polled 23.1 per cent in 1982), it won 20 per cent of the vote in the national elections in 1994 as against barely 8 per cent in 1948 (see Table 9.1). In the provincial elections of 1995, which cannot of course be directly compared to second chamber elections, this percentage had rocketed to an astonishing 27.2 per cent. Given these figures, it is hardly surprising that the charismatic leader of the parliamentary party of the People's Party for Freedom and Democracy, Bolkestein, was widely considered to be a serious candidate to succeed Kok as prime minister, if the former's party were to become the largest party at the 1998 election. This turned out not to be the case, however.

For Labour, the corresponding figures are 24 per cent in 1994 as against 28.3 per cent in 1946 and for the Christian Democrats, 22.2 per cent in 1994 as against 51.5 per cent in 1946. One further remarkable development was, that, in 1994, two new 'single issue' parties entered parliament, the Aged League (AOV) and the Union of those 55 or older (Unie 55+).

It is still difficult to interpret what really happened in 1994. It is certain, however, that specific events played a significant role, particularly in the loss that the Christian Democratic Appeal suffered. Several of these incidents were a direct result of the rapidly deteriorating personal and political relationship between the Christian Democratic Prime Minister Lubbers, who had already indicated in 1990 that he did not want to continue his job after the next election, and his successor, Brinkman, whom Lubbers had himself appointed. This led to increasing tensions between the parliamentary party of the CDA in the Second Chamber, under the leadership of Brinkman, and the Christian Democratic ministers in the Lubbers III cabinet.

In the end, it was unclear for many Christian Democratic voters whether, by voting for the Christian Democratic Appeal, they would be supporting the

Centre–Left policies of the Lubbers III cabinet or the more conservative policies advocated by the parliamentary party. In the case of the Labour Party, their heavy electoral loss can at least in part be attributed to the manner in which they handled the revision of the disability law in 1993.

Structural factors, however, are also likely to have played a role. In particular, it can be argued that, once again, there was a change with regard to the relative importance of the two traditional cleavages in Dutch society, in that social class lost some of the prominence it had as a cleavage during most of the post-war period. As in other Western European countries, the Dutch Labour Party has been so successful in achieving their original political goals that they have, in a sense, become a party without a 'heartland'. The old working class has virtually disappeared, although it can be argued that because of technological developments (with the advent of 'the information age'), new forms of inequality are already emerging.

Religion, on the other hand, still plays a crucial role in Dutch politics and society and it may once again become the most important cleavage as the Netherlands enters the twenty-first century, even though quantitatively speaking the Catholics and orthodox Protestants are significantly smaller in number than in the nineteenth century. Moreover, while at present, still half of the Dutch population regards itself as 'Christian', according to some researchers, this percentage will have dropped to about 20 per cent in the year 2020 (Becker and Vink, 1994).

Consequently, one of the most hotly debated issues in Dutch politics today is whether, as a result of processes of secularization and individualization, the Netherlands is gradually disintegrating as a society. As was argued in a report by the Scientific Council for Government Policy (WRR), there used to be four social groups or pillars. Now there appear to be about 15 million individuals (*Eigentijds burgerschap*, 1992).

As a result, a new cultural dichotomy has gradually developed between the liberal parties, who regard the development of society since the 1960s as predominantly positive and the Christian Democrats who tend to emphasize the potential risks and are therefore more pessimistic in their outlook. In this sense, the Christian Democratic Appeal is a communitarian party, although the ideological differences between communitarians like Amitai Etzioni and Alasdair MacIntyre, on the one hand, and Christian Democratic political philosophies, on the other, should not be underestimated.

The intriguing question is which position Labour will eventually choose in this controversy. At present, the party seems to be paralysed by the tensions between its liberal and communitarian wings. The People's Party for Freedom and Democracy also has a communitarian wing which is currently relatively weak, however.

The renewed importance of the religious or cultural cleavage is demonstrated by the fact that after the elections of 1994 a so-called 'purple' (PvdA red and VVD blue mixed together) coalition of conservative and progressive Liberals and Labour was formed. Apparently, the traditional socio-economic differences between in particular the Labour Party and the People's Party for Freedom and Democracy have become so small that the possibility of them working together in cabinet no longer needs to be definitively excluded.

Consequently, if the national election of 1967 was the first 'historic' election after the introduction of a system of proportional representation and universal suffrage in 1917 because the religious parties lost their combined parliamentary majority, the election of 1994 might well be called the second 'historic' election because the Christian Democrats lost their pivotal position in the process of government formation. One could indeed argue, that the attempt at a 'breakthrough' of the existing party system launched by Labour after the Second World War has finally been successful, even though the liberals are the main party to gain.

It is tempting to draw a comparison between the present political and religious climate and that of the first half of the nineteenth century. Once again, liberalism is dominant. Once again, the Christian Democrats are in opposition to liberalism and the spirit of the French Revolution, the latter in a sense being represented by the coalition of Labour, and conservative (VVD) and progressive (D'66) liberals.

Yet, if one looks carefully, there are already signs that the policies advocated by more or less communitarian parties like the Christian Democratic Appeal and (depending on the outcome of the internal power struggle between its liberal and communitarian wings) the Labour Party might gain popularity once more.

In addition, social class is not likely to completely disappear as a cleavage, and the liberals have an important role to play in the battle against postmodernism, in particular the idea that western political systems are entering a kind of post-institutional era (Guéhenno 1993). This, in combination with the fact that the three traditional groups in Dutch society are still in evidence, reinforces the expectation that the four major Dutch parties will all have important roles to play in the years ahead.

Conclusion: resilience amidst change

The concept of the 'core' of a party system as developed by Gordon Smith seems to be particularly useful as a means of describing the developments which have taken place in the Dutch party system since the Second World War. In an article published in the *Journal of Theoretical Politics* in 1989, Smith concluded that:

What emerges from a review of a cross-section of recent West European experience is that, whatever else may be changing, the essential core of party systems is remarkably unscathed. Typically, we can observe a three-stage process:

1. an initial *reverse* suffered by some or all of the core parties as new parties gain support and electoral volatility rises;
2. a period of *flux* with the core parties in disarray and adopting strategies of adaptation;
3. finally a *restabilization*, the core parties recovering at least a substantial part of their electorate and able to reassert their governing position.

(1989a: 361–2)

As far as the Netherlands is concerned, it can indeed be argued that there have been reverses suffered by several core parties – in particular the Christian Democrats and Labour (in the late 1960s), then a period of flux (the 1970s) and a restabilization of the party system (in the 1980s). Clearly, there has been no complete reversion to the *status quo ante*, if only because the Christian Democrats have recently lost their pivotal position in Dutch politics and the Labour Party was back at a historic low point as well in 1994. In this sense, Wolinetz was certainly correct when he wrote that '[t]he Dutch party system provides fertile ground for exploring party system change' (1988: 130).

There has indeed been party system change in the sense that 'as a result of ideological, strategic, or electoral shifts, there is a transformation of the direction of competition or the governing formula' (Mair, 1989: 257). What is even more striking, however, is the resilience of the party system. Without doubt, the core of the Dutch party system as defined in this chapter has been preserved (Smith, 1989a: 358–9; 1989b). In this sense, the subtitle of a volume on Dutch politics that was published in 1989, *Politics in the Netherlands: How Much Change?* (Daalder and Irwin, 1989), still applies, suggesting as it does both that there have been changes, and that doubts are legitimately possible as to whether there is not also a high degree of continuity.

One of the contributors to that volume, Arend Lijphart, concluded that even without all the measuring that he had performed:

> the adoption of a broad comparative perspective readily shows that the changes in the operation of Dutch democracy should not be exaggerated. The overall pattern of the new Dutch politics in the 1967–88 period still looks a great deal more like the old 1946–67 Dutch politics than like British or New Zealand politics. The Netherlands has merely moved from the politics of accommodation to the politics of relatively less accommodation and relatively more adversarial relations – and it clearly does not qualify yet to be a member of the family of adversarial and majoritarian democracies.

(1989: 151)

Although more recent evidence suggests that the Netherlands is no longer one of the most consensual European democracies, this is largely a result of developments in other countries. According to Mair (1994b: 99, 121), the character of Dutch politics itself has not changed dramatically in the past twenty years, and in any case continues to be consensual. More specifically, the Netherlands appears to have retained its century-old multi-party system as well as its multi-dimensionality. Because of the merger of the three religious parties, on the one hand, and the success of Democrats '66, on the other, there are now four instead of five major parties. Together, however, these traditional parties provided further evidence of long-term stability (Bartolini and Mair, 1990; Mair, 1993), attracting a remarkable 81.7 per cent of the vote in 1994.

One relatively small change to note is that, in 1989, the Communist Party of the Netherlands joined with three other small Leftist parties (the Pacifist Socialist Party, the Radical Party and the Evangelical People's Party that was formed in the 1970s as a protest against the merger of the three confessional parties in the Christian Democratic Appeal) to form the Green Left (GL). In the 1998 parliamentary elections, this combination polled 7.3 per cent. The extreme left-wing Socialist Party (SP) polled 3.5 per cent whereas the extreme right-wing Centre Democrats are not represented any longer in parliament. The Aged League and the Union of Those 55 or Older started to disintegrate almost immediately after the 1994 election had taken place, whereas the three smaller religious parties are more or less stable.

It remains to be seen therefore whether the outcome of the parliamentary election of 1994 and the formation of the first cabinet without Christian Democrats since 1917, has marked the beginning of an era of more or less radical change in the Dutch political and party system. After the substantial gains by the Labour Party and the People's Party for Freedom and Democracy of 5 and 4.7 per cent respectively, and the renewed loss of the Christian Democrats of 3.8 per cent in 1998, there is increasing speculation about the latter being reduced to the status of a 'non-relevant' party. It has been one of the underlying theses of this chapter, however, that what we have experienced thus far is merely another change in the relative importance of the two traditional cleavages in Dutch politics, namely, religion and social class. The overall conclusion must be that, although there has been party system change in the Netherlands, the party system has also demonstrated a high degree of resilience in terms of the parties that comprise its stable and enduring core.

10

Belgium: Party System(s) on the Eve of Disintegration?

LIEVEN DE WINTER AND PATRICK DUMONT

Introduction

The 'classical' party system typologies were applied to the Belgian case in the 'frozen' shape it had assumed from the turn of the twentieth century until the end of the 1960s. Therefore, the typologies do not help us to grasp the dramatic changes that the Belgian party system has undergone since then, transforming it from a simple three-party system into an extreme case of centrifugal multipartism, probably the most complex case in the western world.

As Duverger (1954) put it, most western party systems were at first based on an opposition between two camps. In Belgium the division was religious, opposing Catholics and anti-clerical liberals. In the second half of the nineteenth century the government gradually enlarged the franchise thereby allowing the entrance of the first socialist deputies into the lower parliamentary chamber in 1894. Thus, at the turn of the century, the traditional two-party system was replaced by a three-party system in which the liberals had been gradually reduced to third place. They were saved by the introduction of proportional representation by the Catholic majority government in 1899. This particular feature bothered Duverger: 'As a matter of fact only one of the countries in which a two-party system flourished previously was unable to re-establish it (after the birth of a socialist party): Belgium' (1954: 243). Although Duverger argued that adopting PR would significantly increase the number of parties, tripartism survived until the late 1960s. Introducing his typology in 1954, and thus unaware of the fact that Belgium would move into a strong case of multi-partism soon afterwards, Duverger observed that no real change had occurred in more than 50 years under PR (three main parties with an insignificant communist party) and simply defended his theory by writing that, after all, tripartism was already multipartism.

Blondel's more refined (1968) typology introduced the notion of a 'two-and-a-half-party system'. He initially stipulated that party systems where the two main parties accounted for over 90 per cent of the vote were two-party systems; where they counted for between 66 and 90 per cent a three-party system resulted. Belgium's average two-party vote for the 1945–66 period was 78 per cent, hence Belgium had a three-party system. Considering the Belgian case together with Ireland, West Germany and Canada, however, Blondel concluded that there were no genuine three-party systems, but only 'two-and-a-half-party systems'. Thus, Belgium, from the turn of the century, comprised two major parties and a much smaller third party. Blondel argued that three-party systems were essentially transitional, thus unstable forms of party systems. Blondel wrote his article just after the 1965 Belgian general election that, by coincidence, saw the Liberal Party surge and the two major parties decline, thus making a three-party system emerge (see Table 10.1). As he predicted, the Belgian three party system turned rapidly into a moderate multiparty system with no numerically dominant party. Subsequently, the system evolved into one of extreme fragmentation.

Finally, in Sartorian terms, the current Belgian situation clearly represents a case of extreme multipartism (Sartori, 1976). As far as the direction of competition is concerned, it does not belong to the polarized *type* for the religious and socio-economic founding cleavages, but it certainly does for the third dimension: the linguistic cleavage. On this cleavage, virtually all the Flemish parties are situated at the pole of defence of Flemish interests, while the francophone parties are situated at the pole of the defence of francophone/Walloon interests (De Winter, 1991). Only the Green parties, both Flemish and francophone, are situated near the centre as they constitute the only political family that manages to develop a common programme on linguistic/regional problems.

Figures 10.1 and 10.2 provide a quantitative view of the post-war growth of party system fragmentation in Belgium expressed in terms of the Rae fractionalization index and the effective number of parties.

The first big change in fragmentation occurs in 1965 (the number of effective parties rises from 2.69 to 3.59) due to the breakthrough of the Flemish-nationalist *Volksunie* (VU) and the creation and first success of the *Rassemblement Wallon* (RW) and *Front Démocratique des Francophones* (FDF). The second leap forward occurs in the 1968–78 period due to the split of the traditional parties and the emergence, in 1978, of the *Vlaams Blok* (VB) and the *Union Démocratique pour le Respect du Travail* (UDRT), two extremists parties on the right (the index jumps from 4.97 to 6.77). The emergence of the Green parties in 1981 causes a further increase (from 6.77 to 7.71), while the 'Black Sunday' election of 1991 produces a further jump (to 8.41) due to the breakthrough of protest parties (VB and ROSSEM). The 1995 election shows a small reduction in the effective number of parties yet this

Table 10.1 Belgian general election results, 1946–95

Year	CVP	PSC	BSP	PSB	PVV	PRL	FDF	RW	PCB	VU	AGALEV	ECOLO	VB	UDRT	FN	ROSSEM	OTHER
1946	42.5		31.6		8.9				12.3								4.3
1949	43.6		29.8		15.3				7.5	2.1							1.9
1950	47.7		34.5		11.2				4.8								1.8
1954	41.1		37.3		12.1				3.6	2.2							3.5
1958	46.5		35.8		11.0				1.9	2.0							2.8
1961	41.5		36.7		12.3				3.1	3.5							2.9
1965	34.5		28.3		21.6				4.6	6.7							2.1
1968	22.3	9.4	28.0		20.9		2.2		3.3	9.8							0.1
1971	21.9	8.2	27.2		9.5	7.2	5.9		3.0	11.1							0.7
1974	23.3	9.1	26.7		10.4	6.0	11.4		3.2	10.2							0.2
1977	26.2	9.8	27.0		8.5	7.8	10.9		2.1	10.0							2.3
1978	26.1	10.1	12.4	13.0	10.4	6.0	7.1		3.3	7.0			1.4	0.9			3.0
1981	19.3	7.1	12.4	12.7	12.9	8.6	7.3		2.3	9.8	2.3	2.2	1.1	2.7			2.4
1985	21.3	8.0	14.6	13.8	10.7	10.2	4.2		1.2	7.9	3.7	2.5	1.4	1.2			2.3
1987	19.5	8.0	14.9	15.7	11.5	9.4	1.2		0.8	8.0	4.5	2.6	1.9	0.1			0.9
1991	16.8	7.7	12.0	13.5	12.0	8.1	1.2		0.1	5.9	4.9	5.1	6.6		1.0		2.0
1995	17.2	7.7	12.6	11.9	13.1	10.3*	1.1			4.7	4.4	4.0	7.8		2.3	3.2	3.4

* The PRL and FDF parties joined forces for the 1995 election

Key to party abbreviations

CVP	Flemish Christian Democrats	PCB	Communists
PSC	Francophone Christian Democrats	VU	Flemish Nationalists
BSP	Flemish Socialists	AGALEV	Flemish Greens
PSB	Francophone Socialists	ECOLO	Francophone Greens
PVV	Flemish Liberals	VB	Flemish Extremists
PRL	Francophone Liberals	UDRT	Anti-Tax Party
FDF	Brussels Regionalists	FN	National Front
RW	Walloon Regionalists	ROSSEM	Anarcho–Liberals

Lieven de Winter and Patrick Dumont

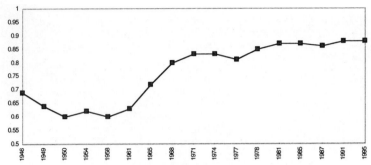

Figure 10.1 Rae fractionalization index, Belgium 1946–95

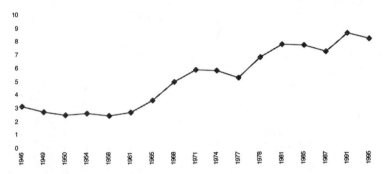

Figure 10.2 Number of effective parties, Belgium, 1946–95

figure remains above the 1980s' average despite the reduction of the number of parties represented in parliament (from 14 in 1981 to 11 in 1995).

Historical background before 1945

At its creation in 1830 the Belgian kingdom was a hybrid state. In the north there was a Catholic, conservative, largely agricultural, Dutch-speaking Flanders, and in the south the more free-thinking, less conservative, industrializing French-speaking Wallonia (Fitzmaurice, 1988; Mabille, 1997).

The cleavage structure of Belgian society

Belgian politics, up to the 1970s, was dominated by three cleavages. These founding cleavages entered the party system at different stages, but by the 1920s all three had been translated into party terms and thereafter they dominated the political agenda to varying degrees.

The opposition between Catholics and anti-clericals is the oldest cleavage in the Belgian polity. This denominational confrontation also had a regional flavour, with a very Catholic Flanders, and a Wallonia and Brussels in which anti-clerical tendencies had more success. In fact, the creation of the Belgian state resulted from the collaboration of the Catholic aristocracy and the liberal bourgeoisie in opposition to the Dutch king. The state, therefore, was based on a compromise between two antagonistic groups: a Catholic elite favouring a state in which the Church would play an important role, and the liberals, who wanted a secular state. The 1831 Belgian constitution reflects this compromise, on the one hand establishing the principle of freedom of religion (thereby acknowledging the separation of State and Church), but on the other hand establishing the principle of freedom of education, allowing the Church to keep a grip on the educational system.

The industrial revolution came early in Belgium and had its strongest impact in Wallonia which soon became the most industrialized region on the continent. In Flanders, there were only some declining industries around Ghent; Antwerp was significant only as a port. The cleavage between workers and employers was translated into the party system via the emergence of the Belgian Workers Party in 1885, following the enlargement of the franchise.

Belgium has been a multi-national state since its creation, with a Flemish community, a French-speaking Walloon community, and a small German-speaking one. The independence movement was, therefore, also based on an alliance between different groups of the French-speaking upper classes: the aristocracy, gentry, provincial bourgeoisie and emergent industrial bourgeoisie in the growing urban centres. By 1830, the once very prosperous Flanders had practically no elites that were integrated culturally with the Flemish people or who identified with the Flemish community for the elites tended to be francophone. Hence, when Belgium gained independence the new political elite was unavoidably a French-speaking one. In addition, as Flanders was mainly poor and agricultural, and Wallonia highly industrialized, the socio-political hegemony of French culture was assured. The official language of the state (used in administration, military affairs, politics and the legal system) was French, and the media and educational system were also French throughout the country. Yet, a majority (57 per cent) of Belgium's inhabitants were Flemish-speaking. Brussels was chosen as the administrative and political capital as it had played the role of administrative centre when the Belgian provinces were part of other states. It soon became a financial centre, too. A former Flemish city situated inside Flemish territory, Brussels gradually became a French-speaking city.

Thus, at the birth of the Belgian state the centre was French-speaking, politically, economically and culturally. Flanders was peripheral in all these fields, while Wallonia was associated through its economic development with the political, administrative, financial and cultural centre, Brussels. Yet, this centre–periphery definition slowly changed, and has been nearly completely reversed today. From the mid-nineteenth century, opposition to francophone predominance in state and society started to grow in Flanders. First, recognition of Dutch as an official language in Flanders was demanded, and gradually granted. Later, demands for measures guaranteeing a fair representation of Flemings in the state apparatus were also voiced. Finally, after the First World War, requests for cultural autonomy were made, while a minority called for independence. Regionalism in Wallonia and Brussels emerged as a reaction of the francophone population to the growing grip of the Flemish on the Belgian state.

The gradual translation of cleavages into the party system

From Unionism to bipartism

Given the fragile international status of the new state, Catholic and liberal politicians who had led the independence movement against the Dutch decided to collaborate in government. For the first 16 years of its existence, 1830–46, Belgium experienced the period of so-called Unionism, i.e. coalitions of Catholics and liberals. As neither group was organized territorially, each consisting only of loose groups of like-minded parliamentary notables before 1846, one can hardly speak of a party system. Until 1893, the electoral system was a plurality one, with the suffrage initially highly restrictive.

The liberals were the first to organize as a national political party, in 1846, on a programme defending free market and anti-clerical principles. The Catholics started organizing national congresses from 1863, but only in 1878 were the local Catholic electoral associations brought under a single nationwide roof. The main issue in the 1846–84 period was denominational: the support for a Catholic, 'free', versus a state educational system. Liberals and Catholics alternated in government.

The emergence of a three-party system

The first socialist organizations appeared on the political scene in the second half of the nineteenth century. For twenty years, until 1885, tensions between the anarchist-influenced Wallonia and the more reformist-inclined Ghent and Brussels blocked the formation of a united national movement – the *Parti Ouvrier Belge*. The Belgian Workers' Party was the political representative of the socialist pillar organizations (consumer co-operatives, trade unions, mutual health insurance organizations, the cultural societies and the press) which were already flourishing before the foundation of the party. From the beginning, they exerted a strong pragmatic influence on the party's strategies and policies. Members of these pillar organizations were automatically members of the party.

From the outset the party's appeal to the working class was restricted by the religious cleavage. The Church and the Catholic Party tried to prevent Catholic workers from joining the socialists by imitating the socialist pillar organization, creating Catholic workers' organizations such as trade unions, co-operatives and mutual aid organizations. Thus the socialists represented on average only half of the Belgian working class.

The Catholic Party was at first mainly a bourgeois, conservative organization, largely dedicated to the defence of the interests of Catholic organizations such as the church, schools and public health networks. Yet, the working-class wing grew in strength within the party, together with the farmers association. Thus by 1914, the Catholic Party consisted of three distinct estates: the bourgeois-conservative *Fédération des Cercles*, the working-class *Ligue Démocratique Belge*, and the peasants' *Boerenbond* (Farmers' League).

The liberals were the major victim of socialist electoral success, for social reformers left to join the socialist ranks. As a result, the Liberal Party evolved into a conservative anti-clerical party. This process of polarization divided the anti-clerical camp in such a way that the Catholic Party became a majoritarian force and controlled all governments in the 1884–1914 period in spite of the enlargement of the franchise and, in 1900, the introduction of PR.

Party proliferation during the inter-war period

The policy success of the socialists' reformist strategy and the strength of the socialist pillar organizations prevented the Belgian Communist Party (PCB-KPB), founded in 1921, from penetrating deeply into the socialist electorate. Under the new electoral system (PR with, from 1919, male universal suffrage) the socialist party became the largest party in the elections of 1925 and 1936. However, in spite of its electoral success in this period, governmental participation was limited.

In the Catholic Party, the estates (a fourth had been added representing the so-called middle classes of shopkeepers, artisans and small entrepreneurs) became more important than the actual party organization. Thus, the *Union Catholique* was a federation of four distinct estates without a common political programme. Each estate enjoyed a large degree of autonomy and collaborated with the others only during the composition of the parliamentary electoral lists. People could not join the party directly, but only through one of its four estates. In 1936, a reorganization took place, creating the *Bloc Catholique Belge*, with a Flemish and a Walloon wing and individual membership.

The centre–periphery cleavage was expressed for the first time in a genuine Flemish-nationalist party in 1919, the *Frontpartij*. The name referred to the war front, where many Flemish soldiers had given their lives while serving under officers who neither spoke nor understood their language. During the First World War, some Flemish nationalists had collaborated with the German occupiers, trying to achieve changes that had been refused before the war, like the 'dutchification' of the State University of Ghent. In 1919, the party won five seats in parliament with 2.6 per cent of the vote. The *Frontpartij* became more radical during the 1920s and 1930s, leading the more moderate nationalists to leave it and to strive for the Flemish cause within the three traditional parties. In fact, Dutch was soon recognized as an official language, and secondary education in Flanders was conducted in Dutch. Yet, Brussels became a more and more francophone city, a francophone island in Flanders, and expanding into the Flemish countryside.

In the 1930s, the VNV (Flemish National Union) became the main Flemish nationalist party. It was a more radically separatist, more explicitly Catholic Party, which also sympathized with national-socialist ideology. In the 1936 election, it captured 10 per cent of the Flemish vote, but it had already declined in the 1939 election before it went on to collaborate with the German invaders. The Germans recognized it as the only representative of the Flemish population and it staffed political and administrative positions in the occupied state. The VNV recruited Flemish volunteers to fight bolshevism with the Nazis and openly adopted fascist ideology. Such open collaboration by the main Flemish nationalist party jeopardized the resurrection of the Flemish movement in the post-war period.

Contextual variables

The electoral system

Since 1919, elections have been conducted according to the PR principle and universal male suffrage. Women were enfranchised for general elections only in 1948, having been given suffrage for local elections in 1920. The d'Hondt system of seat allocation, with second tier allocation of seats at the provincial level, is rather disproportional for a PR system (Mackie and Rose, 1982; Lijphart, 1994). Belgium is one of the few countries still using compulsory voting and although non-voting is rarely punished, participation, at over 90 per cent, remains very high (De Winter and Ackaert, 1994).

Pillarization

The traditional parties are deeply rooted in society and are much more than purely political organizations. Each is the political centre of a densely organized subculture, or 'pillar', which includes a wide spectrum of organizations of which most citizens are members from the cradle to the grave (see Billiet, 1984; Frognier and Collinge, 1984; Hellemans, 1990; Huyse, 1987; Lorwin, 1974b; Pijnenburg, 1984). The parties are visible at all levels of society and in almost all spheres of life. More precisely, the subcultural divisions can be seen, with the parties never far away. At the same time, the parties organize the search for consensus at the level of the political elites who tend to be strong but prudent leaders. They prevent subcultural conflicts (often mobilized by themselves) from exploding into civil war and guarantee that elite political agreements are implemented and respected.

In contrast to the Dutch case, in Belgium these pillar organizations remain politically relevant. First, Belgium has one of the highest degrees of unionization in the world (about 80 per cent of the workforce), workers belonging mainly to the Christian Democratic and socialist trade unions. Second, in the obligatory health insurance sector, Christian mutual insurance organizations represent nearly half of the insured, against only a little over a quarter for the socialist ones. Third, in the socio-medical sector, more than half of the general hospitals and three out of four psychiatric hospitals are associated with *Caritas Catholica*, the Catholic association of socio-medical organizations. Catholic organizations also have a predominant, and usually majoritarian, position *vis-à-vis* old peoples' homes, care for the disabled, homes for juvenile correction, family consulting centres, home medical care, family and aged care, socio-cultural organizations (like adult education) and youth organizations. As far as the politically sensitive educational sector is concerned, in Flanders 70 per cent of the school and university-going population attend Catholic institutions. In Wallonia the figure is 50 per cent.

Despite decreasing church participation, the deconfessionalization of the public at large and the electoral decline of the Christian Democratic parties, most Catholic pillar organizations have managed to maintain their strength and membership by reinforcing the service character of their organizations and by slightly deconfessionalizing their activities at the grass-roots level.

Partyocracy and clientelism

Like Italy, the Belgian political system is often defined as a *partitocrazia* (De Winter, 1981; 1989; 1996). Parties do not, as in any party government, only control parliament and the cabinet in terms of policies and personnel

(Katz, 1986). Their influence is much wider and extends into other public spheres, like the judiciary, the bureaucracy, the media and the educational, health and social systems. The reach of the parties is deeper than usual in party government since patronage extends beyond the elites of those spheres to encompass the lower levels. Party patronage in the recruitment of the civil service is made possible through a variety of measures that circumvent the normal objective recruitment criteria. Until the end of the 1980s, majority parties shared out nearly all graduate grade promotions during regular meetings of an unofficial interparty committee constituted by party representatives and chaired by a trusted ally of the Prime Minister. The recruitment and promotion of judges were until very recently almost completely determined by party patronage. Finally, party patronage is important in sectors such as the public media, education, public, semi-public and quasi-autonomous enterprises and services, local government and public housing, the allocation of governments contracts to particular enterprises and the regional allocation of public investments. In addition, politicians interfere with the allocation of a wide variety of services to individual citizens: social security transfers, draft exemptions, scholarships, tax reductions, rapid telephone connections, car licence plates, divorce, adoption, immigration, legal support, the annulment of traffic fines (De Winter, 1995). The clientelistic nature of the relationship between parties and voters also explains the continuing high member/voter ratio (more than 10 per cent) of Belgian governmental parties, in spite of declining party identification (Maes, 1988; Gabriel and Brettschneider, 1994: 66).

As far as party control of governmental policy-making is concerned, the most crucial moment of party influence occurs during the process of government formation (De Winter, Frognier and Rihoux, 1996; De Winter, Timmermans and Dumont, 1997). Coalition parties draft elaborate and lengthy agreements covering most policy fields in detail. Through these, supporting parties manage to define in detail what kind of policies the government and individual ministers should elaborate, when these should be implemented, and what kind of policies or problems should not be raised due to a lack of consensus. Other matters are also decided in the bargaining process: the distribution of patronage, coalition building at sub-national levels, the selection of parliamentary speakers and the role of parliament in the decision-making process.

Parties also interfere directly with everyday cabinet decision-making. First, the ministers' large personal staffs, which are mostly party appointees, follow the government's conduct of business and prepare ministerial interventions in the cabinet, cabinet committees and parliament. They also exercise control over the minister on behalf of the party. Second, in all governmental parties, most ministers attend a weekly meeting of their party executive as well as a meeting with the party chairman the day before the cabinet meeting. During these latter meetings the cabinet agenda is scrutinized and the positions to be defended by the ministers are defined. Third, parties also influence cabinet decision-making through direct formal and informal contacts between party leaders outside government (and outside the parliamentary arena) during which decisions are reached which are binding on cabinet members. Some crucial denominational and linguistic conflicts have been solved by such party summits, whose final compromises are presented as political pacts not amendable by the cabinet or the parliamentary majority.

In sum, in Belgium, not only have parties occupied the state, in terms both of the nomination of government personnel, from the cabinet to the lowest public servant, and in terms of policy definition, but also, through direct monitoring and the politicization of the government bureaucracy, the implementation of decisions and the allocation of government outputs depend heavily on partisan criteria. While the Italian partyocracy collapsed suddenly in the early 1990s, the Belgian *particratie* underwent a number of gradual modifications that reduced the negative consequences of the grip of political parties on central government actors, structures and processes thus preventing a full collapse of the partitocratic system and, to some degree, restoring the governability of the country (De Winter, 1996).

The resurrection of the pre-war party system, 1944–60

The re-emergence of the traditional parties

By the end of the 1940s, the Belgian party system had reassumed its pre-war two-and-a-half party format (see Figure 10.2 and Tables 10.2 and 10.3). Between 1950 and 1961, the three traditional parties again managed to capture about 90 per cent of the votes, and more than 95 per cent of the seats.

A new Christian Democratic party, the CVP-PSC, was created in 1945 and proved to be quite different to its predecessors. It terminated its formal links with the Church and organized itself on the basis of individual membership instead of indirect membership through the *standen* (estates), although these were not abolished. It became an inter-class party, aiming at the realization of social and economic justice for *all* citizens. It had two wings, the *Flemish Christelijke Volkspartij* (Christian People's Party, CVP) and the francophone *Parti Social Chrétien* (Social Christian Party, PSC), but kept a unitary structure. The renovated Catholic Party soon proved highly successful, obtaining an absolute majority in both chambers in 1950.

Table 10.2 Belgian traditional parties' vote shares, 1946–95

Year	CVP	PSC	BSP	PSB	PVV	PRL
1946		42.5		31.6		8.9
1949		43.6		29.8		15.3
1950		47.7		34.5		11.2
1954		41.1		37.3		12.1
1958		46.5		35.8		11.0
1961		41.5		36.7		12.3
1965		34.5		28.3		21.6
1968	22.3	9.4		28.0		20.9
1971	21.9	8.2		27.2	9.5	7.2
1974	23.3	9.1		26.7	10.4	6.0
1977	26.2	9.8		27.0	8.5	7.8
1978	26.1	10.1	12.4	13.0	10.4	6.0
1981	19.3	7.1	12.4	12.7	12.9	8.6
1985	21.3	8.0	14.6	13.8	10.7	10.2
1987	19.5	8.0	14.9	15.7	11.5	9.4
1991	16.8	7.7	12.0	13.5	12.0	8.1
1995	17.2	7.7	12.6	11.9	13.1	10.3

Table 10.3 Total core party vote, Belgium, 1946–95

Year	CORE
1946	83.0
1949	88.7
1950	93.4
1954	90.5
1958	93.3
1961	90.5
1965	84.4
1968	80.6
1971	74.0
1974	75.5
1977	79.3
1978	78.0
1981	73.0
1985	78.6
1987	79.0
1991	70.1
1995	72.8

In 1945, the Belgian Workers Party was renamed the 'Belgian Socialist Party'. It dropped the term 'workers' in order to attract voters from other social classes. The party remained, however, essentially a party of workers and employees. It underwent some organizational changes, but its basic outlook, strategy and style remained the same. Collective party membership through the socialist pillar organizations was abolished. The socialist-led trade unions took their places as equal partners with the party. Some years later, the party, the unions, the co-operatives and the mutual health insurance organizations set up an organization called Common Socialist Action to co-ordinate their efforts at national, constituency and local level. This organization served both as a mobilization framework enabling the party to back its political demands with public demonstrations, and as a means to spread the cost of party organization, especially of electoral campaigns. The socialist socio-economic organizations were financially far better off than the party itself. Ideologically, the party's strategies became even more reformist and participatory, though it remained strongly anti-clerical until the end of the 1970s. This anti-clerical attitude resulted in the formation of a coalition with the conservative Liberal Party in 1954–58. For the latter party, no significant changes in comparison with the pre-war period occurred.

As far as the other pre-war parties are concerned, the communists, who were very active in the anti-fascist resistance, performed very well in the 1946 election (12.3 per cent) and were rewarded by their inclusion in several post-war governments in the 1944–47 period before the Cold War drove them back into opposition and eroded their electoral appeal. After 1949, they never scored more than 5 per cent. In the 1949 election a new Flemish-nationalist party, the *Vlaamse Concentratie* (Flemish Concentration), participated but did not manage to capture a single seat. In 1954, the Volksunie (VU) won its first seat which it retained at the following elections of 1958. The breakthrough came in 1961 when the VU polled nearly 7 per cent of the national vote, capturing five seats.

Salient cleavages and issues

The hottest issue in the reconstruction period, 1944–50, was the so-called King's Question: the return of Leopold III to Belgium despite the fact that he had favoured a more authoritarian state before the Second World War, refused to follow his government into exile after the German invasion, and held secret negotiations with Hitler in order to keep his position in the new Reich. The Catholics were strongly in favour of the king's return. The socialists and most liberals were against. The government decided to settle the issue through a consultative referendum which produced a majority (58 per cent) in favour of return, with an overwhelming majority (72 per cent) in Flanders. In Wallonia and Brussels, however, a majority, 58 and 52 per cent, respectively, was against. After major riots in Wallonia between demonstrators and the *gendarmerie*, with several casualties, the king was forced to abdicate, to be replaced by his son, Baudouin.

The Catholics, who had won an absolute majority with their support for the king's return, governed the country for four years (1950–54), Belgium's only experience of majority single party government in the post-war period.

They were replaced by an anti-clerical coalition (socialists and liberals) that launched an attack on the Catholic education system. This led to a vast mobilization of the Catholic pillar, with massive public unrest, civil disobedience and violence. This 'School War' revolt forced the government to back down. In 1958, the Catholics captured a majority of seats in the Senate only, and formed a minority government that was soon expanded to include the liberals. In the meantime, the elites of the three traditional parties devised the so-called 'School Pact' in secret – a compromise between the defenders of the Catholic and public education networks which heavily subsidized both. A School Pact Commission was created, with representatives from the three parties, in which all future conflicts were to be debated and solved. Hence, at least as far as the school issue was concerned, the denominational cleavage, which had dominated the Belgian polity for 110 years, was depoliticized.

In 1960, the Centre–Right government launched an austerity programme in order to cope with the effects of the Congo's newly gained independence and the economic recession. In response, the socialist trade union called a general strike which lasted several weeks, at least in the south of the country. In Flanders, however, the strike was not a success, and this division encouraged the government not to give in. After some weeks, the strike collapsed. Socialist Walloon trade union leaders blamed defeat on the hegemonic position of a conservative Flanders that was also benefiting from an economic boom. After 1945, Flanders had attracted a lot of new industries (small and medium-sized enterprises and multinationals) whereas Wallonia, whose economy was based on heavy industry, slowly started to de-industrialize. In the early 1960s, therefore, Walloon socialist leaders started to call for more political autonomy, believing that only public intervention could solve the region's economic problems. Such intervention required a Left political majority which, however, was no longer attainable at the national level given the predominance of conservative public opinion in Flanders. In Wallonia however, a left-wing majority was still within reach.

By the 1960s, then, the nineteenth-century centre–periphery situation had been completely upset: linguistically, Flemish was now on an equal footing with French and the 'frenchification' of Flanders had been stopped by the linguistic laws of 1963 (and had even been reversed as the elites in Flanders became Dutch-speaking). Due to their growing demographic weight and universal suffrage, the Flemish also constituted a political majority while, economically, Flanders was expanding and Wallonia was in decline. This reversal in centre–periphery relations provided the basis for the dramatic changes in the party system in the following two decades: the breakthrough of the VU and the emergence of the Walloon and Brussels francophone regionalist parties in the 1960s, and the break-up of the traditional parties along linguistic lines in the 1970s.

The first wave of party system expansion: the 1960s and 1970s

The emergence and success of regionalist parties

The Flemish *Volksunie* (VU) grew considerably in the 1960s peaking in 1971, with 11 per cent of the national vote. Following this sudden success, the party stalled and even declined slightly in the 1974 and 1977 elections. After its first experience of governmental participation in 1977–8, the VU lost about one-third of its voters, but surprisingly managed to recapture most of them in 1981.

The *Front Démocratique des Francophones* (FDF), the Brussels francophone regionalist movement, grew out of the linguistic laws of 1963. These defined the linguistic border between Flanders, Wallonia, and Brussels and established Dutch and French as the only official language in, respectively, Flanders and Wallonia, while Brussels became bilingual. These same laws made bilingualism a condition of access to higher positions in the national administration and to positions in the Brussels communes that involved social interaction with the public, such as the police and civil service. This measure was felt to be discriminatory towards the Francophone Bruxellois as, in contrast to the Flemish, they were not usually bilingual. Thus, the Flemish became over-represented in the national and Brussels civil service.

The FDF, the party that reacted most strongly to these measures, in no time captured more than half of the francophone vote in Brussels – in 1971, just seven years after its foundation. The party demanded that Brussels become an autonomous and francophone region allowed to expand into the surrounding Flemish communes. In many of these communes, francophone immigration was already high, even to the point that the francophones controlled a political majority in several of these formally Flemish communes. In the 1977–80 period, the FDF participated in three surplus majority governments which aimed at federalizing the unitary state.

The FDF's Walloon sister-party, the *Rassemblement Wallon* (RW), was founded in 1965 as the *Parti Wallon*. From the beginning it demanded federalism, since this would permit the Walloons to halt their economic decline by invoking state intervention. As the RW grew out of the socialist trade union movement it was clearly to the left of the FDF and for some matters it was to the left also of the *Parti Socialiste*, for example in seeking workers' self-management of enterprises. It too reached its electoral peak in 1971. From 1974 to 1977 it participated in government. Thus, in the 1970s, all three regionalist parties (VU, FDF and RW) became relevant to coalition formation.

The effects of the regionalist parties on the traditional parties

Although the Belgian federalist parties were successful in transforming the Belgian unitary state into a federal state, their policy success was not the result of their governmental participation. The 1970 and 1980 institutional reforms were carried through *without* the support of these parties and while the 1988 reform was effected by a government that included the VU, this party also supported the 1993 reforms – from the opposition benches. The process of federalization was, rather, the result of their electoral pressure on the traditional parties. The electoral success of the federalist parties in the 1960s and 1970s provoked the division of the three traditional parties: the Christian Democrats in 1968, the Liberals in 1971, and the Socialists in 1978.

Once liberated from the electorally unprofitable politics of compromise within their former national parties, the linguistically homogeneous wings of the traditional parties gradually took up most of the regionalist parties' issues. Each regional branch rapidly moved towards the extreme position on the linguistic–regional division, leaving a large vacuum in the centre on this most salient conflict dimension. Hence, during the first half of the 1980s the francophone traditional parties managed to crush the electoral appeal of the FDF and the RW, while the VU's vote gradually declined after 1981.

The denominational realignment of the Liberals

With the arrival of a new party leader in 1961 the old unitary Liberal Party (*Parti Libéral/Liberale Partij*) dropped its anti-clerical image. To attract middle-class and conservative Catholic voters to the hitherto anti-clerical movement it placed prominent Catholic right-wingers on the Liberals' lists. To underpin its developing neutrality on the denominational cleavage the party was renamed Party for Liberty and Progress (*Partij voor Vrijheid en Vooruitgang/Parti pour la Liberté et le Progrès*, PVV/PLP). This ideological redefinition, together with the unpopularity of the Christian Democrat/ Socialist coalition (1961–65) boosted the electoral vote tremendously between 1961 (12.3 per cent) and 1965 (21.6 per cent). Accordingly, the Liberals lost their status as a 'halfparty' even though in most subsequent elections they gained less than 20 per cent of the vote.

The other two traditional parties maintained their basic position on this cleavage. The socialists remain fierce defenders of the public education system against the free (i.e. Catholic) dominant educational network and they are also the strongest defenders of the liberalization of abortion legislation. The CVP and the PSC claim to be a deconfessionalized party but they act as fierce defenders of Catholic schools and other pillar organizations. In addition, on many moral issues (abortion, euthanasia) the CVP (and to a lesser degree the PSC) are at the conservative pole of that conflict dimension.

The second wave of party system expansion: the 1980s and 1990s

New parties and agendas

While the elites of the traditional parties were preoccupied by regional–linguistic issues, their failure to implement the 'Egmont pact', the ambitious institutional reform programme of the 1977 Centre–Left government which also included the VU and the FDF, provoked discontent with the traditional and the regionalist parties. The large reservoir of protest votes facilitated the formation of another wave of new parties.

The extreme Right and populists

The parties of the extreme Right were the first to seize the opportunity. The *Vlaams Blok* resulted from the reaction of the Flemish nationalist hard-liners and the right-wing of the *Volksunie* to that party's support for the Egmont pact. The VB was founded in 1978 and managed to get one MP elected the same year. He retained his seat in 1981 and 1985 but the party only broke through at the end of the 1980s when it shifted the focus of its propaganda from separatist to anti-immigration demands. In the 1991 election, it obtained 10 per cent of the Flemish vote and 12 per cent in 1995. On the denominational dimension, the VB defends Catholic conservative issues more strongly than the CVP; on the socio-economic dimensions it is as right-wing as the Liberals, while it calls for full independence of Flanders as a republic. The *Front National*, in ideological outlook a copy of its French homonym, gained one seat in the 1991 election and two in 1995.

In 1978, an anti-tax party was also formed, the UDRT (*Union Démocratique pour le Respect du Travail*). It managed to capture a seat at the 1978 election, and even three in 1981. This poujadist party, successful mainly amongst French-speaking bruxellois, faded away during the reign of the Centre–Right governments of the 1980s, a period in which the traditional liberals radicalized and adopted neo-liberal ideas, including lower taxes. Finally, the anarcho-liberal protest party ROSSEM gained three seats in 1991 but subsequently disintegrated.

The Greens

The ecologist parties, AGALEV and ECOLO, also emerged in the aftermath of the Egmont crisis and naturally have stressed postmaterialist issues such as environmentalism, participation, pacifism, third-worldism and feminism. On the traditional cleavages they are left of the socialists on socio-economic issues, neutral on denominational issues, and try not to polarize the opposition between Flemish and French-speakers on linguistic issues. In fact, they are the only political family that still tries to develop a joint programme with regard to linguistic and regionalist issues. Their first representatives were elected in 1981 and whilst the Flemish AGALEV gradually increased its vote throughout the 1980s, the francophone ECOLO has been relatively more successful since 1991. However, in the first half of the 1990s both parties started losing support due to the breakthrough of the extreme-right and the fact that the Greens have gained in respectability and coalitionability thereby losing their status as a protest party.

The old parties and the old agenda

The predominance of the socio-economic agenda

The focus on community problems in the 1970s impaired the fight against the economic crisis that started with the 1973 oil crisis. Hence, once, in 1980, an important step forward in the federalization of the country had been made, the political elites turned to the country's huge socio-economic problems. The Centre–Right government that came to power in 1981, and remained in office until 1988, took strong austerity measures to enable economic recovery. Still, the public debt grew to 140 per cent of GNP (122 per cent in 1997) with the consequence that nearly 40 per cent of the annual budget now goes on servicing interest payments (Lammens, 1993). The long-lasting Centre–Right coalition caused the Christian Democrats to shift to the right, while the socialists in opposition, especially the Walloon SP, moved leftwards. The SP became more radical with regard to international and defence policies (Zaire, *détente*, nuclear missiles and Third World issues) and strongly criticized the neo-liberal policies of the Centre–Right coalition. Yet, at the end of this opposition period, the SP leadership feared that this strategy might isolate the party jeopardising its coalitionability with the pivotal Christian Democrats. Thus, slowly, it shifted back towards the centre. However, this reverse shift was not appreciated by the new voters the SP had won during its oppositional course and many drained away towards the more radical AGALEV. Losses to their left did not, however, radicalize the socialist parties because they also lost heavily to the extreme right. Hence, the PS and the SP are facing a major problem of redefinition of their programmatic and ideological profiles. First, there is the conflict between the old workerist ideals and the practice of centrist policies of the Centre–Left governments since 1988. The socialist parties accepted the failure of Keynesian politics and seemed able to introduce only minor social corrections to the pro-business policies of the previous Centre–Right coalition. Privatization has not become merely thinkable: the Dehaene I government actually privatized several of the public sector's crown jewels just to keep its budget afloat (De Ruyter *et al.*, 1994).

On the other side of the spectrum, the Flemish Liberals stayed faithful to their neo-liberal creed until 1995 in spite of the decline in popularity of Thatcherite policies in most other countries. In 1992, their party chairman, Verhofstadt, also reformed his party into a 'party of the citizen' (VLD – *Vlaamse en Liberalen Democraten/Partij van de Burger*), democratizing its internal functioning as well as promoting a number of innovations that would boost the influence of individual citizens on decision-making: introducing referendums and the direct election of the leader of the federal, regional and local executives and dismantling neo-corporatist and clientelist networks. For three years, his revolutionary reforms dominated the political agenda. The party soared in the polls and several MPs and lower level elites from other parties defected to the VLD. However, as this polarizing strategy did not produce the expected electoral breakthrough, Verhofstadt resigned and was replaced by a party apparatchik in 1995.

The linguistic conflict

After 1981, support for all three regionalist parties fell rapidly. The RW disappeared completely thanks to the strong radicalization of the francophone PS on Walloon and linguistic issues. The FDF still presents candidates in Brussels but captured only three seats in the 1987 and 1991 elections (with about 1 per cent of the national vote). In 1993, it decided to constitute a federation with the francophone Liberals (*Parti Réformateur Libéral*, PRL), introducing joint lists for all but local elections. Hence, the FDF is also on the verge of disappearance since the expectation is that it will be swallowed up by the PRL. The VU vote has declined gradually since 1981. At its 1993 congress the party shifted to the left and it is now situated between the Greens and the socialists. Partly due to this shift nearly half of its MPs abandoned it for other parties. In the period 1991–95 the VU, like the FDF, conducted negotiations with the Liberals as well as with the CVP about a possible merger. However, as the VU still managed to capture 5 per cent of the national vote in 1995 the party leadership was sufficiently encouraged to continue as an autonomous party.

As far as the traditional parties are concerned, the Liberal–Christian-Democratic coalition tried to put linguistic and regional conflicts on the backburner, at least at the governmental level, and managed rather well until 1987 when the coalition fell again over a linguistic issue. The socialist parties, on the other hand, have radicalized their positions on the community issue. After their split in 1978, the SP rapidly became as nearly as strong a defender of the Flemish cultural and socio-economic interests as the *Volksunie* and the CVP. Meanwhile, the PS became the most outspoken defender of the declining traditional industrial sectors in Wallonia and the vanguard of francophone linguistic claims, especially with regard to the status of the francophone demographic majorities in the Flemish territory (the Fourons area and the Brussels periphery). This strategy brought the PS to a near-majority electoral position in Wallonia in 1987 and it thus became a party which no national coalition could neglect. Since 1988, it has been included in the national and regional executives. In this period two waves of constitutional reform, in 1988 and 1993, transformed the Belgian state into a fully fledged federal state, with 40 per cent of the national budget transferred to the regions and cultural communities. As a consequence, the PS is currently consolidating its quasi-majoritarian positions in these new institutions and taking moderate stands with regard to the community cleavage, having marginalized the minority of fiercer nationalists within its ranks.

The denominational cleavage

Frozen until 1987, despite some potentially explosive issues such as abortion, the political elites do not want to revive the denominational cleavage. The decline in its salience has allowed some attempts at realignment between Catholic and anti-clerical political forces. For instance, at the beginning of the 1980s, the SP launched a 'breakthrough' strategy making the party more attractive to militants in the Christian Workers' movement, left-wing intellectuals with Catholic backgrounds, and former members of the extreme Left (especially the Trotskyites). While the strategy towards the latter two categories proved effective at the beginning of the 1980s, it never really worked for the Catholic workers. As with the failed attempt to constitute a 'progressive Front' a decade earlier, the constituent organizations involved did not want to give up their autonomy or their identities. In the mid-1990s, a further attempt at constituting a single progressive party began, driven by a group of left-wing intellectuals close to the SP led by the leader of the *Volksunie*. This time the plan was not only to merge the socialist with the Catholic Workers' movement, but also to include the Greens and left-wing Flemish nationalists. However, the leadership of the latter three groups were very sceptical, if not entirely hostile, to a strategy which they considered to be aimed essentially at safeguarding the electoral strength of the ailing Socialist Party.

Conclusion: the next decade. awaiting final disintegration?

The future shape and survival of the Belgian party system will depend on the saliency of old and new cleavages and the degree to which they overlap. Although several scenarios are foreseeable, there is no doubt that the system will remain highly fragmented and more complex than that of any other western democracy. In the 1991 election, fragmentation reached its post-war peak. Rae's index rose to 0.88 (0.88 in 1995), whilst the 'effective number of parties' was 8.41 (8.03 in 1995) – higher than any score in Lijphart's 21 democracies study (Lijphart, 1984). Fragmentation decreased between 1991 and 1995 because of the PRL/FDF electoral alliance and the disappearance of ROSSEM.

Of the traditional cleavages, it is clear that the socio-economic one will remain highly salient. High unemployment, a public sector which is virtually bankrupt, budgetary austerity due to the implementation of the Maastricht conversion criteria, the transfer of industrial activity to low-wage countries and the growing number of pensioners all put extremely heavy pressure on the well-established and generous Belgian welfare state. On the other hand, the denominational cleavage will further erode given growing secularization, and this in spite of the fact that organizationally the Catholic pillar has largely kept its predominance, especially in Flanders.

As far as new cleavages are concerned, in spite of the verbal adaptation of the traditional parties to the green creed, post-materialist issues and the parties that politicize them will remain salient. The breakthrough of the *Vlaams Blok* in Flanders at the end of the 1980s, and of the *Front National* in Brussels and Wallonia in 1995, indicate that the issues from the 'silent counter revolution' (Ignazi, 1992a) will also remain salient. Although the traditional parties have formally opted for a policy of active integration of immigrants into Belgian society, the results of this policy will show only in the long term, and will not decrease the current tensions in the big cities. More recently, moreover, the traditional parties have also adopted much tougher positions, especially with regard to illegal immigration and the fight against crime in the urban centres.

As far as the core of the party system under this 'simple' cleavage configuration is concerned, its traditional members, i.e. the Christian Democratic, socialist and liberal parties, will remain the central actors in the competition for government participation. Most likely the Christian Democratic family will remain the central element, given its centrist position on the Left–Right spectrum and the persistent saliency of the religious cleavage. Hence, coalitions will continue to shift between Centre–Right and Centre–Left coalitions, as determined by the pivotal Christian Democrats. Yet, although electoral shifts between the traditional parties are considerable (Aish and Swyngedouw, 1994), on the whole they may continue to lose to non-traditional parties, leaving the core ever smaller (see Tables 10.2 and 10.3). In 1995, the largest core party, the CVP, gained a little over a quarter (27 per cent) of the Flemish vote and just 17 per cent of the national vote.

Table 10.4 Government composition in Belgium, 1946–95

Prime Minister	Date in	Government composition
Spaak I	Mar. 1946	PSB/BSP
Van Acker I	Apr. 1946	PSB/BSP, PL/LP, Comm
Van Acker II	Aug. 1946	PSB/BSP, PL/LP, Comm, UDB
Huysmans	Aug. 1946	PSB/BSP, PL/LP, Comm
Spaak II	Mar. 1947	CVP/PSC, PSB/BSP
Eyskens G. I	July 1949	CVP/PSC, PL/LP
Duvieusart	June 1950	CVP/PSC
Pholien	Aug. 1950	CVP/PSC
Van Houtte	Jan. 1952	CVP/PSC
Van Acker III	Apr. 1954	PSB/BSP, PL/LP
Eyskens G. II	June 1958	CVP/PSC
Eyskens G. III	Nov. 1958	CVP/PSC, PL/LP
Lefèvre	Apr. 1961	CVP/PSC, PSB/BSP
Harmel	July 1965	CVP/PSC, PSB/BSP
Van den Boeynants I	Mar. 1966	CVP/PSC, PL/LP
Eyskens G. IV	June 1968	CVP, PSC, PSB/BSP
Leburton	Jan. 1973	CVP, PSC, PSB/BSP, PL, LP
Tindemans I	Apr. 1974	CVP, PSC, PL, LP
Tindemans II	June 1974	CVP, PSC, PL, LP, RW
Tindemans III	Mar. 1977	CVP, PSC, PL, LP
Tindemans IV	June 1977	CVP, PSC, PSB/BSP, FDF, VU
Van den Boeynants II	Oct. 1978	CVP, PSC, PS, SP, FDF, VU
Martens I	Apr. 1979	CVP, PSC, PS, SP, FDF
Martens II	Jan. 1980	CVP, PSC, PS, SP
Martens III	Apr. 1980	CVP, PSC, PS, SP, PL, LP
Martens IV	Oct. 1980	CVP, PSC, PS, SP
Eyskens M.	Apr. 1981	CVP, PSC, PS, SP
Martens V	Dec. 1981	CVP, PSC, PL, LP
Martens VI	Nov. 1985	CVP, PSC, PL, LP
Martens VII	July 1987	CVP, PSC, PL, LP
Martens VIII	May 1988	CVP, PSC, PS, SP, VU
Martens	Sept. 1991	CVP, PSC, PS, SP
Dehaene I	Mar. 1992	CVP, PSC, PS, SP
Dehaene II	June 1995	CVP, PSC, PS, SP

If the core weakens further, a working majority of Centre–Left or Centre–Right able to embrace both regions may be out of reach. In that case, two alternative types of coalitions are feasible, as long as the extreme Right *Vlaams Blok* and *Front National* are considered uncoalitionable. First, a tripartite (or better hexapartite) grand coalition can be formed including the Flemish and francophone Christian Democrats, Socialists and Liberals. This type of coalition was tried in 1973 and 1980, when a two-thirds majority was required to reform the constitution. However, neither lasted more than a year. Therefore, the second alternative, a Centre–Left coalition with the addition of the Green parties is more likely. The fact that in 1993 the Centre–Left coalition negotiated and passed the constitutional reform bill by co-operating with the opposition Green parties indicates that the latter have become coalitionable in the eyes of the traditional parties. Indeed, the Liberal *formateur* Verhofstadt tried to form a Liberal–Socialist–Green government after the 1991 election.

However, there are less 'optimistic' scenarios as well. First, anti-establishment politics may dominate the political agenda in the years to come. Although the regionalist and Green parties have always favoured a more participatory political life, including greater intra-party democracy, the issue has only become a dominant one on the political agenda through the radicalization of the Flemish Liberals. Although until now this strategy has failed electorally, the campaign for greater citizen participation has stuck, and the other traditional parties have already adopted some of the Liberal innovations in their own party decision-making processes (De Winter, 1993). In addition, Belgium appears vulnerable to the judicial investigation of corruption that, as in Italy, could remove a large number of the current leaders of the traditional parties. Three former Socialist vice-PMs (one of whom had become NATO Secretary-General) resigned from their positions due to investigations into a vast corruption affair possibly linked to the murder of the former Socialist party president, Cools. Many former ministers and leaders of the other parties that were in power in the 1970s and 1980s are equally suspected of taking bribes in exchange for government contracts. The likelihood of such a 'big bang'depends on the extent of past corruption (which most likely was less destructive than in the Italian case) and on the control the parties involved can exert on the judiciary, which seems stronger than in Italy (Della Porta and Vannucci, 1996; Van Outryve, 1996). Still, the issue of clandestine party finance in the 1970s and 1980s remains a time bomb which can go off at any moment or gradually be defused, for example by reinforcing the 1989 law on the public financing of parties.

Another devastating, and more plausible, evolution is the break-up of the country due to insurmountable conflicts between the regions and communities. It is obvious that linguistic and regional problems will remain highly salient, and competition between Flemish and French-speaking parties may become even more centrifugal in spite of the massive federalization of the state. Until 1999, when the next election is due and the law on the financing of the regions is due for review, the party elites will be busy occupying new positions and policy competences acquired through the 1988 and 1993 constitutional reforms. But once this process has been completed, new clashes will occur, most likely resulting in further federal government powers being transferred to the regions and communities. In the end, the federal government will have hardly any powers left: most will be transferred to the regions and communities, while Brussels will take care of monetary and economic policies, foreign policy and defence – to the extent that these are not in any case 'Europeanized'. Hence, if in the future a profound conflict occurs over one of the few remaining federal powers (for instance, the federalization of social security, which some Flemish parties are already calling for), it is likely that the conflicting parties might do away with this troublesome federal level, seeking to become independent regions within the framework of the European Union.

Finally, one should be fully aware that since 1978 and the splitting of the last traditional party, one cannot strictly speak of *a* 'Belgian' party system. There are two distinct party systems: a Flemish one and a Walloon one. In the Flemish constituencies, only Flemish parties compete for votes, and they do not present any lists in the Walloon constituencies – and vice versa. Only in the Brussels-Halle-Vilvoorde constituency do these two party systems overlap with Flemish and francophone parties competing for the same voters. The two party systems differ in terms of the type of parties that are active, as well as their electoral strength and evolution. The splitting of the Belgian party system into two quasi-autonomous regional party systems has strengthened the centrifugal tendencies in the Belgian polity and made an 'ethnic big bang' even more likely.

11

Spain: Political Parties in a Young Democracy

JONATHAN HOPKIN

Introduction

The most recent attempt to classify the Spanish party system (Heywood, 1995a: 174-6) observed that, between 1977 and 1984, nine different classifications had been proposed. This lack of agreement clearly illustrates the difficulty of detecting a settled pattern of party competition in the decade following the end of the Franco dictatorship. In the early 1980s, some authors expressed concern that a fragmented and polarized party system was emerging, threatening an unstable and unconsolidated democracy (Linz, 1980; Maravall, 1981; Bar, 1984). The radical shift provoked by the disintegration of the ruling Union of the Democratic Centre (UCD) in the 1982 elections suggested a volatile electorate with weak connections to the major political parties (Caciagli, 1984). However, the period after 1982 has been marked by a greater degree of stability, making some kind of definition possible. From the perspective offered by almost two decades of democratic party competition, the collapse of the UCD, despite its far-reaching consequences, has had limited effects on the basic definitional features of the party system. The classification of 'limited multi-party system' (Aguilera de Prat, 1988; Ramírez, 1988), applied to the 1977–82 period, remains valid today.

At the level of state-wide parties, a kind of two-party (or two-and-a-half party) system has been established, with the two biggest parties consistently taking around two-thirds of the vote, and a third party taking around 10 per cent. However, while the number of parties enjoying significant electoral support has fallen since 1977 (Montero, 1994: 53–67), the importance of nationalist and regionalist parties in several of the seventeen Autonomous Communities into which the Spanish state is divided, distances Spain from the two-party model. Perhaps the most comprehensive definition is that offered by Ramírez (1982: 17; see also 1988; 1991): 'a limited multi-party system with bipolarity of political options but low degrees of ideological polarization'.

The origins of the Spanish party system

The success of the peaceful transition to democracy after Franco's death and the relative ease with which stable and depolarized party competition has been established are all the more striking in view of Spain's turbulent history. The civil war of 1936–39, and the four decades of dictatorship which resulted from it, are well known, but even before then, Spain had suffered a century of political upheaval and civil war, with the military regularly intervening in politics. This instability made the gradual evolution of a party system impossible, and few of the parties involved in the democratic interlude of the Second Republic (1931–36) could claim any heritage or organizational continuity (Linz, 1980: 101).

The cleavages which provoked high levels of civil conflict in Spain in the first half of this century remained relevant to the structure of party competition which emerged after the dictatorship. They were not, however, the same cleavages which had caused political chaos in the nineteenth century. The civil war simplified a complex combination of sometimes cross-cutting alliances and oppositions into a fight between Republicans and Nationalists. The Franco dictatorship, fiercely opposed to any form of national reconciliation, institutionalized the battle lines of the civil war with a combination of political oppression and social marginalization of those forces associated with the defeated Republic (Preston, 1985). Political alignments formed around three basic cleavages.

The most explosive of these cleavages was between the subject and the dominant culture. State-building in Spain was conditioned by the fact that the unification of the crowns of Aragon and Castile took place when Castile was at its strongest (Elliot, 1963). The subsequent decline of Castile and the ascendancy of Aragon–Catalonia created a disjunction between economic and institutional power which became increasingly visible over the centuries. Catalan nationalism emerged to defend Catalan economic interests against the backwardness of Castile, but also to protect Catalonia's distinctive cultural and linguistic heritage. A similar movement, less linked to economic interests, emerged in the Basque Country.

The Second Republic provided the Catalans and Basques with statutes of autonomy reconstituting their lost institutions of self-government, to the fury of Castilian centralists and, in particular, sectors of the military (Thomas, 1986: 91–6). Crushing these pretensions to home rule became one of the chief objectives of the Nationalist war effort and, after the war, Franco swiftly reasserted the political dominance of the centre, brutally suppressing cultural and linguistic diversity in the Basque Country and Catalonia. This conflict has had a fragmenting and polarizing effect on the development of the party system in the new democracy, creating quite distinct party sub-systems in the two historic nationalities.

The relationship between Church and state has also been a fundamental source of conflict. The Second Republic was founded on an anti-clerical constitution which not only separated Church and state but also banned religious education and abolished the Church's fiscal privileges (Thomas, 1986). Those conservative sectors of the army which ultimately rose against the Republic were also in part motivated by an intense rejection of this secularization of the state, and Franco, particularly in the initial stages of his dictatorship, presented the Church as a guardian of Spanish values. Although the Church later distanced itself from the Franco regime, Catholicism was entrenched as a reactionary force, and generally perceived as an opponent of social change.

While the religious cleavage cross-cut the territorial conflict (the Basque Country, opposed to Franco's centralism, was deeply Catholic), it reflected, and reinforced, what can be described in broad terms as the class cleavage. To an extent, indeed, the religious cleavage can be seen as simply another expression of class conflict.

Class conflict in Spain took two main forms. First of all, landed interests were set against landless labourers and short-term tenants. This conflict was one of the most important causes of the civil war and it acquired an extraordinary virulence in areas such as Estremadura and Andalusia where the landless peasants organized into socialist and anarchist trade unions, establishing a radical left-wing tradition. Although economic development from the 1960s onwards brought an exodus from rural areas to towns, defusing the conflict over land, the south remains a bedrock for the left. Second, in those areas where industrialization took hold, such as Catalonia, the Basque Country, Asturias and Madrid, the familiar workers-versus-employers cleavage was an important source of conflict in the Second Republic. These were also, not by chance, areas which resisted the military coup in 1936 and fought against the Nationalists. As a result they bore the brunt of Francoist oppression during and after the war and they became strong bases of support for the Left.

The electoral environment: institutional and cultural constraints

A peculiarity of the contemporary Spanish party system is that it emerged during a period of radical institutional and cultural change. The 1977 general election, in which the basic features of the system became established, was held in an atmosphere of profound institutional ambiguity: the Francoist constitutional system remained in place, but Adolfo Suárez's government had introduced important reforms which made fully democratic party competition possible. The parliament which emerged from these elections drafted a new democratic constitution which ensured a more stable institutional framework for party politics.

The defining moment of the first democratic election was conditioned by a shifting political landscape in which the electoral law drafted by the Suárez government played a key role in shaping the nature of party competition. This law, notwithstanding minor changes, established the electoral system which has regulated party competition in the new Spanish democracy. Its main features are: the d'Hondt system of proportional representation; the establishment of the province as the electoral district; an upper limit of 350 deputies in the Lower Chamber; a minimum of two seats per district; a threshold of 3 per cent (at district level) for parliamentary representation; and closed lists of candidates (Montero, Llera and Torcal, 1992).

These features have the effect of mitigating proportionality to such an extent that it is difficult to define the system as one of proportional representation. In 1977, the UCD was able to govern alone, with 47.4 per cent of the parliamentary seats, on the strength of just 34.6 per cent of the vote; the Communists (PCE), on the other hand, won only 5.7 per cent of the seats despite obtaining 9.4 per cent of the vote (Pallarés, 1981: 234). As well as under-representing smaller parties, the system encourages tactical voting on a grand scale as in many districts some parties have no hope of winning a seat. The system also over-represents rural areas. Provinces such as Soria, with a small population, are guaranteed the minimum two seats, while the upper limit of 350 deputies constrains the extent to which highly populated provinces, such as Barcelona, can be adequately compensated with more seats (Montero, Llera and Torcal, 1992).

This electoral system, as well as helping the largest parties, also favours parties with geographically concentrated support. In this way, the incentive structure of the electoral rules encourages the territorial fragmentation of the party system. As a result, while the Spanish electoral system has an index of proportionality close to that of majoritarian systems in countries such as Britain and France (Montero, 1992: 280-1), this has not had the effect of creating a two-party system. Alongside the electoral system's encouragement of non-state-wide parties, the radical reform of the state administration in the post-Franco period has created new foci of political representation at the level of the Autonomous Communities. The quasi-federal structure of the new Spanish state, therefore, has an impact on how parties organize and campaign, and it also affects the types of electoral coalitions that can be formed.

The rebirth of party politics after Franco's death

The re-emergence of political parties in post-Franco Spain is difficult to compare with the experience of other Western European democracies in the post-war period since Spanish parties had not been able to operate openly for 40 years. This implied, above all, a high degree of organizational discontinuity (Linz, 1980: 102). Most of the Second Republic parties, including important forces such as the conservative CEDA, simply did not reconstitute themselves after Franco's death. Moreover, in those cases where parties did survive the dictatorship, they were often led by figures who were too young to have been involved in the previous party system.

This suggests that the nature of the new party system was unlikely to be determined by past experience. With the possible exceptions of the communist PCE and the Basque Nationalist Party (PNV), the historic parties had failed to maintain a real presence during the dictatorship at the levels of elites, of grass-roots activists and of identifying voters. This is not to say that the cleavages which had dominated Spanish political life before the civil war had become irrelevant. However, the re-emergence of party politics after 1975 was conditioned in a number of ways by the characteristics of the process of the transition to democracy.

By 1975, the Franco regime was collapsing under the weight of an increasingly active opposition, in which Basque nationalism played a vanguard role (Preston, 1986). The regime's brutal response to terrorism in the Basque Country on top of growing industrial unrest in Madrid, Barcelona and other areas, created an atmosphere of polarization and violence. The threat of a return to civil war could not be excluded, and that threat conditioned the path to democracy which was taken after the dictator's death. Within the regime, an important sector of the higher civil service and the National Movement (the Francoist single party) became concerned that violence would escalate if Spain's sclerotic political structures were not allowed to catch up with the profound socio-economic changes which had taken place. This concern was at the root of the negotiated move towards democracy under Adolfo Suárez in 1976–78, a process of transition which has been described as *ruptura pactada* (a negotiated break with the dictatorship; García San Miguel, 1981).

The most important steps in the rebirth of party politics in Spain took place in the course of this process of transition. The party formations which contested the first democratic elections in June 1977, and even the electoral law regulating these elections, were, to a significant degree, products of the process of *ruptura pactada*. Adolfo Suárez's reform programme was based on a determination to avoid a repetition of the confrontational style of politics which had undermined the Second Republic and to promote dialogue between mutually hostile political forces. Suárez's commitment to dialogue was almost obsessive and owed much to a genuine fear of a return to civil war (Suárez, 1988).

This has been described as a consociational model of transition (Huneeus, 1982) in that political leaders succeeded in reaching compromises in private negotiations which they were then able to cajole their constituencies into accepting. Gunther (1986b: 468) has argued that the consociational model is *not* appropriate, principally because Spanish society in the 1970s lacked the levels of political articulation and vertebration characteristic of consociational systems.

Gunther described the transition as 'the very model of the modern elite settlement', arguing that it:

> helped forge a high and unprecedented level of structural integration among national elites. Mutual respect for political opponents is, for the first time in modern Spanish history, virtually universal among elites at the core of the political system in Madrid. Bonds of personal friendship ... have transcended formerly divisive political and social cleavages.
>
> (1992a: 40)

This atmosphere of elite consensus contributed to the centripetal direction of party competition in the 1977 and 1979 elections, ensuring that the leaders of political parties did not interpret their representative function in as aggressive a fashion as their predecessors. As a result, the class and religious cleavages did not generate the kind of conflictual relationships between parties that had characterized the Second Republic.

The emergence of the new Spanish party system was affected by the nature of the transition in another important respect. Although certain long-standing cleavages remained fundamental in defining the political space, the process of party formation also reflected the positions adopted by elite groups over the transition process itself. This was less true of the left, where communists and socialists initially coincided in arguing for *ruptura*. This involved a 'clean break' with the Franco regime, a strategy which would involve the formation of a provisional government of democratic forces, and immediate elections to a constituent assembly which would define a new institutional and legal structure.

Within the Right, however, there were strong differences over the nature and extent of political change (Amodia, 1990a: 43). The Right was divided most fundamentally between those who had participated in the dictatorship and those who had offered testimonial opposition to it. The Christian Democratic, liberal and monarchist groups which had formed the 'tolerated opposition' to Franco insisted on comprehensive and irreversible political reform and, despite their conservatism over social and economic issues, were deeply suspicious of the Francoist political elite.

Within the regime, the traditionally heterogeneous Francoist elite was deeply split. A small and fanatical sector was bitterly opposed to any form of political change. This group, in its various forms, failed to win parliamentary representation in 1977. The relationship between two other loosely defined groups, however, determined the configuration of the political space to the right of the socialists in the new party system.

On the one hand, a group under the leadership of Manuel Fraga favoured a progressive opening up (*apertura*) of the Franco regime which would gradually 'widen its base of support', making it more representative, but excluding groups such as the communists and the more radical peripheral nationalists (Ortega Díaz-Ambrona, 1984). On the other, a group generally referred to as the reformists was ready to accept that the Franco regime could not be maintained in any recognizable form, and that a fully democratic political system, modelled on other liberal democracies in Western Europe, should replace it. This group was willing to co-operate with the Left in order to achieve the shared goal of democratization, but opposed the idea of a formal *ruptura*, preferring instead to maintain the pretence that democracy could result from an evolution of the existing constitutional order (Tácito, 1975; García San Miguel, 1981; del Aguila, 1982; Morodo, 1984).

These latter two groups formed the basis of the two major parties of the Right which obtained parliamentary representation in the 1977 elections. Fraga, along with a number of other senior conservative Francoists, formed Alianza Popular (AP), which argued for a slower pace of reform using unashamedly reactionary rhetoric (see, for example, Fraga, 1977). The reformists, under the leadership of Adolfo Suárez, joined forces with sectors of the tolerated opposition to form a coalition, later to become a party, the *Unión de Centro Democrático* (UCD).

The UCD, which enjoyed a plurality of votes and seats and governed from 1977 until its dramatic collapse in 1982, was very much a product of the transition process. First of all, UCD was perceived as Adolfo Suárez's party, and would probably not have been formed if Suárez had not enjoyed such a prominent position in the run-up to the 1977 elections. His popularity as the prime minister responsible for introducing the Political Reform Law (Lucas Verdú, 1976) and the extraordinary concentration of political resources around the government of an unreformed authoritarian state (Hopkin, 1995: 49–53), gave Suárez the authority to impose an artificial unity on the various small parties which aspired to occupy the Centre–Right political space in the new party system.

The creation of the UCD was conditioned by the process of political change in other respects too. It was an ideologically heterogeneous party, containing

Christian Democratic, liberal, social democratic and regionalist groups, along with a range of reformists. Such diverse groups, divided over economic management, territorial politics and social issues, were initially able to work together because of their basic agreement over the nature of political reform. As one of the UCD's founders explained in an interview with Richard Gunther:[1]

> UCD emerged as an 'omnibus' party, where perhaps the unifying factor was an idea of political change which contrasted with the *rupturista* position of the PSOE and the more or less *continuista* position of AP in 1977 . . . . It occupied a central position characterized more by its negative assertions than its positive assertions: 'here is where Marxist Socialism is *not* represented; here is where the authoritarian conservative right is *not* represented.'

In sum, the key impulse behind the creation of the UCD was the need to build a coalition of moderate democratic forces which could ensure the continuation of the reform project. In effect, it served as a vehicle for Prime Minister Adolfo Suárez to remain in power. On the Right, at least then, the process of democratic change, and the positions adopted by political elites involved in that process, were fundamental in determining the shape of the party system.

The new party system, 1977–82: a clean break with the past?

The June 1977 elections produced a parliament which elaborated the constitutional framework of the new democracy and laid the foundations for party competition in post-Franco Spain. Its major features were a high concentration of votes and an even higher concentration of seats around the two main parties, the UCD and the PSOE (see Table 11.1); much weaker performances by the less moderate national level parties, AP and the PCE; the elimination of most other national level parties, and the emergence of distinct party sub-systems in the Basque Country and Catalonia.

As mentioned earlier, the new party system had significant features of continuity with the past. The largest party on the left in the Second Republic, the PSOE, remained the largest party on the left in the new democracy, while the PCE remained the most important representative of the 'hard' Left. The PNV retained its position as the main force for Basque nationalism, although since the civil war, it had undergone splits resulting in the emergence of extremist parties favouring terrorism as a means to achieve independence.

The continuity in the names of these parties did not mean, however, with the partial exception of Carrillo in the PCE, that their leaderships and memberships remained the same. The PSOE leadership had been completely renewed after a group of youthful Socialists had wrested control of the party from the old guard in exile (Gunther, Sani and Shabad, 1986: 71–2), and its membership had dwindled so badly during the dictatorship that the party

Table 11.1 Spanish general election results, major parties, 1977–96

Party	1977	1979	1982	1986	1989	1993	1996
PSOE	30.3	30.5	46.5	44.3	39.6	38.7	37.5
AP/PP	8.4	6.5	25.8	26.1	25.8	34.8	38.9
UCD	34.8	35.0	6.7	–	–	–	–
PCE/IU	9.3	10.8	4.1	4.6	9.1	9.6	10.6
CDS	–	–	2.8	9.2	7.9	1.8	-
CiU	2.8	2.7	3.9	5.0	5.0	5.0	4.6
PNV	1.7	1.7	1.9	1.4	1.2	1.2	1.3

Key to party abbreviations

AP   Alianza Popular (Popular Alliance)
CiU   Convergència i Unió (Convergence and Union)
CDS   Centro Democrático y Social (Social and Democratic Centre)
IU   Izquierda Unida (United Left)
PCE   Partido Comunista de España (Spanish Communist Party)
PSOE   Partido Socialista Obrero Español (Spanish Socialist Workers' Party)
PNV   Partido Nacionalista Vasco (Basque Nationalist Party)
PP   Partido Popular (Popular Party)
UCD   Unión de Centro Democrático (Union of the Democratic Centre)

effectively had to be rebuilt. Some of the PCE's civil war leaders remained active in the party, but its role as the main opposition to Franco outside the Basque Country brought a new membership in the 1970s, making it Spain's biggest party as the transition began. For its part, the PNV, despite its leadership being largely too young to have been involved in the Second Republic, remained strongly rooted in the same areas of the Basque Country where nationalist feeling was most intense.

Unsurprisingly, given the 40-year parenthesis of the dictatorship, not all was marked by continuity. Left bourgeois republicanism disappeared (Linz, 1980: 102) and discontinuity was equally striking amongst the national level Right. In particular, a range of conservative and extreme Right forces which had been relevant in the Second Republic's party system either failed to stand, or won scant support, in the 1977 elections. Clearly, some of the potential support for extreme Right options was transferred to AP, which was reactionary in tone in 1977 and had a reasonable chance of winning seats, but it is worth noting that the extreme Right, an important minority force in the 1930s, was in effect eliminated from the political game in the first elections of the new democracy.

The CEDA's disappearance and substitution in 1977 and 1979 by the UCD are also worth close attention. Although it was strongest in the areas which had supported the CEDA in the 1930s (Linz, 1980: 103; Caciagli, 1986), and enjoyed similar prominence as the major party to the right of the PSOE, UCD was a very different kind of party. The CEDA (see Montero, 1977) was fervently anti-Republican, which in the context of the 1930s, can be taken to mean anti-democratic. Indeed, some of the CEDA's leadership were open admirers of Italian Fascism and German Nazism. It was also set against social reform, in particular the redistribution of land and the ending of the privileges of the clergy (Preston, 1986: 33–9), and implicitly encouraged the interventionist aspirations of the military. The UCD, on the other hand, was created with the principal aim of avoiding political conflict and of ensuring a smooth passage to democracy, and although there were profound differences within it, it is difficult to argue that the UCD was intent on blocking reform (Gunther, 1996: 24–31).

The changes in the political space to the right of the PSOE were not only the result of discontinuities at the elite and activist levels. In the course of four decades of authoritarianism, Spanish society had undergone deep transformations, and in some senses was virtually unrecognizable (de Esteban and López Guerra, 1982: 46).

Spain's integration into the international economy after 1959 brought rapid economic expansion and social change on a massive scale. This had particular consequences for the religious and class cleavages which had been so important in the 1930s. In the course of the 1960s, the proportion of the workforce employed in agriculture fell from 40 to 29 per cent, and 1.8 million left the land to work and live in urban areas (Giner and Sevilla, 1984: 138–9). This not only defused the agrarian problem; it also affected the social bases of religious practice in Spain, traditionally linked to rural culture (Murillo Ferrol *et al.*, 1983).

The growing secularization of Spanish society tended to blur the old distinction between the Catholic and anti-clerical subcultures, providing the opportunity to reconcile Catholicism with the idea of a modern democratic state. The movement from agricultural to industrial labour did increase the potential for class conflict in some respects, but the greater prosperity brought by rapid economic growth, and the large numbers of workers employed in the service sector contributed to much higher levels of social integration. The emergence of a modern middle class created a 'constituency for capitalism' for whom 'democracy was acceptable, even desirable, provided that financial security and private property (with cars and seaside holidays) could be preserved' (Bermeo, 1987: 224). The UCD was able to mobilize an important sector of this constituency, as well as winning over sectors of the working class (Linz *et al.*, 1981: 215–22), something a traditional conservative party modelling itself on the CEDA would not have achieved.

Although the religious and class cleavages remained important in articulating political behaviour, their nature had changed and they were unlikely to provoke the levels of social conflict and civil disorder that had been seen in the 1930s (Amodia, 1990a: 42). This is clearly revealed by the various studies on the ideological and attitudinal characteristics of the Spanish electorate in the post-Franco period which document the moderation and lack of ideological commitment of most Spanish voters.[2] On a Left–Right scale, the largest number of voters placed themselves in a central position, with a slight inclination towards the left; very few voters placed themselves in the more radical ideological positions (Linz *et al.*, 1981: 151–228; Maravall, 1981: 44–53).

It is quite accurate to point out that the geographical distribution of support for the two major parties in 1977 corresponded quite closely to those of their predecessors in the 1930s. Linz observed a strong correlation at the provincial level between electoral support for the PSOE in 1936 and 1977, and for the CEDA in 1936 and UCD in 1977, and survey data revealed that voting choices in 1977 appeared to be largely coherent with family allegiances in the civil war (Linz, 1980: 103–5; also Gunther, 1992b: 19–25). However, it is not at all clear whether support for the PSOE or CEDA was 'passed on' down the generations to the post-Franco PSOE and the UCD. Survey research has found little evidence of the survival of strictly partisan loyalties to the PSOE even in those areas where it became the strongest party in 1977 (ibid.: 19).

The substantial differences between the 1930s' and 1970s' parties and party leaders, and between the social and economic circumstances in which both party systems emerged, suggest caution should be exercised in arguing for a causal link. Maravall exercises such caution, arguing that a kind of *'loyalty* towards the left or the right in general, rather than support for parties, survived the forty years and was passed down the generations by families and communities' (1981: 44) and influenced the vote by narrowing the range of available voting options.

In the context of an electorate loosely structured into moderate positions on the Centre–Left and Centre–Right but largely lacking in partisan loyalties or ideological commitments, there was room for the decisions of the party elites themselves to influence the type of party system to emerge (Barnes, McDonough and López Piña, 1986). Richard Gunther, in his extensive work on the development of party competition in democratic Spain (1986a; 1986b; 1992b; with Sani and Shabad, 1986), emphasizes the autonomy of party leaders to structure the vote. His analysis of the 1979 and 1982 votes shows that the most popular party leaders, Suárez and the Socialist, Felipe González, enjoyed support among voters from varied social and attitudinal categories, and that attitude towards party leaders was the strongest variable explaining voters' choice of party (1992b: 31). In their 1986 study, Gunther, Sani and Shabad concluded that:

the behaviour of political elites was by far the most important factor in the emergence of the new party system. Electoral and party financing laws were the product of conscious deliberations and negotiations among party leaders. Elites were the driving force behind the creation or expansion of party organizational infrastructures. ... Finally, in the absence of long-standing partisan attachments, and in the age of television, party leaders themselves served as significant objects of popular identification and electoral support.

(1986: 395)

It is worth emphasizing that the politics of consensus, in which party leaders co-operated over the constitutional project, was the result of Suárez's deter-mination to occupy the centre ground of Spanish politics, while his demise, which led ultimately to the disappearance of the UCD, was the result of a concerted attempt by the right of the party to push for a more confronta-tional strategy (Hopkin, 1995; Gunther and Hopkin, forthcoming). This attempt, despite there being no obvious pressure towards greater ideological polarization on the part of the electorate, led to a profound restructuring of the party system in 1982, as the UCD suffered a fatal electoral defeat to the benefit of the PSOE and AP. Throughout this period, in which radical changes in the dynamics of the party system took place, the ideological positioning and attitudinal characteristics of the Spanish electorate barely shifted (Gunther, 1986a).

The collapse of the centre and party system realignment

The 1977 and 1979 elections produced very similar results. In both elec-tions, the UCD obtained a plurality of votes and seats enabling it to form single-party governments just short of majority parliamentary support. In spatial terms, the new party system was well equipped for Left–Right alternation in power, with the two biggest parties competing for the centre ground (Di Palma, 1980: 180–2). The system was complicated, however, by the bilateral oppositions facing these two parties, and by the presence of Basque and Catalan nationalist parties, at least one of which (EE, later joined by HB) could be regarded as an anti-system party (Maravall, 1981: 38). Given its refusal to support the 1978 constitution, the PNV could also be regarded as an anti-system party.

Both Maravall and Linz (1980), reflecting on the experience of the first two elections, took these complications as threats to the legitimacy of the new democratic system. Linz noted that Sartori's conditions for a two-party system were not fulfilled, since neither the UCD nor the PSOE were likely to win a parliamentary majority alone, and the radical tendencies of the other smaller parties made the prospects for stable coalition formation poor (ibid.: 110–27).

In retrospect, this view appears excessively pessimistic. Certainly, the UCD's failure to win a sufficient majority to govern alone created problems in the 1979–82 legislature, and the party's collapse as a result of internal conflict owed much to the bilateral oppositions it faced from the AP and the PSOE, and the pressures under which it was placed by peripheral nationalists. With hindsight, however, both Linz and Maravall appear to have overestimated the levels of ideological polarization in the system, and underestimated the willingness of the leaders of virtually all the parties in parliament to engage in dialogue and compromise (Gunther, 1992a). Under Santiago Carrillo, the PCE took such pains to present itself as a responsible participant in democratic politics that it often appeared less radical than the PSOE. Moreover, after the crushing defeat of an openly nostalgic AP in 1977, Fraga abandoned authoritarian rhetoric and set out to transform AP into a modern democratic conservative party. The PSOE, despite its formal declarations of Marxist identity, co-operated closely with the UCD in the 'politics of consensus' which dominated the constituent process, the main task of the 1977–79 parliament. This formed a centre bloc which depolarized political debate, and sought to draw the other groups with parliamentary representation into the constituent process. With the significant exception of the Basque nationalist parties, this strategy of negotiation succeeded. The politics of consensus created, at least for the 1977–79 period, a party system characterized by low levels of ideological polarization and high levels of interparty dialogue.

After 1979, the dynamic of the Spanish party system shifted considerably. With the passing of the constitution and the statutes of autonomy for the historic nationalities, pressure began to build for an end to consensus and the opening of what was held to be 'normal' party competition. The PSOE sought to emphasize its role as the main opposition party and alternative government by attacking the UCD and Suárez (Capo Giol, 1981), while the AP attempted to find a role by pushing for a grand coalition of the Right with UCD.

The atmosphere of deep crisis caused by serious governmental failures in regional policy, public order, the economy and relations with the military put the UCD under enormous pressure and strengthened the hand of those within the party who favoured a more confrontational strategy towards the PSOE and close co-operation with AP. The resulting internal conflict dragged on for two years and provoked the departure of several major figures, including Suárez himself, before the 1982 elections.[3]

The pessimistic atmosphere of the 1979–82 period led to talk of a 'crisis of the parties' after only three years of democracy (Caciagli, 1984: 89). The consequences of UCD's disorder were exacerbated by the changes in party strategy which were taking place in the PSOE and the AP. The PSOE's leader,

González, forced a change in the party's statutes whereby it abandoned its commitment to Marxism and sought to associate itself with the more moderate positions of Western European social democratic parties (Share, 1989: 53–62). Similarly, Fraga's AP was attempting, with perhaps less success, to convince electors of the authenticity of its new position on the Centre–Right. Rather than the polarization of the party system, the increasingly competitive nature of party politics after 1979 had the effect of pushing parties towards the centre in search of new electoral support. This put UCD's most direct rivals in a position to take electoral advantage of the governing party's weakness.

The 'cataclysmic' (Caciagli, 1986) election of October 1982 transformed the party system in a manner almost unprecedented in Western European electoral history. The UCD, after governing alone for over five years, was reduced from 35 per cent to 6 per cent of the vote and from 168 to 11 seats. The party which had acted as the mainstay of the new party system went out of existence six months later. The AP was the chief beneficiary of this collapse, leaping to 26 per cent of the vote and becoming the second largest party in parliament, with 107 seats. The PSOE gained a massive 46.5 per cent of the vote and almost doubled its parliamentary representation, winning 202 seats in a 350-seat parliament. The PCE's vote collapsed to 4.1 per cent, and it lost 80 per cent of its seats in parliament. To give an idea of the extent of the transformation in the party system, 47.8 per cent of voters in 1982 voted for the party they had supported in 1979, but 33.4 per cent voted for a different party (Sani, 1986: 8). Total volatility between 1979 and 1982 reached 42.26 per cent, the highest ever detected in a western democracy (Montero, 1992: 283–5).

This election result appears to confirm the limited extent to which the new Spanish party system could be regarded as 'frozen' with regard to the party alignments of the 1930s and it caused some observers to identify extreme instability as being one of the key features of the system (Bar, 1984; Caciagli, 1984). Certainly, it indicated the fragility of the parties' penetration into society and the fluidity of their relationship with their electors (Caciagli, 1984: 84). The transformation of the party system after only five years of democratic party competition also ensured that the system would not be 'frozen' around the faultlines of the transition period. The UCD's inability to institutionalize itself owed much to its creation as a coalition of forces that were united in their approach to the immediate problem of the transition, but divided over longer-term social and economic issues (Hopkin, 1995). This is not to argue that its collapse was inevitable, but the failure to find an adequate organizational formula to hold the component groups together forced a realignment among the forces of the Centre and Right of the Spanish political spectrum (Gunther, 1986b; Gunther and Hopkin, forthcoming).

The most notable feature of this new party system was the extraordinary dominance of the PSOE. With almost twice as many parliamentary seats as its biggest rival and a majority of over 20, there were few constraints on the PSOE's ability to govern alone, and little prospect of a change of government in the medium term. This was not only because of the sheer size of the PSOE's electoral advantage (over 20 percentage points in 1982), but also because of the nature of the parliamentary opposition. The collapse of UCD had left many moderately conservative voters without their natural party of allegiance. For most former UCD voters, especially those in smaller, rural constituencies, the only realistic way to cast a vote against the Socialists was to support the AP. Nevertheless, the AP failed to win over sufficient numbers of ex-UCD voters to reach the levels of support UCD had enjoyed in 1977 and 1979, a failure which had dramatic consequences for the balance of electoral strength in the new system.

Of the over 6 million UCD voters in 1979, an estimated 3 million transferred their support to AP in 1982; but around 1.2 million opted for the PSOE, 1.4 million remained loyal to UCD, and 600,000 backed Adolfo Suárez's newly formed Social and Democratic Centre (CDS) (Sani and Montero, 1986; Montero, 1986). In effect, the elimination of UCD opened up a gap in the ideological centre, part of which the PSOE managed to occupy, thus extending its base of support and taking up a pivotal position in the party system.

The 1982 elections, by presenting the PSOE with a priceless strategic opportunity, ushered in a predominant party system (Caciagli, 1984; Bar, 1984) which lasted until 1993. Sartori's conceptualization of the predominant party system (1976: Chapter 6) requires that a party consistently enjoys majorities in parliament over time, and the PSOE did, in fact, reaffirm its majority position twice, in 1986 and 1989 (see Table 11.1). Another feature of the post-1982 party system was an apparent polarization of party competition: UCD's effective replacement by the AP represented a radicalization of the nature of political debate in the Spanish parliament. Although the AP had striven to present itself as a party of the Centre–Right, most regarded it as more clearly right-wing than UCD, and the majority of voters continued to place themselves in a central position, with a slight preference to the Centre–Left, along a Left–Right ideological scale (Gunther, 1986a; Barnes, McDonough and López Piña, 1986).

There were mitigating features to this polarization: the PSOE since 1979 had abandoned its Marxist roots and undergone an ideological 'Bad Godesberg' (see Share, 1989; Juliá, 1990) and, in consequence, Felipe González's government went to great lengths to emphasize its moderation. Moreover, the collapse of the communist vote was a further indication of the depolarized nature of mass preferences in Spain. The disappearance of the

UCD, a party characterized by a high degree of ideological ambiguity, did allow voting behaviour in Spain to reflect to a greater extent the traditional Left–Right divisions in Spanish society, entrenching the Centre–Left PSOE as a dominant force (Gunther and Montero, 1994: 545).

By 1982, after three elections, the evidence was accumulating that electoral success required ideological moderation and a centrist strategy, if possible tending to the Left. The Right's realization of this in the course of the 1980s led party competition to become ever more centripetal in nature.

Party system stabilization and party organizational change: 1982–89

The development of the Spanish party system in the rest of the 1980s confirmed and institutionalized the realignment of 1982 (see Table 11.1). The UCD, far from recovering, was formally dissolved, and its components either left politics or took up different positions in the new system. Suárez's CDS occupied a central position between the PSOE and the AP similar to that of UCD, but as a minority party. Other offshoots of UCD joined the two major parties: the social democrats who defected from UCD were incorporated into the PSOE, where some of them held ministerial posts, and the former UCD Christian Democrats and liberals formed new parties which joined AP in an electoral alliance.

The disappearance of the UCD gave a radically new shape to the party system which had profound consequences for government formation. Between 1977 and 1979, the two largest parties were, for the purposes of electoral competition, ideologically contiguous (Di Palma, 1980: 180). This meant that the PSOE, in order to win an electoral majority, had to win over part of the UCD's centrist support, and drag more radical Left voters over to the Centre–Left; the UCD, correspondingly, had to win over Centre voters, while maintaining the support of more conservative sectors. This gave party competition a centripetal, moderating dynamic, and provided the opportunity for unpopular governments to be defeated at the polls.

The AP's inability to win over Centre voters as successfully as UCD had done, and the presence of a small party (the CDS) between the AP and the PSOE, made government alternation far less likely. The AP's authoritarian past, and the unpopularity of its leader Fraga among many Centre-oriented voters (Linz *et al.*, 1981; Gunther, 1986a; Montero, 1986) represented a strong limit to electoral growth – the 26 per cent polled in both 1982 and 1986 became known as *el techo de Fraga* (Fraga's ceiling).

The AP's electoral failures in the 1980s stemmed from very fundamental weaknesses. The party was simply out of step with the dominant characteristics of the Spanish electorate: an ideological moderation verging on apoliticism, and a consequent rejection of the authoritarian values propagated by the Franco regime. AP's problems were succinctly described by José Ramón Montero in 1988:

> AP is unable to overcome its lack of democratic legitimacy in the eyes of the electorate, or to adopt a neo-conservative policy framework. AP's image emphasises its excessive conservatism (which is tinged with authoritarianism), and its rigid defence of traditional values, incompatible, to a certain extent, with a secularized and modernized society. These characteristics no longer reflect the values of a majority of Spaniards and help explain the continuing weakness of conservatism in Spain.
>
> (1988: 146)

This distance from the ideological centre of gravity of the electorate is the principal explanation for the AP's poor electoral performance in the 1980s and its inability to threaten the PSOE's grip on government in that period (Montero, 1989).

The 1986 elections confirmed the limitations on the AP's potential for growth (Aguilera de Prat, 1988: 148–50; Robinson, 1987). Its coalition (*Coalición Popular* – CP) with the Christian Democratic PDP (*Partido Demócrata Popular*) and the PL (*Partido Liberal*) polled a similar percentage of the total vote which, given the lower level of abstention, represented a loss of around 300,000 voters in a growing electorate (Montero, 1989). The only positive aspect of this election for Fraga's party was the reduction in the electoral advantage of the PSOE, which fell to a still overwhelming 18.2 per cent (Heywood, 1995a: 177). However, the AP's inability to win over disillusioned Socialist voters demonstrated that Fraga's ambitions to turn the AP into an alternative government were unrealistic: the only party which gained significantly from the PSOE's slight decline was Suárez's rigorously centrist CDS, which leapt to 9.2 per cent of the vote and nineteen parliamentary seats. The CDS's impressive rise indicated that the dissolution of the UCD would not automatically benefit the Right (Robinson, 1987: 120) and suggested that many of the UCD voters who remained loyal to the party in 1982 were genuine 'centre' voters, unwilling to back Fraga's conservatism.

Despite the chaotic nature of the AP's internal politics in 1987–89 which saw the resignation of Fraga as leader, both the origins of the Socialists' decline and the electoral recovery of the Spanish Right can be traced to this period. Again, this provides an opportunity to examine the respective importance of elite decisions and shifts in mass behaviour in explaining changes in the party system and in the way the parties themselves operate. The evidence broadly tends to support the view that, as in the transitional phase, political leaders, acting within the context of known electoral and social constraints, have been able to shape the nature of the party system to a considerable extent.

However, an obligatory step in this analysis is to examine the impact of a case of political change being driven largely 'from below': the general strike of December 1988. The unassailable position of the PSOE in the party system had allowed Felipe González's administration to pursue an orthodox economic policy without losing too much support to the left (Share, 1989; Gillespie, 1989; Boix, 1995). The absence of a viable electoral alternative meant that discontent amongst natural Socialist voters was expressed largely through abstention (almost 10 per cent higher in 1986 and 1989 than in 1982; Justel, 1994). After 1986, this discontent began to be articulated by trade unions: the Socialist-affiliated *Unión General de Trabajadores* (UGT) combined with the communist union *Comisiones Obreras* (CC.OO) to encourage strike action, culminating in a massively successful general strike, in opposition to the PSOE's lack of interest in socially progressive economic policies (Gillespie, 1990; Petras, 1993). This appears to have had a catalytic effect on the party system by revealing the PSOE's vulnerability for the first time, and by forcing it into a strategic shift which has had important implications for party competition in the 1990s.

The PSOE's strategic change involved a marked shift to the left in the government's social and economic policies, consisting of a sharp increase in public expenditure for social ends, a consequent increase in taxation for the middle classes, and growth in the budget deficit (Torcal and Chhibber, 1995: 18–25; Camiller, 1994: 256–9; Gunther, 1996). This was revealing of the way in which mass opinion has interacted with the behaviour of political elites in post-Franco Spain. Under the threat of electoral punishment, the Socialists did not hesitate to undertake a radical change to their governmental strategy in order to avoid electoral 'leakage', and the 1989 election result, in which the party was returned to power with sufficient seats to govern, suggested that it was a successful move.

That electoral support could be 'fine-tuned' in this way is indicative of the fluid nature of the party–voter relationship in Spain. Party identification has remained remarkably low into the 1990s, with Spain unique in Europe in having more voters 'unattached' than 'attached' to any political party (Schmitt, 1989; Heywood, 1995a: 179).

Similarly, party membership is extraordinarily low and does not appear to have increased significantly with the consolidation of the democratic system. In 1990, party members represented just 2 per cent of the Spanish electorate compared with much higher figures for the other new democracies in southern Europe. Analyses of Spanish voting behaviour have generally failed to find statistically significant links between the size of a party's vote in a province and its organizational presence there (Gunther and Montero, 1994:

502–6; see also Montero, 1981). The PSOE itself has always had a much smaller membership than comparable social democratic parties in the rest of Europe and, indeed, in 1982, it had less members than the UCD. Membership doubled to 210,000 in 1988 (Gillespie, 1989: 65), but a high proportion of these new members were holders of public office (Gillespie, 1994: 53).

Given the party's 'thin' social presence, the collapse of its link with the UGT understandably alarmed the Socialist leadership. It is unlikely that the UGT's role as a mobilizer of electoral support was significant enough for it to pressurize the PSOE leadership, as trade union affiliation in Spain is also extraordinarily low by European standards (Gunther and Montero, 1994: 508–13). Instead, the policy shift was a response to the threat posed by the left-wing coalition, *Izquierda Unida* (IU), dominated by the PCE, which had emerged from the anti-NATO campaign in 1986, and which enjoyed the tacit support of sectors of the UGT leadership (Amodia, 1990b: 297).

The election of a new and popular leader, Julio Anguita, gave IU sufficient momentum to present itself as the real party of the left, and the 1989 elections showed that this message did convince some Socialist voters, as the IU almost doubled its vote to 9 per cent, largely at the expense of the PSOE (see Table 11.1).

The PSOE's *giro social* (social turn) gives some idea of the ease with which party leaders – and particularly leaders of parties in government – have been able to make important strategic decisions with minimal party involvement. The PSOE in the 1980s provides a good example of the oligarchical tendencies of contemporary Spanish political parties, and the dominant position of party leaders (Gangas Peiró, 1995). The party, while never a monolith, has generally been a disciplined political machine since González imposed his authority on the party conference during the 1979 crisis, and in particular since the 1982 election victory. Parliamentary rebellions against the González government were conspicuous by their absence, and the party leadership's control over the key regional federations enabled it to push controversial issues through the party conference without major upsets (Share, 1989: 126).

The party's weak implantation and small membership facilitated the concentration of power around the party leader. Leadership dominance was not a matter of straightforward coercion; González was able to offer both regional *barons* and factional opponents important benefits which ensured his position remained unthreatened (Gillespie and Gallagher, 1989). The importance of leadership in election campaigns (Gunther, Sani and Shabad, 1986; Gunther, 1992b; Justel, 1992), and González's remarkably durable popularity, made the leader an indispensable element of the PSOE's continued electoral success. Defeating a leader who can take credit for several election victories is a difficult task, and the fruits of power were enjoyed to a greater or lesser extent by all party members, and particularly by members of the party elite.

The same oligarchical tendencies can be detected on the right of the political spectrum, although the creation of an effective and disciplined political machine took a great deal longer. As early as 1979, Fraga changed the AP's organizational structure, transforming it from a federation with several competing leaders into a *presidentialist* party under his control (López Nieto, 1988; Gangas Peiró, 1995). Despite the statutory changes, Fraga had difficulty imposing his authority on the party for two essential reasons. First, he failed to achieve anything like the electoral success of his socialist opponent, and it became clear in 1986 that he was unlikely to take the Right into government. The internal tensions inevitable in any strategic failure were compounded by the AP's difficult relations with its electoral allies, the PDP and the PL (Jáuregui, 1987: Chapters 9–11). Moreover, Fraga's departure in 1986 set in train a long period of conflict over the succession which created such chaos that he had to take over again in 1988.

By 1989, however, a number of important changes had taken place which allowed the party to enjoy rapid electoral growth and an increase in and rejuvenation of the party membership (Gangas Peiró, 1995: 221). It changed its name to *Partido Popular* (PP), fully integrated the Christian Democrats and liberals into the party, and joined the Christian Democratic International and the European People's Party, thus achieving international recognition as a party of the political Centre rather than of the reactionary Right (Gangas Peiró, 1995: 213). Helped by the decline of the CDS, the PP managed to attract a number of former UCD leaders into the party, confirming its respectability as a moderate political organization. Finally, the PP elected a new leader, José María Aznar, a young figure without associations with the dictatorship. Aznar both moderated the party's ideological position and imposed a rigidly centralized regime of party management.

Oligarchical party organizations with strong, often charismatic, leaders are a natural consequence of the poor links between parties and their social bases. Although the PSOE leadership was forced into strategic change by pressures from its support base, particularly the 1988 general strike, it is striking that the UGT was forced into an open conflict with the government by its failure to influence policy through formal party channels. The PSOE only began to take grass-roots discontent seriously when it started to face competitive pressures from *Izquierda Unida* which, under new leadership, provided the option of *exit* (Hirschman, 1970) for more traditionally left-wing and working-class sectors of the socialist electorate.

The evolution of the Spanish party system has confirmed at every turn that the most successful parties are those that allow leaders sufficient opportunities to respond to the incentives inherent in the electoral opportunity structure. The UCD's initial success was the result of Suárez being able to compete for centre votes while ignoring calls from the more conservative sectors of its social base for more 'representative' policies. Similarly, AP/PP only broke through its electoral ceiling when a determined party leader concentrated power around his circle in order to take advantage of the strategic opportunities made available by the PSOE's shift to the left.

Party competition in the 1990s: government alternation

The change in the nature of party competition in the 1990s can be explained in large part by the PSOE leadership's response to the 1988 general strike, and the quite independent changes in the AP leadership around the same time. Although the 1989 election returned a PSOE government and the PP failed to improve on its 1986 share of the vote, closer analysis reveals the beginnings of party system change. Most obviously, IU's improvement at the expense of the socialists meant that the governing party faced serious bilateral opposition, making its strategic choices more difficult. Also, a less dramatic change was taking place which, in the course of the 1989–93 legislature, provided an opening for the PP. In October 1989, the CDS slipped from 9.2 per cent to 7.9 per cent of the vote, a decline which added to internal disagreements over political strategy and led to Suárez's resignation and the party's virtual disappearance from political life.

By 1992, the social composition of the electorates of the two major parties also seemed to be changing, with social class, for the first time in the new democracy, appearing as an important variable in explaining levels of electoral support. Throughout the 1980s, the social characteristics of the socialist electorate had varied little from those of the electorate as a whole, demonstrating the success of González's 'catch-all' electoral strategy. However, 1992 survey data revealed that the PSOE's support was increasingly limited to older voters, of lower social class and social status, who tended to place themselves further to the left of the ideological spectrum (Torcal and Chhibber, 1995: 13). This implied that the PSOE was becoming a more class-based party and that it was losing significant middle-class support to the PP, a phenomenon which Torcal and Chhibber attribute to the redistributional effects of the Socialists' economic policy after 1988.

These findings were confirmed by the 1993 election in which, for the first time since 1982, the PSOE's grip on power appeared to be under threat, bringing to an end the predominant party system of the 1980s. The PP's assault on the González administration in the early 1990s revolved around an issue indirectly related to the fiscal consequences of the *giro social*: corruption. The emergence into the public domain of a number of cases of abuse of office, illegal party financing and high living on the part of senior

Socialist figures (Heywood, 1995b) coincided with both a sharp economic downturn and an increase in tax rates for the middle classes, damaging the government enormously and allowing the untainted Aznar to establish himself as an honest alternative to a corrupt administration. A well-orchestrated campaign on the part of some newspapers put González under severe pressure, and a number of pre-election opinion polls gave the PP an advantage over the PSOE for the first time.

Although the PSOE campaigned hard in the closing stages of the 1993 campaign and clung on to its position as largest party, it fell short of a majority and had to make parliamentary deals with Catalan and Basque nationalists in order to govern. Socialist support, nevertheless, held up well. The PSOE lost only 0.8 per cent of its vote share, and it actually increased its vote by around a million due to the high turnout (del Castillo and Delgado, 1994: 135). The left coalition, *Izquierda Unida*, only achieved a 0.5 per cent increase. The gradual decline of the PSOE vote after 1982 had been arrested. The threat from the left had proved to be less serious than feared.

What changed in 1993 was that the PP managed to mobilize much greater numbers of voters on the centre and right, almost wiping out the CDS and leaping from 25.6 to 34.6 per cent of the vote, almost 3 million more votes than in 1989 (del Castillo and Delgado, 1994: 135). The PP's success appears to be explained by its ability to mobilize support amongst young voters and voters of higher social status in the cities (Vallés, 1994; Torcal and Chhibber, 1995). It was able to do this partly because of the PSOE's tired image and consequent loss of less committed, centrist voters. Estimates suggest that 50 per cent of CDS voters in 1989 switched to the PP, and around 11 per cent of PSOE voters (del Castillo and Delgado, 1994: 136). Also significant was the ideological renewal which Aznar appeared to have achieved, emphasizing political moderation and opposition to corruption, and drawing attention away from the party's traditionally authoritarian and conservative views on public morality, law and order and religious issues.

The 1996 election brought the alternation in power which had appeared impossible even in the early 1990s (Beltrán, 1993). The PP squeezed ahead of the Socialists by a margin of almost 1.5 per cent becoming the largest party in parliament, 20 seats short of an absolute majority. This represented a growth of a further 4 per cent on top of the remarkable advance of 1993, an extraordinary result, although the party leadership's triumphalism during the campaign led it to perceive the outcome as a disappointment. It appeared that the PP won over former abstainers, disgruntled socialists, surviving voters of the CDS and some Catalan nationalist voters. The biggest surprise of the election was the robustness of the Socialist vote and the stubbornly persistent popularity of Felipe González in spite of a protracted campaign against him centred on the various corruption scandals that had marked his term of office.

The resulting party system appeared to reflect the establishment in Spain of a dynamic of government and opposition. That government responsibility changed hands as a result of a 'normal' shift in the levels of support of the two main parties suggests that unpopular governments can be ousted and replaced without trauma, something that had not happened before in the new democracy. The PSOE resisted the challenge from the Left, with the effective message that a vote for *Izquierda Unida* in the present electoral system would favour the PP. The Socialists thus remained a potential party of government, although that status was threatened by internal problems linked to González's relinquishing the leadership in 1997.

This is not, however, a system of alternation on the Anglo-Saxon model. The PP was unable to form a government alone, and had to resort to a parliamentary arrangement with Basque and Catalan nationalists similar to that which had sustained the 1993–96 PSOE government. Alternation was mitigated by the bargaining power enjoyed by nationalist parties, and concern was expressed over the effects this could have on the territorial integrity of the Spanish state. This situation confirmed that the main threat to government alternation between Left and Right in Spain, rather than the emergence of populist or Green movements, is the presence of party sub-systems in Catalonia, the Basque Country, and to a lesser extent, Galicia and the Canary Islands.

Although the intensity of the religious and class cleavages had died down by the 1970s, the same could not be said for the centre–periphery cleavage, and the question of the territorial organization of the state was the most problematic political issue of the post-Franco period. This issue has, until now, been much more damaging to the Right than the Left, for the simple reason that the Socialists have maintained a strong presence throughout the state, whereas the Right, in particular after 1982, has had serious difficulties in establishing itself as a political force in the Basque Country and Catalonia, both areas of considerable electoral and economic importance. Instead, the middle classes in these areas have supported bourgeois nationalist parties and, as Camiller has suggested,

> their very strength has so far been a net subtraction from the total potential of the Spanish centre and right, as the 'natural' bastions of a self-confident bourgeois politics have become jutting redoubts for the most part turned against it.
>
> (Camiller, 1994: 245)

The state-wide Spanish Right's traditional obsession with national unity has meant that the Catalan and Basque middle classes have had far better relations with the Socialists. The future of government alternation would appear to depend on the PP's ability to overcome this problem, and the inter-party co-operation required by the parliamentary arithmetic after 1996 provided just such an opportunity.

Conclusion: 'volatile parties and stable voters'?

The evolution of the Spanish party system since the end of the Franco dictatorship has been marked by two contradictory features: the consistency of the ideological preferences expressed by Spanish voters, and the extraord-inary organizational fragility of the political parties competing for their votes. Much attention has been paid to the collapse of the UCD in 1982 which brought a radical realignment of the electorate. However, the disappearance of the CDS in 1996, despite having obtained almost 10 per cent of the vote in 1986, and the appearance and disappearance of political forces such as the Christian Democrats, the Liberals and the Reformist Party, confirm that party system instability has owed more to the inability of political elites to organize effective party organizations than to any supposed immaturity on the part of the Spanish electorate.

This 'top-down' perspective should not obscure the undeniable importance of historically important social cleavages in the formation of the post-Franco party system. Social class and religious attitudes have continued to help shape the behaviour of Spanish voters and, indeed, 'class voting', or something approaching it, has increased in the 1990s. Moreover, the centre–periphery cleavage has maintained its political significance, with the last two Spanish governments depending on the parliamentary support of Basque, Catalan and now Canary Island nationalists.

Nevertheless, the social cleavages which led to the tragedy of the 1930s had been largely defused by the time of the first democratic elections, and the socially progressive policies of both UCD and PSOE governments contributed to ever higher levels of social integration. Obviously, workers are more likely to vote for the Left and managers are more likely to vote for the Right, but electoral victories in post-Franco Spain have required the mobilization of broad, socially heterogeneous electorates. To this extent, the UCD, the PSOE after 1979, and the PP after 1989 have all been catch-all parties using a moderate political message to win over the crucial votes of the ideologically undefined centre electorate.

The need for ideological ambiguity and organizational flexibility in order to compete electorally has hampered the institutionalization of Spanish political parties. The disappearance of the UCD is evidence that this type of party competition, in which parties avoid structured relationships with their electoral constituencies, can lead to what Panebianco has described as 'electoral turbulence' (1988).

Since 1982, the Spanish party system has returned to relatively low levels of electoral volatility, and a stable Left–Right competition for power, mediated by the persistence of smaller parties, may be emerging. However, levels of party identification remain extraordinarily low by European standards, and the maintenance of the present party system would appear to depend as much on the high barriers to new entries as on the satisfaction of the Spanish electorate.

Notes

1. The author would like to thank Professor Gunther for making his interview data available; the usual disclaimer applies.
2. The literature on the attitudes, preferences and voting behaviour of the Spanish electorate in the post-Franco period is very comprehensive. Most recently, see Gunther, 1992b; Montero, 1992.
3. The collapse of the UCD is well documented. See most recently: Hopkin, 1995; Gunther and Hopkin, forthcoming.

12

Portugal: Party System Installation and Consolidation

JOSÉ M. MAGONE

Introduction

The making of the Portuguese party system cannot be entirely likened to that of most Western European states given its very late democratization. Politically, it is marked by features of semi-peripheral development. Thus, the capitalist core in countries such as Britain and Germany saw a relatively early development of democracy marked, ultimately, by stable mass participation. In the semi-peripheral countries, by contrast, the incorporation of the masses was vertical and not horizontal, i.e. clientelistic and non-participatory, rather than via the formation of associations, above all political parties. Late industrialization reinforced this pattern of vertical incorporation. Mouzelis argues further that 'the state's tendency to inhibit the formation of autonomous interest groups appears to be a constitutive feature of the semi-peripheral polity' (1986: 74).

Nevertheless, the importation of modern party structures from established parties elsewhere in Western Europe and the similarity of the historico-institutional obstacles to the emergence of a modern nation–state in the rest of southern Europe suggest that the Portuguese party system does have similarities with Western European countries. In order to assess how the historico-institutional and socio-cultural patterns of political organization and incorporation still shape the present political system (Janos, 1988; Mouzelis, 1978), it is necessary to consider the kind of parties and party systems which existed before the emergence of the democratic political and party systems between 1974–76.

Historical background: from oligarchy and dictatorship to democracy

Despite the introduction of a radically liberal constitution as early as 1822, the masses were not successfully incorporated into Portugal's political system until 1974. Rather, the nineteenth and early twentieth centuries saw alternating phases of reformism and even revolution on the one hand, and reaction on the other.

Caciquismo *and* Rotativismo *in the nineteenth century*

Political development in the first half of the nineteenth century was conditioned by the introduction of the 1822 constitution, modelled on that of the new Spanish Cadiz, with one branch of the royal family refusing to recognize it. A civil war between the representatives of absolutist and of constitutional monarchy led to the acceptance of a compromise constitution, the Constitutional Charter, which laid the foundations for a two-party system. From 1834, the radical Progressive Party and the conservative Regeneration Party institutionalized a two-party system via a rotational system (*rotativismo*) of regular alternation in power which was a parody of the British model. In the Portuguese context alternation degenerated into a clientelistic system known as *caciquismo*. The *cacique* was the local boss, usually a landowner, a local priest or some other influential figure able, through his influence in the village, to offer a supply of votes to the government and to gain favours in return. A so-called 'electoral machine' ensured that the clientelistic and patronage system kept the alternating balance of the two parties (Marques, 1981: 60–75; Monica, 1994; Vidigal, 1988: 16–25).

It was, once again, revolution that led to party system change in the early twentieth century. The first decade of the century was characterized by a high level of political violence and instability which the First Republic (1910–26) failed to repress, and which ended only with the introduction of an authoritarian dictatorship (1926–74). The Salazar dictatorship led in turn to the emergence of democracy.

The failed democratic revolution: the First Republic (1910–26)

The Republican Revolution of 1910 did not contribute to the democratization of Portuguese society. The attempt to build a new, more stable and more just political system was doomed because the 1911 Constitution gave a dominant role to the parliament rather than the executive and the originally strong Portuguese Republican Party (PRP) split into factions, proving unable to achieve an absolute majority (Marques, 1980: 80–2; Wheeler, 1978). The executive was a prisoner of the legislature and between 1911 and 1926, Portugal experienced 45 governments with an average duration of four months. In the same period, eight parliaments and eight Presidents were elected, while approximately 30 revolutions, revolts and *coups d'état* were undertaken. Governmental, party and economic instability were intertwined and democracy broke down (Marques, 1981: 285-8).

At the same time, the suffrage remained restricted and largely urban. The new Republican elite excluded the illiterate population from the franchise, arguing that lack of education would hinder making proper decisions. The consequence for the party system was that the vertically orientated structures inherited from the constitutional monarchy were not replaced (Lopes, 1994; Schwartzman, 1989).

The Estado Novo (1926–74)

Seeking to incorporate the social classes into the political system and to harmonize their interests, António Salazar, Portugal's authoritarian dictator (1926–68), built up a different form of representation based on corporatism. Instead of emphasizing party competition, the corporatist system allowed only one party to be active, the National Union. The system emphasized unity, class co-operation and an hierarchical model of decision-making. In fact, the bicameral Parliament – consisting of the National Assembly and the Corporatist Chamber – was subordinated to Salazar (Payne, 1980: 139–60; Wiarda, 1977).

By the end of the Second World War, corporatist representation had lost its original vitality, being regarded as a governmental instrument designed to control civil society. Hermínio Martins describes corporatism as a 'political economy of repression' used to manage the opposition and the more radical classes of civil society, such as the working class in the urban centres, and the land labourers in the southern province of Alentejo (Martins, 1968: 329). Opposition election campaigns, the assignment of locations for rallies, the persecution of candidates after elections and the manufacturing of election results showed the repressive nature of the so-called 'organic democracy' (Eleições, 1979).

Democratic transition: from revolution to the emergence of a party system

The 'Revolution of the Carnations' of 25 April 1974 signalled the start of a wave of democratization around the globe (Huntington, 1991). The Portuguese transition to democracy encouraged similar transitions in other authoritarian regimes such as Spain and Greece (Pridham, 1984). In retrospect, everything seemed inevitable, but the outcome of the revolutionary process of 1974–75 was, in fact, open-ended. Forms of representation other than representative democracy were proposed during this period and it was not certain what the final outcome would be (Manuel, 1995).

The elites carrying out the regime transition, the military of the Armed Forces Movement (AFM), on the one hand, and the civil politicians on the other, had different views of democracy. The radicalization of the revolution and, implicitly, of the military, led Western European countries to fear that Portugal could become a second Cuba (Wettig, 1975). Prior to the first constituent assembly elections in April 1975, the new political formations were unable to play any important role. Only thereafter did the new parties gain importance. Secure in the knowledge of their electoral strength, they were able to lead Portugal towards a West European form of representation.

Thus, while hesitant prior to April 1975, both the Socialist Party (PS) and the People's Democratic Party (PPD, later PSD), the two major parties pushing for a West European-style of democracy, became more assertive. The Socialists won the election with a relative majority of 35 per cent followed by the PPD with 24 per cent (see Table 12.1). There were just two other major parties. The conservative Democratic Social Centre (CDS), comprising many politicians from the former political regime, secured 7 per cent of the vote. At the other extreme, the Communists, who were very close to the AFM, gathered about 12 per cent of the vote, losing their briefly hegemonic position in the political system. In the pre-electoral period they had been engaged in colonizing the state structures and the press, streamlining the trade unions and furthering their control over the economy by socializing private enterprises (Ferreira, 1983: 98–9).

Despite the Communists' defeat, the institutions of the revolutionary legacy (the workers' committees, the Communist-dominated collective production units and the neighbourhood committees) nevertheless continued to build an alternative model of grass-roots-based democracy as advocated by the AFM. The so-called *Aliança Povo-MFA* (Alliance of the People with the AFM) intended to marginalize the parties as just one form of representation alongside the other nationally organized institutions of the revolution (Ferreira, 1983; Bermeo, 1986; Hammond, 1985; Hammond, 1988; Downs, 1989).

Responding to this threat, Mário Soares, a lawyer and regime opponent who had been the crucial figure in refounding the Socialist Party, activated his contacts with the member parties of the Socialist International, asking for help to establish a West European-style political system. A so-called 'Committee of Solidarity with Democracy in Portugal' was established by the Socialist International, the main purpose of which was to make western Socialists aware of the importance of supporting the PS against a possible Communist takeover (Eisfeld, 1984: 44-115; Eisfeld, 1983: 121; Merz and Cunha Rego, 1976). During the summer of 1975, the AFM split, with different currents advocating different models of democracy. In this

Table 12.1 Portuguese general election results, major parties, 1975–95

Party	1975	1976	1979	1980	1983	1985	1987	1991	1995
CDS (PP)[1]	7.0	16.0	–	–	12.5	10.0	4.4	4.4	9.1
AD	–	–	42.5	44.9	–	–	–	–	–
PPD-PSD	24.3	24.4	2.4	2.5	27.2	29.9	50.2	50.6	34.0
PCP/APU/CDU[2]	11.4	14.4	18.8	16.8	18.1	15.5	12.1	8.8	8.6
PS	34.7	34.9	27.3	1.1	36.1	20.8	22.2	29.1	43.9
FRS	–	–	–	26.7	–	–	–	–	–
UDP	0.8	1.7	2.2	1.4	0.5	1.3	1.9	0.1	0.6
PRD	–	–	–	–	–	17.9	4.9	–	–
PSN	–	–	–	–	–	–	–	1.7	0.2

[1] The CDS became the PP in 1995.
[2] PCP: 1975–76, APU: 1979–85, CDU: 1987–1995.

Key to party abbreviations

AD	Aliança Democrática (Democratic Alliance)
APU	Aliança Popular Unitária (United People's Alliance), a communist alliance
CDS	Centro Democrático Social (Social Democratic Centre)
CDU	Coligação Democrática Unitária (United Democratic Alliance), a communist coalition
FRS	Frente Republicana Socialista (Republican Socialist Front)
PCP	Partido Comunista Português (Portuguese Communist Party)
PP	Partido Popular (People's Party)
PPD-PSD	Partido Popular Democrático/Partido Social Democrata (Democratic People's Party/Social Democratic Party)
PRD	Partido Renovador Democrático (Democratic Renewal Party)
PS	Partido Socialista (Socialist Party)
PSN	Partido de Solidariedade Nacional (Party of National Solidarity)
UDP	União Democrática Popular (People's Democratic Union)

situation, the emerging party system seemed to be just one model of representation among several. The small radical parties of the extreme Left in particular were very keen to promote their own models of democracy and to use their influence in the new revolutionary institutions to support the model of the AFM (Mailer, 1976).

The radicalization of the revolutionary process in the autumn of 1975 increased the uncertainty of the situation. The situation of so-called 'double impotence' (Santos, 1984: 22–3) alluded to the 'dual power' situation of revolutionary Russia in 1917 when grass-roots councils (soviets) and the central government shared power, yet also suggested that in Portugal no-one ruled – there was anarchy. Neither the government nor the new social movements were able to gain power and even the Communist leader, Alvaro Cunhal, acknowledged that the late phase of the revolutionary situation was characterized by a situation in which executive power was dispersed among several political actors (Cunhal, 1976). A counter-coup against an imminent extreme Left *coup d'état* put an end to this impasse on 25 November 1975. The leader of the counter-coup, Lieutenant Ramalho Eanes, restored political order and enabled a return to liberal democratic conditions (Antunes, 1979) (see Table 12.2).

Table 12.2 Government composition in Portugal, 1974–98

Period	Prime Minister	From	Coalition
	Palma Carlos	May 1974	PS, PPD, PCP
A Revolutionary	Vasco Gonçalves I	July 1974	PS, PPD, PCP
Period (25 April	Vasco Gonçalves II	Sept. 1974	PS, PPD, PCP
1974 – 25	Vasco Gonçalves III	March 1975	PS, PPD, PCP
November 1975)	Vasco Gonçalves IV	Aug. 1975	PCP
	Pinheiro de Azevedo	Sept. 1975	PS, PPD
	Mário Soares I	July 1976	PS
	Mário Soares II	Jan. 1978	PS, CDS
	Nobre da Costa	Aug. 1978	Presidential, independents
	Mota Pinto	Nov. 1978	Presidential, independents
	Maria Lurdes Pintasilgo	July 1979	Presidential, independents
	Francisco Sá Carneiro	Jan. 1981	AD (PSD, CDS, PPM)
B Constitutional	Pinto Balsemão I	Jan. 1981	AD (PSD, CDS, PPM)
Period 1976–1998	Pinto Balsemão II	Sept. 1982	AD (PSD, PS, PPM)
	Pinto Balsemão III	Dec. 1982	AD (PSD, PS, PPM)
	Mário Soares III	June 1983	PS, PSD
	Aníbal Cavaco Silva I	Nov. 1985	PSD
	Aníbal Cavaco Silva II	Sept. 1987	PSD
	Aníbal Cavaco Silva III	Oct. 1991	PSD
	António Guterres	Oct. 1995	PS

The adoption of the new constitution on 2 June 1976 initiated the process of democratic consolidation in Portugal. The first legislative election of 25 April 1976 stabilized the emerging party system. Although several parties were represented in the first parliament, it was dominated by just four of them: the Socialist Party gained a very fragile relative majority of 34.9 per cent, the PPD 24.4 per cent, the CDS 16.0 per cent and the Communists 14.4 per cent. The major actors and the core Left–Right structure of the party system were already defined but fragmentation remained high and between 1976 and 1979 the party system remained quite unstable, characterized by factionalism and personalism mirrored by governmental instability. A short-term coalition between the Socialists and the Christian Democratic CDS (January to July 1978) ended with the International Monetary Fund auster-ity programme being accepted and subsequently implemented by 'presidential' caretaker governments (Rother, 1984).

Between 1978 and December 1979 these governments, led by inde-pendents and supported by the first elected president (the rapidly promoted

General Ramalho Eanes) concluded the first legislative period of the new political system. Ramalho Eanes's decision to wait until the end of the first legislature before calling for new elections helped to stabilize the party system. In the interim, the Social Democrats (PSD, formerly PPD) successfully built an electoral alliance with the CDS and the People's Monarchist Party (PPM) known as the Democratic Alliance (AD). This alliance gained 44.9 per cent of the vote. The PS won 27.3 per cent and the PCP, in an alliance with the People's Democratic Movement (MDP) won 18.8 per cent. The four main parties (in alliance) had increased their share of the electorate from 89.6 per cent in 1976 to 91.4 per cent in 1979.

The main objective of the AD was to forge a Right–Centre majority government able to undertake constitutional revision diminishing the power of the president and strengthening the government *vis-à-vis* parliament. Confirmation of the electoral situation came in 1980 when the AD won 45 per cent of the vote while the PS, in coalition with splinter parties from PS and PSD, the so-called Republican and Socialist Front (FRS), got 27 per cent, and the Communist coalition 17 per cent. In both 1979 and 1980 the AD's vote was sufficient to gain an absolute majority of seats in parliament, enabling the first constitutional revision, which was, moreover, supported by the PS.

Contextual variables

Although the new Portuguese party system developed rapidly as a two-bloc, four-party system many factors shaped its operation. It matters considerably whether a system has evolved continuously from the nineteenth century or emerged only in the late twentieth century. In the 1970s, Portugal experienced a painful, late transition to a democratic party system and the first steps towards democratic consolidation. Party system transition and consolidation were intimately intertwined with the 'freezing' of cleavages which endured through the 1980s and into the 1990s. The Portuguese case shows that party systems are conditioned not only by past political experience. Party systems are also shaped by institutional variables, party strategies and social cleavages.

The institutional variables

One of the most important aspects of the nascent Portuguese party system is that it was a highly important factor in the consolidation of the new political system. The parties had a major role in moderating the originally highly socialist constitution which resulted largely from Communist and radical military influence. The so-called 'hidden' fluidity of an ultra-stable party system helped to define the new democracy's rules of the game (Aguiar, 1985).

The major difference from the previous regimes, of course, was that universal suffrage was introduced for all citizens over 18. Parties had, for the first time, to build territorial organizations to reach the electorate and the outcome of the early elections was highly unpredictable, particularly as the AFM campaigned against competitive party politics. Until 1985, the Portuguese political system was characterized by a high level of governmental instability and the constitutionally powerful president was required to play a major role. Only in the second half of the 1980s can one speak of a stabilization and institutionalization of the party and the political systems. Thus, after an initial period of institutional ambiguity, Portugal settled down as a parliamentary and capitalist democracy. On the one hand, the more strongly presidential aspects of the constitution were modified by parliament, against the will of the president (Eanes), in 1982. On the other hand, the socialist principles enshrined in the constitution were progressively removed, the dominance of market mechanisms being assured in the 1980s by combined constitutional reform and preparations for joining the European Union. With the return to power of the Socialists in 1995, alternation seems to have been established as a principle underlying the functioning of the party system.

For electoral purposes, the country is divided into the 18 electoral districts of continental Portugal and the islands of Madeira and Açores, plus two constituencies outside Portugal (Europe and Extra-Europe) allowing migrants to vote (Ramos and Torres, 1992: 15–16). The distribution of the districts favours the cities and urban areas. The electoral system is proportional, based on the d'Hondt method which favours larger parties to the detriment of smaller ones. The proportional system was enshrined in the constitution in order to hinder revision but reform may be enacted in the future. The two main parties (Socialists and Social Democrats) have been very keen to further reinforce the 'imperfect' two-party system which the survival of the smaller flank parties challenged.

The parties

The shape of the new party system, and in the medium term also the constitution, were significantly determined by the nature of the political parties which emerged in and after 1974. Apart from the Communists, none of the parties had any long-standing organization inside Portugal. The Socialist Party was founded only in 1973, and in Germany at that. By contrast, the Communist Party could lay claim to a long history and a prominent, well-defined identity, one linked to the international Communist movement (Comintern) co-ordinated by Moscow from 1921. The new parties respected and paid tribute to the PCP's organizational strength and its resistance to the authoritarian regime from the early 1930s. Deference towards the Communist Party ended after the April 1975 election, however, when the Socialists (PS) and the People's Democratic Party (PPD) gained the majority of the vote.

Although the Socialist Party stuck to an ideological identity based on 'democratic socialism', it became more flexible and electorally orientated after 1976. The structure of the PPD was, from the beginning, very similar to that of a 'catch-all' party, integrating all possible currents from the Centre to the conservative Right. Both these parties attracted more and more voters from election to election. The Christian Democratic CDS remained a party of notables, including many figures from the former authoritarian regime. Its ideological identity was based on a conservative interpretation of Christian Democracy which drew most of its strength from a fierce anti-communism. The ideological identity of the parties influenced the relationships between them and helped define the party system which evolved, at the national level, from imperfect multipartyism (which excluded the Communist Party from governmental responsibility) to imperfect bipartyism (Corkill, 1993b) which led to a permanent hegemonic dominance of the two centre parties, the PS and the PSD (formerly the PPD), by the end of the 1980s.

The Socialist Party was founded on 19 April, 1973 in Bad Münstereiffel near Bonn. It relied on the strong support of the German SPD. Although the first Portuguese Socialist Party had been founded in 1875 it was never strong, even during the First Republic. After the Second World War, several attempts were undertaken to re-found a Socialist party. Mário Soares succeeded by integrating the Portuguese socialists in exile via international socialist organizations. This development was a major advantage for the Socialists during the revolution (Nosty, 1975: 79–82, 89–92; Soares, 1976: 202). Ideologically, the party changed considerably after the revolution. It moved away from the Marxist ideas of its 1973–74 programme and became more like the other social democratic parties of Western Europe (Nosty, 1975: 97–101; Declaração, 1975; Declaração, 1986; Declaração, 1991; Robinson, 1992: 15–18).

After Mário Soares stepped down as secretary-general in 1985, a move necessitated by his candidature for the presidency of Portugal, the party became even more technocratic and electoralist. The former secretary-general, Vitor Constâncio, and the present one, António Guterres, were classified as technocrats whose sole purpose was to generate a parliamentary majority (Robinson, 1992: 12–15; Gallagher, 1990: 30). Although Mário Soares became president of the Republic in 1986, he continued to exert influence upon the party via his supporters, the so-called *Soaristas* or *Históricos* (Cruz, 1995: 144–5).

In the pre-electoral campaign of 1994–95 the Socialist party presented a 'legislative contract' to the electorate emphasizing many aspects of the Bad Münstereiffel programme such as social justice, cultural revolution, better education and sustainable development. However, the party's 'catch-all' nature is a major impediment to achieving such an ambitious programme. The party's internal structure is still highly centralized and the party can be characterized as a cartel party because most of its membership is passive. The highest levels of mobilization occur only at election time.

The Democratic People's Party (PPD), from 1976 the Social Democratic Party (PSD), was founded on 6 May 1974 by Francisco Sá Carneiro. It consisted of a group related to the Society for Economic and Social Studies (SEDES) which was active in the late phase of the authoritarian regime as an independent think-tank promoting modernization and democratization. Some of the leaders of the PPD/PSD were active as MPs in the National Assembly, the façade legislature of the authoritarian regime, but they gave up their seats in 1972 when the regime stopped the move towards liberalization and democratization.

The ideology of the party was flexible from the outset, placing the modernization and democratization of the country at its core. After the first congress of November 1974 it even advocated 'socialism by democratic means' (*Eleições*, 1975: 244–7) but moderation prevailed after the Revolution. From 1976, it adopted a more technocratic liberal line and changed its name from People's Democratic Party to Social Democratic Party. This pragmatic liberal approach has been retained. It is sustained by an ideology of modernization and economic and social development. In a sense, it kept the imprint of the SEDES. This ideologically very indeterminate make-up is related to the fact that the party is highly decentralized and factions still prevail (Stock, 1989a: 14; Lopes, 1989). Therefore, the PSD has been dependent on charismatic leaders such as Sá Carneiro and Aníbal Cavaco Silva. Nevertheless, from the late 1970s until 1995, the PSD was in power without interruption and it provided the innovative element in Portuguese politics. The social democrats were the pivotal party in creating intra- and cross-bloc alliances, as well as minority and absolute majority governments. In this sense, they were responsible for extending the 'repertoire' of governmental coalitions.

A crucial turning point for the PSD's role within the party system was the election of Aníbal Cavaco Silva as party president at the 1985 congress. His charismatic style increased stability both inside the PSD and in the party system. The Portuguese party system enjoyed this high stability until the second half of 1992 when the economy entered into a deep crisis. After a decade of government, Aníbal Cavaco Silva decided to step aside at the party congress of February 1995. He was replaced by Defence Minister, Fernando Nogueira, characterized as an 'eternal number two'. Given the party's highly decentralized nature it was likely that the party's factions would become strong again. The so-called *baronatos* grouped around prominent party figures such as the president of the government of the autonomous island of Madeira, João Alberto Jardim, or the president of the municipal chambers of Oeiras, Isaltino Morais, were likely to be prominent actors in any such factional revival (Lopes, 1989; Stock, 1989a; Corkill, 1995). Deep divisions inside the party were already witnessed at the sixteenth party congress in late 1992 over the question of regionalization which Cavaco Silva fiercely opposed and which Isaltino Morais and Mendes Bota advocated (*Expresso* 25 July 1992: A5; *Expresso*, 14 November 1992: A4). This 'most Portuguese of political parties' was accused of being the new UN/ANP, the former single party in the authoritarian regime, i.e. of creating an *Estado Laranja* (Orange State, referring to the colour of the party's emblem) based on clientelism and patronage within and over administrative structures and semi-official organizations (*Expresso-Revista*, 16 April 1994: 27–30). Electoral defeat in 1995 contributed to the party's malaise, further exacerbating factional tensions. The new party leader from March 1996, Marcelo Rebelo Sousa, a professor at the Law Faculty of the University of Lisbon, also faced the thankless task of balancing the financial difficulties that the party faced after losing a substantial amount of its state subsidy (*Expresso*, 10 August 1996: 4).

The Portuguese Communist Party (PCP) was founded in 1921 and was closely linked to the Communist Third International (Comintern) until the latter's collapse in 1943. The party was highly sectarian with a very small membership until the end of the Second World War. Moreover, during the early period of the authoritarian regime the party was badly organized and highly factionalized (Pereira, 1983: 4–8; Cunhal, 1985).

The turning point came in 1943 when Alvaro Cunhal took over the *de facto* leadership of the party. During the 1940s and 1950s the PCP was the pivotal party in creating electoral alliances to confront the governmental party and promoting candidates in legislative and presidential elections. Such a strategy was doomed to failure because the regime did not intend to give any representation to the opposition in the institutions of government (Raby, 1989: 107–49). In the 1960s, the party called for a 'democratic and national revolution', defined as the armed struggle of the people and the revolutionary military. This strategy was presented by Cunhal at the sixth extraordinary party congress in 1965 (Cunhal, 1974: 137–8). Cunhal's analysis was very close to what happened a decade later in the Revolution of the Carnations. In the late 1960s, the party penetrated the official trade unions and founded a parallel confederation consisting of eighteen communist *sindicatos*, called the Intersindical. This communist expansion within the official trade unions could not be tolerated by the regime and in 1972–73 a phase of repression was initiated. The whole project of political liberalization initiated by Salazar's successor, Marcelo Caetano, was abruptly halted (Barreto, 1990).

The systematic exclusion of the PCP from governmental responsibility after the revolution was related to its role during the pre-constitutional period. The party was deemed responsible for having contributed substantially to the radicalization of the revolutionary process. The communists never abandoned Marxist–Leninist ideology and party structures continued to be ruled by the principle of 'democratic centralism'. Such factors hindered other parties, particularly the PS, from seeking to form a coalition government with the PCP. Hence the PCP followed a strategy of alliances with smaller parties such as the Portuguese Democratic Movement/Electoral Democratic Coalition (MDP/CDE), and the Greens. At the local level, the PCP has been more successful. It is dominant in the southern districts of the Alentejo and in the peripheral suburban centres of Lisbon and Setúbal.

The party is committed to Leninism, identified as a third way between Stalinism and Eurocommunism and defined in terms of 'communist morality' based on equality and solidarity as against capitalist 'bourgeois morality'. The party is, therefore, against the European Union, although it has become less dogmatic on certain aspects of European integration, such as the social charter, with the passage of time. It has, however, remained a fierce defender of the constitution, voting against the conservative revisions of 1982, 1989 and 1992. The party thus continues to be a party with a radical programme though it gave up seeking to establish a 'dictatorship of the proletariat'. It now acts within the legal framework of the Portuguese constitution.

Alvaro Cunhal remained the leader of the party until 1992, indicating clearly that its structures remained highly centralized. Nor did the election of Carlos Carvalhas as secretary-general at the 1992 congress end Cunhal's influence. He remained a member of the central committee and of the political commission and continues to be regarded as an important symbol of unity (*Expresso*, 12 December 1992: 12R–23R; Patricio and Stoleroff, 1996: 116).

Although the Communist Party has been losing members and voters since 1987, it still plays an important role in local elections and as a coalition partner in local government. Moreover, its control of the largest trade union CGTP-In makes it an important actor in Portuguese politics. Nevertheless, its militants are old and prospects for rejuvenation are bleak due to the fact that the party's image does not appeal to the young. Electoral support is stagnating.

The Social Democratic Centre Party (CDS), from 1992 the People's Party (PP), has suffered severe decline since 1987. Founded on 24 July 1974 by Freitas do Amaral, Amaro da Costa and Basilio Horta, most of the leaders originated from the technocratic structures and institutions of the Salazar and Caetano administrations. Many notables of the authoritarian regime became members of the new party (Pinto, 1989: 202). The CDS follows the ideological principles of West European Christian Democracy and is a member of the various international Christian Democratic organizations. It has received considerable support from the German Christian Democratic Union (CDU).

The CDS/PP opposes the 1976 constitution as 'patronizing', and Christian Democratic MPs voted against it in the Assembly of the Republic. Nevertheless, the CDS accepted the democratic majority in parliament which voted for the adoption of the constitution (Lopes, 1976). A conservative party, the CDS played an important role until 1983. This climaxed with its participation as a junior partner in the right-wing government based on the AD. Although the party rank-and-file was discontented by the tactical policies of their leaders Amaro da Costa and, after his death, Freitas do Amaral, the alliance pushed through the 1982 revision of the constitution which undercut the military's continuing supervision of the political process and the institutional framework.

The party lost its importance after 1983. Thereafter, its presidents (Francisco Lucas Pires, 1983–85, Adriano Moreira, 1985–87 and Freitas do Amaral, 1987–92) were unable to generate electoral support for the party. Steady decline seemed inevitable. From 1992 the new leader of the party, the 32-year-old Manuel Monteiro, attempted to revitalize it by changing its name to People's Party and equipping it with a more populist discourse. He was a leading figure in the opposition to the Maastricht Treaty on European Union and he targeted those who lost out by the introduction of the Single European Market. This did not immediately generate more electoral support, but the decline of the already small electorate was stopped and in 1995 Monteiro was able to reverse the downward trend, more than doubling the party's electoral support (to over 9 per cent) and tripling its seats from five to fifteen. This achievement did not prevent a challenge to Monteiro's leadership and long-term strategy taking place the following year, led by Paulo Portas. Portas became the new leader at the end of 1997.

A further six to ten small parties regularly present candidates in legislative elections, representing some 3 to 6 per cent of the electorate between them. Most belong to the extreme Left and were founded shortly before or during the revolution. Some of these tiny parties have achieved representation in the Assembly of the Republic: the Maoist UDP's single MP in 1976, 1979 and 1980; or more recently, in 1991, the PSN representing the interests of pensioners. On the left, four parties should be mentioned as they were present throughout the 1980s and 1990s. The People's Democratic Union (UDP) is by far the most important. It followed a Maoist ideological programme in the 1980s and was the only party of the extreme left to achieve representation in the Assembly. In the 1991 election it lost almost all its electorate. More interesting has been the steady rise of the Trotskyist Socialist Revolutionary Party (PSR) led by Francisco Louçã, who almost gained a seat in the 1991 election. The Communist Party of the Portuguese Workers – Movement for the Reorganization of the Party of the Proletariat (PCTP/MRPP) – is known particularly for having been highly active during the revolution and for having extremely hostile views on the Communist Party (Pereira, 1989). Last, but not least, the Greens (*Partido Ecologista 'Os Verdes'*, PEV) are a permanent partner of the PCP. Their political views are related to the establishment of a grass-roots democracy which would focus on the promotion of environmentally friendly behaviour. On the Right, the oldest party is the monarchist PPM, the ideology of which is nationalist–ecological. It was prominent as a junior partner in the 1979–83 AD coalition government.

More important than all these tiny parties together was the moderate left-wing Democratic Renewal Party (PRD) between 1985 and 1991. Founded by former president Antonio Ramalho Eanes, it attracted almost 18 per cent of the vote in 1985 but declined rapidly thereafter. A flash party, it was conjured into existence by Eanes's appeal to highly volatile voters who thereafter largely transferred their votes to the Right, to the PSD, in 1987.

To make a concluding general point, Portuguese parties have never been membership parties, with the possible exception of the Communist Party. On the contrary, political cadres have always dominated. The predominantly electoral orientation of the parties has been clear since the 1975 election ended the other parties' deference to the communists, as discussed above. Membership data are still very unreliable. In 1992, the largest parties were the PCP and PSD with 163,506 and 143,075 members, respectively. The PS and CDS had 70,000 and 27,092, respectively, though the figure for the Socialist Party may well be an overestimate (*Expresso*, 4 July 1992).

Social and territorial cleavages

Although Portugal is a unitary nation–state, the 1990s have witnessed the emergence of regionalism. This has to do with the decentralization of the Portuguese political system and the process of European integration which offers the regions the opportunity to enhance their political significance (Cruz, 1992). In the wake of the revolution it has become evident that the main territorial cleavage lies between a conservative and Catholic north, largely comprising small farmers and predominantly voting CDS and PSD, and a more lay, socialist–communist south (Gaspar and André, 1989: 274–7). A secondary cleavage distinguishes the rich, western coastal fringe where more than 70 per cent of the population is located, voting for the PS or PSD or, among the urban working class of Lisbon, Almada and Setúbal, for the PCP. By contrast, less than 30 per cent of the population lives in the poor eastern regions bordering Spain and the exodus of young people from this region to the larger towns, leaving behind an ageing population with no hope of improving their lives, is further reinforcing this cleavage.

Even a sketchy characterization of the parties' electorates reveals that the PSD is mainly a party of the small rural and urban petty bourgeoisie, the new middle classes and the farmers. The party's absolute majorities of 1987 and 1991 were explained as being related to the fact that Aníbal Cavaco Silva was, as a charismatic figure, able to attract votes from other parties. This long dominant party has strong affinities with the business organization (*Confederação Industrial Portuguesa*) as well as with the small farmers' association (*Confederação de Agricultores Portuguesa*). It is, moreover, also well represented in the General Workers' Union (UGT) which was founded by social democrats and socialists as an alternative to the communist union (*Confederação Geral de Trabalhadores Portugueses-Intersindical*, CGTP-In) in 1978 (Optenhogel and Stoleroff, 1985).

The PS is dominant among the new middle classes, the industrial proletariat in the north and the farmers of central Portugal. The relationship between the UGT and the Socialists is very close. The leader of the union, Torres Couto, is a leading Socialist MEP. In 1995 the UGT came under criminal investigation because several of its leading functionaries were involved in various cases of fraud relating to EU structural funds.

The PCP is hegemonic among the land labourers in the southern province of Alentejo and the lesser-skilled strata of the industrial working class in the south's urban centres. The party has strong connections with the CGTP-In. Recently, there has been growing co-optation of Communist trade unionists into the leading bodies of the Communist party and vice versa. The CGTP-In can be seen as the party's main power resource. The union follows a more pragmatic position than the Communist Party in the question of European integration. Nevertheless, several leading union functionaries such as José Barros Moura, an independent MEP, and José Miguel Judas, mayor of the fishing town and bourgeois summer resort of Cascais near Lisbon, were expelled from the confederation and the party, indicating that the leadership of the CGTP-In remains highly dogmatic and unsympathetic to reform proposals.

The traditional electoral basis of the CDS is eroding. The economic and social decline of the northern and north-eastern regions has had a dramatic effect on the CDS's traditional conservative clientele (Gaspar and André, 1989: 273). The new leader, Manuel Monteiro, wants to enlarge the party's social base by developing a more nationalist discourse *vis-à-vis* the European Union. The election result of October 1995 may have been the first fruits of this strategy. In 1993 the CDS was excluded from the Christian Democratic European People's Party and it had to join the French Gaullists' European Democratic Alliance in the European Parliament.

Party system consolidation in the 1980s: preparing for European integration

The main political issue in the 1980s was integration into the European Community. The political elite geared all their efforts to achieving this goal as soon as possible. The application in 1977 by Prime Minister Mário Soares and the EC's positive response to it in 1978 led to the assumption that accession would be achieved within two or three years. Instead, Portugal had to wait eight years before becoming a Community member.

The election of the conservative Democratic Alliance in 1979 and 1980 seemed to ensure that greater political and party system stability could be achieved, contributing to a stronger position in the negotiation process with the European Community. However, the death in an aeroplane crash of the PPD/PSD leader, Sá Carneiro, in December 1980 reactivated party faction-alism and after the adoption of the constitutional revision of August 1982, the unstable coalition collapsed.

The April 1983 election led to the victory of the Socialists who gained 36 per cent of the vote compared to the Social Democrats' 27 per cent. The two major parties then entered into negotiations to build a centrist coalition so that the austerity policies demanded by the IMF could be implemented. The cross-bloc coalition that resulted, the so-called Centre Bloc, surmounted the Left–Right cleavage aided by both electoral volatility and ideological fluidity in the centre ground. Neither the PS nor the PSD wanted to enter into a coalition with the PCP which had been marginalized within the new constitutional democracy from the outset, largely because of the ambivalent role this large party played during the revolutionary process (Stock, 1989b: 159–61). This anomalous coalition lasted until the socially very costly austerity measures imposed by the IMF were fully implemented.

In the 1985 election the newly-formed Democratic Renewal Party (PRD) of the outgoing president, Ramalho Eanes, gained 18 per cent of the vote and briefly destabilized the party system to the long-term benefit of the Centre–Right. Orientated to the left, the PRD comprised mainly the urban new middle classes who wanted to protest against the austerity policies of the Centre Bloc. The PRD contributed to the fragmentation of the Left, occupying the electoral space between the Socialist and Social Democratic parties, and facilitated the PSD's rise to a hegemonic position on the centre and right of the party spectrum (Aguiar, 1989: 227–8).

While the PRD's votes came from all four major parties, with reference to the 1983 elections, most came from the PS and the PCP rather than the PSD and CDS (Bacalhau, 1989: 247). The PSD increased its vote to nearly 30 per cent in 1985 whereas the Socialist vote declined from 36 per cent to just 21 per cent. The Communist Alliance vote dropped slightly to 15 per cent. In this sense, the party to suffer most was the Socialist Party, the party most affected by the unpopular austerity measures introduced by the Centre Bloc coalition.

On the whole, one can argue that voter fidelity increased between 1976 and 1983 but that thereafter a realignment took place within the party system. A massive vote switch from the PRD to the PSD in 1987 confirmed the stable and responsible 1985–87 minority government of Aníbal Cavaco Silva (Bacalhau, 1989: 250) and enabled the PSD to achieve an absolute majority of the vote. This was the first such majority in the history of the new democracy. At the same time, the PS recovered minimally, while the wings of the party system declined. The Communist Alliance slipped to 12 per cent whilst the conservative CDS secured barely over 4 per cent.

The reasons for such massive electoral volatility are various. First, in March 1987 the government of Cavaco Silva was brought down by a censure motion initiated by the PRD and supported by the PS and PCP. The public was not happy with this manoeuvre and protested by voting massively for the PSD. Second, the charismatic personality of Aníbal Cavaco Silva, a professor of economics, appealed to the electorate. His whole style reminded voters of Salazar, for Cavaco Silva was extremely assertive about the future of Portugal. Besides, he presented himself as an almost independent candidate representing all Portuguese people and the elections had the aura of presidential elections about them. The consequent 'presidentialism of the prime minister' could be seen as creating a new kind of political regime without constitutional reform (Moreira, 1989). Third, the American-style campaign and the electorally mobilizing slogans ('Portugal cannot stop now') presented the PSD as a party going forward, of modernization. Accession to the EC in January 1986, presided over by Cavaco Silva, was a fourth major factor behind such electoral mobility. Finally, the electorate was tired of being called to elections every two years. It yearned for stability, as is shown by the confirmation of the PSD's absolute majority in 1991.

The late 1980s, then, was a period of ultra-stability of the party system (see Table 12.3). The absolute majority stabilized the political and party systems, while the EC's structural funds helped to stabilize the economy. Between 1989 and 1992 Portugal experienced an economic boom and a

Table 12.3 Trends in electoral volatility, Portugal, 1976–91

Year	Total electoral volatility	Cross-bloc volatility
1976	11.3	6.6
1979	10.5	3.2
1980	4.6	1.7
1983	11.2	7.8
1985	22.5	0.5
1987	23.2	15.5
1991	9.5	1.2

Source: Morlino, 1995: 318, 320.

policy-making process more orientated to the long-term (Eaton, 1994; Hudson, 1994; Corkill, 1993a).

Examination of Table 12.3 shows total electoral volatility to be much higher than cross-bloc volatility. More particularly, the highest degree of electoral instability was registered in the elections of 1985 and 1987 when the PRD destabilized existing cleavages by occupying a position between the Socialists and Communists. Yet this volatility did not, in 1985, affect the share of votes *between* the blocs. In 1987, however, the 1985 change became very important, for when the PRD's vote declined from 18 to 4 per cent, much of the lost vote crossed to the PSD. This switch led to the hegemony of the Right–Centre bloc and to the decline in importance of the Left–Centre Socialists. In 1991, total electoral volatility was much reduced, while the new distribution of the vote between Left and Right remained highly stable.

Even more revealing is the evolution of partisan loyalty between elections. In a remarkable study by Mário Bacalhau on electoral mobility and vote transfer based on opinion polls conducted in 1984, 1986 and 1987, he concludes that until 1985 party loyalty was very high, with 84 per cent of the electorate voting for the same parties in the 1983 and 1985 elections. The highest scores were registered by the communists, with 87 per cent of 1975 voters choosing the same party eight years later, followed by the socialists, the PSD and the CDS (84, 75 and 69 per cent, respectively) (Bacalhau, 1989: 245). The appearance of the PRD in 1985 upset this pattern considerably. Only 45 per cent of 1983 voters backed the PS in 1985 while the other parties were able to secure most of the 1983 voters (PSD 81 per cent, PCP 86 per cent, CDS 72 per cent). The PRD gained nearly a quarter of the PS's voters, more than double that of the Communist party's and four times that of the Social Democrats and Christian Democrats (Bacalhau, 1989: 247). In 1987, over 90 per cent of the PSD's 1985 voters remained faithful to the party. The fidelity of the Communist alliance voter was also high (86 per cent). Although the loyal electoral vote between 1985 and

1987 increased (from 45 to 62 per cent) compared to 1983–85, the Socialist share of the vote stagnated. The electoral stability that existed before 1985 continuing to elude the party. The PS lost a further 14 per cent of its 1985 voters to the PSD. The smaller conservative CDS was also a big loser in 1987, its core electorate declining by half compared to 1985. About 30 per cent of its 1985 voters went over to the PSD (Bacalhau, 1989: 250).

In an excellent study carried out by Franz Wilhelm Heimer in 1988, the ideological make-up of these core electorates of the four main parties was analysed in depth. Heimer discovered that in his sample more than 70 per cent of PS voters were convinced democrats, with only 3 per cent expressing an anti-democratic attitude. Among the communist voters, nearly two-thirds (65 per cent) were convinced democrats, though 15 per cent preferred a non-liberal–democratic regime. The two right-wing parties, the PSD and CDS, both had a lower share of convinced democrats – just over half (56 per cent) (Heimer, 1991: 143–4). Heimer subsequently asked about the regime preferences of the different core electorates. This question shed further light on the cleavages between the parties. The Socialist core electorate over-whelmingly preferred a democratic regime (80 per cent) as did that of the PSD (78 per cent). Although the majority of the CDS voters felt at home in a democratic regime (57 per cent), a large minority (37 per cent) supported an authoritarian–corporatist regime. Communist voters were clearly adherents of a communist regime (66 per cent). These findings show that the share of supporters of democracy is stronger in the two centre parties (Heimer, 1991: 144–5). The study also shows that the PCP is the most anti-fascist party, consequent upon its role as the main resistance party challenging the authoritarian regime, whereas in the CDS and PSD the anti-communist perspective is predominant (Heimer, 1991: 146–7). PS voters also express a strong anti-fascist attitude (49 per cent). The greatest importance to political participation is given by the PCP (57 per cent) and the lowest by the CDS (19 per cent). The other centre parties (PSD and PS) lie in between with 33 and 47 per cent respectively. Nevertheless, the overwhelming majority of the voters of all four parties are supporters of an average or a strong level of participation. It seems, too, that a large share of the electorate of the four parties was satisfied with the democracy of the late 1980s (Heimer, 1991: 149–50).

Paradoxically, the new party system consolidated itself in the 1980s partly via the brief destabilization of 1985–87. Fundamental ideological cleavages between the parties became more salient, yet electoral availability in the centre of the party spectrum became more flexible and less ideologically defined. Less sub-cultural, more 'political market' (Bartolini and Mair, 1990: 295–8) behaviour, became evident from 1985 with the emergence of the Democratic Renewal Party. Suddenly, electoral availability led to the breakdown of the left-wing bloc in favour of the right-wing one. The absolute majority of the PSD in 1987 consolidated this shift to the predominance of the Right over the Left. Moreover, it increased the openness of the political market for more flexible electoral strategies by political parties. This trend towards the development of a marketplace in electoral politics became even more noticeable in the 1990s.

The 1990s: party system institutionalization or transformation?

Joaquim Aguiar has argued strongly that the Portuguese party system may be undergoing a transition from neo-patrimonial representational structures to modern and post-modern forms. In the former, parties treat the state as their private property, colonizing it in order to protect the interests of certain clienteles. In the latter, there is a more open and competitive relationship between the parties. In Aguiar's opinion the nature of the party system has to be put in the context of democratic regime change. He expected that the election of 1995 would see voters' choices becoming less predictable (Aguiar, 1994: 230–6).

Certainly, the prominence of political scandals in the 1990s made it evident that the Portuguese party system could not be seen independently from Portuguese society (Magone, 1994). Electoral volatility and availability have increasingly been conditioned by conjunctural developments. In Portugal, mass membership parties other than the Communist Party never existed. The late development of parties and of a modern party system are also contingently influenced by party change and transformation elsewhere. The impact of transnational party organizations on the development of the Portuguese party system is clear. International networks, particularly those related to the European integration process, influence and reinforce the stability and institutionalization of party competition in Portugal.

Up to the end of 1992 the growth of the Portuguese economy led to the misleading assumption that Portugal was becoming similar to the other Western European countries. The party system had, correspondingly, to adapt to new forms of politics. The party of electors in the American style, which conditioned the spectrum of programme choice for the electorate, seemed to have become reality in Portugal (Aguiar, 1988).

In the 1991 election the PSD under Aníbal Cavaco Silva, a prototype of this supposedly technocratic party, again gained an absolute majority. Yet the situation changed in 1993 when the introduction of the Single European Market plunged Portugal into an economic crisis. All the main opposition parties became more radical. The CDS became a nationalist–patriotic party hostile to Maastricht and for a 'Europe of the Nations', the Communists continued to be an anti-EU party, whilst the Socialists attempted to act as a constructive 'shadow government' presenting themselves as a credible alternative. The outcome of the autumn 1995 election was unpredictable, especially as the charismatic Aníbal Cavaco Silva stepped down as prime minister to be replaced by the number two of the party, Fernando Nogueira. Speculation was strong that Cavaco Silva was positioning himself to stand as a candidate for the presidential elections in early 1996. After eight years of an absolute majority government, it was interesting to ask whether the party system would change from a predominant one to a multi-party one (Blondel, 1968). Much depended on whether the PSD would be able to maintain its cohesion after Cavaco Silva's departure. The party's leadership change would test whether the PSD had become a 'charismatic party' (Panebianco, 1988: 65–7) like the Greek PASOK under Andreas Papandreou, or whether it had been able to develop towards a stably structured modern mass party. Hitherto the 'most Portuguese of the political parties' had needed a strong charismatic leader to keep the factions within the party together (Stock, 1989a).

The election of October 1995 did not confirm the trend towards a predominant party system. On the contrary, the victory of the Socialist Party with 44 per cent of the vote re-established the predominance of the Left over the Right. Yet, and moreover, the defeated social democrats gathered just over one-third of the vote which gave them a strong role in opposition. Furthermore, the revival of the CDS-PP, which attracted 9 per cent of the vote, and of the PCP with nearly as much, seems to indicate that the four-party format remains very much alive. An analysis of the pre-campaign period and the campaign itself confirms that the two main parties are becoming less ideologically distinct, and that political market behaviour is increasingly becoming the main feature of elections (Corkill, 1996; Frain, 1996).

In sum, the Portuguese party system has a four-party format (Sartori, 1976) within which the two main parties alternate in power despite the brief period in the late 1980s when the rise of the PSD made it appear to be a predominant party. From the early 1990s, the two smaller parties attempted to present radical programmes to attract the social groups disadvantaged by the European integration process – fishermen, farmers and the industrial working class. This strategy showed little initial success because neither party seemed able to attract support beyond their traditional clienteles, but this changed with the revival of the CDS-PP in 1995, confirming the four-party-format. It is always possible that the government-opposition dynamic will encourage the development of a two-party system based on the Socialists and Social Democrats. The trend from 1976 is for these two parties to increase their joint share of the vote while the two smaller parties lose votes. However, the revival of the CDS-PP suggests that such a trend faces major obstacles.

The two main parties have increased their share of the vote from 59 per cent in 1976 to almost 80 per cent in the 1990s. The appearance of the PRD in 1985 contributed substantially to speeding up the concentration of the vote on the two main parties. Conversely, the share of the vote gained by the two smaller parties declined from 30 to just 13 per cent by 1991, although this trend was notably reversed in 1995. On the other hand, as a consequence, the 1995 election reinforced the trend towards electoral aggregation around the four main parties with fully 96 per cent of votes going to them. This process of concentration, however, has to be balanced against increasing abstention. By 1995, fully one third of the population had abstained from voting. The highest levels of abstention are found in the eastern regions of Portugal, with whole villages sometimes boycotting elections. The level of political participation and engagement in politics in Portugal is generally low as we noted earlier in describing Portuguese parties as non-membership parties.

Conclusion: a fluid, ultra-stable party system

The comparability of party system change in Portugal with other Western European states is only partial. Portugal's democratic transition began only in the mid-1970s and this gives the party system some unique features, for example a still large Communist Party and a Centre–Right party which is, nominally, social democratic. The Portuguese party system is embedded in a democracy that is still in the process of consolidation and institutionalization. The transition did not only end an authoritarian dictatorship of 48 years. It also introduced universal suffrage for Portuguese citizens over 18 for the very first time. Hitherto the electorate had been highly restricted. With no electoral history worthy of the name, the democratic party system developed by trial and error. Only after the first election of April 1975 was it possible to have any idea of the future party system format (two large parties, two small parties). In effect, this original party format remained stable throughout the 1980s and 1990s.

Despite this stability, electoral volatility and hence availability were dominant in the early 1980s. Within the four-party system several intra- and cross-bloc alliances and coalitions were attempted so that a ruling majority could be achieved. In 1985 the appearance of the Democratic Renewal Party supporting President Ramalho Eanes split the Left and then saw its votes substantially captured by the Right in 1987, leading to absolute majority government notwithstanding the proportional representation electoral system. In 1991 this absolute majority was repeated, contributing to the stabilization of the party and political systems. Nevertheless, economic and social crisis, the stepping aside of the charismatic Aníbal Cavaco Silva from the office of prime minister, and growing electoral abstentionism introduced a potential for renewed electoral volatility and availability. Much depended, after 1995, on whether the once-ruling PSD would be able to maintain itself as a cohesive united party in opposition. The pre-Cavaco Silva history of the party suggested that this was unlikely. On the contrary, it was probable that factionalism and personalism among the regional barons would reappear once more. Yet the comfortable relative majority (112 of 230 seats) of the Socialists gained in 1995 was a further variation of the four-party format and in this sense, Joaquim Aguiar's characterization of the Portuguese party system as 'fluid, ultra-stable' continues to be a valid interpretation.

Acknowledgment

I am grateful to Franz Wilhelm Heimer and his colleagues for providing me with a wealth of information of direct relevance to this chapter. In addition, I wish to thank Mark Donovan for his comments forwarded to me during editing.

13

Party System Change in Western Europe: Positively Political

MARK DONOVAN AND DAVID BROUGHTON

Understanding party system change

Party systems are central to the functioning of modern representative democracies. It is scarcely exaggerated to say that no aspect of contemporary politics is uninfluenced by them. However, the reverse is also inevitably true, and the high number of variables influencing the structure and functioning of party systems has engendered despair regarding the possibility of identifying specific types of party system (Ware, 1996). Were such a typology available it would not only yield a set of independent variables able to further political analysis, it would also provide a simple way of identifying party system change, that is, in terms of 'from what to what?'. The non-typological approach to the analysis of party system change, based on analysing various indicators of change, for example the increase in the number of parties in a system, is not a satisfactory alternative. Quantitative data need to be placed in a qualitative context identifying what degree and what sort of change is significant. The problem is not merely analytical. Normatively, a fear has come to be expressed that party systems are not merely changing, but have become *vulnerable* to change, potentially leading to instability and even collapse.

With regard to the analytical problem, a body of research has developed which proposes that a qualitative response may be given to the questions of 'how' and 'in what way' party systems are changing. As argued by Gordon Smith the 'from what to what' question can be answered with reference to the changing definition of a party system's 'core' meaning, as developed by Peter Mair (1996, 1997), its enduring structure of competition for government. The precise meaning of this is elaborated below, but the key point is that the core approach retains a fundamental idea of the typological method, that is, Sartori's crucial insight that a party system, as a system, is defined by the structure of the whole, that is, by the pattern of interaction between the parties rather than by the sum of the parties themselves. In other words, the argument is a substantially structural one. The crucial notion that there is some element of 'systemness' which is an independent variable is maintained. The major problem with Sartori's typology is that it is difficult to find cases that are not of 'moderate pluralism' whilst the other two key categories, 'polarized pluralism' and the 'two-party system', though important, find few examples to illustrate them. The focus on party system cores stressing the importance of coalition dynamics and change through the redefinition of coalitional blocs is a more flexible approach. This chapter surveys the case study contributions to this volume in terms of core change. It asks two principal questions: *what are the implications of the concept of core change?*, and *how much core change have party systems in Western Europe seen in recent decades?*

The second part of this conclusion starts by outlining the debate in the study of party system change, suggesting that currently its major preoccupation, amply demonstrated by our contributors, is party system 'defreezing'. At the extreme, such defreezing raises the spectre of an entirely destructured politics in which the electorate is atomized, comprising individuals devoid of collective identities. Such an electorate may well spurn parties (Appleton, 1995; Richardson, 1995). Hence, party systems may be giants with feet of clay, as De Tocqueville described the *ancien régime* nobility before its fall (Mair, 1995). Such an electorate may be tempted to support charismatic leaders, turning party democracy into a plebiscitary pseudo-democracy. Pessimists and certain critics of liberal democracy, especially the presidential and specifically American variant, see this situation as already close to reality (Lipow, 1996). The second part continues by outlining a response to the premise underlying this critique, identifying what will be called a 'neo-orthodoxy'. This stresses continuing structural stability of a systemic, political nature independent of sociological transformation and ideological collapse. The historical context of contemporary change is then clarified with the help of a 'stages' model of development of European party systems and the contemporary presence of both flux and structure emphasized.

The third part argues that the country which has seen *the* most radical challenge to any contemporary Western European party and political system, including the outside risk that charismatic, presidential and even authoritarian politics would assert themselves, namely Italy, nevertheless has seen the reassertion of party government based on competitive party politics. Overall, the contributions to this volume identify not the danger of party system collapse but, rather, *challenges* to their existing structuration. Three challenges are identified: 1 the weakening of established 'people's parties'; 2 the transformation of predominant party systems into balanced, or alternating, systems; and 3 territorial differentiation. The third part concludes by assessing the significance of parties themselves, both old and new, to party system change, suggesting that the emergence of new parties paradoxically bears testimony to the continuing importance of the established parties.

The fourth part develops the concept of the party system core to assess the extent of core change in Western European party systems. This assessment emphasises the expressly *political* contribution to the structuring of party systems. From this perspective we conclude that the more alarmist views about party system change are too pessimistic. In some respects there is less change than the pessimists perceive. In some respects, however, there is more than the 'continuists' allow. But stability should not be confused with stasis. Change may be conducive to stability. We need to appreciate that competitive party systems may be stable yet dynamic structures. As such, they provide political systems with an architecture which permits the interaction of structural constraint and human agency, or political will, thus providing both resilience and flexibility. To a great extent social conflict is still institutionalized and organized via competitive party systems which, thanks to the construction, destruction and reconstruction of political blocs (governmental parties or alliances of parties) competing for government, constitute enduring yet innovative learning structures for both elites and voters.

Party system breakdown?

The extent of change in contemporary party systems has inspired a range of analyses specifying the parameters that need to be considered in order to understand it. Thus, Jan-Erik Lane and Svante Ersson have sought to operationalize five aspects of party system change in a series of indicators designed to facilitate its measurement (1994: 177 ff.). These indicators cover: the extent of electoral participation; the number of parties in the system; the degree of ideological polarization; the sociological nature of party support; and the volatility of the electorate. Peter Mair (1989) has argued that obsessive attention to the electoral dimension has entailed the neglect of the organizational and ideological dimensions of party system structure and in this context Gordon Smith's identification of patterns of government and opposition as a systemic property of party systems is highly significant (see Table 13.1).

In this volume, party system change has been analysed within national historical contexts in accordance with the logic of identifying national party system cores, while nevertheless using a common framework to ease comparison. While the contributors have stressed electoral change and the so-called 'defreezing' of party systems, they have also, in line with the elite and political structure focus of Mair and Smith, pointed to ideological and organizational change, often emphasizing the innovative role of party

Table 13.1 Systemic properties of party systems

	Properties
1	The number of parties and their relative sizes
2	The ideological distances between parties
3	Changes in parties' electoral support
4	Change and continuity in cleavage salience
5	Patterns of government and opposition
6	The arenas in which a party system operates (electoral, including its different levels; governmental, including neo-corporatist aspects; and parliamentary).

Source: Adapted from Smith, 1989a.

leaderships. Particular attention has been paid to changing patterns of coalition formation. Let us first turn to the debate on defreezing.

Defreezing stands in contrast to the 'freezing' of party systems identified by Seymour Martin Lipset and Stein Rokkan as having taken place by the 1920s, and as having endured through to the 1960s when they were writing (Lipset and Rokkan, 1967a). Since then there has been a dramatic shift in perspective. Sartori has spoken of the mid-1960s to mid-1970s as a phase of defreezing, with the 1990s seeing 'a new defreezing and, this time, a deeper one' (1994: 50). Others have suggested that 'There are no frozen party systems in Western Europe any more' and that 'The Lipset–Rokkan model should be abandoned' (Ersson and Lane, 1996: 13). The perception of change led to a shift in analytical emphasis away from stability as early as the 1970s (Dalton, Flanagan and Beck, 1984; Mair, 1990a). This did not go unchallenged, yet the 'neo-orthodox' re-emphasis on stability discussed below has not sought to deny the reality of change (Mair, 1985; 1993). Rather, it has sought to specify change more precisely and to normalize it within a long-term and more political, less sociologically determined, perspective (Bartolini and Mair, 1990).

In what might be called a 'neo-orthodox' perspective, Mair challenges the theoretical premise underpinning the radical view of change. In this latter view, socio-economic and cultural change must eventually produce party system instability since increasingly high levels of electoral volatility have, so to speak, pulled the carpet out from beneath the parties. Mair has highlighted two counter-arguments. Empirically, electoral volatility in the past, not least during the 'frozen' inter-war period, was extensive. In historical perspective, it is the electoral stability of the 1950s and 1960s which was exceptional rather than the increased volatility of the 1970s onwards. Theoretically, Mair asks what does freezing refer to. For Mair, freezing is not necessarily disproved by electoral volatility since the concept properly refers to the stability of voting *within blocs* defined by cleavages, not to the share of votes won by individual parties. Thus, electoral volatility between a socialist and a communist party is compatible with the freezing hypothesis since there is no volatility across the dominant worker–owner cleavage. Empirically, Mair emphasizes, recent increases in volatility have indeed been largely within either the left bloc or the right bloc. Thus, more controversially, vote shifts between a social democratic and a green party might also be considered intra-bloc where the latter has taken on a left-wing coalition identity as in Italy, France and, at regional level, Germany.

At this point, the cleavage-based, rather than party-based, argument blends with more substantial methodological and theoretical points concerning the underpinnings of party system structuration. The analytical approach rooted in cleavages developed by Lipset and Rokkan is prone to sociological reductionism meaning parties are easily seen as being no more than the necessary *product* of social or socio-economic factors. In fact, cleavages are only formed where there is successful political mobilization, located where, in modern terms, party formation takes place. Cleavages, then, are as much politically as socially constructed (Zuckerman, 1982). Indeed, party system structuration stems from the interaction of party strategies, including ideological mobilization and the institutional requirements of government formation (typically coalition formation) in parliamentary democracies as well as from sociological factors. A shift in focus beyond the merely electoral aspects of party systems is needed (Pennings, 1996). As Sartori has forcefully argued, voters should not be seen as sociological constructs who in turn determine party system structure. Rather, voters are, in part at least, themselves constructed by the existing (or even emerging) party system. Moreover, while party system structures tend to become something of a 'cage' for party elites too, such elites are relatively autonomous. This emphasis on political sociology, rather than the sociology of politics (Sartori, 1969) appears to be carried through forcefully in Peter Mair's most recent work (1997). In sum, a political analysis should lead us to switch our focus not merely from party to cleavage but, more radically to that noticeably under-theorized concept, the 'bloc'. Successful bloc formation leading to a sustained pattern of government formation, like the failure to build or maintain such structures, is the stuff of political history (see Esping-Andersen, 1985; Luebbert, 1991).

This emphasis on the political bases of party system structure arguably corresponds to the institutionalization of party democracy in twentieth-century Europe. This may seem a rather optimistic view given that the shift in emphasis from stability to change has been accompanied by a discourse of crisis. Yet, even while recognizing that Western Europe's contemporary circumstances present major political challenges (Hayward, 1995), one can still be optimistic about the changes that have been occurring in party systems over the past quarter century. They can be seen as ending a period of immobilism and stagnation. A more positive hypothesis still would be that the changes under consideration signal processes of learning, adaptation and innovation among elites, on the one hand, and between elites and voters, on the other. These are processes which the rigid, one-party political systems of Eastern Europe were unable to entertain.

This optimistic hypothesis can be briefly contrasted with the pessimistic one. A starting point is Sartori's powerful analysis of party systems (1976). As briefly indicated, and despite his emphasis elsewhere on the autonomy of the political, Sartori's analysis of party systems as *systems*, not fluidly changing configurations, stresses their comprising stable patterns of inter-action with, consequently, identifiable 'mechanics'. Accordingly, elites may appear to be trapped in structures determined by mass electoral behaviour. In other words, within Sartori's political approach, there is a tension between structure and agency. In practice, recent change has signalled a decline in 'mechanical' certainties, arguably due to elite initiatives: new parties have been founded and compete successfully (green parties generally, or the Austrian FPÖ and Dutch Democrats '66); unprecedented coalitions formed; party organizations and ideologies transformed. In sum, structural determination has weakened and political agency has come to the fore.

Sartori's analysis of the way structural determination became dominant stressed the importance of party organization and ideology. Sartori identified what he called party system *consolidation* with the domination of the sig-nificantly named mass integration party (1968). That party type is no more. The literature on political parties makes it abundantly clear that today's parties, be they catch-all (Kirchheimer, 1966), electoral-professional (Pan-ebianco, 1988), modern cadre (Koole, 1994) or cartel parties (Katz and Mair, 1994), see a fundamentally different relationship between their elites and the electorate and membership. Voters are less tied by ideological identifica-tion to specific parties and more likely to switch their votes between elections. Party members are losing influence in some respects yet sometimes also gaining influence in others (Katz and Mair, 1992; 1994).

The strengthening of agency over structural constraints is clear in the growing prominence of party leaders. In the traditionally dominant parties a presidential image is often projected on to their leaders. But many of the newer parties have been characterized by charismatic leaders with a far more radical image, e.g. Italy's Umberto Bossi, though these too may aim at an eventual presidential role – as with Austria's Jörg Haider. Increasingly significant too, since the 1960s, has been the role of media and marketing professionals in national party headquarters and the role of television in communicating with the electorate. This change has been especially evident in Britain and Ireland, as noted respectively by Paul Webb and Justin Fisher and by David Farrell. But such modernization can come about very quickly.

In Italy, Silvio Berlusconi updated Italian campaign style in only a few months over the winter of 1993–94.

Research into mass political behaviour also points to growing political activism, either simultaneously, or in reaction to greater elite entrepreneurialism: citizens' initiatives, new social movements and the rise of new grass-roots-inspired parties indicate a 'democratic transformation' of the representative democracies at a level largely below that of party politics (Fuchs and Klingemann, 1995). We would argue that the increase in political agency at both levels, and that very differentiation itself, can be welcomed. We recognize the arguments of those who seek greater citizen participation in politics but we also concur with those who seek to supplement, rather than replace, competitive party democracy (Keane, 1988: Chapter 4). If the citizen is to have adequate impact on government, then competitive party systems must remain a feature of western democracies (Ware, 1987).

The fear, however, is that increasing political agency means the structural *de*consolidation of party systems. We can capture the fears concerning the present flux via reference to another definition of the origins of our party systems. Alessandro Pizzorno (1981) defined the initial stage of party system construction as 'generative'. Is the present stage, then, one of *de*generation? To answer this question an understanding of historical context is needed. In an attempt to grasp the historical dimension of party system change, Gordon Smith developed a three-stage model of European party system development (1990). The model (see Table 13.2) comprised an initial, exceptionally long-lasting, mobilization and alignment stage; a second stage starting roughly in the 1960s; and a third stage, from the 1970s. The stages overlap. Some features of the first and second stages remain operative today. The major features of the second stage, captured by Kirchheimer in his analysis of the 'catch-all' party, were party organizational change and ideological depolarization (Kirchheimer, 1957; 1966). Parties became vehicles for ambitious leaders and professional advisors and parties became more competitive in a situation in which competition was increasingly centripetal, avoiding the extremes. The third stage was one of flux, with both 'deconcentration' and 'diffusion'. Deconcentration indicated the rise of new parties and the declining size of existing parties, not least the large 'people's parties'. A variety of indices, most notably Rae's, were devised to measure party system 'fractionalization'. Diffusion referred to the corresponding propensity of voters to spread their votes among more parties.

For many pessimistic observers, electoral diffusion signalled citizen disenchantment and gathering political crisis but, as Smith pointed out in an earlier article, such diffusion may also indicate a more adventurous electorate 'secure in the knowledge of the basic consensus in society' (Smith,

Table 13.2 Stages and phases of party system development
in Western Europe

Stage	Dates	Types
1	1880s–1920s:	*Generative stage*. Mobilization and alignment in transitions to liberal democracy marked by crises, innovation and fluidity.
	By/in 1920s:	*Stabilization* (with notable exceptions e.g. Italy, Germany, Spain, Portugal and Greece).
2	1920s–60s:	*Mobilized stability*. Structurally consolidated systems (with the addition from the late 1940s of Italy and Germany).
3	From 1960s:	*Growing competititveness and depolarization*. 'Catch-all' parties expand their range of appeal; voters tend towards party dealignment.
4	1970s on:	*Structured flux*. Party deconcentration and voter diffusion. Challenge, innovation and learning among elites and between elites and citizens.
	A 1970s:	Increasing volatility. (Greece, Spain and Portugal added.)
	B 1980–90s:	Core resilience, innovation and transformation. (Emergence of central/east European party systems.)

Source: Adapted from Smith, 1979, 1989a, 1990; Pizzorno, 1981.

1979: 140). This interpretation may downplay the extent of continuing conflict, sounding overly sanguine. Yet, equally, electorates have not polarized around two juxtaposed alternatives. Ideological uncertainty and continuing party system fragmentation suggest that citizens are able, or perhaps are required to be, more expressive. There is experimentation.

Writing before the 'deeper defreezing' of the 1990s identified by Sartori, Smith (1989a, b) suggested that a period of flux had largely given way to a period of restabilization. Party system cores had reasserted themselves, often through the organizational and ideological adaptation of the dominant 'people's parties' (see below). Since 1989, the 'flux' which Smith identified especially with a realignment of the Left has come to affect the Centre and Right as well. *Both* types of mass integration party, the class and the religious-based, social democratic and Christian Democratic, have undergone significant decline. As Hans-Martien ten Napel puts it in his chapter on the Netherlands, the two major communitarian or solidarist parties have fallen victim to increasing individualism. We can add that the related 'silent revolution' of the post-materialist Left identified by Inglehart (1977) has been matched by a silent 'counter-revolution' of the Right (Ignazi, 1992a). Thus, several contributors indicate that flux, and the challenge to the cores identified by Smith, continues unabated. Nevertheless, David Arter signals that while electoral volatility now seems to be a norm, Sweden sees only a 'mild case' of the syndrome of inter-related changes and even ten Napel speaks of 'resilience', despite the historic magnitude of the changes he discusses in the Dutch case. Flux, it seems, remains subject to structural constraints. Indeed, Jonathan Hopkin and José Magone contrast electoral volatility to the consolidation of new party systems in Spain and Portugal. Neither electoral defreezing nor party system deconsolidation seem to equate to party system (let alone political system) degeneration.

The challenge to party system cores in Western Europe

Events in Italy provide a yardstick for the challenges faced by party system cores in Western Europe, both for what has actually happened and for what some fear might happen. Italy's crisis is three-fold, involving the state, a political class and the party system (Bull and Rhodes, 1997). By mid-1998, change was limited to massive turnover in the political class and the attempted consolidation of a new party system. Constitutional reform was probable, but this seemed more likely to reinforce party government than overthrow it. Indeed, the reformists sought to consolidate a two-bloc party system conducive, unlike the old one, to alternation. Thus, even in this case of the greatest dissatisfaction with democratic performance, the political solution sought was mainly a better functioning party democracy. Indeed, the weakening of party government from 1992 and its brief abeyance in 1995 (Fabbrini, 1996) were countered by the reassertion of the importance of the politics of coalition and competition based on Left–Right structuring in the elections of 1994 and 1996, as described by Philip Daniels in Chapter 5.

While competitive party government was not abandoned, a powerful anti-party and anti-politics current favouring a presidential and plebiscitary solution to Italy's governmental problem was nevertheless reinforced by the collapse of the old party system. Democracy can not only take different forms, as José Magone reminds us in his discussion of the rebirth of democracy in Portugal, it can also be more or less democratic (Beetham, 1994). It is the anti-party, presidential–plebiscitary programme which represents the maximum challenge facing party government and, thereby, party systems. Yet not even Italy has seen such political degeneration. Rather, party system *regeneration*, albeit full of difficulties and uncertainties seems to be taking place.

Putting party and political degeneration aside, then, the changes identified by the contributors can be grouped under three broad headings: the setbacks suffered by what Smith calls 'large, moderate' 'people's parties'; the continuing decline of the predominant party; and 'territorial differentiation'. Having outlined these developments, this section concludes by considering the role of old and new parties in bringing these changes about.

The challenge to the 'people's parties'

The term 'people's party' was introduced by Gordon Smith in relation to his development of the concept of the party system core. According to Smith, the 'people's party' is one of the major factors underlying party system continuity and persistence. These parties are 'large and moderate', adjectives which indicate their key role in underpinning government formation on the basis of size and their 'coalitionability'.

With regard to their size, Smith suggested that a vote of 30 per cent could be taken as a benchmark for defining them, since this would largely limit the number present in any system to one or two (Smith, 1989b: 158). If we adopt this criterion, we can see how significant the challenges of deconcentration and electoral diffusion have become. In the Christian Democratic family the Italian DC saw its share of the vote fall fractionally under 30 per cent in 1992 immediately prior to its collapse, while the Dutch CDA fell below this level in 1982 and again in 1994, and the Austrian ÖVP in 1994 and 1995. In Ireland, support for Fine Gael fell below 30 per cent from 1987. In the social democratic family, the British Labour Party fell below this level in 1983, very narrowly avoiding displacement as the UK's second party. More recently, in 1994, the Dutch Labour party (PvdA) fell to 24 per cent.

While none of these parties faces the melt-down experienced by the DC, it is clear that the challenges confronting them are substantial. Indeed, in the Dutch and Italian cases, Christian Democratic predominance has been overthrown *and* no party now has over 30 per cent of the vote. In Ireland and Austria too, although Fianna Fáil and the SPÖ still gain over 30 per cent of the vote, both have lost their predominant position.

The shift from predominance to balance and alternation

The domination of some party systems, and governments, by specific parties has weakened in favour of a situation of balance and alternation since the 1960s. Smith charts the erosion of social democratic predominance in Scandinavia from that decade and points to a similar loss of more temporary Centre–Right dominance in Germany and France (Smith, 1989c). The shift from imbalance, or predominance, to balance is no small matter. The significance of alternation as a modern 'social invention' has been hailed and highlighted (Dahl, 1966; Kolinsky, 1987). Recently, alternation has been prominent in the new Mediterranean democracies of Spain and Portugal. In Portugal, in 1995, the Left confirmed that it had a moderate governing orientation, not merely a radical one, as its association with the overthrow of the Salazar dictatorship might have suggested. In Spain, a year later, the post-Franco Right demonstrated its legitimacy as a government party, blocking the development of a predominant party system based on the PSOE. These alternations confirmed the importance of competition for government.

In Italy, imbalance, that is the predominance of a party and a bloc centred on it, ended dramatically in the 1990s. A shift to a balanced system where alternation was likely, was explicitly sought by reformers. Daniels shows that the elections of 1994 and 1996 achieved this, albeit perhaps provisionally. At least two other cases examined in this volume have seen a similar shift to balance and alternation. Both the Irish and the Swedish party systems contained predominant parties, Fianna Fáil and the SAP. Both parties have lost this status. In both cases, moreover, predominance was overcome by the initiative of existing elites in forming alternative coalitions – Fine Gael and Labour in Ireland, and what David Arter calls the bourgeois *ménage à trois* in Sweden. A further case of interrupted predominance is the Dutch one, dating back to 1918, where the Catholic KVP was incorporated into the Christian Democratic Appeal in the 1970s and then ejected from government in 1994.

Territorial differentiation

Italy, Belgium, Spain, the UK, and Germany have all seen territorial differentiation become a significant feature of their party systems in recent years. Italy has always had territorially distinct political regions but it did not, until the late 1980s, have major regional parties. By the mid-1990s, the Northern League challenged the country's national identity and, as a third, territorially-based pole, hostile to both Left and Right it threatened to destabilize government formation. In so doing, it challenged the domination of the nascent Left–Right 'core cleavage'. In Belgium, territorial differentiation has had dramatic effect. By the 1990s, as Lieven De Winter and Patrick Dumont point out, Belgium comprised not one but two party systems, with a 'big bang' separation of Wallonia and Flanders not out of the question. In newly democratic Spain, distinct regional–national party systems, most notably that of Catalonia, have come to play a key role in coalition formation at the Spanish state level.

In the UK, the election of a New Labour government in 1997, accompanied by the Conservative 'wipe out' in Scotland and Wales, brought to a head a long-brewing constitutional crisis regarding the territorial governance of this multi-national state. The promised creation of regional (national) assemblies, legitimized in Wales and Scotland by popular referendums, signalled a major change in state structure. In Germany, unification in 1990 brought a single national parliament and capital – once more to be Berlin – but also the formation of different party systems in east and west. This difference was emphasized by the federal nature of the German state and threatened to kill off the liberal FDP, barely present in the east and floundering in the west. Such a development, as Charlie Jeffery points out, would definitively end the pattern of centripetal coalition building already ruptured in the 1980s.

These different developments indicate the salience of the territorial dimension within party systems but also the way in which it tends to be subordinated to Left–Right structuration. More generally, the diversity of ways in which territorial politics are articulated also indicates the flexibility and resilience of multi-party polities in the face of major political challenges.

The contained significance of new parties

The *coup de grâce* to Italy's old party system was administered in 1994 when voters overwhelmingly supported new parties (notably the Northern League and *Forza Italia*) and transformed and transforming non-governmental parties (the PDS and MSI-AN). Many long-term and contingent factors contributed to the demise of Italy's old party system, the former going under such rubrics as secularization and modernization, the latter ranging from the collapse of the Soviet empire to electoral reform and television's 'spectacularization' of the judicial uncovering of corruption. However, if one focuses on the direct causes of the collapse of the old system, electoral behaviour and the appearance of new parties to vote for, then even in Italy new parties did *not* transform the old party system. The mould-breaking role of the Lega Nord *should* be acknowledged, but the other new parties which pre-dated the crisis (e.g. the Radicals, Proletarian Democracy, the Greens, the Network) were of marginal importance. Rather, phoenix-like, a new party system rose from the ashes of the old, constituted by old, albeit transformed and transforming parties, and by parties (*Forza Italia*) created in response to the conflagration. Party system transformation did not result from any sustained challenge by new parties.

If we look beyond Italy, new parties remain surprisingly marginal, the Austrian FPÖ, French FN and Dutch Democrats '66 being notable exceptions to this observation. In Ireland and Sweden, we have seen, it was old parties which overthrew the dominant party. Furthermore, whilst in the Netherlands the Democrats '66 played a key role in dumping the CDA into opposition, it was the innovative alliance between two old parties, Labour and Liberal (VVD), which was decisive in bringing this about. So, while the rise of new parties undoubtedly does undermine the people's parties and challenge predominant parties, party system change does not appear to be only a consequence of the electoral success of new parties – even when one focuses narrowly on voting behaviour and the parties on offer, excluding the wider environmental causes of change.

Nevertheless, the emergence of new parties has been welcomed for their innovative impact. Ralf Dahrendorf shocked the German establishment by welcoming the Greens on these grounds. Hindsight confirms Dahrendorf's viewpoint. Thus, Andreas Schedler (1996) concludes that the primary role of most anti-establishment parties is to act as '"shakers" who redefine the political agenda, revitalize inter-party competition, stir up waves of counter-mobilization, or else act as agents of party system dealignment' (Schedler, 1996: 306). Robert Harmel and Lars Svåsand have identified six ways in which new parties can have an impact on an existing party system (1990). To this list (see Table 13.3) can be added the organizational and campaign-style innovations introduced as part of some new parties' mobilizational appeal.

Table 13.3 Possible impacts of (new) parties on party systems

	Impact
1	Organizational innovations inspired
2	Campaign-style innovations inspired
3	Range of alternatives available to the electorate increased
4	Level of participation increased by mobilizing new voters and/or energizing old ones
5	Existing party/parties forced to alter its/their platform/s
6	Number of potential coalition alternatives increased
7	Number of viable coalitions increased
8	Nature of political debate shifted; possibly even the prevailing consensus shaken or shifted.

Source: Adapted from Harmel and Svåsand, 1990.

Against this, the impact of new parties is limited by their extraneity to the existing structure of competition. Even when partisan identity is minimal, there is an incentive for voters not to 'waste' their vote on small new parties which won't stop the most disliked party or bloc from winning. This sort of vote may not be positive support voting, but it is not usually considered protest voting and, indeed, voting 'against' rather than 'for' may have motivated even 'aligned' voters in the past (Dunleavy, 1990). In addition, new parties are constrained by state regulation, even though regulations also provide opportunities. As Wolfgang Müller (1993) has pointed out, a variety of constitutional rules, not least to do with the electoral system but also regarding, for example, party financing, influence the viability and sustainability of new party challenges to established parties. Given that modern party government renders the state substantially a tool of the established parties (Katz and Mair, 1995; 1996), it is the latter which tend to benefit from state regulation. As early as the beginning of the twentieth century electoral reform in the direction of proportionality cushioned the impact of the rise of the mass integration, especially class parties, to the benefit of the established liberal parties. Even when new parties are elect-orally successful and break into government, continued success is not guaranteed as De Winter and Dumont's analysis of the rise and fall of the Belgian language parties shows. In an extreme case of adaptation the traditional parties split, allowing these transformed 'old' parties to champion the language issue. The language parties waned – making way for another wave of new parties to crash against the established system.

Given the evidence that established parties have ever adapted and innovated, and bearing in mind the limited electoral, and even more limited governmental success, of new parties, it seems reasonable to argue that the 'entrepreneurialism' of old parties should be emphasised. Old parties have (see Table 12.3) transformed their organizations and their campaign styles, energized old voters and mobilized new ones, forced other existing parties to amend their platforms and even increased the number of coalition alternatives available. Old parties can even shift the prevailing consensus – as most notoriously achieved by Margaret Thatcher's commandeering of the Conservative Party in Britain. Of course, new parties may catalyse such developments, as Schedler's 'shaker' metaphor suggests, but no crude dichotomy between old and new should be drawn. Instead, party systems should be seen as resilient, flexible systems in which learning takes place in and via both old and new parties. We now turn to consideration of this process by looking at the process of core change.

The party system core and core change

We have seen that the challenge to the people's parties has intensified and the predominant party become rare. We have also seen that territorial differentiation can challenge prevailing state structures and make coalition formation more complex. Here we want to focus on the question of the party system core. We start with consideration of what comprises a core party and then move on to consider the role of political blocs in structuring party systems.

The core party

The term party system core was introduced by Smith alongside his argument concerning the persistence of the 'people's parties'. The size and moderation of these parties made them key players in government formation. However, small parties can also be core parties. For Smith, a core party must be 'influential' in the system's functioning and in the pattern of alignments, 'especially coalitional' (1989b: 161). Hence, a party as small as the German FDP can be a core party. By contrast, Smith was uncertain whether a party as large and influential as the Italian PCI should count as a core party given its semi-permanent exclusion from government. Finally, Smith asked whether a single party (the Italian Christian Democrats or the Swedish SAP) might form a system core.

A core comprising a single party suggests a substantially non-interacting party system which is close to being a contradiction in terms. For such a condition to be met there would have to be both voter immobility and a lack of interest among opposition elites in providing alternative government. Both may have been true to some extent in Sweden where post-war electoral volatility was low and the bourgeois parties were reconciled to social democratic 'hegemony' given that their resources nevertheless influenced policy-making. Still, when it came to the 'crunch' in 1976 the bourgeois parties did form an alternative governmental bloc – just as they already had in Norway a decade earlier (Urwin, 1987).

Turning to the Italian case, it is even less clear that it was non-competitive given the near-doubling of the PCI vote, 1946–76, to 34 per cent, and sustained conflict over the definition of the coalition 'formula'. The extent to which voters were 'immobile' is also debated (Allum and Mannheimer, 1985). The PCI was a hugely significant party both in terms of electoral competition and in its effects on coalition formation. One can draw a contrast with the French PCF (and *Front National*). These have neither prevented the formation of Centre–Left and Centre–Right coalitions, nor forced a centrist or grand coalition. Arguably, whereas, in David Hanley's terms, the FN and PCF have been 'peripheral', the PCI was what might be called an 'external core party'. It clearly influenced the pattern of government formation and with it the structure of the party system.

The same terms might be used elsewhere. For example, when the Austrian Grand Coalition came to an end, the FPÖ moved slowly from irrelevance to peripherality, briefly achieving (provisional) core status. Under Haider, it then returned to irrelevance but, in 1987, achieved external core status when it forced the reconstitution of an SPÖ–ÖVP grand coalition. Austria's new parties, the Greens and centre liberals (LiF), can be regarded as peripheral rather than irrelevant. Irrelevance denotes an inability to influence government competition patterns stemming from both arithmetical weakness, i.e. lack of parliamentary strength, and political weakness, i.e. the lack of partners willing and able to form a governing bloc. The uncertainty of status that surrounds peripheral relevance indicates the power of existing core parties to grant or withhold core status. In France, Hanley hints that even the FN could become a government partner. It is more than simply irrelevant.

With this development of the notion of the party system core, we have a four-fold typology: *irrelevant* (weak and with no potential bloc partner); *peripheral* (weak, but potentially part of a governmental bloc); *external core* (strong enough to influence government formation, but not part of a governmental bloc) and *core* (part of a bloc, or able to govern alone). The key discriminator is relevance to government formation. This approach emphasizes the politico-institutional aspect of party system structuration over the sociological aspects. Thus, whereas Lane and Ersson distinguish structural from non-structural parties in sociological terms (1994: 159–70, 185–9) finding that conservative and liberal parties (as well the residual 'other parties' comprising discontent, ultra-right and green parties) are non-structural, a political analysis will see many such parties as structural in terms of patterns of competition for government. The German liberal party (FDP), for example, was a 'king-maker' until 1982 thanks to its ability to establish core status in two alternative blocs.

Core change in West European party systems

The establishment of alternation in Sweden is an interesting case for considering what change to a party system core means. The passage into opposition of the SAP in 1976 established a two-bloc party system, challenging the notion that the SAP was the 'hegemonic' party of government. An arithmetically conceivable coalition became a political reality. This ended the peripherality of the bourgeois parties. Moreover, as David Arter stresses, this core change had nothing to do with electoral volatility.

The development was significant, too, for what did *not* happen. Competitiveness for government on a two-bloc basis was not inevitable. A coalition of the SAP with a centre-orientated bourgeois party was possible. If it happened, it would create a tripolar system, the government bloc facing 'bilateral' opposition (i.e. from both Left and Right). This would render both the two excluded bourgeois parties and the Left (ex-Communist) Party peripheral. The split between the SAP and the Left Party would become a structural one. By contrast, a minority SAP government which excludes the Left, yet is generally supported by it, albeit externally, does not deny the existence of a single left-wing bloc.

A similar core change, to a two-bloc structure, has been seen in Ireland where a governing party no longer confronts a range of opposition parties, as had been the case between 1957–73 (Mair, 1987). The change favoured the hitherto peripheral Labour Party and Fine Gael and while the former's electoral surge of 1992 receded in 1997, the consolidation of the Fine Gael–Labour coalition formula from 1973 undoubtedly ended Fianna Fáil's claim to have been, from 1933, *the* party of government. The competitive, two-bloc logic of government formation was confirmed by Fianna Fáil's coalition with the Progressive Democrats in 1989, repeated in 1997 after the failure of the brief coalition with Labour in 1992.

What is also interesting about the Irish case is that the Fine Gael–Labour coalition challenged existing understandings of Ireland's Left–Right structure. While the importance of Europe's dominant twentieth-century cleavage (class or socio-economic status) in Ireland has been disputed, and Farrell suggests that Ireland's apparent 'politics without social bases' might be a precursor of developments elsewhere in Europe, an alternative view would be that core structural change has paralleled a recasting of party and bloc identities. On the one hand, Fine Gael and Labour became a modernizing alliance. On the other, the Progressive Democrats split from Fianna Fáil and, even though they now co-operate, Fianna Fáil is not what it was.

The 'anomalous' Irish coalition probably did not, therefore, represent a case of coalition 'promiscuity'. A new structure has stabilized. There is not fluidity. It seems unlikely that Europe will see a shift to what is sometimes referred to as *Allgemeinkoalitionsfähigkeit* whereby all parties are open to coalition with all other parties. Contemporary extreme or non-mainstream parties of the Right have found it difficult, if not impossible, to gain access to government (e.g. the Finnish Rural and Danish Progress parties). None have become stable bloc members. We see lingering exclusion on the left too: in Spain (IU), Italy (Communist Refoundation) and Greece (the communist KKE).[1] Parties challenging the Left–Right dimension have fared little better. In Belgium, the language parties had only ephemeral success while the more enduring green party phenomenon achieved core status only in 1996 and 1997 (in Italy and France).

The exclusion of new and 'extreme' parties depends crucially on the strategies of the dominant parties. Integral to such strategies is the fact that new party elites and ever-changing electorates thereby undergo lengthy process of learning and socialization. In Germany, even the sudden rise of the Republikaner in the late 1980s, which raised the spectre of renewed Neo-Nazism, served to confirm that radical right-wing parties are ostracized by the establishment and tend to self-destruct. It remains to be seen whether Germany's party elites will be forced into a less shocking but nevertheless innovative pattern of coalition formation, as discussed by Charlie Jeffery. The SPD might prefer a return to the CDU-CSU/SPD grand coalition formula to coalition with the Greens since these would be difficult to fob off with the single minister obtained by their French and Italian counterparts. In either case, however, the German party system core would be transformed.

It is too early to say whether the post-1994 Dutch coalition has installed a new party system core structure. Certainly, the 'purple' coalition of Labour and Liberals, Left and Right, is innovative, having pushed the Centre religious bloc into the opposition, where it had not been since 1918. The switch is explicable in terms of changing cleavage saliency, but this is neither clear cut nor to be taken lightly. As ten Napel's chapter emphasizes, such changes have been of historic import. Moreover, the switch may represent more than a shift in cleavage salience. A process of ideological redefinition is taking place. Thus, the assertion of the lay-clerical *or* individual versus communitarian/solidarist cleavage did not favour the traditional left so much as *liberal* forces, on left and right. In other words, the political and institutional dimension of party system structuring may be interacting with the redefinition of the left.

It is not only the Dutch and Irish cases which see the definition and meaning of the core cleavage or axis challenged. Sartori has described Italy's new party system as binary rather than bipolar, so heterogeneous are its two core governmental blocs. Furthermore, if one accepts Anthony King's view of the dominant British parties cited by Webb and Fisher, then the model which many reform-minded Italians aspire to is no less ideologically confused. One tentative answer to these changes is that the European Left is increasingly taking on a left–liberal rather than social democratic colouration. Such ideological change may be linked with changing electoral sociologies. However, an alternative hypothesis would emphasize instead an increasingly 'Schumpeterian' model of competition-for-government by teams of elites using parties. Thus, parties might even be seen almost as 'falling prey' to successive leaderships, becoming, in some sense, enduring vehicles for transient packages of people and ideas.

The parallels between the British, Dutch, Irish and Italian cases regarding the redefinition of Left and Right and the role of party elites' coalition strategies in structuring party systems can be extended. Thus, in both Italy and the Netherlands, the Left (or parts of it) has sought at different times in different ways to establish a two-bloc system and consequent alternation in order to gain a prominent governmental role. The currently highly successful Dutch Democrats '66 came into existence specifically to promote this aim. Britain's contrary case of two-party dualism possibly giving way to coalitional competition represents the other side of the same coin of the interaction of party strategy and party system structuration. Thus, some Labour strategists seek to release Britain's suppressed multi-partism in order to secure the party long-term advantage, the two-party format having overwhelmingly benefited the Conservatives.

To conclude this overview of core change, the Spanish and Portuguese cases are new party systems which have undergone processes of core consolidation. In both cases, alternation between two blocs has been established as a fundamental systemic principle despite, in Portugal, especially, high levels of electoral volatility. In Spain, indeed, Aznar's Popular Party has become a people's party in Smith's terms, likes its rival the PSOE, gaining over 30 per cent of the vote and capturing the government. Both cases confirm the importance of competition for government and the tendency to form two competing blocs, albeit the Spanish case also sees national, sub-state party systems playing a core role. Thus, in the 1990s the Catalan Convergence and Union has become a core party despite being only half the size of the United Left which remains, so far, irrelevant.

In summary, then, in different ways, change is pervasive and flexibility in coalition patterns is marked, but it does not seem limitless. Flux is structured by competition for government conceived in left/right terms, and by bloc structures built to that end. Thus, if a trend to increasing coalition innova-tion and flexibility exists, it may be a sign of systemic *regeneration*. There is elite turnover, programmatic innovation and experimentation in policy-handling capabilities, but not complete promiscuity of coalition-making, and certainly not a rejection of party government and competition for govern-ment.

Conclusion

It is difficult to overstate the significance of Western Europe's multi-party systems. As one commentator has put it: 'Democratic party systems are an early modern invention of bold and pathbreaking dimensions' (Keane, 1988: 140). The historical novelty and import of such systems are easily over-looked. When their significance is not underestimated, their possible transience tends to be a cause of concern. The question which analysts of party system change seek to answer is: what lies beyond the generative stage of party systems and their subsequent embedment? We suggest it is flexible experimentation rather than decay.

In the century since Western Europe's party systems emerged, the context and challenges of European politics have changed dramatically. The origins of Western Europe's party systems lie in the transition to 'modern' demo-cracy. Such democracy is representative and it has been structured by sociological, ideological and political criteria, and bound territorially within the context of nation–states. Today, the relationships between party system structure, social structure and ideology are the subject of intense political debate and experimentation. Indeed, Europe's states and the state–national level of government themselves are fundamentally challenged. Economic policy demands, in particular, challenge the relevance of national govern-ments and, hence, national parties and party systems. Moreover, as the debates on the nature of the European Union demonstrate, economic policy is hard to separate from social policy, while environment policy is a paradig-matic 'global' issue. It should not surprise us, then, to find that voters have changed sociologically and cognitively, and that party systems are undergoing significant change too.

The most complex issue for understanding party system change concerns the relationships between sociology, ideology and patterns of government formation. We believe that the role of party elites in mediating these relationships is fundamental to understanding the evolution of party systems. We also believe that the concept of the political bloc points usefully to the strategic articulation of sociological, ideological and partisan organizational concerns and that further theoretical elaboration of this concept would be useful. Our brief mention of the idea that the European Left is being redefined in a Left–liberal rather than social–democratic sense (for example in the UK, the Netherlands and Italy) indicates one path such exploration might pursue. At the same time, 'silent' revolutions of Left and Right offer new, non-economic identity agendas so that even at the merely ideological level the range of issues to be considered is daunting.

Whether party systems have entirely lost their sociological anchors or not is still unclear. Whether new political sociologies and ideological configurations are emerging in response to contemporary party strategies is a matter of intense debate. However, to conclude, on these are not necessarily grounds for despair. We would argue that party system change might usefully be regarded positively, as a macro-political learning process comprising both multi-faceted innovation and resilience. This combination is possible thanks to the existence of a political architecture which conjoins pluralism with order, stability with change. This political architecture comprises, above all, the pervasiveness of party-based ideological patterning and the underpinning of this patterning by political blocs oriented towards competition for government.

Acknowledgments

The authors wish to thank Peter Mair and Gordon Smith for their comments on an early draft of this conclusion and Peter Mair for providing us with part of his 1997 work when still in proof stage.

Note

1. Notwithstanding the necessarily limited communist/conservative coalition of 1989–90 which ousted the increasingly inept and corrupt socialist party (PASOK), leading to early elections and a conservative government. This was also, notably, a case of party predominance being nipped in the bud.

Glossary of Key Terms

———

Agency   The influence of actors, individual or collective (e.g. parties), in contrast to *structure*, on institutions, processes and outcomes. See also *systemness*.

Alford index   Classically, the percentage of manual workers voting Labour minus the percentage of non-manual voters voting Labour. The maximum score of 100 indicates total class voting.

Atomized electorate   An unstructured electorate, with individuals lacking in collective identities and so likely to change their vote from election to election. See *structural consolidation, partisan identification* and *dealignment*.

Bipolar   The aggregation of the electorate around two dominant points on the Left–Right spectrum.

Bloc   An alliance of government-oriented parties. The term further implies a significant degree of ideological and sociological congruity between the parties.

Cadre party   Loosely organized, essentially parliamentary party, which preceded the *mass party*. Elections were won thanks to the social authority of notables and their patronage.

Catch-all party   Term coined by Otto Kirchheimer to signal the development by which both bourgeois cadre parties and mass parties increasingly appealed to the electorate more generally rather than to specific, limited social categories. This implies a more competitive stance and may have encouraged *dealignment*.

Centrifugal dynamic   Growth of parties closer to the left and/or right extremes and corresponding decline of more moderate/centre parties due to aggregate electoral movements. The opposite of a *centripetal* dynamic.

Centripetal dynamic   Growth of moderate/centre parties at the expense of more extreme parties due to aggregate electoral movements. The opposite of a *centrifugal* dynamic.

Clientelism   The gaining of votes in return for personal favours based on patronage rather than on the basis of a programme or party identity.

Contagion   *From the left*: the idea that socialist mass party organization led to the competitive modernization of liberal-conservative, cadre parties in the immediate post-war period. *From the right*: that the elite autonomy and consequent strategic flexibility of modern centre-right parties has influenced modern centre-left parties, for example New Labour in Britain.

Core party   A party which is regarded as a governmental party, whether in government or in opposition, and which influences the process of government formation.

Dealignment   When aligned voters cease to identify with a party or cease to vote for parties based on established cleavage patterns there is, respectively, partisan or class dealignment. Working-class voters switching from a communist to a social democratic party would indicate partisan dealignment and *realignment* but not class dealignment. If voters do not realign, they may remain *atomized*. See *volatility*.

Effective number of parties   Denotes the number of hypothetical equal-sized parties that would have the same total effect on party system fractionalization as have the actual parties of unequal size. Intuitively more meaningful than *Rae index*.

Electoral-Professional party   Modern party type identified by Pane-bianco. The stress is on the use of professional marketing techniques to identify and target electoral categories. Can be seen as typifying *contagion from the right* and *catch-all* development.

External core party   A party which is strong enough to influence government formation in the sense that the coalition formed deliberately excludes this challenging party.

Five-party system   A party system comprising five parties (communist or left-socialist, left liberal, agrarian/centre, liberal and conservative) argued to have been typical of Scandinavia, especially Sweden.

Flash party A party that gains parliamentary representation, but only briefly, often only for the duration of a single legislative period.

Mass party Typically the socialist, but also the religious/denominational parties, which emerged from the late nineteenth century and gained access to parliament thanks to the strength of their organization based on formal, large-scale membership. They underpinned *structural consolidation*.

Multi-party system A 'one-party system' is a contradiction in terms unless the term is an abbreviation for 'one-party political system'. All genuine party systems are multi-party systems, but conventionally a distinction is made between two-party systems and more-than-two or multi-party systems.

Partisan identification An explanation of voting behaviour stressing voters' (weak or strong) identification with a particular party, and hence their voting for it. At the aggregate level, such identification is also known as alignment. If voters cease to identify with a party, there is *dealignment* and increasing *volatility*.

Party system The structure of interactions between the parties comprising it. See *systemness*.

Party system core The individual parties or alliances of parties which determine the structure of competition for government.

Pedersen index A measurement of *volatility* defined as 'the net change within the electoral party system resulting from individual vote transfers'.

People's party Parties which emphasize competition for government and the representation of broad, national identities rather than specific identities. In Smith's usage, such parties typically gain over 30 per cent of the vote.

Peripheral party A party which may become part of a governmental bloc.

Personalism An extreme form of candidate-centred politics in which votes are attracted by socially prominent, often local figures, rather than parties. Often associated with *clientelism*.

Plebiscitary democracy Political system in which a leader endorsed by a mass vote uses his/her charismatic authority to govern. This may be revolutionary, using such legitimacy to challenge constraints, including parliamentary and constitutional; or it may be conservative, with populist distributive measures but no specific reform programme.

Rae's index Perhaps the best-known measure of party system fragmentation, or fractionalization. It is based on the probability that any two randomly selected voters will have chosen different parties in any given election. The index is 1 minus the sum of the squares of each party's decimal share of the vote. The higher the value, the more fragmented the system, with a theoretical range from 0 (total concentration in one party) to 1 (as many parties as voters).

Realignment If voters switch their *partisan identification* or formerly unaligned voters take up such identification, there is said to be partisan realignment. This may or may not be associated with new cleavage formation.

Structural consolidation According to Sartori, the stabilization of electoral interaction by organizational and ideological means effected by the mass parties. Otherwise, according to Mair, the stabilizing of party interaction by competition for government.

Systemness The influence of a stabilized structure of interactions (i.e. system) on *agency*. See *party system*.

Tripolar The aggregation of the electorate around three points on the left-right spectrum, i.e. with the centre occupied by a large party or bloc of parties.

Volatility The switching of votes between elections by individuals (individual volatility, or vote-switching) or by the electorate as a whole (aggregate volatility). This may result from *dealignment*. Aggregate volatility is often less than the sum of individual vote-switching due to transfers mutually cancelling each other out, hence the term 'net' volatility is also used – see *Pedersen index*.

Vulnerability *Of parties*: the possibility that these may suffer significant and rapid vote losses due to weakening *partisan identification* and the decline of *structural consolidation*. Consequently, the notion that party systems are prone to instability with potential knock-on effects on government stability and performance.

References

Abrams, M., Rose, R. and Hinden, R. (1960) *Must Labour Lose?*, Harmondsworth: Penguin.

Aguiar, J. (1985) The hidden fluidity in a ultra-stable system, in E. Sousa-Ferreira and W.C. Opello Jr. (eds), *Conflict and Change in Portugal 1974–1984*, Lisbon: Editorial Teorema, pp.101–207.

Aguiar, J. (1988) Democracia pluralista, partidos políticos e relação de representação, *Análise Social*, **24**, 59–76.

Aguiar, J. (1989) Dinâmica do sistema a partidário – condições de estabilidade, in M.B. Coelho (ed.), *Portugal: O Sistema Político e Costitucional*, Lisbon: Instituto de Ciências Sociais, pp. 295–335.

Aguiar, J. (1994) Partidos, eleições dinâmica política, *Análise Social*, **29**, 171–236.

Aguila, R. del (1982) La transición democrática en España: reforma, ruptura y consenso, *Revista de Estudios Políticos*, **25**, 107–27.

Aguilera de Prat, C.R. (1988) Balance y transformaciones del sistema de partidos en España (1977–87), *Revista Española de Investigaciones Sociológicas*, **42**, 137–53.

Aish, A-M. and Swyngedouw, M. (1994) Stabilité et instabilité du vote en Wallonie: déalignement et réalignement des électeurs, in A-P. Frognier and A-M. Aish-Van Vaerenbergh (eds), *Elections: la fêlure? Enquête sur le comportement des Wallons et des Francophones*, Brussels: De Boeck, pp. 61–76.

Allum, P. and Mannheimer, R. (1985) Italy, in I. Crewe and D. Denver (eds), *Electoral Change in Western Democracies: Patterns and Sources of Electoral Volatility*, London: Croom Helm, pp. 287–318.

Amodia, J. (1990a) Taxonomía e inestabilidad del sistema de partidos en España, *ACIS. Journal of the Association for Contemporary Iberian Studies*, **3**, 39–48.

Amodia, J. (1990b) Personalities and slogans: the Spanish election of October 1989, *West European Politics*, **13**, 293–8.

Anderson, M. (1974) *Conservative Politics in France*, London: Allen and Unwin.

Andeweg, R.B. (1989) Institutional conservatism in the Netherlands: proposals for and resistance to change, in H. Daalder and G.A. Irwin (eds), *Politics in the Netherlands. How Much Change?*, London: Frank Cass, pp. 42–60.

Andeweg, R.B. and Irwin, G.A. (1993) *Dutch Government and Politics*, Basingstoke: Macmillan.

Andics, H. (1968) *Der Staat, den keiner wollte. Österreich von der Gründung der Republik bis zur Moskauer Deklaration*, Vienna: Molden.

Antunes, J.F. (1979) *O Segredo do 25 de Novembro*, Lisbon: Europa-América.

Appleton, A. (1995) Parties under pressure. Challenges to 'established' French parties, *West European Politics*, **18**, 52–77.

Arnim, H.H. von (1990) Entmündigen die Parteien das Volk? Parteienherrschaft und Volkssouveränität, *Aus Politik und Zeitgeschichte*, **B21**.

Arter, D. (1989) A tale of two Carlssons: the Swedish general election of 1988, *Parliamentary Affairs*, **42**, 84–101.

Arter, D. (1994) 'The war of the roses': conflict and cohesion in the Swedish Social Democratic Party, in D.S. Bell and E. Shaw (eds), *Conflict and Cohesion in Western European Social Democratic Parties*, London: Pinter, pp. 70–95.

Åsard, E. and Lance Bennett, W. (1995) Regulating the marketplace of ideas: political rhetoric in Swedish and American national elections, *Political Studies*, **43**, 645–63.

Bacalhau, M. (1989) Mobilidade e tranferência de voto através das sondagens, in M.B. Coelho (ed.), *Portugal: O Sistema Político e Costitucional*, Lisbon: Instituto de Ciéncias Sociais, pp. 237–56.

Bar, A. (1984) The emerging Spanish party system. Is there a model?, *West European Politics*, **7**, 128–55.

Bardi, L. (1996) Anti-party sentiment and party system change in Italy, *European Journal of Political Research*, **29**, 345–63.

Barnes, J. (1994) Ideology and factions, in A. Seldon and S. Ball (eds), *The Conservative Century: The Conservative Party Since 1900*, Oxford: Oxford University Press, pp. 315–45.

Barnes, S.H. and Kaase, M. (1979) *Political Action: Mass Participation in Five Western Democracies*, Beverly Hills: Sage.

Barnes, S.H., McDonough, P. and López Piña, A. (1981) The Spanish public in political transition, *British Journal of Political Science*, **11**, 49–79.

Barnes, S.H., McDonough, P. and López Piña, A (1986) Volatile parties and stable voters in Spain, *Government and Opposition*, **21**, 56–75.

Barreto, J. (1990) Os primórdios da Intersindical sob Marcelo Caetano, *Análise Social*, **25**, 57–117.

Bartolini, S. (1984) Institutional constraints and party competition in the French party system, *West European Politics*, **7**, 103–27.

Bartolini S. and Mair, P. (1990) *Identity, Competition and Electoral Availability: The Stabilisation of European Electorates, 1885–1985*, Cambridge: Cambridge University Press.

Becker, J.W. and Vink, R. (1994) *Secularisatie in Nederland, 1966–1991. De Verandering van opvattingen en enkele gedragingen*, Rijswijk: SCP.

Beedham, B. (1993) A better way to vote. Why letting the people themselves take the decisions is the logical next step for the West, *The Economist*, 11–17 September.

Beetham, D. (1994) *Defining and Measuring Democracy*, London: Sage.

Bell, D. and Criddle, B. (1994a) *The French Communist Party in the Fifth Republic*, Oxford: Clarendon Press.

Bell, D. and Criddle, B. (1994b) The French party system: from polarised pluralism to consensus fatigue, *Aston Papers in European Politics and Society*, **2**.

Beltrán, A. (1993) La cuestión del acceso al poder del Partido Popular. Una aproximación desde la Teoría Espacial, *Revista de Estudios Políticos*, **81**, 211–40.

Bennulf, M. and Holmberg, S. (1990) The Green breakthrough in Sweden, *Scandinavian Political Studies*, **13**, 165–84.

Berglund, S. and Lindström, U. (1978) *The Scandinavian Party System(s)*, Lund: Student litteratur.

Bergström, H. (1991) Sweden's politics and party system at the crossroads, *West European Politics*, **14**, 8–30.

Bermeo, N. (1986) *The Revolution Within the Revolution: Workers' Control in Rural Portugal*, Princeton, NJ: Princeton University Press.

Bermeo, N. (1987) Redemocratisation and transition elections. A comparison of Spain and Portugal, *Comparative Politics*, **19**, 213–31.

Beyme, K. von (1985) *Political Parties in Western Democracies*, Aldershot: Gower.

Billiet, J. (1984) On Belgian pillarization: Changing perspectives, *Acta Politica*, **1**, 117–28.

Birk, F. and Traar, K. (1987) Der durchleuchtete Wähler in den achtziger Jahren, *Journal für Sozialforschung*, **27**, 3–74.

Birnbaum, P. (1979) *Les petits contre les gros*, Paris: Grasset.

Blecha, K., Gmoser, R., and Kienzl, H. (1964) *Der durchleuchtete Wähler. Beiträge zur politischen Soziologie in Österreich*, Vienna: Europa Verlag.

Blom, J.C.H. and van der Plaat, G.N. (1986) *Wederopbouw, Welvaart en Onrust. Nederland in de Jaren Vijftig en Zestig*, Houten: De Haan.

Blondel, J. (1968) Party systems and patterns of government in Western democracies, *Canadian Journal of Political Science*, **1**, 180–203.

Boix, C. (1995) *Building a Social Democratic Strategy in Southern Europe: Economic Policy Under the González Government (1982–93)*, Working Paper 1995/69. Madrid: Instituto Juan March.

Boje, T.P. and Nielsen, L.D. (1993) Flexible production, employment and gender, in T.P. Boje and S.E. Olsson Hort (eds), *Scandinavia in a New Europe*, Oslo: Scandinavian University Press, pp. 137–70.

Boyer, J. (1981) *Political Radicalism in Late Imperial Vienna: Origins of the Christian Social Movement 1848–1897*, Chicago: University of Chicago Press.

Brand, J. (1989) Faction as its own reward: groups in the British Parliament 1945–1986, *Parliamentary Affairs*, **42**, 148–65.

Brand, J. (1992) *British Parliamentary Parties*, Oxford: Clarendon Press.

Breen, R., Hannan, D., Rottman, D., Whelan, C. (1990) *Understanding Contemporary Ireland: State, Class and Development in the Republic of Ireland*, Dublin: Gill and Macmillan.

Bruckmüller, E. (1996) *Nation Österreich. Kulturelles Bewußtsein und gesellschaftlich-politische Prozesse*, 2nd edn, Vienna: Böhlau.

Brügel, L. (1922–1925) *Geschichte der österreichischen Sozialdemokratie*, 5 vols, Vienna: Verlag der Wiener Volksbuchhandlung.

Bruins Slot, J.A.H.J.S. (1952) *Bezinning en Uitzicht. De Motieven der Huidige Wereldontwikkeling en Onze Roeping Daarin*, Wageningen: Zomer en Keuning.

Bull, M. and Rhodes, M. (1997) Between crisis and transition. Italian politics in the 1990s, in M. Bull and M. Rhodes (eds), *Crisis and Transition in Italian Politics*, London: Frank Cass; a special issue of *West European Politics*, **20**, 1–13.

Bundesministerium für Inneres (ed.) (1996) *Nationalratswahl vom 17 December 1995*, Vienna: Bundesministerium für Inneres.

Bürklin, W. and Roth, D. (1994) Das Superwahljahr 1994. Deutschland am Ende einer Ära stabilen Wahlverhaltens?, in W. Bürklin and D. Roth (eds), *Das Super-wahljahr 1994. Deutschland vor unkalkulierbaren Regierungsmöglichkeiten?*, Cologne: Bund-Verlag, pp. 9–26.

Butler, D. and Kavanagh, D. (1992) *The British General Election of 1992*, Basingstoke: Macmillan.

Caciagli, M. (1984) Spain: parties and the party system, in G. Pridham (ed.), *The New Mediterranean Democracies*, London: Frank Cass, pp.84–98.

Caciagli, M. (1986) *Elecciones y partidos en la transición española*, Madrid: Centro de Investigaciones Sociológicas.

Calvi, G. and Vannucci, A. (1995) *L'Elettore Sconosciuto*, Bologna: Il Mulino.

Camiller, P. (1994) Spain: the survival of socialism?, in P. Anderson and P. Camiller (eds), *Mapping the Western European Left*, London: Verso, pp. 233–65.

Capo Giol, J. (1981) Estrategias para un sistema de partidos, *Revista de Estudios Políticos*, **23**, 153–67.

Cartocci, R. (1994) *Fra Lega e Chiesa*, Bologna: Il Mulino.

Carty, R.K. (1983) *Electoral Politics in Ireland: Party and Parish Pump*, Dingle, Co. Kerry: Brandon.

Castillo, P. del and Delgado, I. (1994) Las elecciones legislativas de 1993: movilidad de las preferencias partidistas, in P. del Castillo (ed.), *Comportamiento político y electoral*, Madrid: Centro de Investigaciones Sociológicas, pp. 125–48.

Castles, F.G. and Mair, P. (1984) Left–Right political scales: some 'expert' judge-ments, *European Journal of Political Research*, **12**, 73–88.

Charlot, J. (1989) Les mutations du système de partis français, *Pouvoirs*, **49**, 27–35.

Childers, T. (1983) *The Nazi Voter. The Social Foundations of Fascism in Germany 1919–1933*, Chapel Hill, NC: University of North Carolina Press.

Childers, T. (1986) *The Formation of the Nazi Constituency*, London: Croom Helm.

Chubb, Basil (1991) *The Politics of the Irish Constitution*, Dublin: Institute of Public Administration.

Clemens, C. (1991) Helmut Kohl's CDU and German unification: the price of success, *German Politics and Society*, **22**, 33–44.

Clemens, C. (1995) Second wind or last gasp? Helmut Kohl's CDU/CSU and the elections of 1994, in D.P. Conradt, G.R. Kleinfeld, G.K. Romoser and C. Søe (eds), *Germany's New Politics*, Tempe, AZ: German Studies Review, pp. 115–30.

Coakley, J. and Gallagher, M. (1993) *Politics in the Republic of Ireland*, 2nd edn, Dublin: Folens/PSAI Press.

Cole, A. (1990) The evolution of the party system, in A. Cole (ed.), *French Political Parties in Transition*, Aldershot: Dartmouth, pp. 3–24.

Cole, A. (1998) *French Politics and Society*, Hemel Hempstead: Prentice Hall.

Cole, A. and Campbell, P. (1989) *French Electoral Systems and Elections since 1789*, Aldershot: Gower.

Conradt, D. (1993) The Christian Democrats in 1990: saved by unification?, in R. Dalton (ed.), *The New Germany Votes*, Oxford: Berg, pp. 59–76.

Cook, C. (1989) *A Short History of the Liberal Party 1900–88*, Basingstoke: Macmillan.

Corkill, D. (1993a) *The Portuguese Economy since 1974*, Edinburgh: Edinburgh University Press.

Corkill, D. (1993b) The political consolidation of democracy in Portugal, *Parliamentary Affairs*, **46**, 517–33.

Corkill, D. (1995) Party factionalism and democratization in Portugal, in R. Gillespie, M. Waller and N. Lourdes Lopez (eds), *Factional Politics and Democratization*, London: Frank Cass, pp. 64–76.

Corkill, D. (1996) Portugal votes for change and stability: the election of 1995, *West European Politics*, **19**, 403–9.

Courtney, J. (1995) Mail order democracy: one member, one vote leadership election in Canada, paper presented at the Party Politics in the Year 2000 Conference, Manchester, 13–15 January.

Crewe, I. (1985) Introduction: electoral change in western democracies: a framework for analysis, in I. Crewe and D. Denver (eds), *Electoral Change in Western Democracies: Patterns and Sources of Electoral Volatility*, London: Croom Helm, pp. 1–22.

Crewe, I. (1986) On the death and resurrection of class voting: some comments on *How Britain Votes*, *Political Studies*, **34**, 620–38.

Crewe, I. (1993) Parties and electors, in I. Budge and D. McKay (eds), *The Developing British Political System: The 1990s*, London: Longman, pp. 83–111.

Cruz, M. Braga da (1992) Europeísmo, nacionalismo, regionalismo, *Análise Social*, **27**, 827–53.

Cruz, M. Braga da (1995) *Instituções Políticas e Proçessos Sociais*, Venda Nova: Bertand.

Cunhal, A. (1974) *Rumo A Vitória*, Lisbon: Edições Avante.

Cunhal, A. (1976) *A Revolução Portuguesa. O Passado e o Futuro. Relatório Aprovado pelo CC do PCP para o VIII Congresso*, Lisbon: Edições Avante.

Cunhal, A. (1985) *O Partido Com Paredes de Vidro*, Lisbon: Edições Avante.

Curtice, J. (1988) Great Britain: social liberalism reborn?, in E. Kirchner (ed.), *Liberal Parties in Western Europe*, Cambridge: Cambridge University Press, pp. 93–123.

Daalder, H. (1966) The Netherlands: opposition in a segmented society, in R.A. Dahl (ed.), *Political Oppositions in Western Democracies*, New Haven: Yale University Press, pp. 188–236.

Daalder, H. (1975) Extreme proportional representation: the Dutch experience, in S.E. Finer (ed.), *Adversary Politics and Electoral Reform*, London: Anthony Wigram, pp. 223–48.

Daalder, H. (1986) Changing procedures and changing strategies in Dutch coalition-building, *Legislative Studies Quarterly*, **9**, 507–31.

Daalder, H. (1987) The Dutch party system: from segmentation to polarization – and then?, in H. Daalder (ed.), *Party Systems in Denmark, Austria, Switzerland, the Netherlands, and Belgium*, London: Pinter, pp. 193–284.

Daalder, H. and Irwin, G.I. (1989) *Politics in the Netherlands. How Much Change?*, London: Frank Cass.

Daalder, H. and Koole, R. (1988) Liberal parties in the Netherlands, in E.J. Kirchner (ed.), *Liberal Parties in Western Europe*, Cambridge: Cambridge University Press, pp. 151–77.

Daalder, H. and Mair, P. (eds) (1983) *Western European Party Systems: Continuity and Change*, London: Sage Publications.

Daalder, H. and Schuyt, C.J.M. (1986) *Compendium voor politiek en samenleving in Nederland*, Houten: Bohn Stafleu Van Loghum.

Dahl, R.A. (1966) *Political Oppositions in Western Democracies*, New Haven, Conn.: Yale University Press.

D'Alimonte, R. and Bartolini, S. (1995) Il sistema partitico italiano: una transizione difficile, in S. Bartolini and R. D'Alimonte (eds), *Maggioritario ma non troppo*, Bologna: Il Mulino, pp. 429–66.

Dalton, R. (1989) The German voter, in G. Smith, W. Paterson and P. Merkl (eds), *Developments in West German Politics*, Basingstoke: Macmillan, pp. 99–121.

Dalton, R.J., Flanagan, S.C. and Beck, P.A. (1984) *Electoral Change in Advanced Industrial Democracies: Realignment or Dealignment?*, Princeton, NJ: Princeton University Press.

Daniels, P. and Bull, M. (1994) Voluntary euthanasia: from the Italian Communist Party to the Democratic Party of the Left, in M.J. Bull and P. Heywood (eds), *West European Communist Parties after the Revolutions of 1989*, Basingstoke: Macmillan, pp. 1–30.

Daudt, H. (1980) De ontwikkeling van de politieke machtsverhoudingen in Nederland sinds 1945, in J.E. Ellemers *et al.* (eds), *Nederland na 1945. Beschouwingen over ontwikkeling en beleid*, Deventer: Van Loghum Slaterus, pp. 178–97.

Declaração de Príncipios (1975) *Programa e Estatutos do Partido Socialista, aprovado no congresso do PS em Dezembro de 1974*, Lisbon: Jornal do Comércio.

Declaração de Príncipios (1986) *Programa e Estatutos do Partido Socialista, aprovado no congresso do PS em Dezembro de 1986*, Lisbon: Jornal do Comércio.

Declaração de Príncipios (1991) *Programa e Estatutos do Partido Socialista*, Lisbon: Jornal do Comércio.

Deisler, R. and Winkler, N. (1982) *Das politische Handeln der Österreicher*, Vienna: Verlag für Gesellschaftskritik.

Della Porta, D. and Vannucci, A. (1996) Controlling political corruption in Italy: what did not work and what can be done, *Res Publica*, **38**, 353–69.

De Ruyter, K., Michielsen, S. and Mortelmans, J. (1994) *België verkoopt. De stille privatisering van de Belgische overheidsbedrijven*, Groot-Bijgaarden: Scoop.

Deschouwer, K., De Winter, L. and della Porta, D. (1996) *Partitocracies between Crises and Reforms: The Cases of Italy and Belgium*, Special Issue of *Res Publica*, **38**, Leuven: Politologisch Institut.

De Wilde, J.A. and Smeenk, C. (1949) *Het Volk ten Baat. De Geschiedenis van de AR-Partij*, Groningen: Haan.

De Winter, L. (1981) De partijpolitisering als instrument van de particratie. Een overzicht van de ontwikkeling sinds de Tweede Wereldoorlog, *Res Publica*, **23**, 53–107.

De Winter, L. (1989) Parties and policy in Belgium, *European Journal for Political Research*, **17**, 707–30.

De Winter, L. (1991) Socialist Parties in Belgium, in E.Maravall *et al.* (eds), *Socialist Parties in Europe*, Barcelona: Institut de Sciencies Politiques i Socials, pp. 123–56.

De Winter, L. (1993) The selection of party presidents in Belgium. Rubber-stamping the nominee of the party elites, *European Journal of Political Research*, **24**, 233–56.

De Winter, L. (1995) Le service aux électeurs en tant que forme de l'échange politique, in P-H. Claeys and A-P. Frognier (eds), *L'échange politique*, Brussels: Editions de l'Université de Bruxelles, pp. 209–22.

De Winter, L. (1996) Party encroachment on the executive and legislative branch in the Belgian polity, *Res Publica*, **38**, 325–52.

De Winter, L. and Ackaert, J. (1994) Abstentionnisme et vote blanc ou nul: le non-vote en Wallonie, in A-P. Frognier and A-M. Aish-Van Vaerenbergh (eds), *Elections: la fêlure? Enquête sur le comportement des Wallons et des Francophones*, Brussels: De Boeck, pp. 77–98.

De Winter, L., Frognier, A-P. and Rihoux, B. (1996) Belgium. Still the age of party government?, in J. Blondel and M. Cotta (eds), *The Relationship between Governments and Supporting Parties in Europe*, London: Macmillan, pp. 153–79.

De Winter, L., Timmermans, A. and Dumont, P. (1997) 'Belgien: Über Regierungsabkommen, Evangelisten, Gläubige und Häretiker', in W.C. Müller and K. Ström (eds) *Koalitionsregierungen in Westeuropa*, Vienna: Signum, pp. 371–442.

Diamant, A. (1958) The group basis of Austrian politics, *Journal of Central European Affairs*, **18**, 134–55

Diamant, A. (1960) *Austrian Catholics and the First Republic: Democracy, Capitalism and the Social Order, 1918–1934*, Princeton, NJ: Princeton University Press.

Di Palma, G. (1980) Founding coalitions in Southern Europe: legitimacy and hegemony, *Government and Opposition*, **15**, 162–89.

Donovan, M. (1995) The politics of electoral reform in Italy, *International Political Science Review*, **16**, 47–64.

Downs, C. (1989) *Revolution at the Grassroots: Community Organizations in the Portuguese Revolution*, Albany, New York: State University of New York Press.

Dreijmanis, J. (1982) Austria: the 'Black'–'Red' coalitions, in E.C. Browne, and J. Dreijmanis (eds), *Government Coalitions in Western Democracies*, New York: Longman, pp. 237–59.

Dunleavy, P. (1979) The urban basis of political alignment: social class, domestic property ownership and state intervention in consumption processes, *British Journal of Political Science*, **9**, 409–33.

Dunleavy, P. (1980) The political implications of sectoral cleavages and the growth of state employment, *Political Studies*, **28**, 364–83 and 527–49.

Dunleavy, P. (1987) Class dealignment revisited: why odds ratios give odd results, *West European Politics*, **10**, 400–19.

Dunleavy, P. (1990) Mass political behaviour. Is there more to learn?, *Political Studies*, **38**, 453–69.

Dunleavy, P. and Husbands, C. (1985) *British Democracy at the Crossroads*, London: Allen and Unwin.

Dunleavy, P., Margetts, H., O'Duffy, B. and Weir, S. (1997) Remodelling the 1997 General Election: How Britain would have voted under alternative electoral systems, paper delivered to the Elections, Public Opinion and Parties Conference, University of Essex, 26–8 September.

Dunleavy, P., Margetts, H. and Weir, S. (1992) *Replaying the 1992 General Election: How Britain would have Voted under Alternative Electoral Systems*, LSE Public Policy Paper Number 3, London: JRRT/LSE Public Policy Group.

Dunleavy, P., Margetts, H. and Weir, S. (1994) The 1992 election and the legitimacy of British democracy, in D. Denver, P. Norris, D. Broughton and C. Rallings (eds), *British Elections and Parties Yearbook, 1993*, Hemel Hempstead: Harvester Wheatsheaf, pp. 177–92.

Dupoirier, E. and Grunberg, G. (1986) *Mars 1986: la drôle de défaite de la gauche*, Paris: PUF.

Duverger, M. (1964) *Political Parties. Their Organisation and Activity in the Modern State*, London: Methuen, 3rd English edn. Also (1954) original edition.

Eaton, M. (1994) Regional Development funding in Portugal, *Journal of the Association for Contemporary Iberian Studies*, **7**, 36–46.

Eigentijds burgerschap (1992) WRR-publikatie vervaardigd onder leiding van H.R. van Gunsteren, The Hague: Sdu uitgeverij.

Eisfeld, R. (1983) A 'Revolução dos Cravos' e a Política Externa: O Fracasso do Pluralismo Socialista em Portugal a Seguir a 1974, *Revista Crítica de Ciências Sociais*, **11**, 95–128.

Eisfeld, R. (1984) *Sozialistischer Pluralismus in Europa. Ansätze und Scheitern am Beispiel Portugal*, Cologne: Verlag Wissenschaft und Politik.

Eleições em Abril. Diário de Campanha (1975). Lisbon: Ediçao Liber.

Eleições no regime fascista (1979) Lisbon: Presidência do Conselho de Ministros. Comissão do Livro Negro sobre o Fascismo.

Elliot, J.H. (1963) *Imperial Spain: 1469–1716*, London: Penguin.

Elliott, G. (1993) *Labourism and the English Genius: The Strange Death of Labour England*, London: Verso.

Engelmann, F.C. (1966) Austria: the pooling of opposition, in R.A. Dahl (ed.), *Political Opposition in Western Democracies*, New Haven, Conn: Yale University Press, pp. 260–83.

Engelmann, F. and Schwartz, M. (1974) Partisan stability and the continuity of a segmented society: the Austrian case, *American Journal of Sociology*, **79**, 948–66.

Ersson, S. and Lane, J-E. (1996) Electoral instability and party system change in Western Europe, paper presented at the Workshop on Party System Change in Europe, European Consortium for Political Research, Oslo, 29 March–3 April.

Esping-Andersen, G. (1985) *Politics Against Markets: The Social Democratic Road to Power*, Princeton, NJ: Princeton University Press.

Esping-Andersen, G. (1990) Single-party dominance in Sweden: the saga of social democracy, in T.J. Pempel (ed.), *Uncommon Democracies. The One-Party Dominant Regimes*, Ithaca, NY: Cornell University Press, pp. 33–57.

Esteban, J. de and López Guerra, L. (1982) *Los partidos políticos en la España actual*, Barcelona: Planeta.

Fabbrini, S. (1996) Italy: the decline of a parliamentary party government, *Res Publica*, **38**, 307–23.

Farneti, P. (1983) *The Italian Party System*, London: Pinter.

Farrell, B. (1970) Labour and the Irish political party system: a suggested approach to analysis, *Economic and Social Review*, **1**, 477–502.

Farrell, B. (1984) *Communications and Community in Ireland*, Dublin: Mercier.

Farrell, B. (1985) Ireland: from friends and neighbours to clients and partisans, in V. Bogdanor (ed.), *Representatives of the People?*, Aldershot: Gower, pp. 237–64.

Farrell, D. (1986) The strategy to market Fine Gael in 1981, *Irish Political Studies*, **1**, 1–14.

Farrell, D. (1989) Ireland: the 'Green Alliance', in F. Müller-Rommel (ed.), *New Politics in Western Europe*, Boulder, Co.: Westview Press, pp. 123–30.

Farrell, D. (1992) Ireland, in R.S. Katz and P. Mair (eds), *Party Organizations: A Data Handbook on Party Organizations in Western Democracies 1960–90*, London: Sage, pp. 216–41.

Farrell, D. (1993) Campaign strategies, in M. Gallagher and M. Laver (eds), *How Ireland Voted 1992*, Dublin: Folens/PSAI Press, pp. 21–38.

Farrell, D. (1994) Ireland: centralization, professionalization and competitive pressures, in R.S. Katz and P. Mair (eds), *How Parties Organize: Change and Adaptation in Party Organizations in Western Democracies*, London: Sage, pp. 216–41.

Farrell, D. (forthcoming) The transition of Irish election campaigning from the traditional to the modern, in T. Garvin, M. Manning and R. Sinnott (eds), *Government, Politics and the Media in Ireland*.

Farrell, D., Mackerras, M. and McAllister, I. (1996) Designing electoral institutions: STV systems and their consequences, *Political Studies*, **44**, 24–43.

Ferreira, J.M. (1983) *Ensaio Histórico sobre a Revolução de 25 de Abril*, Lisbon: Casa da Moeda.

Fianna Fáil (1993) *Commission on the Aims and Structures of Fianna Fáil: Final Report*, Dublin: Fianna Fáil.

Fine Gael (1993) *Report of the Commission on Renewal of Fine Gael*, Dublin: Fine Gael.

Fisher, J. (1992) Trade union political funds and the Labour Party, in P. Norris, I. Crewe, D. Denver and D. Broughton (eds), *British Elections and Parties Yearbook 1992*, Hemel Hempstead: Harvester Wheatsheaf, pp. 111–23.

Fisher, J. (1994a) Political donations to the Conservative Party, *Parliamentary Affairs*, **47**, 61–72.

Fisher, J. (1994b) Why do companies make donations to political parties?, *Political Studies*, **42**, 690–9.

Fisher, J. (1995) The institutional funding of British political parties, in D. Broughton, D. Farrell, D. Denver and C. Rallings (eds), *British Elections and Parties Yearbook 1994*, London: Frank Cass, pp. 181–96.

Fisher, J. (1996a) *British Political Parties*, Hemel Hempstead: Prentice Hall/Harvester Wheatsheaf.

Fisher, J. (1996b) Party finance, in P. Norton (ed.), *The Conservative Party*, Hemel Hempstead: Harvester Wheatsheaf, pp. 157–69.

Fitzmaurice, J. (1988) *The Politics of Belgium: Crises and Compromise in a Plural Society*, London: Hurst.

Fraga, M. (1977) *Alianza Popular*, Bilbao: Albia.

Frain, M-T.F. (1996) Portugal's legislative and presidential elections: a new socialist majority, *South European Society and Politics*, **1**, 115–20.

Franklin, M. (1985) *The Decline of Class Voting in Britain: Changes in the Basis of Electoral Choice, 1964–83*, Oxford: Clarendon Press.

Franklin, M., et al. (1992) *Electoral Change: Responses to Evolving Social and Attitudinal Structures in Western Countries*, Cambridge: Cambridge University Press.

Frears, J. (1991) *Parties and Voters in France*, London: Hurst.

Frognier, A-P. and Collinge, M. (1984) La problématique des 'Mondes sociologiques' en Belgique, *Les Cahiers du CACEF*, **114**, 3–12.

Fuchs, D. and Klingemann, H-D. (1995) Citizens and the state: a relationship transformed, in H-D. Klingemann and D. Fuchs (eds), *Citizens and the State*, Oxford: Oxford University Press, pp. 419–43.

Fusaro, C. (1995) *Le regole della transizione: La nuova legislazione elettorale italiana*, Bologna: Il Mulino.

Gabriel, O. and Brettschneider, F. (1994) *Die EU-Staaten im Vergleich. Strukturen, Prozesse, Politikinhalte*, Opladen: Westdeutscher Verlag.

Gallagher, M. (1987) Does Ireland need a new electoral system?, *Irish Political Studies*, **2**, 27–48.

Gallagher, M. and Komito, L. (1993) Dáil deputies and their constituency work, in J. Coakley and M. Gallagher (eds), *Politics in the Republic of Ireland*, 2nd edn, Dublin: Folens/PSAI Press, pp. 150–66.

Gallagher, M., Laver, M. and Mair, P. (1995) *Representative Government in Modern Europe*, 2nd edn, New York: McGraw-Hill.

Gallagher, T. (1990) The Portuguese Socialist Party: the pitfalls of being first, in T. Gallagher and A. Williams (eds), *Southern European Socialism: Parties, Elections and the Challenge of Government*, Manchester: Manchester University Press, pp. 12–32.

Galli, G. (1966) *Il bipartitismo imperfetto*, Bologna: Il Mulino.

Galli, G. (1975) *Dal bipartitismo imperfetto alla possibile alternativa*, Bologna: Il Mulino.

Gangas Peiró, P. (1995) *El desarrollo organizativo de los partidos políticos españoles de implantación nacional*, Madrid: Instituto Juan March.

García San Miguel, L. (1981) *Teoría de la transición. Un análisis del modelo español 1975–78*, Madrid: Editora Nacional.

Garelli, F. (1996) Destra e cattolici in Italia, *Aggiornamenti Sociali*, **47**, 549–58.

Garvin, T. (1974) Political cleavages, party politics and urbanisation in Ireland: the case of the periphery-dominated centre, *European Journal of Political Research*, **2**, 307–27.

Gaspar, J. and André, I. (1989) Portugal-Geografia eleitoral 1975–1987, in M.B. Coelho (ed.), *Portugal. O Sistema Político e Costitucional*, Lisbon: Instituto de Ciências Sociais, pp. 257–77.

Gerlich, P. (1992) A farewell to corporatism, in K.R. Luther, and W.C. Müller (eds), *Politics in Austria: Still a Case of Consociationalism?*, London: Frank Cass, pp. 132–46.

Gerlich, P., Grande, E. and Müller, W.C. (1985) *Sozialpartnerschaft in der Krise. Leistungen und Grenzen des Neokorporatismus in Österreich*, Vienna: Böhlau.

Gibowski, W. (1995) Germany's general election in 1994. Who voted for whom?, in D.P. Conradt, G.R. Kleinfeld, G.K. Romoser, and C. Søe (eds), *Germany's New Politics*, Tempe, AZ: German Studies Review, pp. 91–114.

Giddens, A. (1994) What's left for Labour?, *New Statesman and Society*, 30 September, 37–40.

Gillespie, R. (1989) Spanish Socialism in the 1980s, in T. Gallagher and A. Williams (eds), *Southern European Socialism: Parties, Elections and the Challenge of Government*, Manchester: Manchester University Press, pp. 59–85.

Gillespie, R. (1990) The break-up of the 'socialist family': party–union relations in Spain, 1982–89, *West European Politics*, **13**, 47–62.

Gillespie, R. (1994) The resurgence of factionalism in the Spanish Socialist Workers' Party, in D.S. Bell and E. Shaw (eds), *Conflict and Cohesion in Western European Social Democratic Parties*, London: Pinter, pp. 50–69.

Gillespie, R. and Gallagher, T. (1989) Democracy and authority in the Socialist Parties of Southern Europe, in T. Gallagher and A. Williams (eds), *Southern European Socialism: Parties, Elections and the Challenge of Government*, Manchester: Manchester University Press, pp. 163–87.

Gilljam, M. and Holmberg, S. (1992) Väljarna inför 90-talet, *Valundersökningar 14*, Stockholm: Statistiska Centralbyrå.

Gilljam, M. and Holmberg, S. (1995) Väljarnas val, *Valundersökningar 15*, Stockholm: Statistiska Centralbyrå.

Giner, S. and Sevilla, E. (1984) Spain: from corporatism to corporatism, in A. Williams (ed.), *Southern Europe Transformed: Political and Economic Change in Greece, Italy, Portugal and Spain*, London: Harper and Row, pp. 113–41.

Giovagnoli, A. (1996) *Il partito italiano: La Democrazia cristiana dal 1942 al 1994*, Rome-Bari: Laterza.

Goguel, F. (1946) *La Politique des partis sous la Troisième République*, Paris: Fayard.

Goldthorpe, J.H., Lockwood, D., Bechhofer, F. and Platt, J. (1968) *The Affluent Worker: Political Attitudes and Behaviour*, Cambridge: Cambridge University Press.

Groen van Prinsterer, G. (1922 [1847]) *Ongeloof en Revolutie. Een Reeks van Historische Voorlezingen*, Kampen: Kok.

Guéhenno, J-M. (1993) *La Fin de la Démocratie*, Paris: Editions Flammarion.

Gunther, R. (1986a) El realineamiento del sistema de partidos en 1982, in J. Linz and J.R. Montero (eds), *Crisis y cambio. Electores y partidos en la España de los años 80*, Madrid: Centro de Estudios Constitucionales, pp. 27–69.

Gunther, R. (1986b) El hundimiento de UCD, in J. Linz and J.R. Montero (eds), *Crisis y cambio. Electores y partidos en la España de los años 80*, Madrid: Centro de Estudios Constitucionales, pp. 433–92.

Gunther, R. (1992a) Spain: the very model of the modern elite settlement, in J. Higley and R. Gunther (eds), *Elites and Democratic Consolidation in Latin America and Southern Europe*, Cambridge: Cambridge University Press, pp. 38–80.

Gunther, R. (1992b) *The Dynamics of Electoral Competition in a Modern Society: Models of Spanish Voting Behaviour 1979 and 1982*, Working Paper No.28. Barcelona: Institut de Ciències Polítiques i Socials.

Gunther, R. (1996) *Spanish Public Policy: From Dictatorship to Democracy*, Working Paper 1996/84. Madrid: Instituto Juan March.

Gunther, R. and Hopkin, J. (forthcoming) A crisis of institutionalisation: the collapse of the UCD, in R. Gunther, J. Linz and J.R. Montero (eds), *Political Parties: Changing Roles in Contemporary Democracies*.

Gunther, R. and Montero, J.R. (1994) Los anclajes del partidismo: Un análisis comparado del comportamiento electoral en cuatro democracias del sur de Europa, in P. del Castillo (ed.), *Comportamiento político y electoral*, Madrid: Centro de Investigaciones Sociológicas, pp. 467–548.

Gunther, R., Sani, G. and Shabad, G. (1986) *Spain After Franco: The Making of a Competitive Party System*, Berkeley: University of California Press.

Guyomarch, A. (1995) The European dynamics of evolving party competition in France, *Parliamentary Affairs*, **48**, 100–23.

Habert, P. and Ysmal, C. (eds) (1988) *Les Elections législatives de 1988*, Paris: Le Figaro/FNSP.

Haerpfer, C. (1983) Nationalratswahlen und Wahlverhalten seit 1945, in P. Gerlich and W.C. Müller (eds), *Zwischen Koalition und Konkurrenz. Österreichs Parteien seit 1945*, Vienna: Braumüller, pp. 111–49.

Haerpfer, C. (1985) Austria, in I. Crewe and D. Denver (eds), *Electoral Change in Western Democracies: Patterns and Sources of Electoral Volatility*, London: Croom Helm, pp. 264–86.

Haerpfer, C. and Gehmacher, E. (1984) Social structure and voting in the Austrian party system, *Electoral Studies*, **3**, 25–46.

Hailbronner, O. (1992) The failure that succeeded: Nazi Party activity in a Catholic region of Germany, 1929–1932, *Journal of Contemporary History*, **27**, 531–49.

Hamilton, R. (1982) *Who Voted for Hitler?*, Princeton, NJ: Princeton University Press.

Hammond, J. (1985) Popular power and the Portuguese Far Left, *European Journal of Political Research*, **13**, 207–25.

Hammond, J. (1988) *Building Popular Power*, New York: Monthly Review Press.

Hanley, D. (1986) *Keeping Left? CERES and the French Socialist Party*, Manchester: Manchester University Press.

Hanley, D. (ed.) (1994) *Christian Democracy in Europe: A Comparative Perspective*, London: Pinter.

Hardiman, N. and Whelan, C.T. (1994) Values and political partisanship, in C.T. Whelan (ed.), *Values and Social Change in Ireland*, Dublin: Gill and Macmillan, pp. 136–86.

Harmel, R. and Svåsand, L. (1990) *The Impact of New Political Parties: The Case of the Danish and Norwegian Progress Parties*. Paper presented at the Annual Meeting of the American Political Science Association, San Francisco, 30 August–2 September.

Hay, C. (1994) Labour's Thatcherite revisionism: understanding the politics of 'catch-up', *Political Studies*, **42**, 700–8.

Hayward, J. (1995) *The Crisis of Representation in Europe*, London: Frank Cass. Originally, special edition of *West European Politics*, **19**.

Heath, A., Jowell, R. and Curtice, J. (1985) *How Britain Votes*, Oxford: Pergamon.

Heath, A., Jowell, R. and Curtice, J. (1987) Trendless fluctuation: a reply to Crewe, *Political Studies*, **35**, 256–77.

Heath, A., Jowell, R., Curtice, J., Evans, G, Field, J. and Witherspoon, S. (1991) *Understanding Political Change*, Oxford: Pergamon.

Heimer, F-W. (1991) Eleitorados e atitudes face à democracia. Uma nota de pesquisa, *Sociologia. Problemas e Práctica*, **9**, 139–59.

Hellemans, S, (1990) *Strijd om de moderniteit*, Leuven: Universitaire Pers K.U. Leuven.

Herrnson, P. (1988) *Party Campaigning in the 1980s*, Cambridge, Mass: Harvard University Press.

Heywood, A. (1994) Britain's dominant party system, in L. Robins, H. Blackmore and R. Pyper (eds), *Britain's Changing Party System*, London: Leicester University Press, pp. 10–25.

Heywood, P. (1995a) *The Government and Politics of Spain*, London: Macmillan.

Heywood, P. (1995b) Sleaze in Spain, *Parliamentary Affairs*, **48**, 726–37.

Hirschman, A. (1970) *Exit, Voice and Loyalty*, Cambridge, Mass.: Harvard University Press.

Hobsbawm, E. (1981) The forward march of Labour halted?, in M. Jacques and F. Mulhearn (eds), *The Forward March of Labour Halted?*, London: New Left Books, pp. 1–19.

Hoffmann, S. (1956) *Le mouvement Poujade*, Paris: Armand Colin.

Hofmann, G. and Perger, W. (1994) Ohnmächtige Riesen. Die strategische Basis der Volksparteien in Superwahljahr 1994, in W. Bürklin and D. Roth (eds), *Das Superwahljahr 1994. Deutschland vor unkalkulierbaren Regierungsmöglichkeiten?*, Cologne: Bund-Verlag, pp. 293–307.

Holmes, M. (1994) The establishment of Democratic Left, *Irish Political Studies*, **9**, 148–56.

Hölzl, N. (1974) *Propagandaschlachten. Die österreichischen Wahlkämpfe 1945 bis 1971*, Vienna: Verlag für Geschichte und Politik.

Hopkin, J. (1995) *Party Development and Party Collapse: The Case of Unión de Centro Democrático in Post-Franco Spain*, Florence: European University Institute, PhD thesis.

Horner, F. (1987) Austria 1945–1979, in I. Budge, D. Robertson and D. Hearl (eds), *Ideology, Strategy and Party Change: Spatial Analyses of Post-War Election Programmes in 19 Democracies*, Cambridge: Cambridge University Press, pp. 270–93

Horner, F. (1997) Programme – Ideologien: Dissens oder Konsens, in H. Dachs *et al.* (eds), *Handbuch des politischen Systems Österreichs. Die zweite Republik*, 3rd edn, Vienna: Manz, pp. 235–47.

Houska, J. J. (1985) *Influencing Mass Political Behaviour: Elites and Political Subcultures in the Netherlands and Austria*, University of California: Institute of International Studies.

Huber, J. and Inglehart, R. (1995) Expert interpretations of party space and party locations in 42 societies, *Party Politics*, **1**, 73–111.

Hudson, M. (1994) *The Portuguese Economy, 1974–1993*, paper presented at the University of Reading Workshop on Portugal, 18 February.

Hughes, C. and Wintour P. (1990) *Labour Rebuilt: The New Model Party*. London: Fourth Estate.

Hugill, B. (1995) Mandelson wants Labour to form Lib-Lab pact, *The Observer*, 24 December.

Huneeus, C. (1982) La transición a la democracia en España. Dimensiones de una política consociacional, in J. Santamaría (ed.), *Transición a la democracia en el sur de Europa y América Latina*, Madrid: Centro de Investigaciones Sociológicas, pp. 243–86.

Huntington, S. (1991) *The Third Wave: Democratization in the Late Twentieth Century*, Norman, Oklahoma: University of Oklahoma Press.

Huyse, L. (1987) *De verzuiling voorbij*, Leuven: Kritak.

Ignazi, P. (1992a) The silent counter-revolution: hypothesis on the emergence of extreme-right wing parties in Europe, *European Journal of Political Research*, **22**, 3–34.

Ignazi, P. (1992b) *Dal Pci al Pds*, Bologna: Il Mulino.

Ignazi, P. (1994) *Postfascisti? Dal Movimento sociale italiano ad Alleanza nazionale*, Bologna: Il Mulino.

Ingle, S. (1994) Britain's third party, in L. Robins, H. Blackmore and R. Pyper (eds), *Britain's Changing Party System*, London: Leicester University Press, pp. 93–109.

Inglehart, R. (1977) *Silent Revolution: Changing Values and Political Styles Among Western Publics*, Ann Arbor: University of Michigan Press.

Irwin, G.A. and van Holsteyn, J.J.M. (1989a) Decline of the structured model of electoral competition, in H. Daalder and G. Irwin (eds), *Politics in the Netherlands: How Much Change?*, London: Frank Cass, pp. 21–41.

Irwin, G.A. and van Holsteyn, J.J.M. (1989b) Towards a more open model of competition, in H. Daalder and G. Irwin (eds), *Politics in the Netherlands: How Much Change?*, London: Frank Cass, pp. 112–38.

Israel, J.I. (1995) *The Dutch Republic: Its Rise, Greatness, and Fall, 1477–1806*, Oxford: Clarendon Press.

Janos, A. (1988–89) The politics of backwardness in Continental Europe, 1780–1945, *World Politics*, **41**, 325–58.

Jáuregui, F. (1987) *La derecha después de Fraga*, Madrid: Ediciones El País.

Jackson, J. (1988) *The Popular Front in France: Defending Democracy, 1934–38*, Cambridge: Cambridge University Press.

Jeffery, C. (1995) *Social Democracy in the Austrian Provinces, 1918–1934: Beyond Red Vienna*, London: Leicester University Press.

Jeffery, C. and Green, S. (1995) The sense of malaise in Germany, *Parliamentary Affairs*, **48**, 675–87.

Jones, L.E. (1979) Inflation, revaluation and the crisis of middle class politics, *Central European History*, **12**, 143–68.

Juliá, S. (1990) The ideological conversion of the leaders of the PSOE, 1976–79, in F. Lannon and P. Preston (eds), *Elites and Power in Twentieth Century Spain: Essays in Honour of Sir Raymond Carr*, Oxford: Clarendon Press, pp. 269–85.

Justel, M. (1992) *El líder como factor de explicación del voto*, Working Paper 51, Barcelona: Institut de Ciències Polítiques i Socials.

Justel, M. (1994) Composición y dinámica de la abstención electoral en España, in P. del Castillo (ed.), *Comportamiento político y electoral*, Madrid: Centro de Investigaciones Sociológicas, pp. 19–48.

Kadan, A. and Pelinka, A. (1979) *Die Grundsatzprogramme der österreichischen Parteien. Dokumentation und Analyse*, St. Pölten: Niederösterreichisches Pressehaus.

Katz, R. (1986) Party government: a rationalistic conception, in F. Castles and R. Wildenmann (eds), *Visions and Realities of Party Government*, Berlin: De Gruyter, pp. 31–71.

Katz, R. (1996) Electoral reform and the transformation of party politics in Italy, *Party Politics*, **2**, 31–53.

Katz, R.S. and Kolodny, R. (1992) The USA: the 1990 congressional campaign, in S. Bowler and D. Farrell (eds.), *Electoral Strategies and Political Marketing*, Basingstoke: Macmillan, pp. 183–203.

Katz, R.S. and Mair, P. (1992) *Party Organizations in Western Democracies: A Data Handbook*, London: Sage.

Katz, R.S. and Mair, P. (eds) (1994) *How Parties Organize: Change and Adaptation in Party Organizations in Western Democracies*, London: Sage.

Katz, R.S. and Mair P. (1995) Changing models of party organization and party democracy: the emergence of the cartel party, *Party Politics*, **1**, 5–28.

Katz, R.S. and Mair, P. (1996) Cadre, catch-all or cartel? A rejoinder, *Party Politics*, **2**, 525–34.

Katz, R.S., *et al.* (1992) The Membership of Political Parties in European Democracies, 1960–1990, *European Journal of Political Research*, **22**, 329–45.

Keane, J. (1988) *Democracy and Civil Society: On the Predicaments of European Socialism, the Prospects for Democracy, and the Problem of Controlling Social and Political Power*, London and New York: Verso.

Keatinge, P. (1991) *Ireland and EC Membership Evaluated*, London: Pinter.

Kellner, P. (1997) Virgin MPs set a radical agenda, *The Observer*, 11 May.

Kelly, R.N. (1989) *Conservative Party Conferences*, Manchester: Manchester University Press.

Kergoat, J. (1983) *Le Parti socialiste*, Paris: Le Sycomore.

King, A. (1992) The implications of one-party government, in A. King *et al.* (eds), *Britain at the Polls*, Chatham, NJ: Chatham House, pp. 223–48.

Kirchheimer, O. (1957) The waning of opposition in parliamentary regimes, in F.S. Burin and K.L. Shell (eds), *Politics, Law and Social Change: Selected Essays of Otto Kirchheimer*, New York: Columbia University Press, 1969, pp. 292–318.

Kirchheimer, O. (1966) The transformation of the Western European party systems, in J. LaPalombara and M. Weiner (eds), *Political Parties and Political Development*, Princeton, NJ: Princeton University Press, pp. 177–200.

Kohl, H. (1991) *Our Future in Europe*, London: Konrad-Adenauer Stiftung.

Kolinsky, E. (1987) Introduction, in E. Kolinsky (ed.), *Opposition in Western Europe*, London: Croom Helm, pp. 1–8.

Koole, R.A. (1992) *De opkomst van de moderne kaderpartij*, Utrecht: Spectrum.

Koole, R.A. (1994) The vulnerability of the modern cadre party in the Netherlands, in R.S. Katz and P. Mair (eds), *How Parties Organize: Change and Adaptation in Party Organizations in Western Democracies*, London: Sage, pp. 278–303.

Koole, R.A. and ten Napel, H.-M. (1991) De Riante Positie in het Vermaledijde 'Midden'. Confessionele Machtsvorming op Nationaal Niveau, in P. Luykx and H. Righart (eds), *Van de Pastorie naar het Torentje. Een Eeuw Confessionele Politiek*. The Hague: SDU, pp. 72–92.

Kulemann, P. (1979) *Am Beispiel des Austromarxismus. Sozialdemokratische Arbeiterbewegung in Österreich von Hainfeld bis zur Dolfuß-Diktatur*, Hamburg: Junius.

Laakso, M. and Taagepera, R. (1979) 'Effective' number of parties: a measure with application to West Europe, *Comparative Political Studies*, **12**, 3–27.

Labour Party (1992) *It's Time to Get Britain Working Again*, London: Labour Party.

Lammens, A. (1993) *Het Bankroet van België. Het verhaal van 10.000.000.000.000 frank staatschuld*, Antwerp: Darbo.

Lane, J-E. and Ersson, S.O. (1994) *Politics and Society in Western Europe*, 3rd. edn, London: Sage.

Laver, M. (1992) Are Irish parties peculiar?, in J.H. Goldthorpe and C.T. Whelan (eds), *The Development of Industrial Society in Ireland*, Oxford: Oxford University Press, pp. 359–81.

Laver, M. and Hunt, W.B. (1992) *Policy and Party Competition*, London: Routledge.

Laver, M., Marsh M. and Sinnott R. (1987) Patterns of party support, in M. Laver, P. Mair and R. Sinnott (eds), *How Ireland Voted*, Dublin: Poolbeg, pp. 99–140.

Lhomme, J. (1960) *La grande bourgeoisie au pouvoir, 1830–80*, Paris: Presses Universitaires de France.

Lijphart, A. (1968) Typologies of democratic systems, *Comparative Political Studies*, **1**, 3–44.

Lijphart, A. (1969) Consociational democracy, *World Politics*, **21**, 207–25.

Lijphart, A. (1975) *The Politics of Accommodation: Pluralism and Democracy in the Netherlands*, 2nd edn, Berkeley: University of California Press.

Lijphart, A. (1984) *Democracies: Patterns of Majoritarian and Consensus Government in Twenty-One Countries*, New Haven, Conn: Yale University Press.

Lijphart, A. (1989) From the politics of accommodation to adversarial politics in the Netherlands: a reassessment, in H. Daalder and G. Irwin (eds), *Politics in the Netherlands: How Much Change?*, London: Frank Cass, pp. 139–53.

Lijphart, A. (1994) *Electoral Systems and Party Systems. A Study of Twenty-Seven Democracies 1945–1990*, Oxford: Oxford University Press.

Linz, J. (1980) The new Spanish party system, in R.Rose (ed.), *Electoral Participation: A Comparative Analysis*, London: Sage, pp. 101–90.

Linz, J. *et al.* (1981) *Informe sociológico sobre el cambio político en España 1975–81. IV Informe FOESSA, Vol. 1*, Madrid: Euramérica.

Lipow, A. (1996) *Political Parties and Democracy: Explorations in History and Theory*, London: Pluto Press.

Lipset, S.M. (1960) *Political Man*, London: Heinemann.

Lipset, S.M. and Rokkan, S. (1967a) *Party Systems and Voter Alignments: Cross-National Perspectives*, New York: Free Press.

Lipset, S.M. and Rokkan, S. (1967b) Cleavage structures, party systems and voter alignments: an introduction, in S.M. Lipset and S. Rokkan (eds), *Party Systems and Voter Alignments: Cross-National Perspectives*, New York: Free Press, pp. 1–64.

Lopes, F.F. (1994) *Poder Político e Caciquismo na 1ª República*, Lisbon: Editorial Estampa.

Lopes, P.S. (1989) PPD/PSD: A dependência do carisma, in M.B. Coelho (ed.), *Portugal. O Sistema Político e Costitucional*, Lisbon: Instituto de Ciências Sociais, pp. 181–92.

Lopes, V.S. (1976) *Constituição da República Portuguesa 1976 (anotada)*, Lisbon: Editus.

López Nieto, L. (1988) *Alianza Popular: Estructura y evolución electoral de un partido conservador (1976–82)*, Madrid: Centro de Investigaciones Sociológicas.

Lorwin, V.R. (1974a) Segmented pluralism: ideological cleavages and political cohesion in the smaller European democracies, *Comparative Politics*, **3**, 141–75.

Lorwin, V.R. (1974b) Belgium: conflict and compromise, in K. McRae, (ed.), *Consociational Democracy, Political Accommodation in Segmented Societies*, Toronto: McClelland and Stewart, pp. 175–94.

Lucardie, P. (1988) Conservatism in the Netherlands: fragments and fringe groups, in B. Girvin (ed.), *The Transformation of Contemporary Conservatism*, London: Sage, pp. 78–97.

Lucardie, P. (1991) Fragments from the pillars: small parties in the Netherlands, in F.

Müller-Rommel and G. Pridham (eds), *Small Parties in Western Europe: Comparative and National Perspectives*, London: Sage, pp. 115–34.

Lucardie, P. and ten Napel, H-M. (1994) Between confessionalism and liberal conservatism: the Christian Democratic parties of Belgium and the Netherlands, in D. Hanley (ed.), *Christian Democracy in Europe: A Comparative Perspective*, London: Pinter, pp. 51–70.

Lucas Verdú, P. (1976) *La octava ley fundamental*, Madrid: Tecnos.

Luebbert, G. (1991) *Liberalism, Fascism or Social Democracy: Social Classes and the Political Origins of Regimes in Interwar Europe*, New York: Oxford University Press.

Luther, K.R. (1987) The Freiheitliche Partei Österreichs: protest party or governing party?, in E. Kirchner (ed.), *Liberal Parties in Western Europe*, Cambridge: Cambridge University Press, pp. 213–51.

Luther, K.R. (1989) Dimensions of party system change: the case of Austria, *West European Politics*, **12**, 3–27.

Luther, K.R. (1992) Consociationalism, parties and the party system, in K.R. Luther and W.C. Müller (eds), *Politics in Austria: Still a Case of Consociationalism?*, London: Frank Cass, pp. 45–98.

Luther, K.R. (1995) An end to the politics of isolation? Austria in light of the 1994 elections, *German Politics*, **4**, 122–39.

Luther, K.R. (1996a) Friedrich Peter, in H. Dachs, P. Gerlich and W.C. Müller (eds), *Die Politiker. Karrieren und Wirken bedeutender Repräsentanten der zweiten Republik*, Vienna: Manz, pp. 435–45.

Luther, K.R. (1996b) Norbert Steger, in H. Dachs, P. Gerlich and W.C. Müller (eds), *Die Politiker. Karrieren und Wirken bedeutender Repräsentanten der zweiten Republik*, Vienna: Manz, pp. 548–57.

Luther, K.R. (1997a) Die Freiheitlichen, in H. Dachs *et al.* (eds), *Handbuch des politischen Systems Österreichs. Die zweite Republik*, 3rd edn, Vienna: Manz, pp. 286–303.

Luther, K.R. (1997b) Bund-Länder Beziehungen: Formal- und Realverfassung, in H. Dachs *et al.* (eds), *Handbuch des politischen Systems Österreichs. Die zweite Republik*, 3rd edn, Vienna: Manz, pp. 907–19.

Luther, K.R. and Deschouwer, K. (eds) (1998) *Political Parties and Party Elites in Divided Societies: in Consociational Democracy*, London: Routledge.

Luther, K.R. and Müller, W.C. (eds) (1992) *Politics in Austria: Still a Case of Consociationalism?*, London: Frank Cass. Originally a special issue of *West European Politics*, **15**.

Lyne, T. (1987) The Progressive Democrats, *Irish Political Studies*, **2**, 107–14.

Mabille, X. (1997) *Histoire Politique de la Belgique. Facteurs et acteurs de changement*, Brussels: CRISP.

Machefer, P. (1974) *Ligues et fascismes en France, 1918–39*, Paris: PUF, Dossiers 'Clio'.

Machin, H. (1989) Stages and dynamics in the evolution of the French party system, *West European Politics*, **12**, 59–81.

MacIvor, H. (1995) Changing party leadership selection in Canada: causes and consequences, paper presented at the Party Politics in the Year 2000 Conference, Manchester, 13–15 January.

Mackie, T. and Rose, R. (1982) *The International Almanac of Electoral History*, London: Macmillan.

Maderthaner, W. and Müller, W.C. (1996) *Die Organisation der österreichischen Sozialdemokratie 1889–1995*, Vienna: Löcker Verlag.

Maes, M. (1988) *De ledenaantallen van de politieke partijen in België*, Leuven: Departement Politieke Wetenschappen.

Magone, J.M. (1994) Political corruption and democratic consolidation in the Southern European semiperiphery. Some notes on the Portuguese case (1974–1993), in P. Dunleavy and J. Stanyer (eds), *Contemporary Political Studies*, Belfast: Political Studies Association, pp. 751–64.

Magone, J.M. (1996) *The Changing Architecture of Iberian Politics: An Investigation of the Structuring of Democratic Political Systemic Culture in Semi-peripheral Southern European Societies*, Lewiston: Mellen University Press.

Mailer, P. (1976) *Portugal: The Impossible Revolution?*, London: Verso.

Mair, P. (1979) The autonomy of the political: the development of the Irish party system, *Comparative Politics*, **11**, 445–65.

Mair, P. (1983) Adaptation and control: towards an understanding of party and party system change, in H. Daalder and P. Mair (eds), *Western European Party Systems: Continuity and Change*, London: Sage, pp. 405–29.

Mair, P. (1987) *The Changing Irish Party System*, London: Pinter.

Mair, P. (1989) The problem of party system change, *Journal of Theoretical Politics*, **1**, 251–76.

Mair, P. (1990a) Introduction, in P. Mair (ed.), *The West European Party System*, Oxford: Oxford University Press, pp. 1–22.

Mair, P. (ed.) (1990b) *The West European Party System*, Oxford: Oxford University Press.

Mair, P. (1992) Explaining the absence of class politics in Ireland, in J.H. Goldthorpe and C.T. Whelan (eds), *The Development of Industrial Society in Ireland*, Oxford: Oxford University Press, pp. 383–410.

Mair, P. (1993) Myths of electoral change and the survival of traditional parties: the 1992 Stein Rokkan Lecture, *European Journal of Political Research*, **24**, 121–33.

Mair, P. (1994a) Party organizations: from civil society to the state, in R.S. Katz and P. Mair (eds), *How Parties Organize*, London: Sage, pp. 1–22.

Mair. P. (1994b) The correlates of consensus democracy and the puzzle of Dutch politics, *West European Politics*, **17**, 97–123.

Mair, P. (1995) Political parties, popular legitimacy and public privilege, *West European Politics*, **18**, 40–57.

Mair, P. (1996) Party systems and structures of competition, in L. LeDuc, R.G. Niemi and P. Norris (eds), *Comparing Democracies: Elections and Voting in Global Perspective*, London: Sage, pp. 83–106.

Mair, P. (1997) *Party System Change: Approaches and Interpretations*, Oxford: Clarendon Press.

Mair, P. and Smith, G. (eds) (1989) *Understanding Party System Change in Western Europe*, London: Frank Cass.

Mandelson, P. and Liddle, R. (1996) *The Blair Revolution: Can New Labour Deliver?*, London: Faber and Faber.

Mannheimer, R. and Sani, G. (1987) *Il Mercato Elettorale*, Bologna: Il Mulino.

Manuel, P.C. (1995) *Uncertain Outcome: The Politics of the Portuguese Transition to Democracy*, Lanham: University Press of America.

Maor, M. (1997) *Political Parties and Party Systems: Comparative Approaches and the British Experience*, London: Routledge.

Maravall, J.M. (1981) *La política de la transición*, Madrid: Tecnos.

Marques, O.A.H. (1980) *A Primeira República Portuguesa*, Lisbon: Livros Horizonte.

Marques, O.A.H. (1981) *História de Portugal. Vol. III: Das Revoluções Liberais aos nossos Dias*, Lisbon: Palas Editora.

Marsh, M. and Sinnott, R. (1990) How the voters decided, in M. Gallagher and R. Sinnott (eds), *How Ireland Voted 1989*, Galway: Centre for the Study of Irish Elections/PSAI Press, pp. 94–130.

Marsh, M. and Sinnott, R. (1993) The voters: stability and change, in M. Gallagher and M. Laver (eds), *How Ireland Voted 1992*, Dublin: Folens/PSAI Press, pp. 93–114.

Marshall, G., Newby, H., Rose, D. and Vogler, C. (1988) *Social Class in Modern Britain*, London: Hutchinson.

Martins, H. (1968) 'Portugal', in S.J. Woolf (ed.), *European Fascism*. London: Weidenfeld and Nicolson, pp. 302–36.

Mayer, N. and Perrineau, P. (1992) *Les Comportements politiques*, Paris: Armand Colin.

Mayer, N. and Perrineau, P. (1994) *Le Front National à découvert*, Paris: FNSP.

McAdams, A.J. (1990) Towards a new Germany? Problems of unification, *Government and Opposition*, **25**, 304–16.

Menasse, R. (1992) *Das Land ohne Eigenschaften. Essay zur österreichischen Identität*, Vienna: Sonderzahl.

Merkl, P. (ed.) (1980) *Western European Party Systems*, New York: Free Press.

Merkl, P. (1988) The SPD after Brandt: problems of integration in a changing urban society, *West European Politics*, **11**, 40–53.

Merz, F. and Cunha Rego, V. (1976) *Testfall Portugal-Freiheit für den Sieger*, Zürich: Schweizer Verlagshaus.

Miller, W. (1983) The denationalization of British politics: the reemergence of the periphery, *West European Politics*, **6**, 103–29.

Mockler, F. (1994) Organisational change in Fianna Fáil and Fine Gael, *Irish Political Studies*, **9**, 165–71.

Monica, M.F. (1994) A lenta morte da Câmara dos Pares (1878–1896), *Análise Social*, **29**, 121–52.

Montero, J.R. (1977) *La CEDA: El catolicismo social y político en la II República*, Madrid: Ediciones de Revista de Trabajo (2 vols).

Montero, J.R. (1981) Partidos y participación política: Algunas notas sobre la afiliación política en la etapa inicial de la transición española, *Revista de Estudios Políticos*, **23**, 33–72.

Montero, J.R. (1986) El sub-triunfo de la derecha: Los apoyos electorales de AP, in J. Linz and J.R. Montero (eds), *Crisis y cambio. Electores y partidos en la España de los años 80*, Madrid: Centro de Estudios Constitucionales, pp. 343–432.

Montero, J.R. (1988) More than Conservative, less than Neoconservative: Alianza Popular in Spain, in B. Girvin (ed.), *The Transformation of Contemporary Conservatism*, London: Sage, pp. 145–63.

Montero, J.R. (1989) Los fracasos políticos y electorales de la derecha española (1976–87), in J. Tezanos, R. Cotarelo and A. de Blas (eds), *La transición democrática española*, Madrid: Sistema, pp. 495–542.

Montero, J.R. (1992) Las elecciones legislativas, in R. Cotarelo (ed.), *Transición política y consolidación democrática. España (1975–86)*, Madrid: Centro de Investigaciones Sociológicas, pp. 243–97.

Montero, J.R. (1994) Sobre las preferencias electorales en España: fragmentación y polarización (1977–1993), in P. del Castillo (ed.), *Comportamiento político y electoral*, Madrid: Centro de Investigaciones Sociológicas, pp. 51–124.

Montero, J.R., Llera, F. and Torcal, M. (1992) Sistemas electorales en España. Una recapitulación, *Revista Española de Investigaciones Sociológicas*, **58**, 7–56.

Moreira, A. (1989) O Regime: Presidencialismo do Primeiro-Ministro, in M.B. Coelho (ed.), *Portugal. O Sistema Político e Costitucional*, Lisbon: Instituto de Ciéncias Sociais, pp. 31–7.

Morlino, L. (1995) 'Political Parties and Democratic Consolidation in Sourthern Europe', in R. Gunther, N. Diamandouros and H.-J. Pühle (eds) *The Politics of Democratic Consolidation: Southern Europe in Comparative Perspective*, Baltimore, MD: Johns Hopkins University Press, pp. 315–88.

Morlino, L. (1996) Crisis of parties and change of party system in Italy, *Party Politics*, **2**, 5–30.

Morlino, L. and Tarchi, M. (1996) The dissatisfied society: the roots of political change in Italy, *European Journal of Political Research*, **30**, 41–63.

Morodo, R. (1984) *La transición política*, Madrid: Taurus.

Mossuz-Lavau, J. (1994) *Les Français et la politique*, Paris: Odile Jacob.

Mouzelis, N. (1978) 'On Greek Formalism: Political and Cultural Aspects of Under-development', in N. Mouzelis (ed.) *Modern Greece: Facets Of Underdevelopment*, London: Macmillan, pp. 134–48.

Mouzelis, N. (1986) *Politics in the Semi-periphery: Early Parliamentarianism and Late Industrialization in the Balkans and Latin America*, Basingstoke: Macmillan.

Müller, W.C. (1985) Die Rolle der Parteien bei Entstehung und Entwicklung der Sozialpartnerschaft. Eine handlungslogische und empirische Analyse, in P. Ger-lich, E. Grande and W.C. Müller (eds), *Sozialpartnerschaft in der Krise. Leistungen und Grenzen des Neokorporatismus in Österreich*, Vienna: Böhlau, pp. 135–224.

Müller, W.C. (1992a) Austria (1945–1990), in R. Katz and P. Mair (eds), *Party Organization: A Data Handbook on Party Organizations in Western Democracies, 1960–90*, London: Sage, pp. 21–120.

Müller, W.C. (1992b) Austrian governmental institutions: do they matter?, in K.R. Luther and W.C. Müller, (eds), *Politics in Austria. Still a Case of Consociationalism?*, London: Frank Cass, pp. 99–131.

Müller, W.C. (1993) The relevance of the state for party system change, *Journal of Theoretical Politics*, **5**, 419–54.

Müller, W.C. (1996) Wahlsystem und Parteiensystem in Österreich 1945–1995, in F. Plasser, P. Ulram and G. Ogris (eds), *Wahlkampf und Wahlentscheidung. Analysen zur Nationalratswahl 1995*, Vienna: Signum, pp. 235–52.

Müller, W.C. (1997) Das Parteiensystem, in H. Dachs *et al.* (eds), *Handbuch des politischen Systems Österreichs. Die zweite Republik*, 3rd edn, Vienna: Manz, pp. 215–34.

Müller, W.C., Philipp, W. and Jenny, M. (1995) Ideologie und Strategie der österreichischen Parteien: Eine Analyse der Wahlprogramme 1949–1994, in W.C. Müller, F. Plasser and P. Ulram (eds), *Wählerverhalten und Parteienwettbewerb. Analysen zur Nationalratswahl 1994*, Vienna: Signum, pp. 119–66.

Müller, W.C., Plasser, F. and Ulram, P. (1995) *Wählerverhalten und Parteienwettbewerb. Analysen zur Nationalratswahl 1994*, Vienna: Signum.

Murillo Ferrol, F. *et al.* (1983) *IV Informe FOESSA. Informe sociológico sobre el cambio social en España (1975–83)*, Madrid: Eurámerica.

Neumann, F. (ed.) (1956) *Modern Political Parties: Approaches to Comparative Analysis*, Chicago: University of Chicago Press.

Nordisk Kontakt 9, 1994 (Vänstervind både i riksdags- och kommunalvalen).

Norpoth, H. and Roth, D. (1993) Unification and electoral choice, in R. Dalton (ed.), *The New Germany Votes*, Oxford: Berg, pp. 209–31.

Norris, P. (1990) *British By-Elections: The Volatile Electorate*, Oxford: Clarendon Press.

Norton, P. (1975) *Dissension in the House of Commons, 1945–74*, London: Macmillan.

Norton, P. (1980) *Dissension in the House of Commons, 1974–79*, Oxford: Oxford University Press.

Nosty, B.D. (1975) *Mário Soares. O Chanceler Português*, Lisbon: Liber.

O'Leary, C. (1979) *Irish Elections, 1918–1977*, Dublin: Gill and Macmillan.

Optenhogel, U. and Stoleroff, A. (1985) The logics of politically competing trade union confederations in Portugal 1974–1984, in E. de Sousa Ferreira and W.C. Opello (eds), *Conflict and Change in Portugal 1974–1984*, Lisbon: Teorema, pp. 179–90.

Ortega Díaz-Ambrona, J.A. (1984) Fraga y Suárez ante la transición, in *Diario 16, Historia de la transición*, Madrid: Diario 16, pp. 234–5.

Padgett, S. (1987) The West German Social Democrats in opposition 1982–1986, *West European Politics*, **10**, 333–56.

Padgett, S. (1989) The party system, in G. Smith, W. Paterson and P. Merkl (eds), *Developments in West German Politics*, Basingstoke: Macmillan, pp. 122–46.

Padgett, S. (1993) The new german electorate, in S. Padgett (ed.), *Parties and Party Systems in the New Germany*, Aldershot: Dartmouth/Association for the Study of German Politics, pp. 25–46.

Padgett, S. (1995) *Superwahljahr* in the new *Länder*: Polarisation in an open electoral market, *German Politics*, **4**, 75–94.

Padgett, S. and Burkett, T. (1986) *Political Parties and Elections in West Germany: The Search for a New Stability*, London: Hurst.

Pallarés, F. (1981) La distorsión de la proporcionalidad en el sistema electoral español. Análisis comparado e hipótesis alternativas, *Revista de Estudios Políticos*, **23**, 233–67.

Panebianco, A. (1988) *Political Parties: Organisation and Power*, Cambridge: Cambridge University Press.

Pappalardo, A. (1996) Dal Pluralismo Polarizzato al Pluralismo Moderato. Il Modello di Sartori e la Transizione Italiana, *Rivista Italiana di Scienza Politica*, **26**, 103–45.

Pappi, F. (1984) The West German party system, West European Politics, 7, 7–26.

Pasquino, G. (1980) Italian Christian Democracy: a party for all seasons? in P. Lange and S. Tarrow (eds), Italy in Transition: Conflict and Consensus, London: Frank Cass, pp. 88–109.

Passmore, K. (1993) The French Third Republic: stalemate society or cradle of Fascism?, French History, 7, 417–49.

Patricio, M.T. and Stoleroff, A.D. (1996) The Portuguese Communist Party: Perestroika and its aftermath, in M.J. Bull and P. Heywood (eds), West European Communist Parties After the Revolutions of 1989, New York: St. Martins Press, pp. 90–118.

Payne, S.G. (1980) Fascism: Comparison and Definition, Wisconsin: University of Wisconsin Press.

Pedersen, M. (1979) The dynamics of European party systems: changing patterns of electoral volatility, European Journal of Political Research, 7, 1–26.

Pedersen, M.N. (1983) Changing patterns of electoral volatility in European party systems, 1948–1977: exploration in explanations, in H. Daalder and P. Mair (eds), Western European Party Systems: Continuity and Change, London: Sage, pp. 29–66.

Pelinka, A. and Welan, M. (1971) Demokratie und Verfassung in Österreich, Vienna: Europa Verlag.

Pennings, P. (1996) The triad of party system change: votes, office and policy. Paper presented at the Workshop on Party System Change in Europe, European Consortium for Political Research, Oslo, 29 March–3 April.

Pereira, J.P. (1983) O PCP na Primeira República: Membros e Direcção, Estudos Sobre o Comunismo, 1, 2–21.

Pereira, J.P. (1989) O Partido Comunista Português e a esquerda revolucionária, in M.B. Coelho (ed.), Portugal. O Sistema Político e Costitucional, Lisbon: Instituto de Ciências Sociais, pp. 79–109.

Perkins, D. (1996) Structure and choice: the role of organizations, patronage and the media in party formation, Party Politics, 2, 355–75.

Perry, J. et al. (1994) Honderd Jaar Sociaal-Democratie in Nederland, 1894–1994, Amsterdam: Bert Bakker.

Petersson, O. and Särlvik, B. (1975) The 1973 Election, Stockholm: Central Bureau of Statistics.

Petras, J. (1993) Spanish socialism: the politics of neoliberalism, in J. Kurth and J. Petras (eds), Mediterranean Paradoxes: Politics and Social Structure in Southern Europe, Oxford: Berg, pp. 95–127.

Pierce, R. (1992) Toward the formation of a partisan alignment in France, Political Behavior, 14, 443–69.

Pijnenburg, B. (1984) Pillarized and consociational-democratic Belgium: the views of Huyse, Acta Politica, 19, 57–72.

Pinto, J.M. (1989) A direita e o 25 de Abril: ideologia, estratégia e evolução polítical, in M.B. Coelho (ed.), Portugal. O Sistema Político e Costitucional, Lisbon: Instituto de Ciências Sociais, pp. 193–212.

Piretti, M.S. (1995) Le elezioni politiche in Italia dal 1848 a oggi, Rome-Bari: Laterza.

Pizzorno, A. (1981) Interests and parties in pluralism, in S. Berger (ed.), Organizing Interests in Western Europe: Pluralism, Corporatism, and the Transformation of

Politics, Cambridge: Cambridge University Press, pp. 247–84.

Plant, Lord (1993) *Final Report of the Party Commission on Electoral Reform*, London: Labour Party.

Plasser, F. and Seeber, G. (1995) In search of a model: Multivariate Analysen der Exit Polls 1986–1994, in W.C. Müller, F. Plasser and P. Ulram (eds), *Wählerverhalten und Parteienwettbewerb. Analysen zur Nationalratswahl 1994*, Vienna: Signum, pp. 227–64.

Plasser, F. and Ulram, P. (1982) *Unbehagen im Parteienstaat. Jugend und Politik im Parteienstaat*, Vienna: Böhlau.

Plasser, F. and Ulram, P. (1988) Großparteien in der Defensive. Die österreichische Parteien und Wählerlandschaft nach der Nationalratswahl 1986, in F. Plasser and A. Pelinka (eds) *Das österreichische Parteiensystem*, Vienna: Böhlau, pp. 79–102.

Plasser, F. and Ulram, P. (1991) *Staatsbürger oder Untertanen? Politische Kultur Deutschlands, Österreichs und der Schweiz im Vergleich*, Frankfurt a.M.: Peter Lang.

Plasser, F., Ulram, P. and Grausgruber, A. (1992) The decline of '*Lager* mentality' and the new model of electoral competition in Austria, in K.R. Luther and W.C. Müller (eds), *Politics in Austria: Still a Case of Consociationalism?*, London: Frank Cass, pp. 16–44.

Plasser, F., Ulram, P. and Ogris, G. (1996) *Wahlkampf und Wahlentscheidung. Analysen zur Nationalratswahl 1995*, Vienna: Signum.

Plasser, F., Ulram, P. and Seeber, G. (1996) (Dis-)Kontinuitäten und neue Spannungslinien im Wahlverhalten: Trendanalysen 1986–1995, in F. Plasser, P. Ulram and G. Ogris (eds), *Wahlkampf und Wahlentscheidung. Analysen zur Nationalratswahl 1995*, Vienna: Signum, pp. 155–209.

Plasser, F., Ulram, P., Neuwirth, E. and Sommer, F. (1995) *Analyse der Nationalratswahl vom 17. Dezember 1995*, Vienna: Zentrum für angewandte Politikforschung.

Plumyène, J. and Lasierra, R. (1963) *Les fascismes français, 1923–63*, Paris: Seuil.

Portelli, H. (1980) *Le socialisme français tel qu'il est*, Paris: Presses Universitaires de France.

Powell, G.B. (1970) *Social Fragmentation and Political Hostility: An Austrian Case Study*, Stanford: Stanford University Press.

Preston, P. (1985) *The Triumph of Democracy in Spain*, London: Methuen.

Preston, P. (1986) *Las derechas españolas en el siglo XX: Autoritarismo, fascism y golpismo*, Madrid: Sistema.

Pridham, G. (1984) *The New Mediterranean Democracies*, London: Frank Cass.

Puchinger, G. (1969) *Colijn en het Einde van de Coalitie, I, De Geschiedenis van de Kabinetsformaties 1918–1924*, Kampen: Kok.

Puchinger, G. (1979) *Ontmoetingen met Historici*, Zutphen: Terra.

Puchinger, G. (1980) *Colijn en het Einde van de Coalitie, II, De Geschiedenis van de Kabinetsformaties 1925–1929*, Kampen: Kok.

Puchinger, G. (1993a) *Colijn en het Einde van de Coalitie, III, De Geschiedenis van de Kabinetsformaties 1933–1939*, Leiden: Groen.

Puchinger, G. (1993b) Verzuiling??-Ontzuiling??, *Transparant, Orgaan van de Vereniging van Christen-Historici*, **4**, 4–8.

Pugh, M. (1992) *The Making of Modern British Politics*, Oxford: Basil Blackwell.

Pugh, M. (1985) *The Tories and the People*, Oxford: Basil Blackwell.

Pulzer, P. (1962) Western Germany and the three party system, *Political Quarterly*, **33**, 414–26.

Raby, D.L. (1989) *Fascism and Resistance in Portugal: Communists, Liberals and Military Dissidents in the Opposition to Salazar, 1941–74*, Manchester: Manchester University Press.

Rae, D. (1967) *The Political Consequences of Electoral Laws*, New Haven, Conn.: Yale University Press.

Ramírez, M. (1982) El sistema de partidos en España tras las elecciones de 1982, *Revista de Estudios Políticos*, **30**, 7–20.

Ramírez, M. (1988) El sistema de partidos en España, 1977–87, *Revista de Estudios Políticos*, **59**, 7–26.

Ramírez, M. (1991) *El sistema de partidos en España (1931–1990)*, Madrid: Centro de Estudios Constitucionales.

Ramos, I. and Torres, L. (1992) Análise dos Sistemas Eleitorais dos Estados Membros da Comunidade Européia, *Eleições*, **3**, 11–22.

Rémond, R. (1968) *La Droite en France*, Paris: Aubier-Montaigne.

Rémond, R. (1969) *La Vie politique en France depuis 1789*, (2 vols), Paris: Armand Colin.

Rémond, R. (ed.) (1981) *Léon Blum, chef de gouvernement*, Paris: Presses de la FNSP.

Rhodes, M., Heywood, P. and Wright, V. (eds) (1997) *Developments in West European Politics*, Basingstoke: Macmillan.

Richardson, J. (1995) The market for political activism: interest groups as a challenge to political parties, *West European Politics*, **18**, 116–39.

Riedlsperger, M. (1978) *The Lingering Shadow of Nazism: The Austrian Independent Party Movement since 1945*, Boulder, Co.: East European Quarterly.

Rieken, M. (1995) The financing of political parties in France, paper presented to conference on Party Politics in the Year 2000, University of Manchester, 13–15 January.

Roberts, G.K. (1989) Party system change in West Germany: *Land*–Federal linkages, *West European Politics*, **12**, 98–113.

Robinson, R. (1987) From change to continuity: the 1986 Spanish election, *West European Politics*, **10**, 120–24.

Robinson, R.A.H. (1992) The evolution of the Portuguese socialist Party 1973–1986, an international perspective, *Portuguese Studies Review*, **1**, 6–26.

Rogier, L.J. and de Rooy, N. (1953) *In Vrijheid Herboren. Katholiek Nederland 1853–1953*, The Hague: Pax.

Rose, R. and McAllister, I. (1985) *Voters Begin to Choose: From Closed-Class to Open Elections In Britain*, London: Sage.

Rother, B. (1984) Wirtschaftspolitik von Sozialisten in der Krise: Der Fall Portugal, *Politische Vierteljahresschrift*, **25**, 156–68.

Rottman, D. and O'Connell, P. (1982) The changing social structure of Ireland, in F. Litton (ed.), *Unequal Achievement: The Irish Experience, 1957–1982*, Dublin: Institute of Public Administration, pp. 64–88.

Rovati, G. (1996) Il voto dei cattolici alle elezioni politiche del 21 aprile, *Vita e Pensiero*, **79**, 322–34.

Rudzio, W. (1971) Entscheidungszentrum Koalitionsausschuß – Zur Realverfassung Österreichs unter der großen Koalition, *Politische Vierteljahresschrift*, **12**, 87–118.

Sainsbury, D. (1986) The 1985 Swedish election: the conservative upsurge is checked, *West European Politics*, **9**, 293–7.

Sani, G. (1986) Los desplazamientos del electorado: Anatomía del cambio, in J. Linz and J.R. Montero (eds), *Crisis y cambio. Electores y partidos en la España de los años 80*, Madrid: Centro de Estudios Constitucionales, pp. 1–26.

Sani, G. (1996) I verdetti del 21 aprile, *Il Mulino*, **365**, 451–8.

Sani, G. and Montero, J.R. (1986) El espectro político: Izquierda, derecha y centro, in J. Linz and J.R. Montero (eds), *Crisis y cambio. Electores y partidos en la España de los años 80*, Madrid: Centro de Estudios Constitucionales, pp. 155–200.

Sani, G. and Sartori, G. (1983) Polarization, fragmentation and competition in western democracies, in H. Daalder and P. Mair (eds), *Western European Party Systems: Continuity and Change*, London: Sage, pp. 307–40.

Santos, B. de Sousa (1984) A Crise e a Reconstituição do Estado em Portugal (1974–1984), *Revista Crítica de Ciências Sociais*, **14**, 7–27.

Särlvik, B. (1980) European elections: Sweden, *West European Politics*, **3**, 253–6.

Sartori, G. (1968) Political development and political engineering, *Public Policy*, **17**, 261–98.

Sartori, G. (1969) From the sociology of politics to political sociology, in S.M. Lipset (ed.), *Politics and the Social Sciences*, New York: Oxford University Press, pp. 65–100.

Sartori, G. (1976) *Parties and Party Systems: A Framework for Analysis, Volume I*, Cambridge: Cambridge University Press.

Sartori, G. (1994) *Comparative Constitutional Engineering: An Inquiry Into Structures, Incentives and Outcomes*, Basingstoke: Macmillan.

Scalisi, P. (1996) La dissoluzione delle strutture organizzative di base dei partiti, *Polis*, **10**, 221–42.

Schedler, A. (1996) Anti-political-establishment parties, *Party Politics*, **2**, 291–312.

Scheuch, E. and Scheuch, U. (1992) *Cliquen, Klüngel und Karrieren*, Reinbek: Rowohlt.

Schmitt, H. (1989) On party attachment in Western Europe and the utility of the Eurobarometer data, *West European Politics*, **12**, 122–39.

Schwartzman, K. (1989) *The Social Origins of Democratic Collapse: The First Portuguese Republic In the Global Economy*, Kansas: Kansas University Press.

Scoppola, P. (1991) *La repubblica dei partiti*, Bologna: Il Mulino.

Secher, H. (1960) Representative democracy or chamber state?: the ambiguous role of interest groups in Austrian politics, *Western Political Quarterly*, **13**, 890–909.

Share, D. (1989) *Dilemmas of Social Democracy: The Spanish Socialist Workers Party in the 1980s*, New York: Greenwood.

Shaw, E. (1994) *The Changing Labour Party Since 1979*, Oxford: Clarendon Press.

Sickinger, H. (1995) *Politikfinanzierung in Österreich – ein Handbuch*, Vienna: Thaur.

Simon, W.B. (1957) *The Political Parties of Austria*, New York: Columbia University, unpublished PhD.

Sinnott, R. (1984) Interpretations of the Irish party system, *European Journal of Political Research*, **12**, 289–307.

Sinnott, R. (1986) Party differences and spatial representation: the Irish case, *British Journal of Political Science*, **16**, 217–41.

Sinnott, R. (1995) *Irish Voters Decide: Voting Behaviour in Elections and Referendums since 1918*, Manchester: Manchester University Press.

Smith, G. (1976) West Germany and the politics of centrality, *Government and Opposition*, **11**, 387–407.

Smith, G. (1979) Western European party systems: on the trail of a typology, *West European Politics*, **2**, 128–42.

Smith, G. (1989a) A system perspective on party system change, *Journal of Theoretical Politics*, **1**, 349–63

Smith, G. (1989b) Core persistence: change and the 'People's Party', in P. Mair and G. Smith (eds), *Understanding Party System Change in Western Europe*, London: Frank Cass, pp. 157–68. Originally a special edition of *West European Politics*, **12**.

Smith, G. (1989c) *Politics in Western Europe*, 5th edn, Aldershot: Gower.

Smith, G. (1990) Stages of European development: electoral change and system adaptation, in D.W. Urwin and W.E. Paterson (eds), *Politics in Western Europe Today: Perspectives, Policies and Problems since 1980*, London: Longman, pp. 251–69.

Smith, G. (1993) Dimensions of change in the German party system, in S. Padgett (ed.), *Parties and Party Systems in the New Germany*, Aldershot: Dartmouth/Association for the Study of German Politics, pp. 87–101.

Smith, J. and McLean, I. (1994) The poll tax and the electoral register, in A. Heath, R. Jowell and J. Curtice (eds), *Labour's Last Chance?*, Aldershot: Dartmouth, pp. 229–53.

Smith, M.J. (1994) Understanding the politics of 'catch-up': the modernization of the Labour Party, *Political Studies*, **42**, 708–15.

Soares, M. (1976) *Portugal: Que Revoluçao? Diálogo com Dominique Poudrin*, Lisbon: Perspectivas e Realidades.

Søe, C. (1993) Unity and victory for the German liberals: little party, what now?, in R. Dalton (ed.), *The New Germany Votes*, Oxford: Berg, pp. 99–134.

Stäuber, R. (1974) *Der Verband der Unabhängigen (VdU) und die Freiheitliche Partei Österreichs (FPÖ). Eine Untersuchung über die Probleme des Deutschnationalismus als Einigungsfaktor einer politischen Partei in Österreich seit 1945*, St. Gallen: Kolb.

Stiefbold, R. (1975) Elites and elections in a fragmented political system, in R. Wildenmann (ed.), *Sozialwissenschaftliches Jahrbuch für Politik*, Munich: Günther Olzog Verlag, pp. 119–227.

Stock, M-J. (1989a) *Elites, Facções e Conflito Intra-Partidário. O PPD/PSD e o Processo Político Português de 1974 a 1985*, unpublished PhD thesis, Universidade de Évora.

Stock, M-J. (1989b) O centrismo político e os partidos do poder em Portugal, in M.B. Coelho (ed.), *Portugal: O Sistema Político e Costitucional*, Lisbon: Instituto de Ciéncias Sociais, pp. 147–79.

Streek, H.J. van de, ten Napel, H.-M. and Zwart, R.S. (eds) (1997) *De strijd om de Ether. Christelijke Partijen en de Inrichting van het Radio- en Televisiebestel*. The Hague: Sdu.

Sturm, R. (1993) The territorial dimension of the new party system, in S. Padgett (ed.), *Parties and Party Systems in the New Germany*, Aldershot: Dartmouth/Association for the Study of German Politics, pp. 103–25.

Suárez, A. (1988) Consideraciones sobre la transición española, *Cuenta y Razón*, **41**, 13–22.

Taal, G. (1980) *Liberalen en Radicalen in Nederland (1872–1901)*, The Hague: Nÿjhoff.

Tácito (1975) Madrid: Ibérico Europeo de Ediciones.

Taggart, P. and Widfeldt, A. (1993) 1990s Flash party organisation: the case of new democracy in Sweden. Paper presented at the Political Studies Association of the UK Annual Conference, University of Leicester, 20–22 April.

Tálos, E., Dachs, H. and Hanisch, E. (1995) *Handbuch des politischen Systems Österreichs Erste Republik 1918–1933*, Vienna: Manz.

Ten Napel, H.-M. (1992) *'Een Eigen Weg'. De Totstandkoming van het CDA (1952–1980)*, Kampen: Kok.

Ten Napel, H.-M. (1995) Rudolphus (Ruud) Lubbers, in D. Wilsford (ed.), *Political Leaders of Contemporary Western Europe: A Biographical Dictionary*, Westport, CT: Greenwood Press, pp. 279–87.

Thomas, H. (1986) *The Spanish Civil War*, 3rd edn, London: Penguin.

Topf, R. (1994) Party manifestos, in A. Heath, R. Jowell and J. Curtice (eds), *Labour's Last Chance?*, Aldershot: Dartmouth, pp. 149–71.

Torcal, M. and Chhibber, P. (1995) Elites, cleavages y sistema de partidos en una democracia consilidada: España (1986–92), *Revista Española de Investigaciones Sociológicas*, **69**, 7–37.

Tromp, B. (1989) Party strategies and system change in the Netherlands, *West European Politics*, **12**, 82–97.

Tudesq, A.-J. (1964) *Les grands notables en France, 1840–49: étude historique d'une psychologie sociale*, Paris: Presses Universitaires de France.

Ulram, P. (1990) *Hegemonie und Erosion: Politische Kultur und politischer Wandel in Österreich*, Vienna: Böhlau.

Ulram, P. (1997) Politische Kultur der Bevölkerung, in H. Dachs *et. al.* (eds), *Handbuch des politischen Systems Österreichs. Die zweite Republik*, 3rd edn, Vienna: Manz, pp. 514–25.

Urwin, D. (1987) Do resources decide, but votes count – in the end? A review of some recent Norwegian literature, *West European Politics*, **9**, 297–315.

Vallés, J. (1994) The Spanish general election of 1993, *Electoral Studies*, **13**, 87–91.

Van Gunsteren, H. and Andeweg, R.B. (1994) *Het Grote Ongenoegen. Over de Kloof tussen Burgers en Politiek*, Haarlem: Aramith.

Van Outrive, L. (1996) The political role of the judiciary: the Belgian case, *Res Publica*, **38**, 371–84.

Van Schendelen, M.P.C.M. (1984) *Consociationalism, Pillarization and Conflict-Management in the Low Countries*, Special Issue of *Acta Politica*.

Van Spanning, H. (1988) *De Christelijk-Historische Unie (1908–1980) Enige Hoofdlijnen uit haar Geschiedenis*, PhD, University of Leiden.

Verzichelli, L. (1996) I gruppi parlamentari dopo il 1994. Fluidità e riaggregazioni, *Rivista Italiana di Scienza Politica*, **26**, 391–413.

Vidigal, L. (1988) *Cidadania, Caciquismo e Poder*, Lisbon: Livros Horizonte.

Vinen, R. (1993) The *Parti Républicain de la Liberté* and the reconstruction of French conservatism, 1944–51, *French History*, **7**, 183–204.

Vinen, R. (1995) *Bourgeois Politics in France, 1945–51*, Cambridge: Cambridge University Press.

Wald, K.D. (1983) *Crosses on the Ballot: Patterns of British Voter Alignment Since 1885*, Princeton, NJ: Princeton University Press.

Wandruszka, A. (1954) Österreichs politische Struktur: Die Entwicklung der Parteien und politischen Bewegungen, in H. Benedikt (ed.), *Geschichte der Republik Österreich*, Vienna: Verlag für Gesellschaft und Politik, pp. 289–485.

Ware, A. (1987) *Citizens, Parties and the State: A Reappraisal*, Cambridge: Polity Press.

Ware, A. (1996) *Political Parties and Party Systems*, Oxford: Oxford University Press.

Webb, P.D. (1992a) Election campaigning, organisational transformation and the professionalisation of the British Labour Party, *European Journal of Political Research*, **21**, 266–88.

Webb, P.D. (1992b) *Trade Unions and the British Electorate*, Aldershot: Dartmouth.

Webb, P.D. (1993) The Labour Party, the market and the electorate: a study in social democratic adaptation, in J.S. Sheldrake and P.D. Webb (eds), *State and Market: Aspects of Modern European Development*, Aldershot: Dartmouth, pp. 108–25.

Webb, P.D. (1994) Party organizational change in Britain: the iron law of centralization?, in R.S. Katz and P. Mair (eds), *How Parties Organize: Change and Adaptation in Party Organizations in Western Democracies*, London: Sage, pp. 109–33.

Webber, D. (1992) Kohl's *Wendepolitik* after a decade, *German Politics*, **1**, 149–80.

von Weizsäcker, R. (1992) *Richard von Weizsäcker im Gespräch mit Gunter Hofmann and Werner Perger*, Frankfurt/Main: von Eichorn.

Wettig, G. (1975) *Die sowjetische Portugal-Politik (1974–1975)*, Cologne: Berichte des Bundesinstituts für Ostwissenschaftliche und Internationale Studies, no. 60.

Wheeler, D.L. (1978) *Republican Portugal: A Political History, 1910–1926*, Madison: University of Wisconsin Press.

Whiteley, P., Seyd, P. and Richardson, J. (1994) *True Blues: The Politics of Conservative Party Membership*, Oxford: Clarendon Press.

Whiteman, D. (1990) The progress and potential of the Green Party in Ireland, *Irish Political Studies*, **5**, 45–58.

Whyte, J. (1974) Ireland: politics without social bases, in Richard Rose (ed.), *Electoral Behaviour: A Comparative Handbook*, New York: Free Press, pp. 619–51.

Whyte, J. (1980) *Church and State in Modern Ireland, 1923–1979*, Dublin: Gill and Macmillan.

Wiarda, H. (1977) *Corporatism and Development: The Portuguese Experience*, Amherst: University of Massachusetts Press.

Wickham-Jones, M. (1995) Recasting social democracy: a comment on Hay and Smith, *Political Studies*, **43**, 698–702.

Wiesendahl, E. (1990) Der Marsch aus den Institutionen, *Aus Politik und Zeitgeschichte*, **B21**.

Wildenmann, R. (1989) *Volksparteien. Ratlosen Riesen?*, Baden-Baden: Nomos.

Williams, P. (1964) *Crisis and Compromise: The Politics of the Fourth French Republic*, London: Longman.

Wilson, F. (1982) *French Political Parties Under the Fifth Republic*, New York: Praeger.

Witte, E., Craeybeckx, J. and Govaert, S. (transl.) (1987) *Belgique politique de 1830 à nos jours. Les tensions d'une démocratie bourgeoise*, Brussels: Labor.

Wolinetz, S.B. (1988) The Netherlands: continuity and change in a fragmented party system, in S.B. Wolinetz (ed.), *Parties and Party Systems in Liberal Democracies*, London: Routledge, pp. 130–58.

Wolinetz, S.B. (1991) Party system change: the catch-all thesis revisited, *West European Politics*, **14**, 113–28.

Wolinetz, S.B. (1993) Reconstructing Dutch social democracy, *West European Politics*, **16**, 97–111.

Wolinetz, S.B. (ed.) (1997) *Party Systems*, Aldershot: Ashgate.

Worre, T. (1980) Class parties and class voting in the Scandinavian countries, *Scandinavian Political Studies*, **3**, 299–320.

Ysmal, C. (1989) *Les Partis politiques sous la Cinquième République*, Paris: Montchrestien.

Zeldin, T. (1958) *The Political System of Napoleon III*, London: Macmillan.

Zuckerman, A.S. (1982) New approaches to political cleavage: a theoretical introduction, *Comparative Political Studies*, **15**, 131–44.

Index

abortion   36, 37, 156, 198–9, 202
agency   257, 260, 261, 275
Aguiar, J.   251, 254
Alford index   132, 149, 152, 275
alignment, electoral   8, 16, 18, 21, 113,
     116, 208, 261, 262, 268
anti-party sentiment   57, 68, 76, 95,
     109–11, 113, 115, 117, 158, 165,
     171, 205, 256, 263, 267, 270
anti-system parties/leagues   3, 51–2, 74,
     79, 91, 92, 99, 100, 121, 123,
     139–40, 218
Arter, D.   2, 262, 265, 270
atomized electorate   165, 179, 256, 275
Austria   2, 118–42, 264, 269
   civil war   121
   cleavages
      centre–periphery (including Pan-
         German and national/ethnic)
         119, 120, 129
      class   119, 123, 129, 130, 132–3
      post-material   130
      regime type   129
      religion   119–20, 123, 129, 130,
         132–3
      urban–rural   120
   coalition   118, 120, 122, 125, 129,
      134–41 passim
   consociationalism   118, 124, 141
   'core elements'   126–138
      government/opposition relations   134–6
      ideological distance   128–30
      movements in party support   130–4
      party number and size   126–8
      site of decisive encounters   137–8
   'cultural' variables   123–6
   electoral system   122, 126, 137
   federalism   122–3
   institutional variables   122–3
   Lager   119–26 passim, 128, 129, 130,
      131, 137, 138, 140
   parties
      christian democratic (ÖVP)   118, 119,
         121, 123–41 passim, 264, 269

Communist (KPÖ)   119, 120, 121,
     124, 135, 136
Green   122, 127, 129, 130, 132, 133,
     135, 136, 139, 140, 269
liberal (FPÖ)   118, 122, 124, 126,
     127, 128, 129, 130, 132–41
     passim, 260, 269
Liberal (Lif)   122, 127, 129, 133, 135,
     136, 139, 140, 269
Socialist (SPÖ)   118, 119, 121,
     123–41 passim, 264, 269
party and party system emergence   118–
     21
party system structure
   four-party   128
   moderate pluralism   118, 139
   polarized pluralism   139–140
   predominant 118, 139
   two-party 118, 121, 128, 139
pillarization/depillarization   123–5,
     130–2, 140
politicians
   Figl, L.   134, 135
   Haider, J.   118, 124, 129, 132, 134,
      129, 140–1, 260
   Kreisky, B.   131–2, 135
   Steger, N.   124, 140
post-war rebirth of party system   121–2
Proporz   125, 130
social partnership   125–6, 130, 141

Bacalhau, M.   249
Bartolini, S.   48
Belgium   2, 6, 45, 183–206, 265, 271
   alternation   188
   cleavages
      centre–periphery   184, 186–90, 196,
         201, 202, 205–6
      class   183, 184, 186, 188–9, 196,
         197, 200, 203
      immigration   199, 203
      post-material   200, 203
   clientelism   191–2, 201
   coalition   188, 192, 197, 204–5

contextual variables 190–3
Egmont pact 199–200
electoral system 183, 188, 189, 190
first expansion wave 197–9
historical background 186–90
 cleavage structure 186–8
 three-phase party system
  formation 188–90
King's Question 195–6
parties
 Catholic 183, 184, 185, 189, 191,
  193, 194, 198–205 *passim*
 communist 183, 185, 189, 195
 extreme right 184–5, 199, 200, 203,
  205
 Flemish 184, 185, 190, 195, 196,
  197, 198, 199, 201, 202
 Francophone 184, 185, 196, 197,
  198, 199, 201, 203
 Green 184, 185, 200, 201, 202, 203,
  205
 liberal 183, 184, 185, 194, 195, 198,
  201, 202, 203, 204, 205
 socialist 183, 185, 187, 189, 193–5,
  197, 198, 200, 201–3, 205
partyocracy 191–3
party system structure
 fragmentation 184–6, 203
 three-party 183–4
 two-and-a-half party 183–4, 193
 two-party 183–4, 193
pillarization 188–9, 191, 194, 198, 203
politicians
 Cools, A. 205
 Dehaene, J.-L. 201, 204
 Verhofstadt, G. 201, 205
resurrection of pre-war party system,
 1944–60 193–6
'School War' 196
second expansion wave 199–203
territory *see* cleavages, centre–periphery
Berglund, S. and Lindström, L. 145–6,
 153, 159, 160
Bergstöm, H 146, 159
bipolarism 48, 60, 64, 68, 75, 78, 79,
 84–6, 88, 89, 91–4, 139, 144, 161,
 207, 272, 275
blackmail potential 5, 139
blocs 28, 48, 57, 88, 91, 93, 109, 144,
 147, 150, 162, 189, 219, 238, 241,
 247–8, 249, 251, 253, 256, 257,
 258, 259, 263, 265, 267–74 *passim*
Blondel, J. 6, 27, 32, 183–4
bourgeois parties 97–8, 102, 107, 128,
 144, 150, 161, 229, 269–70
Brand, J. 19
Britain 2, 6, 8–29, 41, 45, 105, 163, 210,
 260, 265
 alternation 8, 15, 27–8
 change and adaptation 16–27

adaptation of party organization 24–7
adaptation of policy and ideology 22–4
electoral change 20–22
cleavages
 class 8, 10–11, 15
 ethnic (centre–periphery/national) 18
 imperialism 11
 public/private 17–18
 religion 10–11
coalition 12, 24
Conservative dominance 15, 19–20,
 28–9, 272
contextual factors 12–14
electoral reform 29
electoral system 8, 10, 12–14, 20, 28
historical background 10–12
parties
 Conservative 8–11, 13–20 *passim*,
  22–29 *passim*, 265, 268
 Labour 8–20, 22, 23, 24, 25, 27, 28,
  29, 264
 Liberal/Liberal Democrat 9–14 *passim*,
  18, 20, 22, 23, 24, 26, 27, 28,
  29
 Plaid Cymru 13
 Scottish National Party 13, 18, 29
party system structure
 suppressed two-and-a-half party 27–9
 two-party 8, 10, 15–19 *passim*, 27–9
politicians
 Attlee, C. 9, 15
 Bevin, E. 15
 Blair, T. 9, 24, 29
 Butler, R.A.B. 16, 21
 Churchill, W. 9, 14, 15
 Cook, R. 29
 Disraeli, B. 11
 Gaitskell, H. 16
 Gladstone, W.E. 11
 Kinnock, N. 23, 24
 MacDonald, R. 12
 Major, J. 9, 22–3
 Mandelson, P 24
 Smith, J. 24
 Thatcher, M. 9, 22, 268
post-war party system 14–16
referendums
 electoral reform 29
 Scotland 8, 14, 18, 29 n.2, 265
 Wales 8, 14, 18, 29 n.2, 263

cadre party 25, 53, 119, 124
Camiller, P. 229
cartel 6, 14, 40, 44, 52, 63, 82, 91, 241,
 260
catch-all thesis/party 4, 5, 34, 38, 99,
 102, 230, 240, 241, 260, 261
Catholicism *see* cleavages, religion *under individual countries*

caucus party 25, 138, 177
centre party 12, 56, 59, 72, 79, 84–7,
    92–3, 97–8, 102, 105, 139, 143–50,
    152–8, 160, 161, 162, 172, 207,
    218, 219, 220, 221, 226, 240,
    247–8, 250, 269, 275–6
Charlot, J. 48
christian democratic parties 2, 262, 264–5
cleavages 1, 258–9, 265, 271, 272
    see also under individual countries
clientelism 276
coalition 256, 258, 259, 260, 263–73 *pas-
    sim*
    see also under individual countries
Cold War 2, 56, 65, 99, 195
communist parties 259, 270, 271
    see also parties, communist *under individual
        countries*
competition
    centrifugal 5, 74, 92, 94, 139–40, 183,
        205–6, 275
    centripetal 5, 27–8, 71, 75, 92–4, 108,
        212, 222, 262, 266, 275–6
    for government 94, 134, 141, 161–2,
        255–7, 265, 270, 272, 273, 274
    structures of 267
consociationalism 118, 124, 141, 177,
    212
core party/parties 8, 65–70, 107–8,
    112–17 *passim*, 181, 194, 203–4,
    268–71, 273
corruption 44, 68, 78, 110–11, 113, 131,
    205, 228–9, 266, 274

Dahl, R. 6, 137
Daniels, P. 263, 265
Denmark 2, 6, 143–9 *passim*, 158, 162
DeWinter, L. 265, 268
dominant party *see* predominant party sys-
    tem
Dumont, P. 265, 268
Duverger, M. 4, 6, 119, 124, 183

Eastern Europe 3, 62, 77, 80, 260
electoral-professional party 24, 171, 260,
    277
electoral system 3, 267
    see also under individual countries
electoral volatility 5, 257–9, 262, 278
Ersson, S. 257, 270
Esping-Andersen, G. 147, 148–9
Etzioni, A. 179
Europe 3, 19, 22, 23, 24, 36, 37, 64, 67,
    68, 69, 130, 146, 157–8, 170, 206,
    239, 243, 244, 247–8, 251–2, 273
external core party 269–70, 276
extreme party exclusion 141, 204, 271,
    276

Farneti, P. 71, 75

Farrell, D. 260, 271
Finland 146, 148, 153
Fisher, J. 260, 272
five-party system 143, 276
'flash' parties 3, 55, 159, 245, 276
France 2, 6, 36, 48–70, 210, 259, 264,
    269, 271
    absorptive party system 53–3, 70
    alternation 52, 54, 55, 56
    cleavages
        centre–periphery 50
        class 49–50, 65
        nationalism 51, 55, 68
            Algerian 56
        religion 50, 61, 65
        urban/rural 50, 65
    coalitions 48, 52, 54–6, 64, 69
        National Union/Republican Concentra-
            tion 52
    electoral system 53, 54, 58, 59, 60, 61,
        67–8
    Fifth Republic 57–8
    foundations 53–4
    Fourth Republic 54–7
    genesis 48–53
    leagues 51–2, 55
    parties
        christian democratic 51, 55, 57–58,
            61, 63, 64, 65
        communist 51–9, 61–3, 66, 67, 68,
            69, 70, 269
        Front National 52, 58, 59, 60, 65,
            67, 68, 69, 266, 269
        Gaullist 55, 56, 57, 58, 61, 63, 64,
            65, 66, 67; *see also* RPR
        green 59, 65, 66, 67, 68, 69
        Poujadist 55
        Socialist Party 57–62 *passim*, 66, 67,
            68, 69; *see also* SFIO
        Radicals 48, 51, 52, 53, 54, 55, 57,
            58, 66
        Republican 58, 63, 66
        RPR 36, 57, 58, 60, 63, 64, 66, 70
        SFIO 51–7 *passim*, 59, 66
        UDF 36, 57, 58, 60, 63, 64, 65, 66,
            70
    party system structure
        bipolar (dualist) 48, 57
        fluid 48, 54
        multi-party 48, 58, 65
        polarized 48, 65
        predominant 48
    party system today 58–64
    politicians
        Balladur, E. 64, 66
        Chaban-Delmas, J. 63, 66
        Chevènement, J.-P. 61, 69
        Chirac, J. 57, 58, 60, 63, 66, 68
        Defferre, G. 61
        de Gaulle, C. 55–7 *passim*, 60, 63

Giscard d'Éstaing, V. 57, 60, 63
Guèsde, J. 51
Hue, R. 63, 68–9
Jaurès, J. 51
Jospin, L. 58, 60, 66, 68, 69
Le Pen, J.M. 69
Marchais, G. 63
Mitterrand, F. 57–8, 60–3 *passim*
Poincaré, R. 52
Pompidou, G.J.R. 57, 60, 63, 66
Rocard, M. 61, 66
Voynet, D. 69
Popular Front 51, 52
referendums 57, 68
republicanism 49–52 *passim*, 61
territory
  Algeria 56–7
  Alsace 50
  Basque country 50
  Brittany 50, 61

Galli, G. 71, 75
Garvin, T. 34
Germany 2, 6, 45, 96–117, 184, 239,
  259, 264, 265–6, 271
  alternation 101, 104, 109–110
  anti-party sentiment 109–11, 113, 115,
    117
  cleavages
    class 105–7, 113
    religion 105–7, 113
  coalition 98–104 *passim*, 108–9,
    115–16
  contextual variables 99–102
  electoral system 99–100
  historical background 97–9
  Machtmonopol 110, 114
  modernization trap 109–10
  parties
    CDU 110, 115–16
    CDU/CSU 96, 100, 101, 102, 103,
      104, 106–16 *passim*, 271
    CSU 97
    far right 111, 115, 271
    Liberal (FDP) 97, 100, 101, 102, 103,
      104, 108, 111, 112, 114, 115,
      266
    Greens 97, 100, 103, 108, 109, 111,
      115, 116, 267, 271
    SED 97
    SPD 97, 100–16 *passim*, 152, 271
  party system, 1949–82 102–8
  party system structure
    balanced 108
    bifurcated 97, 116
    fluid 97
    four-party 116
    three-party 116
    two-and-a-half party 97, 107–9
    two-bloc 109

Weimar 96–7
politicians
  Adenauer, K. 103, 104
  Barschel, U. 110–11
  Brandt, W. 103, 104
  Genscher, H.-D. 114
  Gerhardt, W. 114
  Kinkel, K. 114
  Kohl, H. 104, 114, 117
  Lafontaine, O. 114
  Merkel, A. 114
  Scharping, R. 114
  Schäuble, W. 114
  Schmidt, H. 104
  Thierse, A. 114
  von Weizsäcker, R. 113
politics of centrality 97, 101, 108
post-unification change and
    adaptation 112–16
pre-unification change and
    adaptation 109–12
territory, bifurcated party system 97,
  116
Giddens, A. 23
Gilljam, M. and Holmberg, S. 149, 157,
  160
Goguel, F. 49
Greece 234, 271
green parties 259, 260, 266, 267, 269,
  270, 271
  see also parties, green *under individual*
    countries
Gunther, R. 217

Hanley, D. 269
Hardiman, N. and Whelan, C.T. 45
Harmel, R. 267
Heimer, F.W. 250, 254
Hopkin, J. 262

ideology 5, 22–4, 28, 35, 48, 50, 51, 52,
  54, 59, 61, 62, 63, 64, 65, 71, 75,
  80, 90, 91, 94, 97, 99, 101, 102,
  103, 104, 105, 106, 108, 109, 110,
  119, 121, 125, 128–31, 133, 136,
  140, 148, 156, 166, 171–2, 179,
  181, 190, 195, 198, 199, 201, 207,
  213, 217–19, 221, 222, 223, 226,
  227, 228, 230, 240, 241, 243, 244,
  245, 247, 250, 252, 256–62, 272,
  273, 274
Ireland 2, 6, 11, 30–47, 184, 260, 264–6
  passim, 270–1
  alternation 39, 47
  Anglo-Irish Treaty 30
  change and adaptation 36–44
  civil war 30, 41
  cleavages
    centre–periphery 33–4
    class 32–8

national 33, 35, 36
religion 33, 35, 37, 45
urban–rural 34, 45
coalition 32, 39–40, 47
electoral system 32
historical context 31–2
IRA 31, 42
parties
Democratic Left 31, 33, 39, 40, 41, 42
Fianna Fáil 30–6, 38–43, 45, 46, 47, 264, 265, 270–1
Fine Gael 31–6 *passim*, 38–43 *passim*, 46, 264, 265, 270–1
Greens 31, 41
Labour 30, 32–6, 38–43, 45, 46, 265, 270–1
Progressive Democrats 31, 33, 38, 39, 40, 41, 47, 271
Sinn Féin 30, 31, 34, 40, 47
Workers' Party 31, 38, 39, 40, 41, 42
party system structure
'Mediterranean' 36
moderate pluralist 46
multi-party 46
predominant 32, 46
two-and-a-half party 32, 46
politicians
Burke, R. 44
Haughey, C. 33, 41, 44
McAleese, M. 47 n.2
O'Malley, D. 40–1
Robinson, M. 45, 47
referendums 37, 45, 47 n.1
territory, N. Ireland 30, 36, 40, 47 n.2
Italy 2, 6, 71–95, 205, 256, 259, 260, 263, 264, 265, 266, 271
alternation 71, 86, 94
Bicameral Constitutional Committee 94
change and adaptation 75–81
cleavages 74, 76
class 80
religion 80, 93
regional 77, 80, 85, 86, 88, 92
coalition 71, 72, 74, 75, 78, 83, 84, 87, 90–1, 93, 94, 95
election (1994) 82–5
election (1996) 85–9
electoral alliances
Freedom Pole 79, 82, 83, 84, 86, 87, 88, 89, 93
Olive Tree 83, 85–91 *passim*, 93
Good Government Pole 83–4, 87
Progressives 78, 79, 82, 83, 84, 85
electoral system 72, 76,78, 79, 81, 84, 89, 90, 93, 94
electorate 80–1
new party system 89–93
number of parties 90–1
ideological distance 91

competition dynamics 91–3
parties ('First Republic')
Christian democratic (DC) 71–81, 85, 91, 264, 269
Communist (PCI) 71, 72, 73, 74, 75, 77, 80, 81, 87, 91, 269
Liberal (PLI) 72, 73, 79, 81
Neo-Fascist (MSI) 72, 73, 74, 78, 79, 81, 83, 84, 91
Proletarian Democracy 73, 77, 266
Radicals 73, 266
Republican (PRI) 72, 73, 79, 81, 87
Social Democratic (PSDI) 72, 73, 79, 81
Socialist (PSI) 73, 75, 76, 78, 79, 84
parties ('Second Republic')
christian democratic 78, 83, 86, 87
(CDU), 78, 82, 83, 86, 87 (CCD), 78 (CS), 78, 82–7 passim (PPI)
Communist Refoundation 77, 82–7 passim, 91, 92, 271
Democratic Left (PDS) 77, 78, 81, 82, 83, 84, 87, 91, 93, 266
Forza Italia 78, 79, 81, 82, 83, 84, 86, 91, 92, 93, 266
Greens 82, 83, 84, 266
National Alliance (AN) 78, 79, 81, 82, 83, 84, 86, 91, 92, 93, 266
Neo-Fascist (MSFT) 79, 86, 87, 91, 92
Network/Rete 78, 82, 84, 266
Northern League (LN) 77, 79, 81–9, 91, 92, 92, 265, 266
party landscape 77–9
party system structure
bipolar 75, 78, 79, 84, 85, 86, 88, 89, 91–4
tripolar 83–4, 86, 88
politicians
Berlusconi, S. 5, 78, 79, 83, 91, 93, 95
Bianco, G. 78
Bossi, U. 260
Buttiglione, R. 78
Craxi, B. 78
Dini, L. 77, 85, 87, 95
Fini, G. 79
Occhetto, A. 77
Orlando, L. 78
Prodi, R. 78, 85, 87, 91, 94, 95
Segni, M. 78
post-war party system, 1945–92 72–5
subculture 75, 78, 80
territory 77, 87, 92
see also Northern League

Jeffery, C. 266, 271

Kelly, P. 25–6
King, A. 19, 272

Kirchheimer, O. 4, 6, 261, 275
Koole, R. 171

labour parties *see* socialist parties
Lane, J.-E. 1, 257, 270
Laver, M. 35–6
Lijphart, A. 6, 163, 170, 181, 203
Linz, J. 218–9
Lipset S.M. and Rokkan S. 3, 4, 6, 33–4,
    49, 96, 98, 105–7, 113, 118–19,
    146, 258, 259

Machin, H. 48
MacIntyre, A. 179
Magone, J. 262, 263
Mair, P. 5–7, 35, 134, 135, 141, 154,
    182, 255, 257–9, 274, 278
Maor, M. 28
Maraval, J. 217, 218, 219
Martins, H. 234
mass media 13, 21, 37, 41, 42, 79–81,
    125, 130, 131, 165, 187, 192, 218,
    260, 266
mass (integration) party 118–19, 124,
    171, 260, 262, 268, 275, 276
modern cadre party 174, 260
Montero, J.R. 223
Mouzelis, N. 232
Müller, W. 267

Netherlands, the 2, 6, 45, 163–82, 262,
    264, 265, 271–2
  anti-establishment sentiment 165
  breakthrough strategy 163, 164, 171,
    176, 180
  Calvinism 167
  change and adaptation 176–80
  cleavages
    class 164, 169, 172, 175, 179–80,
        182
    religion 164–5, 169, 172, 175,
        179–80, 182
  coalition 168 ('the'), 170, 172, 177–8
        (Roman-Red), 179–80 (purple)
  consensus democracy 163, 170, 177,
        181
  contextual variables 169–71
  depillarization 165, 176, 178, 179
  Dutch Reformed Church 167
  electoral system 169–70
  historical background 164–9
  individualization 165, 179
  parties
    Anti-Revolutionary (ARP) 166, 167,
        168, 169, 172, 175–7
    Catholic People's (KVP) 171–2, 176,
        265
    Christian Democratic Association
        176–82 *passim*, 264, 265, 266

Christian Historical Union 167, 168,
    169, 172, 176–7
Communist 169, 182
Democrats '66 175, 176, 177, 178,
    180, 182, 260, 266, 272
Green Left 182
Labour (PvdA) 172, 176–81 *passim*,
    264, 266
liberal 166, 167, 168, 170, 176–7,
    179
Pacifist Socialist 169, 175, 182
People's Party for Freedom and Democ-
    racy (VVD) 171, 175, 177, 178,
    179, 180, 266
radical (PPR) 175, 177, 182
party system structure
  multi-dimensional 169, 172, 182
  one-dimensional 163, 171
  polarized 175
  re-dichotomization 164
  two-party 163, 171
pillarization 164–5, 171, 176
plural society 163–4, 169
politicians
  Bolkestein, F. 178
  Brinkman, E. 178
  Colijn, H. 168, 170
  Den Uyl, F.M. 175, 177
  De Savornin Lohman, A.F. 167, 168
  Domela Nieuwenhuis, F. 168
  Drees, W. 172, 175, 178
  Kok, W. 170, 175, 178
  Kuyper, A. 167, 168
  Lubbers, R. 175, 177, 178
  Oud, P.J. 171
  Schaepman, H.J.A.M. 167, 168
  Thorbeke, J.R. 166
  Troelstra, P.S.A. 168
  van Prinster, G. Groen 166, 71
post-war party system 171–5
sub-cultures 165–6, 176
new parties 3, 11, 31–2, 40, 41, 44, 57,
    71, 76–7, 79, 95, 97, 118, 123,
    133, 141, 143, 145, 150, 151, 153,
    155, 157, 158, 161, 162, 181,
    199–200, 222, 235, 240, 244,
    256–7, 260, 261, 263, 266–8, 269,
    271
Norton, P. 19
Norway 2, 6, 143–9 *passim*, 153, 156,
    158, 162

Panebianco, A. 4, 230
Pedersen index 6, 20, 40–1, 147–8, 277
Pennings, P. 1, 259
people's party 6, 145, 148–9, 256, 261–9
    passim, 273, 277
peripheral party/parties 65, 67–8,
    269–70, 277
Pizzorno, A. 261

plebiscitary democracy   256, 263, 277
polarization   5, 28, 48, 52, 59, 65, 71, 74,
       91, 96–7, 99, 139, 163, 184, 207,
       211, 219, 256, 257
political architecture   257, 274
Portugal   2, 3, 232–54, 263, 264, 272
   alternation   233 (*rotativismo*), 239
   civil war   233
   cleavages
       class   246
       religion   245–6
       territorial   245–6
   clientelism   232–3, 242, 251
   coalitions   237, 241, 243, 245, 247,
       248, 253
   contextual variables   238–47
   electoral system   239, 253
   Europe   243, 244, 247, 248, 251–2
   historical background   232–8
   International Monetary Fund (IMF)   237,
       247
   1980s   247–51
   1990s   251–3
   parties
       communist   235–40 *passim*, 242–3,
           245, 246, 248–53 *passim*
       Democratic Alliance (AD)   236, 237,
           238, 244, 245, 247
       Democratic Renewal Party
           (PRD)   236, 245, 247–8, 249,
           253
       Republican Socialist Front (FRS)   236,
           238
       Social Democratic Centre (CDS)/People's
           Party   236–7, 240, 244–53
           passim
       Social Democratic Party (PPD-
           PSD)   235–42 *passim*, 245–54
           passim
       Socialist (PS)   235–41 *passim*, 245–54
           passim
   party system structure
       fluid, ultra-stable   236, 238–9, 244–5
       four-party   238, 252
       Left–Right structure   237
       predominant   242, 252
       two-party   233, 239, 252
       two bloc   238
   personalism   237, 254
   politicians
       Caetano, M.   243, 244
       Carneiro, F. Sá   241, 247
       Cavaco Silva, A.   237, 241, 242, 246,
           248, 251, 252, 253
       Cunhal, A.   236, 242, 243
       Eanes, General R.   237, 238, 239,
           245, 147, 153
       Guterres, A.   237, 240
       Monteiro, M.   244, 247
       Nogueira, F.   242, 252

Salazar, A.   233, 243, 244, 248
Soares, M.   235, 237, 240–1, 247
predominant party system   15, 28, 32, 48,
       118, 146–7, 154, 161, 221, 227,
       252, 256, 262–6, 272, 274

Rae's index   184–6, 203, 261, 278
Rhodes, M.   2, 302

Sartori, G.   5, 6, 27, 28, 46, 48, 52, 65,
       71, 75, 91, 139, 147, 163, 218,
       221, 255–62 *passim*, 272, 278
Schedler, A.   267, 268
silent counter-revolution   262
silent revolution   262, 274
Sinnott, R.   33, 34, 35, 40, 45
Smith, G.   5–6, 101, 112, 143–4, 145,
       149, 159, 180–1, 256–7, 261, 262,
       263, 264, 268, 269, 273, 274
socialist parties   262, 264
Spain   2, 3, 207–31, 263, 264, 265
   alternation   218, 227–30
   centre party collapse and
           realignment   218–22
   cleavages
       centre–periphery   208–9, 227,
           229–30
       church–state   209, 216–17, 229, 230
       class   209, 216–17, 220–1, 229
   coalition   219, 223
   electoral environment   209–10
   electoral system   210
   elite autonomy   217, 224–7
   general strike, 1988   224, 225, 226,
       227
   new party system   214–18
   1982–9   222–7
   1990s   227–30
   origins   208–9
   parties
       Basque (PNV)   211, 214, 215, 218
       Catalan (CiU)   218, 273
       CDS   221, 222, 223, 226, 227, 228,
           229, 230
       CEDA   211, 216–17
       communist   210, 211, 212, 214, 215,
           220, 225, 226, 227, 228, 229,
           271, 273
       Popular Alliance/Party   213–15,
           218–23, 226, 227, 228, 229,
           230, 273
       Socialist (PSOE)   212–30 *passim*
       UCD   297, 210, 213, 214, 216–27
           passim, 230
   party system structure
       predominant   221, 227
       two-and-a-half   207
       two-party   207, 210, 218–19
   politicians
       Anguila, J.   225

Aznar, J.M. 226, 228
Carrillo, S. 214
Fraga, M. 213, 220, 222–3, 226
González, F. 217–8, 220, 222, 225, 226, 227, 228, 229
Súarez, A. 209–14, 217, 218, 219, 221, 223, 227
rebirth of party politics 211–14
territory 207, 208, 209, 210, 214, 228–30, 265
terrorism 211, 214
structural parties 270
Svåsand, L. 267
Sweden 1, 143–62, 262, 265, 266, 269, 270
alternation 144, 161–2
cleavages
centre–periphery 157–8
class 144, 146, 148–9, 152–4, 160
pluralization 160
post-material 155–8, 160, 161
urban–rural 146
coalition 154, 156, 159, 161–3
electoral volatility containment 143
new conflict dimensions, new parties 154–9
new issue containment 161–2
parties
Agrarian 143, 146, 148, 153, 159
Centre 143, 145–50, 152–8, 160, 161, 162
Christian Democratic 143, 145, 146, 147, 150, 153, 156–61 *passim*
Communist/Left 143, 145, 150, 155, 156, 158, 270
Green 143, 145, 150, 151, 153, 156, 157, 158, 160, 161
Liberals 143–8 *passim*, 150, 155, 156, 157, 158, 160, 161, 162
Moderates 143–8 *passim*, 150, 151, 153, 155, 156, 158, 159, 160

New Democrats 143, 144, 145, 153, 156–61
Social Democratic (SAP) 143–56, *passim*, 158, 159, 160, 161, 162, 265, 269, 270
party system structure
bipolar 144, 162
five-party 143, 145–6, 148, 159, 160
predominant 147, 161
'people's party' 148–9, 152
politicians
Bildt, C. 147, 156, 160, 161
Carlsson, E. 156
Carlsson, I. 146–7
Fälldin, T. 147, 155, 161
Hansson, P.A. 148
Johansson, O. 161
Karlsson, B. 158–9
Odell, M. 157
Palme, O. 156
Persson, G. 146–7
Schyman, G. 156
Svensson, A. 156–7
Wachtmeister, I. 158–9
Westerborg, B. 160
post-1973 149–54
pre-1973 147–9
referendum 155, 157–8
wage-earner funds 154–5

ten Napel, H.-M. 262, 272
territorial differentiation 256, 263, 265–6

volatility containment 143

Webb, P. 260, 272
Whyte, J. 33–4, 37–8
Wildenmann, R. 111
Wilson, F. 48
Wolinetz, S.B. 7, 144, 181
Worre, T. 149, 159